THE FACT OF
RESONANCE

INVENTING WRITING THEORY

Jacques Lezra and Paul North, series editors

THE FACT OF RESONANCE

MODERNIST ACOUSTICS AND NARRATIVE FORM

JULIE BETH NAPOLIN

Fordham University Press *New York* *2020*

Fordham University Press gratefully acknowledges financial assistance and support provided for the publication of this book by Eugene Lang College, The New School for Liberal Arts.

Fordham University Press has no responsibility for the persistence or accuracy of URLs for external or third-party Internet websites referred to in this publication and does not guarantee that any content on such websites is, or will remain, accurate or appropriate.

Fordham University Press also publishes its books in a variety of electronic formats. Some content that appears in print may not be available in electronic books.

Visit us online at www.fordhampress.com.

Library of Congress Control Number: 2020903278

Printed in the United States of America

22 21 20 5 4 3 2 1

First edition

for Marsha
&
in loving memory of Leah Napolin

CONTENTS

NOTE ON ABBREVIATIONS

For major primary sources, I have used an abbreviation system.

SBF   W. E. B. Du Bois, *The Souls of Black Folk: Authoritative Text, Contexts, Criticism*, ed. Henry Louis Gates Jr. and Terri Hume Oliver (New York: Norton, 1999)

Unless otherwise noted, all references to Conrad's works are to Joseph Conrad, *The Collected Works*, 26 vols. (Garden City, NY: Doubleday, Page, and Co., 1926), and are abbreviated as follows:

AF   *Almayer's Folly*
IJ   *Lord Jim*
NN   *The Nigger of the "Narcissus"*
PR   *A Personal Record*
TU   *Tales of Unrest*
Y   *Youth and Two Other Stories*

The most frequently cited works by William Faulkner are abbreviated as follows, less frequently cited works being noted in the text:

AA   *Absalom, Absalom!*, corrected text ed. (New York: Vintage, 1990)
SF   *The Sound and the Fury*, corrected text ed. (New York: Vintage, 1984)

THE FACT OF
RESONANCE

If there is a space of thinking, either real or virtual, then within it there must also be sound, for all sound seeks its expression as vibration in the medium of space.

—Bill Viola

And the sound of the novel, sometimes cacophonous, sometimes harmonious, must be an inner-ear sound or a sound just beyond hearing, infusing the text with musical emphasis that words can do sometimes even better than music can.

—Toni Morrison

OVERTURE: THE SOUND OF A NOVEL

What is the sound of a novel? It is a motivating force, one that brings narrative into being. Samuel Beckett dramatizes this performative of literary appearance when he begins *Company*, "A voice comes to one in the dark. Imagine."[1] The sentence is remarkable in eliding the grammatical subject of the verb's mode of action. A "voice" says that a voice comes to one.[2] Reflexive, a third-person voice narrates itself into existence. It brings into being but is not itself called forth; it simply instantiates the fictive space and is instantiated.

The elliptical power of this novel's opening is testimony to the fact that we have yet to understand the acoustics underlying legibility, audibility, and visibility in the production and reception of narrative. Narrative discourse, Gérard Genette famously insists, is the only level "directly available to textual analysis."[3] To ask after the forces that determine that availability, but also that disclose its availability as the realm of the apparent, is to exit the realm of narrative theory as it concerns itself with representation. Pursuing that project to its own logical conclusion opens up a series of questions regarding a level that does not, and cannot, come under the purview of narrative theory without at the same time becoming an "acoustics," rather than, strictly speaking, a poetics or rhetoric.[4]

In 1921, the formalist literary critic Percy Lubbock praised the techniques of Henry James and Gustave Flaubert in order to ratify what would become the now-standard terminology of literary criticism and modernism studies: "I speak of his 'telling' the story, but of course he has no idea of doing that and no more;

1

the art of fiction does not begin until the novelist thinks of his story as a matter to be *shown*, to be so exhibited that it will tell itself."[5] James encourages this terminology when he proposes in "The Art of Fiction" to "show you" character, such that it may be contained in the image of a woman's fleeting gesture. "The house of fiction has in short not one window, but a million. . . . These apertures, of dissimilar shape and size, hang so, all together, over the human scene."[6] Showing, the dramatic scene, the aperture—James initiates the visualist terms of the first wave of novel theory. "The book is not a row of facts," Lubbock writes, "it is a single image; the facts have no validity in themselves, they are nothing until they have been used."

In French, *récit*, or narrative, discloses its premise in an act of recitation, an imputed act of memory and orality. Something has happened in the past and is now being told by a narrator ("X happened," a narrator recounts). James's incredible gesture of beginning in *The Portrait of a Lady* transformed the *récit* in its claim to narrate the past: "Under certain circumstances there are few hours in life more agreeable than the hour dedicated to the ceremony known as afternoon tea. . . . Real dusk would not arrive for many hours; but the flood of summer light had begun to ebb, the air had grown mellow, the shadows were long upon the smooth, dense turf."[7] The tense of this sentence hovers between past (had grown) and future (would not arrive) in this threshold space of light's transformation.[8]

The grammar converts narrative chronology ("X" happened, followed by "Y") into temporality. Of course, we can presume that light's passage has already happened, but the description seeks to make it move once again before us. Grammatically, James's sentence means two realities at once: It has happened, and it had not yet happened. The future falls under the sway of the past perfect and its positivity, so containing is the sentence in its sensibility. The subject of this remarkable sentence is no one. It is the light itself.

Paradoxically, Genette names this work of grammar a "voice." In Genette's lexicon, voice is merely the textual effect of the verb's mode of action. There are no persons, there are no subjects. There is, still less, a sound. When Genette writes, as a confession, that "there is an enunciating instance . . . always present in what is indeed for me, I fear, an act of communication,"[9] his statement posits a remainder. Orality is the model for a theory of narrative voice—writing represents someone speaking, telling someone else something—and yet, the spatial acoustic of the voice is displaced.

In *Social Formalism*, Dorothy Hale leads me in this direction when she argues that Genette and the second wave of novel theory simply placed "inside" the novel, as language, the consolidating subjectivity that the first wave had posited as being "outside" the novel, as the artist's intention or "vision." Whether we write of "vision" or "voice," these concepts refer back, Hale argues, to a phenomenological subject.[10] The work of James's opening scene is to consolidate phenomena as the presence of substance, a here and now of imperial self-possession sensing itself.

With James's dusk, we are in the presence of what Edward Said calls a "consolidated vision."[11] This is an England without borders, a total and all-encompassing space. The most profound external determinant of the scene is nonetheless internal to it, metonymized through the presence of tea.[12] The consolidated vision is paired with the consolidated voice, soundless and implicitly neutral. In its account, the function of narrative voice is harnessed in and as the enunciating instance and not stratified or invocative of what is not immediately present in and as enunciation itself. The consolidated vision thus pushes out of view as much as (or perhaps more than) it presents for view. The acoustics of what it pushes out of view is what this book seeks to recuperate.

The consolidated vision struggles to maintain itself against what Georg Lukács calls "the power of time."[13] In the modernist novel, one place from which that power emanates is the colonial and postcolonial encounter, for the consolidated vision must maintain itself against the fact that from the moment there is colonization and imperial possession, there is the threat of its coming to an end. Threatening that vision are elements of difference—sexual, cultural, linguistic, but especially, as we will explore in detail, racial—and the forms of violence they can both embody and incite. These elements require displacement, repression, or liminalization if the consolidated vision and the neutral voice are to be achieved and preserved. With regard to race, what ultimately is displaced, repressed, or liminalized are the fact and memory of European colonization of nonwhite territories and the forced migration of slavery's Middle Passage. To recuperate these and other displacements, this book examines a body of work exemplary of this domain—that of Joseph Conrad. It seeks through his translingual formation, political exile, and colonial encounter what in the consolidated vision and voice is not instantiating. It seeks what is grounded in the fact of resonance, neither showing nor telling but sounding.

Conrad wrote from a premise inassimilable to the European tradition of the novel, with a single maxim grounded neither in an authorial personality that tells nor in its evacuation that shows: "My task which I am trying to achieve is, by the power of the written word to make you hear, to make you feel—it is, before all, to make you *see*" (*NN* 14). Between 1895 and 1900, the years that Conrad developed Marlow, his famous storytelling voice, Conrad's only maxim was grounded in a processual and often vibratory movement of hearing to feeling to seeing that, while it returns to the premodern oratorical arts—as the conjuring of a third space between speaker and listener—is not reducible to it.[14]

It is through resonance that each time Conrad's early works begin, they open within narrative what Hannah Arendt calls "the space of appearance"—the space without which speech and action cannot occur. The space is opened not in a priori ways, prior to writing as its referent, but in the fictional orientation of the narrator's hypothetical body to space and to a real or imagined listening other. (While Genette returns to a number of Greek terms, "ellipsis" and "prolepsis," for a theory of narrative, none of these terms relate to space.) Conrad calls it a "clearing."[15] There, fictive voices don masks and share aspirations for other ways of being. It is a spatial clearing while also being a temporal threshold of light and sound through which an event might break: a *chora*.[16] In the same semantic field of *chora* and chorus, we find *dechomai* (to admit), which includes both the active and passive states, to give and receive hospitality: "to give ear to."[17] We also find *chōreō*, or "to make room for another by withdrawing."[18] Such spaces of chore-ography act as both "limit and passage . . . both extending and complementing."[19] In this clearing, something has not yet happened and perhaps not been admitted or sanctioned in its possibility as an event. In its exuberance, such a possibility cannot be positively recuperated by the logic of what has already happened. What founds and exceeds the *récit* cannot be *réciter*.

"Resonance," according to the *Oxford English Dictionary*, is a sympathetic vibration or "the condition in which an oscillating or periodic force acting on an object or system has a frequency close to that of a natural vibration of the object."[20] One system acts upon another near it spatially or akin to it vibrationally. It is the physical, social, linguistic, and psychological fact of the more than one.

In citing the *OED* in this instance, I invoke resonance as the remainder of its linguistic consolidation. Throughout this book, I pursue the resonances in and between literary passages, which only became the dominant object of literary study in the early twentieth century, on the heels of the mid-Victorian, "eminently colonial" project of the *OED* and in tandem with the allusive writing practices of the English modernists.[21] What Christopher GoGwilt calls "the passage of litera-ture" instead moves fitfully through "multiple, overlapping, and contested liter-ary systems of culture" and leaves behind it a wake, one documented for GoGwilt in the linguistic turn of critical theory and in the pages of Conrad and other trans-national modernists. The document is at times no more than an echo between words.[22] We will find these to be audible traces of what the consolidated vision of literary study cannot synthesize. At the same time, they are the linguistic traces of the unsynthesized colonial and postcolonial encounter within the contemporary study of sound. The first requires a turn to sound studies, the second a (re)turn to the passage of literature. These are the twin aims of *The Fact of Resonance*.

Resonance, rather than "sound" more generally, provides the form, content, and method of this book because it is fundamentally relational or, as W. E. B. Du Bois would say, split into two. While resonance is defined by relating, it is also defined by a spaciotemporal delay. A sound is a wavelength, and it takes time to travel to a wall, for example, off which it reflects. The composer Alvin Lucier made this traversal famous in his work for tape and voice "I Am Sitting in a Room" (1969). Recording his voice, playing it back, and recording the result, again and again, he wished to disclose the spatial possibility of his speech in the resonance of the room that hosted its event, his words slowly decaying until the semantic register of his voice was annihilated, leaving only resonance. Such a "physical fact," according to Lucier, is nonetheless determined by the social conditions of speech and, above all, the desire to be heard and received.[23]

This movement at the moment of reading is what the determinate "voice" cannot by itself disclose. It is, as Jean-Luc Nancy writes, "suspended and straining between arrival and departure."[24] Resonance is "an intensive spacing of a rebound that does not end in any return to self."[25] Not "posed in itself to its *point of view*, the subject of listening is always still yet to come, spaced, traversed, and called by itself, *sounded* by itself."[26] Conversely, "To sound . . . is not only to emit a sound, but it is also to stretch out, to carry itself and be resolved into vibrations that both return it to itself and place it outside itself."[27] Nancy understands that the fact of resonance is powerfully disclosed by the *récit* when he writes of narrative as "repercussion in a yawning gap . . . that opens the subject and that opens itself to him so that he can be called to it, so that he can cite and recite himself there."[28] For Nancy—as for Philippe Lacoue-Labarthe in "The Echo of the Subject"—resonance is ultimately "the structure of the subject and of sense."[29]

But this structure in Nancy is also a pure possibility of listening, a pure possibility of referral. When Nancy turns to the elliptical instantiation of narrative as recitation (as when a voice says "a voice comes to one"), he stops at the tautology, as if at a door.[30] In Conrad, we will find, the pure possibility of listening becomes sensible in the novel as the effect of a colonial displacement.

My interest in this book is drawn to this difficult-to-retrieve auditory threshold as the ground of a theory of narrative that I hope will renew an urgent sense of the shared psychic and social life of listening and reading. The threshold between sound studies and literary studies has yet to be elaborated, given the turn away from the linguistic upon which sound studies is so often premised. It revolves around two questions and their corollaries: "Who speaks?" ("Who can speak?") and "Who hears?" ("Who can hear?")—questions asked and answered not in terms of the modernist "voice" and "vision" or the classical subject of reading but the spatial acoustic of the voice that is the displaced ground of such positions, the space from which "a voice comes to one in the dark." One reads through what Jennifer Lynn Stoever calls, after Du Bois, "the sonic color line."[31] Resonance, in this way, is the condition of possibility of Bakhtinian dialogics and heteroglossia. The spoken and written utterance is heterogeneously populated not only by others' words (the glossic) but their corporeal, sonic traces (the phonic) through which readerly voices become gendered and racialized—a heterophonia.

The Fact of Resonance thus reopens for inquiry the simple question that Barthes once asked in "The Death of the Author" of a sentence from Balzac: "Who speaks thus [*qui parle ansi*]?" Barthes begins his essay by forcefully resolving this question: "As soon as a fact is narrated no longer with a view to acting directly on reality but intransitively, that is to say, finally outside of any function other than that of the very practice of the symbol itself . . . the voice loses its origin, the author enters into his own death, writing begins."[32] The literary is fundamentally acousmatic (a literary sound acts with no visible source except the page): "No one, no 'person,' says it: its source, its voice, is not the true place of writing, which is reading."[33]

But what is reading?[34] Barthes transfers power from the hypothetical voice (of the writer) to the hypothetical ear (of a reader or *narrateé*). He concludes his essay by leaving the space of reading to invoke a scene of listening and auditory perception; he involves us, in other words, with extratextual sensation as the basis of the "transference" that is metaphor (μεταφορά, or "transfer"). He recalls the ambiguity of Greek tragic utterance, or words woven with "double meanings" and misunderstandings that lend drama its tragic dimension: "There is, however, someone who understands each word in its duplicity and who, in addition, hears the very deafness of the characters speaking in front of him—this someone being precisely the reader (or here, the listener)."[35] Listening appears to be both an attribute of reading and its metaphor.

My aim is not to supplant theories of written narrative in favor of what Ann Banfield influentially calls "unspeakable sentences" but rather to take seriously such metaphors and recuperate their displaced acoustics.[36] Writing of displacement in relation to the feminine, Naomi Schor reminds us that it is "the principle by which libidinal energy can be transferred from the significant to the insignificant." She continues, "It is the theory of displacement rather than of sublimation that makes intelligible, and, more important, legitimate the multiple modes of investment in the trivial everywhere at work in modern society."[37] In resonance, a displacement of one quantity within another, we have to wait for a sound—at times no more than a trivial thing—to be physically completed, heard, or understood. In decay, the sound is not telegraphed but choreographed, transferred to some other place than its original attack.

Resonance is, in this way, what Rodolphe Gasché might call a "minimal thing." These are things that are "at the verge of ceasing to be things, but also things that are already something other than things."[38] Linguistic and geographic passage in the making of modernity become possible through minimal things. "Encounter, arrival, address, contact, touch, belonging, distance, accord, agreement, determination, measuring, translation, and communication are some such forms of relation."[39] Resonance would seem to be the primary basis of comparatism, of the comparatist impulse—what it means to say that one passage relates to another. We lack a critical vocabulary for the affective substance of that experience. We say that passages or works "resonate" when the reasons for their return or hold on us and on each other are difficult to demonstrate (the Greek sense of *apodeixis*, or the proven and demonstrable, is also to make visible, the primary quality of action in Aristotle). We say they "strike a chord," as if a string vibrates.

Resonance thus becomes in this book a way of thinking through and with the sonorous modality of the relations also explored in Emily Lordi's *Black Resonance*, where resonance involves pairing. It is transhistorical but also transgressive and redressive, a way to access "relationships that are not causal or inevitable but are nevertheless *there*."[40] As conceived by the Caribbean scholar Édouard Glissant, relation is a creolizing methodology where objects and consciousness, like languages, tend toward being transformed by what they come in contact with. Abyssal, such forms of relation allow the Pacific and Atlantic spaces of Conrad's memory to become legible and audible through one another in ways that exceed his moment of writing. Among the most prominent endeavors to think within this field is Said's "contrapuntal analysis," which sets dominant European cultures in relation to the non-European peripheries. Said draws this term from tonal harmony whose forms and logics in many ways sought to contain the most exuberant dimension of sound. In "A Theory of Resonance," Wai Chee Dimock already opens an alternative course when she proposes that literary resonance, the circumambience generated by a text's "feat of motion," orients diachronic historicism. Occupying a space between history and theory, historicism and formalism, *The Fact of Resonance* takes up Dimock's call that literary history be reorganized by resonance while it also theorizes the "aural transposition" of the printed page.[41]

A literary resonance lacks the definition afforded by a traditional acoustic instrument where the shape and substance of a physical object produces timbre. A temporal fact, literary resonance—which is not acoustic but *acoustical*—means that what was in one moment on the verge of ceasing to be a thing becomes in another moment significant, the experience of reading being not only diachronic but anachronic and translative—the present resounds into and against the past.[42] In this way, resonance presages mutuality and reciprocal encounter. Acousticality is at the fold between matter and metaphor. It determines the composition, structure, and prose of this book.

I have composed the book around three figures (or sound figures, in Theodor Adorno's phrase): voice (Chapter 1), echo (Chapter 2), and sinister resonance (Chapter 3). Positioned between Chapters 2 and 3 is what I call an "Intersonority." Though I mean to invoke a sonorous counterpart to the intertext,[43] I conceive of it as a resonator, the site in and through which the other chapters resonate as a medium.

The book comes up against the limitation of writing as a serial form. Built into its composition is what I theorize as preaudition and retroaudition, or a hearing before and a hearing after. The chapters also include preludes and codas, musical moments where the argumentative structure, largely devoted to single works, begins to drift between relations. They engage a series of moments that open a text inward and outward toward new pairings. The autonomy of an individual work is weakened by the pressure exerted by relation. The book ends with a fourth figure, reverberation, in and through which the texts previously encountered return as a reprise.

I draw the notion of "drift" from among the most well-known passages in Freud concerning the "evenly suspended" attention. The analyst, he writes, should "not to try to fix anything that he heard particularly in his memory, and by these means to catch the drift of the patient's unconscious with his own unconscious [*nichts von dem Gehörten sich besonders im Gedächtnis fixieren wolle, und solcher Art das Unbewußte des Patienten mit seinem eigenen Unbewußten auffange*]."[44] The unconscious "catches" in the manner of a transmission received (a radio message is caught, for example, as in *einen Funkspruch auffangen*, where *auffangen* is "to catch" or "collect"). The "drift," however, is implied by the space of the scene, its atmospherics. One unconscious transmits and another receives, but through a third and indeterminate intermediary of resonating space. *Auffangen* is further suggestive of an object that is liable to become lost; I catch it just before it falls. The second sense merges with this first. To drift, in Glissant's lexicon in *Poetics of Relation*, is to be "errant," which "is not so much to be mistaken, as to be in transit, to be in imaginative flight across the world."[45]

This book's structure approaches the single work as a quantity that comes in contact with other quantities. My hope is that upon reading the codas, the reader circles back to a memory of having read the main body, then feels as if the ideas of the other texts were already "there" in it all along. The *dejá entendu*—"haven't I heard this before?"—is part and parcel of a text's resonance.

Chapter 1, "Voice at the Threshold of the Audible: Free Indirect Discourse and the Colonial Space of Reading," is a study of Conrad's first novel, *Almayer's Folly* (1895), and it concentrates on the first two words of the novel, neither of which is in English. The chapter asks what it means to approach the entire novel through the filters of these words' racial and colonial sound effects. For Said, beginnings matter; they are minimal things that determine what follows.[46] In one sense, *The Fact of Resonance* is an extended rehearing of this event, the power of the first two words—and their speaker, a Malay woman—to begin Conrad's fictional enterprise. Her sound is the return of the repressed of the modernist doxa of impersonality. The colonial ways of listening in this novel allow me to return to the work of Friedrich Kittler to argue that although he provides some of the most important terminology of literary sound studies, it is premised upon an imperial listening consciousness and an exclusion of the sonic traces of colonial sexual violence. These are sonic traces whose displaced memory populates Conrad's sound spaces.

The historical work of Saidiya Hartman and the anthropologists Ann Laura Stoler and Nancy Rose Hunt, as theorists of the archive, assist in the chapter's retrieval of those traces and toward transformative ends. At stake in Conrad's experiments with imagining inner voices in free indirect discourse—what I argue to be a sound technology—is a series of open-ended questions concerning how to "hear" the subaltern consciousness in narrative. Conrad negotiates the late-nineteenth-century rise of discourse networks, such that the novel is an archive of (post)colonial sound and listening. Conrad's prediction of sound cinema and his critical, highly reflective adoptions of the technologies of colonial knowledge production, the phonograph and ethnography, allow me to conclude the chapter with a coda on Chantal Akerman's adaptation of *Almayer's Folly* and lip sync as a postcolonial strategy.

Chapter 2, "The Echo of the Object: On the Pain of Self-Hearing in *The Nigger of the 'Narcissus'* and 'The Fact of Blackness,'" searches for a mode of reading that might repair the sonorous afterlife of racialized objects in narrative and text. Echo is defined by slapback, or a doubling. This doubling locates, as a counterpart to the Freudian subject (the ego ideal), a "voice ideal." It is defined by the at times painful experience of hearing oneself speak, particularly in relation to an idealized sound, one that could be neutralized, cleansed of foreign traces or colonial accent. These traces bear profoundly on Conrad as a non-native speaker of English—he was hailed by this language in the moment of its ascending global dominance. The instantiating case for the voice ideal is a study of Conrad's third novel, *The Nigger of the "Narcissus"* (1897), his first to document an English crew on a journey home to England. It is a counterpart to Freud's "On Narcissism" and Frantz Fanon's "The Fact of Blackness," each of these texts heard, conjoined, and interpreted through the psychodynamics described by Anne Cheng in *The Melancholy of Race*. The structure of echo is repetitive, and as a form of relation, it mandates "echolocation," that is, finding something not in its place. Such echolocation provides a way of relating textual moments, sonorities, and bodies across the Atlantic and Pacific.

In a coda, I consider the sound effects produced by Faulkner's intensive engagement with Conrad in *The Sound and the Fury* and Faulkner finding his "voice" as a writer of the American South through the echo of Conrad's racial melancholy. In this way, the coda is a companion to Peter Mallios's historicist recuperation of Conrad within the annals of American modernism, *Our Conrad*. I develop a technical vocabulary for the racialized acoustics of echolocation, sounding modernism across the oceans.

These effects continue into the Intersonority, "Unclaimed Voices Circum-1900, or Sound and Sourcelessness in *The Souls of Black Folk*." The Intersonority is precisely that, a diachronic and anachronic space in a linear format. In it, I approach Du Bois as a contemporary of Conrad and Freud, but one who was listening to memory, song, and the unconscious in ways they could not. I read Du Bois as a theorist of sound through his strategies of beginning in resonance, asking how melody, for Du Bois, is a sonic trace of experiences and their counterpotentials that cannot be narrated.

When Conrad wrote *Heart of Darkness* and Du Bois *The Souls of Black Folk*, they wrote these works without awareness of each other (Conrad gained prominence in the United States only in the 1920s). Du Bois compiled the essays on black life in America between 1896 and 1903, and Conrad began his diaries in the Congo in 1890, transmuting them into the novel in 1898 (collected again in 1902). Those familiar with both texts will be "hearing" Du Bois well in advance of himself and "hearing" Conrad after himself, but the Intersonority presumes no such familiarity, instead introducing sonic traces to allow the reader to hear the relation in preparation for Chapter 3. In his thinking of the acousmatic event, Freud writes of listening with ears "pricked" (*aufgestellt*)—the techniques in the Intersonority aim to incite such alertness.

By the time we arrive at Chapter 3, "A Sinister Resonance: On the Extraction of Sound and Language in *Heart of Darkness*," the reader will have experienced the way these texts exist as companions, unknown to each other as such—they resonate, but through the position of a third term (the reader). The chapter is a study of Conrad's *Heart of Darkness* (1899), a novel narrated in a single night aboard a ship, when Marlow, its narrator, remembers his journey to the Congo. Searching for a way to describe this novel, Conrad wrote that it was like "a sinister resonance" and "continued vibration." These sound figures, based in his memories of music and at the fold of matter and metaphor, issue a profound challenge to the transcendental signifier that supports narrative levels: the "voice." At the same time, I seek out the linguistic sign in the material substratum of vibration. Both the linguistic sign and the history of telecommunications cannot be thought outside of the colonial extraction of sound in its ongoing, global violence. In 1903, the final tract of oceanic cable completing a global communications system—one preface to the internet—was laid in Manila, facilitated by US colonial rule; there is perhaps no better allegory of the transpacific as it is always already transatlantic. It is there that *Heart of Darkness* resonates. Asking how his novel communicates, I argue that the "sinister resonance" redefines the foundational exclusion of sound from structuralist linguistics but also appropriates the (racializing and libidinal) experience of consciousness defined as an "inner voice." It is a narrative of transformation through listening.

The "Reprise" departs from Conrad to take up among his most sensitive readers, William Faulkner in *Absalom, Absalom!*. Through Conrad, Faulkner was seeking a literary racial form for the historical present and not yet determined future of a segregated and unreconstructed South.

I hope the reader will learn to read for and listen to resonance as I have, to read not for the political unconscious but for the acoustical unconscious of canonical texts that register noncanonical historical trajectories.[47] My practice of collecting material began as an analog one, circling the recurrence of single words and phrases across books and notations of spoken occurrences, long before the digital afforded a search function. But as a book, *The Fact of Resonance* is less analog than it is digital, conceived as a series of sonorous hyperlinks. When possible, I send the reader backward or forward in a note or an aside.

Caught between epistemes, some of the resonances are not entirely known to me, notwithstanding the fact that texts pass on their repressions.[48] Resonance in this way can involve reading for the way one acoustical unconscious contacts or drifts into another. *The Fact of Resonance* indicates a way of writing of, thinking with, and listening to resonance that exceeds the very form—the modernist novel—that instantiates my inquiry. It is common in this book that I leave certain points unsaid, not wishing to determine their resonance in other people, leaving an opening or space. In some cases, I provide a footnote with a strong indication of the background and direction, but it is ancillary to the musical precision of withholding, indirection, and not knowing that I privilege on a stylistic and intellectual level, the opening of the sentence and the thought itself toward the other, who is unknown to me.

I wish to search out that single sound which is in itself so strong that it can confront silence.

—Toru Takemitsu

I do not intend to speak about. Just speak nearby.

—Trinh T. Minh-ha

1

VOICE AT THE THRESHOLD OF THE AUDIBLE: FREE INDIRECT DISCOURSE AND THE COLONIAL SPACE OF READING

THE POWER TO BEGIN

He begins with the shout of a woman:

"Kaspar! Makan!"

I leave the quotation suspended, lingering on its interruptive power of beginning. Who is speaking? What is the voice saying? Where is the voice coming from?

The woman who calls will be referred to by the narrator simply as "Mrs. Almayer," a married name, Dutch and paternal. The name bears no trace of her Sulu origins yet showcases her rank within the colonial household: She is by Dutch law a proper wife yet not separable conceptually from a "concubine," "mistress," "maid," or, in colonial Malay, a *nyai*.[1] We will never know by what name she might have been originally called. She calls out a first name, but she is not herself called by one. The name is uninscribed.

The shout, the reader quickly learns on its heels, is addressed to Kaspar Almayer, a Javanese Dutch trader who gazes out absentmindedly at the Pantai River. The anonymous, third-person narrator obeys Almayer's desire and ignores the woman, floating into his reveries. For Almayer, the shout's only significance is its nonsignificance. Left untranslated on the page, the phrase appears as a mere signifier, a racial linguistic mark. It takes approximately eight pages for the shout to be translated and even then, obliquely, when Almayer awakens from his day-

13

dreams of gold and wealth: We learn that "he had a hazy recollection of having been called some time during the evening by his wife. To his dinner probably" (*AF*, 11).

One anticipates that a Victorian work of fiction will begin with some sort of utterance that is in close proximity to authorial speech, an authoritative "voiceover" in the third person that overlays the world of the novel, establishing a time and place.[2] This shout, quickly followed by the consciousness of someone who refuses to listen, is a puzzling beginning for a writer who would worry so much about reaching and convincing his English readers.

Yet something of Conrad's beginning flouts late-nineteenth-century conventions. The shout erupts onto the page as the return of the repressed of the modernist doxa of showing—the belief, epitomized by James, that the writer "should recede into the background" to narrate "a succession of dramatically presented fictional scenes."[3] For James, the novel is illustrative, driven by the artist's "power to guess the unseen from the seen" and to "convert" the impression of the moment into the reality of the "concrete image."[4] It is as if Conrad predicts a much later moment, one memorably described by Mark McGurl as the period in which Anglo-American fiction writers abandoned the Jamesian ideal to advocate writing as an act of "miming the emotional, improvisational rhythms of a *spoken* voice . . . necessarily an embodied voice."[5] Yet Conrad's opening shout, his first words as a published novelist, is neither "impersonal" nor "improvisational."

The shout, issued across a colonial fictional space, forces us to confront an aesthetic principle for which impersonality has no descriptive power.[6]

What if, in pursuit of this colonial fictional space, we were to presume for this shout a series of textual sound effects? These effects send us not to the quantum of Conrad's "voice," an ethical causality of his identity and exoticism, but to sensorial contact with the page. As an optical artifact, the words "Kaspar! Makan!" are invested with some ability to communicate a phonemic sound to the English-speaking reader. The words are syllabic. I sound them out, recognizing the first as a name. But the second remains without sense, untranslated from a language unknown by me.

Readers unfamiliar with Malay only learn later, as Almayer's reverie draws to a close in the first chapter, that the opening shout is a command (*makan*, "eat"). Yet the exclamation mark in the text allows the English-speaking reader to call upon an imperative verb and, with it, the modal dimension of grammar, that is, its "mood."[7]

When Gérard Genette begins the chapter in *Narrative Discourse* dedicated to mood, he returns to the famous section on poetry in Plato's *Republic* to account for the origins of the distinction between telling and showing, diegesis and mimesis. It is a foundational distinction between the poet who speaks as himself and the poet who speaks "as if he were someone else."[8] All of narrative comes down to "two data," Genette writes, "the quantity of narrative information" and "the absence (or minimal presence) of the informer."[9] It's on the basis of this data that Genette critiques the cardinal distinction between showing and telling, finding them to be interrelated: "Pretending to show is pretending to be silent."[10] But really, Genette should have said "pretending to be 'silent,'" for he never entertains a sonic trace, a claim upon writing and reading for sounding. This "voice" is haunted by a displaced acoustics (making *chōreō*, or the opening of space for sound and movement, its Greek twin). But so, too, is modernism. When James and Lubbock argue that the art of the novel is not to tell but to show, a series of aural events get cast out, such as voices that do not tell but shout, cry, or scream, and voices that are never actually vocalized.

Though Genette begins with textual effects, he never sheds a dependence on orality, which becomes in his system what Hale argues to be an ontological referent, neutral and transcendental.[11] His sense of writing is attenuated by an oral paradigm that achieves a priori autonomy: The storyworld is a totality whose vocal qualities writing simply represents. Genette's system presumes that one knows what the words on the page mean, what they say, what they sound like. In relation to narrative theory, then, we find ourselves on unfamiliar ground.

With the exclamation point, I imagine a shout, even if I do not yet fantasize its timbre; it is a kind of shape of a sound that calls across a distance. Untranslated, unattributed, and unnarrated, a vocal shard simply erupts into the world that, in that same instant, claims to create it. In imagining the shout, I imagine it has been transliterated and inscribed. (One could just as easily claim that from an inscription, one imagines a shout and that it has been transliterated.) If the exclamation marks, for the English-speaking reader, the existence of the imperative mood, then it marks a demand for immediate presence, that is, an absence, a paradox heightened by the delayed translation of Malay into English.

It is through punctuation and grammatical mood, then, that text becomes sound. "Hear me! Hear that I am addressing you!" says the exclamation and the imperative. It also says, "Listen! Listen to what I am saying!" There is an elliptical movement between inscription and sound, sound and inscription. It would seem, then, that from the moment we try to think the untranslated shout within Genette's system, it thrusts us outside: The oral is not a stable referent outside of the text but caught up in a transposition or sliding between text and sound.

The demand is to "hear" difference, to recognize its imperative on the scene.

"Conrad confronts his readers with these unexplained foreign sounds at the very threshold of his first work to emphasize the radical difference of what is to follow," writes Michael North.[12] For North, Conrad inaugurates a "dialect modernism" but also a studied reflection on the transformations and standardization of English. By this logic, Conrad "speaks," as it were, through the foreign woman; he speaks "as if he were someone else," announcing the difference of *his* modernism, the foreignness of *his* "voice." The shout would then be akin to Gustave Flaubert's famous announcement "Madame Bovary c'est moi." But to make such a claim would be to overleap the ambiguously erotic-affective dimension—a hegemonically gendered and racialized dimension—of Conrad's announcement (if, indeed, it is an announcement at all). It is precisely the dimension that the shout, in its textual sound effects, demands we consider.

Such a consideration will prove to be significant to the theory of the novel as a sound technology—in its production of space and an imaginary acoustics—and an acousmatic technology of voice—in the invention of free indirect discourse, the writer "speaking" as if he were someone else. Someone, a subaltern woman, is narrated into existence. A narrator simultaneously voices itself; it "speaks" in her borrowed sound and name.[13] Though we take Conrad as our point of departure, we will find that such an invention cannot be thought outside of colonial difference. This difference is not a "content" that can be removed from or added to the novel: The novel and its sound are colonial-racial forms. The question "who hears?" is never far from "who speaks?" or from "who can speak?" and "who can hear?" and "where is the voice heard?"

Writing himself into existence as an English author, Conrad already gives up some authorial impulse. He abandons the armature of both showing and telling. Conrad once fantasied that his pseudonym could be a Malay one, "Kamudi" (Malay for "rudder"). One wonders if he wanted the English to believe that he was a Malay writing to them, and what kind of voice they would have imagined themselves to "hear" "behind" or "within" his written tone. To annotate the shout, then, we have to annotate the threshold between text and sound. This threshold creates the pseudo-three-dimensional space of narrative but also the fiction of the space of reading, the space through which voices on the page arrive in consciousness. Where there is "world," there is relation to space and place—an acousticality.

The entirety of the narrative, its linguistic, acoustical, and temporal effects, rests on the fact of Almayer's refusal to listen. The shout opens the possibility of narrative, of the novel's relationship to space, time, and perceiving and remembering consciousness. We learn of Almayer's disregard for his wife as "a slave" but also something of the geopolitical coordinates that have brought him here to the present hour, coordinates that organize the novel's space and time.

Later, when the third-person narrative enters the consciousness of Mrs. Almayer, we learn little of her story, only an outline or simple trajectory. When still a young girl among Sulu pirates (perhaps, though we can't be certain, in what is now called the Philippines), she had been captured by Captain Lingard, an English trader. Lingard sent her to school with the nuns in Samarang to learn religion and the English language. Coming of age, she returned to Borneo not to be married to her English "father," as she had hoped, but to be brokered in a marriage to a man she had never met, Almayer.

On the heels of the call, in the novel's second sentence, Almayer snaps out of a reverie filled with elliptical and proleptical temporal and geographical coordinates. But this reverie had already been underway long before we arrived on the scene, such that the novel's "present," its first instance, is set in sharp relief against an uncoverable ellipsis:

"Kaspar! Makan!"
The well-known shrill voice startled Almayer from his dream of splendid future into the unpleasant realities of the present hour. An unpleasant voice too. He had heard it for many years, and with every year he liked it less. No matter; there would be an end to all this soon.
He shuffled uneasily, but took no further notice of the call. (*AF*, 3)

"Shrill." The voice is a woman's and grates his bodily being.[14] The subject who is called seeks distance from some haunting figure of "woman, native, other," as Trinh T. Minh-ha might say ("Easy enough to dispose of a Malay woman, a slave after, after all," Almayer later thinks to himself in his reveries [*AF*, 10–11]).[15] But is not something of "woman" imputed from the moment the shout appears, even before any predicate? If I immediately recognize that "Kaspar" is a name (a foreign name) and that what follows is a verb (a foreign verb), imperative or at least commanding, do I not immediately recognize the presence of a listener who occupies a space defined by physical distance (calling from afar) and, with it, an emotional demand? If not a mother calling to a child, demanding belief, then Mother, a vocalic figure who does not in this moment soothe but occupies a terrifying and castrating place merged with the Orientalized body of the other: the robber of dreams.

In *Discourse Networks*, the media theorist Friedrich Kittler describes at length the place of the "mother's mouth" in Romantic discourses of the nineteenth century. She is Nature and not "the woman," or even "a woman," but Woman, whose "function consists in getting people—that is, men—to speak."[16] Metaphysically, the maternal gift is language itself in a pure, nascent state. This organizing discourse of 1800 mandates that Woman initiates the opening for speech and culture but that she not herself speak. Here, that nascence is all the more charged by its Orientalizing and primitivizing inflections, as if the shout were a natural or virgin artifact, unexplored and issuing directly from the source.

As a quotation, however, the shout has been heard by someone in some hypothetical space. That is where the novel gains its importance as a technology of sound: A sound in narrative space is always as heard, as reported. The narrator that mediates the shout is never described; it simply arrives in narrative space through an anonymous power of citation and, more implicitly, audition. The shout thus creates the literary fiction of space, the space in which all other subsequent events will or can take place. She makes space. The vocal signifier summons what James was among the first to posit as the novel's exceptional capacity to build a "world."[17] Again, where there is "world," there is an acoustical relation to space and place.

But between Conrad and this woman intercedes the third voice, the third-person narrator. In beginning with the citation of a voice, the narrative begins with a kind of vocal imitation or impersonation, as if the shout has simply landed on the page, unmediated. The third-person narrator, in this way, claims to seize completely its object, to merge with it—but that is simply part of the fiction or mimetic illusion in which Conrad's novel involves us. The mimetic illusion, integral to the realist novel in Conrad's moment, is also a colonial fiction of a world from "afar" being brought "near." The minimum quantity for a call, a shout across some distance, is immediately charged with or inflected by the gendered geopolitics of spatialization and temporalization. In other words, Conrad's novel confronts the fact that, as a novel, it must generate itself autotelically; it must begin and initiate time and space.

The novel plays out the creation and extractive use of the river settlement of Sambir by Lingard's hands: Captain Lingard, Ruth Nadelhaft observes, is a fundamentally coercive figure, Conrad recognizing that colonialism is but one expression of patriarchy.[18] From the novel's first instance, its fiat out of nothing, then, the shout elliptically addresses "the world he thinks he has created."[19] Conrad understood that the mimetic illusion of a novel's fictional world is, too, premised upon an imperial demand for space. A novel must "take place," a phenomenological issue quickly charged with the historical fact of primitive accumulation.[20] The mimetic illusion falters in the delayed translation. The shout gains not in its unalloyed purity but in its instability. It remains insistently outside the (English) narrative discourse, a colonial parabasis.[21]

We move quickly on the heels of the shout into Almayer's consciousness, the consciousness of a colonizing man who won't listen. Yet the shout marks the urgency of "the present hour," daydream being defined by anxious suppression or attenuation. The name Dain, a Balinese prince and anticolonial insurgent, drifts into Almayer's reverie. We have not yet the means to understand his importance. In these reveries, nearly every temporal coordinate of the novel's plot is elliptically and proleptically mapped, though Almayer, "deaf" to the present hour, fails to recognize it as such. That misunderstanding—a displacement not simply in time but space—is *where* the anticolonial effects of the novel begin to gather or how these effects will *take place*: acoustics, resonance.

The shout hangs suspended in a pseudo-three-dimensional space created by the acoustical valence, the threshold between text and sound.

"Kaspar! Makan!"

That penetration is, by definition, caught between the physical and the conjectural. Imaginary spatial acoustics begins to localize and temporalize the ambiguous ground of the theory of narrative "voice": its displacement of acoustics.

Years have passed, and some trajectory, for Almayer, is waning. The woman has become in Almayer's eyes insane, intolerable, a mad woman blocking the gates of his desire. She crouches in the corner of their ramshackle house, with a pile of uncombed hair, spitting betel nuts, torturing his waking moments with epithets and condemnation.

It is her shout that calls Conrad's entire fictional project into being.

THE THRESHOLD OF THE AUDIBLE:
INNER SPEECH AND EMPLACEMENT

With the shout across a distance, a relational ontology of sounding in written narrative becomes necessary, one that reconceptualizes the interaction between an inward voice of reading, the narrative "voice," and the physical page or screen, while also confronting the rhetorical sliding between listening as metaphor and listening as act. The shout is in three "voices."

At issue is how both "vision and voice" in novel and narrative theory depend upon a deeper imbrication in and refusal to abandon a submerged colonial relation. Colonial sound is the repressed of the novel, of James's belief, contemporary to Conrad, in the novel as "picture" and "world," but also of more recent theories of fiction's essential "unspeakability." With the vocal shard of a subaltern woman, Conrad marks a different beginning for the theory of the novel in the threshold of the audible.

I draw this phrase in part from Conrad's phrase in *Heart of Darkness* "the threshold of the invisible," which has opened up provocative readings along the axis of sexuality and desire.[22] In Conrad, the unseen is often heard, issuing from outside the "frame," as it were, in an acousmatic voice. The film theorist Michel Chion names such a voice the *acousmêtre*, or the "not-yet-seen," which is defined by the cinematic principle "that at any moment these faces and bodies *might* appear."[23] Chion genders, racializes, and eroticizes the invisible.[24]

In "The Mirror Stage as Formative of the *I* Function," Jacques Lacan writes, "the specular image seems to be the threshold of the visible world."[25] In the reflection, the infant sees himself, but he sees himself alongside of the other (the mother) who holds up the infant near the surface that he touches. Here, we find the earliest formation of the bodily ego, its idealization and identification in a constituted image. Yet it is a surprisingly sonorous scene in that the voice of the mother, not yet attached to the field of the symbolic, also encourages the infant to link the image to itself and says, "That is you." These are words spoken in a tone of recognition, of affirmation prior to meaning. This is a tone that becomes the sonorous ground of the self's perennial internal voiceover. It is sealed to the image in the moment the infant places its hand against the mirror. The subject forever moves asymptotically in what Lacan calls "a fictional direction."[26]

Film theory, the Anglo-American strains of which began as an extension of novel theory, has already answered the question of how perception, in the context of classic narrative cinema, requires a visual and sonic *vraisemblable*, or credulousness, of its world. The spectator perceives a synchronous relation between voice and body, losing herself in the story and forgetting the sound-image's technological regulation. In the terms proposed by the "apparatus" school of film theory, a "primary identification" with the camera gives way to a "secondary identification" with the story. These issues seem more immediate or less conjectural in the case of cinema because of the existence of the screen. The cinematic *vraisemblable*, or its reality effect, sets to work at solving the essential problem of "suturing" the physical distance between the screen and spectator. In the case of cinema, this work is less easily concealed from the critic because, as an audiovisual event, cinema is fundamentally external.

But the problem of suture, which stitches up the affective "holes," as it were, in the image's reality effect, is no less the case with the novel. Film theory remains the most sophisticated theory of representation.[27] If film theory and narrative theory have long drawn from each other to understand the parameters of story and discourse, then it stands to reason that cinema offers a robust point of beginning for theorizing how the imaginary voices and bodies of literature are to be perceived, how the affective and identificatory distance between page and reader is, too, to be sutured. In other words, narrative voice requires a suture to be experienced as "it speaks." What form this suture might take in colonial narrative is precisely at issue in Conrad's opening shout, that is, not only how colonial space can be represented through sound but also how the introduction in narrative of unseen sound can involve a destructive component, one that rails against the fictional world that also censors it. The fictional world can be a normative world whose imagination by the reader the unseen sound is asked to assist.[28] In this case, the unseen sound straddles two dimensions, being both assistant and puncture, a sign of another form of life.

The case of classic narrative cinema is instructive, for it conceals its fetishistic operation, one by which the cinematic image claims to reproduce visual reality. In what Kaja Silverman calls, after Guy Rosalto, the "acoustic mirror," cinema only conceals its lack by way of its plentitude of sounds and voices that "sound" adequately reproduced, that is, with fidelity and synchronized with the image. Silverman makes it clear how, through synchronization, cinema generates veracity by way of the long metaphysical tradition that "locates the subject of speech in the same ontological space as the speaking subject, so that the former seems a natural outgrowth of the latter."[29] The opening shout unsettles this tradition.

In the case of cinema, this achievement is not merely technological, Silverman insists, but psychical. Christian Metz defines suture through the structure of narcissism, an idealization by which I forget the camera and screen to see only its unified *imago*, or what is known as its "world." "Film is like the mirror," Metz writes.[30] "But it differs from the primordial mirror [of Lacan] in one essential point: . . . there is one thing and one thing only that is never reflected in it: the spectator's own body. In a certain emplacement [*emplacement*], the mirror suddenly becomes clear glass."[31] An emplacement is also a setting in place; that is, it involves a setting and settling. In Metz's terms, emplacement is produced by cinema's demand for a "passionate" attachment to the images. In that attachment, also an identification, it is *there* that I am, or that I find myself where I do not see myself—that is the definition of suture. This fantasy is also an acoustic one. I have the sense that voices and sounds emanate not from speakers but from the screen, or still more radical in its forgetting, I believe the sounds and voices to emanate from its characters and world. If the speaking voice of a character before us on the screen suddenly lags behind the movements of the mouth, we lose the fantasy of a sound's "source," which is so integral to cinema's reality effect. It is the effect through which I locate myself, my affective being, in the story, its "picture."

One readily speaks of seeing narrative or of reading as an ideational space in which characters, settings, and scenes appear in acts of what the phenomenologist Wolfgang Iser has called "image-building," a phrase that promises the substantiality of architecture.[32] "The process of image-building begins . . . with the schemata of the text, which are aspects of a totality that the reader himself must assemble; in assembling it, he will occupy the position *set out* for him, and so create a sequence of images that eventually results in his constituting the meaning of the text."[33] But there are various forms of support for this space that are nonideational because they produce no images.

If the human being in the novel, as Mikhail Bakhtin famously argues, is first and foremost a speaking human being, then what can the fantasy of the cinematic screen and its abundance of sound tell us about reading as an event of identification? If it is to achieve its "worlding" effect, the novel must also convince its reader that the reported voices and sounds "match" its implied spaces and images. Reading the novel precedes by the work of identification with a "setting." Such work is more difficult to theorize and retrieve, however, because its event is more synthetic. The "screen" of literary images, sounds, and voices is nowhere locatable, except "inwardly," that deep and invisible space of metaphysics. Reader-response theory and the phenomenology of reading are profoundly eidetic, unwilling to ask after the traversal of an "invisible distance,"[34] the rhetorical sliding between listening as metaphor and listening as act.

To the extent that reading is imputed an invisible, metaphysical space, it is imputed the medium of an inward "voice." In nineteenth-century discussions of hearing and disability, it was thought that the deaf could not be taught to read silently, being without speech and therefore without inner speech[35]—so entrenched is the notion that the written word is "articulated," "said," or "enunciated" in the mind (a notion whose essential metaphysical premise would not have been unfamiliar to Conrad and other modernists who experimented with voices on the page). Communicational theorists of narrative describe the enunciation as "pronounced." But where is it pronounced? Inwardly, we can presume. The enunciating instance is the wordless temporal event that binds an inner pronouncement to the page. If the words themselves were difficult to pronounce or unfamiliar—as they are in Conrad's opening shout—something of this temporal event would begin to stagger, become noninstantaneous or desynchronized, its

otherwise tight spatial relay made palpable. This sound effect will prove crucial
to the way the novel registers the fact of decolonization.

McGurl influentially writes of novel theory's continued phonocentrism in
positing "the 'voice' that we cannot help but 'hear' in even the most impersonal
modern narratives [that] should be understood as issuing from what [Wayne]
Booth called an 'Implied Author' who unifies the text as the product of a coherent intention and/or moral sensibility."[36] In this same way, Marc Blanchard
suggests that when Genette says "voice," this grammatical notion is nonetheless
founded on the sense that "the text resonates" with someone who transcends a
narrator's persona.[37] Blanchard telegraphs in "resonance" a kind of feeling; that
is how it becomes possible for critics to describe these various voices as both
inaudible yet sounding at the same time.[38]

The overarching inquiry of this book is to reconsider resonance not as a false
metaphor but as a physical event that has been displaced. What critics seem to
ignore is that if, in Genette's structuralism, the enunciation can so easily move
between spoken and written discourse and maintain its identity, writing always
being attenuated by the oral paradigm, it is because the enunciating or narrating
instance as a category—"voice"—is in principle *soundless*. For when Émile Benveniste notes that subjectivity (the "I") refers to "the act of individual discourse
in which it [the pronoun] is pronounced," this pronunciation could be a mental
act.[39] What Blanchard names "resonance" invokes a phonocentric attachment; it
is a dead metaphor.

I draw this notion, of course, from Jacques Derrida, among the foremost critics of structuralism and a contemporary of novel theory's second wave. When he
argues against "phonocentrism," he deconstructs phenomenology's insistence
upon an essential tie between expression and *phone* (sound). He underscores
the distinction between a phonic element in its "phenomenological sense" and
as a "real sound."[40] Derrida writes, "the phenomenological 'body' of the signifier seems to fade away at the very moment it is produced; it seems already to
belong to the element of ideality."[41] "Where does this complicity between sound
and ideality, or rather, between voice and ideality come from?" he asks. The
self-revising form of the question implies that the two—voice and sound—are
nonsynonymous. The phenomenological voice makes use of sound, but it disappears, used up, as it were, in the fading of the signifier into the ideality of the
signified, which is "immediately present in the act of expression."[42]

When phenomenology idealizes the voice, what it idealizes is not the sound
but rather the essence of the operation "*I hear myself* [je m'entende] *at the*

same time that I speak."[43] Thus when Genette makes recourse to what Blanchard pinpoints as "the aboriginal voice of an elusive pre-textual subject," he makes recourse to the soundlessness that preserves its ontological referentiality. In the essence of its operation, the "voice" is the one signifier that seems to escape a worldly and spatial fate. "It does not fall into the exteriority of space, into what one calls the world, which is nothing but the outside of speech."[44] It is not as if it is "outside" me but rather "is in absolute proximity to me."[45] It is all as if in an instant. That is why I suggest that to recover an analytic for sound—for colonial sound—is already to be ejected from Genette's system.[46]

"'Language' may first of all signify a physiologically conditioned psychic function, either as speech with someone or as so-called internal speech with oneself," writes Roman Ingarden in his seminal work of phenomenological aesthetics *The Literary Work of Art.*[47] By this notion, to read a novel is to assume (take on, take up, absorb) words on a page by way of the medium of an inwardly pronouncing voice. The fiction writer Eudora Welty vividly describes such an experience of a "reader-voice":

> Ever since I was first read to [by my mother], then started reading to myself, there has never been a line read that I didn't *hear*. As my eyes followed the sentence, a voice was saying it silently to me. It isn't my mother's voice, or the voice of any person I can identify, certainly not my own. It is human, but inward, and it is inwardly that I listen to it. It is to me the voice of the story or the poem itself. The cadence, whatever it is that asks you to believe, the feeling that resides in the printed word, reaches me through the reader-voice. I have supposed, but never found out, that this is the case with all readers—to read as listeners—and with all writers, to write as listeners.[48]

Reading inwardly: It is most close and most far, personal and impersonal. The concept of a reader "voice" is perhaps only a terminological convenience, one that borrows from the long tradition of inner speech and consciousness. "I'm aware of it *sounding* in a very thin version of my own tone of voice," Denise Riley writes. "I catch myself in its silent sound, a paradox audible only to me."[49] By "silent sound" Riley describes the immediacy of the experience that Derrida named autoaffection, or "hearing (understanding) oneself-speak" (*s'entendre parler*), yet in the "paradox," she marks its heterogeneity.[50] Silence, across multiple discourses, is a portmanteau, denoting not only the lack of sound but inwardness and self-presence. When Genette says that "pretending to show is pretending to be silent," his conceptualization of telling is already premised upon a displacement of sound.

It is precisely through this displacement that it becomes possible for Georges

Poulet to call the voice of reading "alien to me and yet in me"—he simply means the first-person "voice," or the everyday event of reading silently to oneself a text's grammatical "I."[51] Poulet does not directly state the acoustic problem of its relation to a "physical" voice. In a logical continuation, however, we can pursue resonance not as authenticity but as the elliptical threshold or space of relay between sound, inner voice, and text.

For would not the differential event that Poulet experiences in the grammatical "I," the distance between his "I" and the "I" of another, make itself felt through some event of timbre, even if that timbre is not to be heard with the ears but only *sensed* as the difference between the page and its articulation?[52] This difference is an opening in the essence of the operation "I hear myself at the same time that I speak." "I mentally pronounce an *I*, and yet the *I* which I pronounce is not myself," Poulet writes.[53] It matters little where an imputed reader sits in the spectrum of hearing and ability, since the *essence* of the autoaffective operation is not tethered to a physical sound (heard with the ear or sensed with the body) but to its idealization.[54] Poulet's beautiful essay leaves the acoustic question of *pronunciation* to the side, unthought in his investment in the grammatical subject; it is the very question so forcefully introduced by Conrad's opening.

As a question of pronunciation, of sonic production, this resonance is not localized in the ear, except in conjectural ways. It is sensed, or, rather, what Barthes posits as the pure "holding together" of language begins to stretch and to *sense itself* not reflexively but through the mediation of the sign.[55] Resonance names not a sound but this differential and differentiating sound effect. Without it, Conrad could not have begun as he did. Poulet does not think this event of the "voice" as a sensorial one—it is only with enough substance to provide the material of the figure "pronunciation." However, what is it that makes reading an "alien principle" if not the fact of an alien substance, a conjectural sound with an imputed location or place (what he calls the "alien to me and yet *in* me")?

What marks the "foreignness" of Conrad's beginning in fact orients fictional reading as such, except that some sonic event is often diminished or muted. In other words, Conrad emphasizes what is already pervasive in reading, such that the two are separated by a difference in degree: Both involve us in the alien principle of pronouncing a grammatical "I" that is not mine. For Poulet's thesis to work, there would have to be a sound of this alien principle—*a neutral or otherwise unapparent sound*—that I can hold close enough to myself that I do not deem it foreign or a hostile invasion. For do I not readily take up what I read, readily allow my consciousness to shelter their event? (Shelter: one archaic meaning of the root of *logos* in *legein*. Other archaic meanings include gathering, binding, joining, and counting, as in, recounting a sequence.)[56] These spaces and settings immediately relate, then, to what may count as the reader voice, a question not only of degree but value.

In the shelter of the reader voice there is something that is multiply determined by what may count as an object to be apprehended through it, what can be permissibly heard in its warm, spontaneous, and intimate timbre of interiority, and what must instead be distanced as not "of" me, alien to my inward tonality and its words. In the act of reading, my consciousness, Poulet writes, is "on loan." But would this loan (to the page, to its voices and sounds) not also include the inner voice? If so, then the "loan," in its transfer, is a differential event. A reader voice carries and transports—transmits—the words into consciousness. In inwardly pronouncing "Kaspar! Makan!" that relay or carrying loses its imputed immediacy such that the words are in the middle of becoming sensible in their mediation.

In seeking the enunciating body behind the shout and, with it, the words on the page, we move from or transpose the visual to the audible register. However, I cannot claim to "see" the body of Mrs. Almayer or the narrator who quotes her, nor can I claim to hear them. I can claim to do so only to the extent that a written figure might simulate something other than what it is. Sound, in this space, is pushed through into an alternate dimension. When I read, there is nothing that, properly speaking, separates written voices from one another: No surface of another body emerges by which to posit their limit.

In the reader voice, the immediate, internal voice of reading, there is a veil or, perhaps more precisely, a screen. Sonic object relations divide that sheltering space, mark inclusions and exclusions. The voice of reading does not appear; it cannot be made manifest. I hear both myself and what cannot possibly be admitted as me.

Hearing (understanding) oneself speak is marshaled by Conrad's opening shout in vexed ways. In the words "Kaspar! Makan!" the problem of pronunciation takes on a new dimension for an English-speaking reader. How to pronounce these words (what is their sound), one asks, before (or perhaps at the same time) one asks, what do the words mean (what is their sense)? Genette's major inheritor, Seymour Chatman, metaphorizes narrative as "transmission." But if a reader voice carries and transmits words into consciousness, then what is the nature or structure of the invisible distance that the shout of a subaltern woman traverses? How might this traversal—as a transmission—announce not the signal but the displaced ground of its traversal? In the tonality that I reject as not "of me," I "hear" the traversal itself, that some signal is in me yet not of me.

In Chapter 2, I address the vexed relationship between a physical voice and a narrative voice, but already we can begin to sense that from the beginning, Conrad's prose is organized by protracted misunderstandings and the struggle to hear in fraught spaces. These are spaces in which understanding comes only too late or with a long delay, if it arrives at all. In narrative theory, the spatiality of the sound that falls into the world has not been canceled and destroyed by its idealization but is displaced.

Silverman insists in a Lacanian vein that "language preexists and coerces speech—that it can never be anything but 'Other.'"[57] If to speak and write in one's own language, the mother tongue, nonetheless demands spontaneity, that language conceal its own coercive conditions, then such concealment (a silencing and displacing) was unavailable to Conrad, as a writer who wrote, spoke, and lived in a language that was not his own. It was on loan, under what Aaron Fogel describes as fundamentally coercive, Oedipal conditions.[58] This notion of coercive speech will prove important to Conrad's opening shout as a vexed act of translation, a colonial Malay voice entering (or being thrown into) an Anglophone context via the print form. To be sure, Conrad begins with the shout of a Malay woman, a wife and mother, calling to her husband, a father lost in thoughts of their daughter and wealth, a mixed-race daughter and extractive wealth. These coordinates are not merely triangular or determined by Oedipal psychobiography but colonial.

In "Kaspar! Makan!" we already find some ground over which we cannot quickly move. If we ask of this voice, "Where are you?" this voice could only respond—and perhaps in some language that is not English, "I am somewhere other than 'here.'" Conrad's opening shout is framed at the outset by questions of translation and language, both in the simplest sense (this voice doesn't speak English) and in its utter complexity; for example, what kind of Malay is being spoken and inscribed? Conrad learned English by overhearing it aboard ships, a lingua franca of trade. He stood at the threshold of the audible world he desired to enter and live within. At this threshold, he did not always hear (understand) himself speak.[59] His fictional techniques demand sensitivity to the differentiating and nonunifying effects of listening. At this point, if we were to follow the well-worn path of literary criticism, the question "Who speaks?" would be posed. However, with this shout, a call across an invisible distance, the question becomes, "Who hears?"

FOCALIZATION AND THE COLONIAL EAR

The phonograph and ethnography are modern, technological systems of inscription and knowledge production that depend upon what Barthes was among the first to describe, in relationship to realism in the novel, as the rhetoric of the "detail."[60] These are apparatuses that, in their earliest definition, seek verisimilitude and what Rey Chow calls "fidelity," a term both epistemic and passionate in its charge.[61] Through a certain imperialist logic, one could argue that the representational impulse of ethnographic writing "develops" with photography, followed by the phonograph, and finally ethnographic sound film, as if each involved a progressive move from the imaginary to the real, ultimately seeing and hearing the other from afar.[62] Conrad writes in the moment of the first and second transformations, such that his modernist techniques predict while also preemptively intercede in and imagine later developments.

Almayer's Folly was published in 1895, not long after Edison spoke into the phonograph in 1877. This machine does not appear in the novel, but in the conclusion of chapter 6, Babalatchi, a Malay servant, plays a hand-organ rendition of Verdi's *Il Trovatore* for Lakamba, the rajah of Sambir, who commands him to "fetch the box of music the white captain gave me" (*AF*, 88). This formal position of mechanical reproduction and technological sound makes the image the "center" of the novel, while its moment of acousmatic sound brings the chapter to a close: "Through the open shutter the notes of Verdi's music floated out on the great silence over the river and forest" (*AF*, 88).[63] The chapters continually end at the point where text reaches its limits in sound.

As a form, the novel was made possible by many technologies while also surviving them; it tends toward incorporating technologies that follow it.[64] These include the phonograph, which was adopted almost immediately for ethnographic purposes of capturing and storing what Roshanak Khesthi calls, in relation to a libidinal economy of desire and the rise of "world music," the "aural other."[65] Conrad inscribed the voices and sounds of the Malay Archipelago in the moment of the phonograph's nascence, when the earliest cylinders were not only too fragile but too short and noisy to capture voices and sounds with any fidelity. In Conrad's moment, the novel still superseded the phonograph in its ability to "render," as it were, a reproduction of a three-dimensional sense of acoustics. Conrad turned to novel writing as a particular kind of form, one that offered a mode of representing coloniality different from those of existing colonial technologies: the phonograph (in its logic of storage and preservation) and ethnography (in its logic of capture).

Speaking of Conrad during an interview, the Indonesian novelist Pramoedya Ananta Toer said, "In Conrad's work there are historical facts which have not been recorded elsewhere."[66] As an archive of coloniality and decolonization, Conrad's fiction underscores the novel as a memory system, but one that is essentially violent in the way it gathers together signs.[67] In *Discourse Networks 1800/1900* (in German, *Aufschreibesysteme*, or "notation system"), Kittler turns to physical archives, finding pages and pages of European training manuals that "delegated to mothers first the physical and mental education of their children, then their alphabetization."[68] If, philosophically, Romanticism imagines a primordial Mother's mouth, then, domestically, this same figure teaches reading, pronunciation, and syllabic form. Enclosed, she trains the reading eye into symmetry with pronunciation. Kittler follows the primacy of the letter and alphabetization in 1800 to the differentiation of the senses wrought by the gramophone, film, and typewriter in 1900, but it has gone largely unnoticed that Kittler's archive is exclusively Western.[69] If there is what Ann Laura Stoler calls "a colonial order of things," then there is, too, a colonial system of storage, transmission, and reproduction: the colonial system of education, a system of the linguistic conversion.

Such conversion bears centrally on *Almayer's Folly* in its recording of facts and its production of domestic and colonial space. In reverie, Almayer invokes the fact that Lingard has sent Nina to Singapore for linguistic and religious acculturation by the nuns (where Lingard also sent his kidnapped "daughter," brokered in marriage). This coordinate, which appears in Almayer's first reverie in chapter 1, marks Mrs. Almayer's shout in Malay as something of a refusal of linguistic conversion. However, Mrs. Almayer's origins are quickly said to be Sulu, such that the opening shout indexes forcible transport. Its narrating instance, its spatial acoustics, is shot through with geographic displacement. The sonic trace of Sulu—which is heard in the narrative but not transcribed or even summarized for the reader—demarcates and delimits the social, affective, and economic zones of the household.[70] At issue is how colonial outposting makes itself felt, on the one hand, in a narrative's acoustical production of space (in the diegesis and the space of reading), and, on the other, in what Gerald Prince calls the "threshold of narratability," where events or objects lacking in value or interest do not enter into narrative discourse.[71] Sulu is heard by Almayer (or overheard, since he does not understand it) but not inscribed in the text. Conrad's first words as a writer essentially split the analytic of the discourse network that would account for them. They are the sonic trace of the colonial practices that guarantee the Kittlerian object of memory.

The shout posits itself like a bell, calling the world and then vibrating into it.[72] It is as if the narrative desires the moment when the mystique of the verb could still be believed as what Kittler calls, after Foucault, the "pure poetic flash that disappears without a trace, leaving nothing behind it but the vibration suspended in the air for one brief moment."[73] The voice of a woman vibrates onto the page, yet the fleeting image of the hand organ (subtended by the missing image of the phonograph) makes belatedly sensate the beginning shout as a kind of recording. The opening vibration is also a vocal shard or fragment, a phonographic trace, but it is also a kind of cut or laceration, a mark of separation. The first words manifest on the other side of some loss.

"Phonography means the death of the author; it stores a mortal voice rather than eternal thoughts and turns of phrase," Kittler writes.[74] In Kittler's invocation of Barthes to underscore phonographic inscription's supposed separation of voice and body, suddenly we are not so far from the discourse of the novel. The possibility of posthumous speech, captured in fragments along with its noisy, contingent background, is closely linked for Kittler to the rise of the detail as corporeal evidence in aesthetics but also to the nascence of psychoanalysis and criminology, for which the "meaningless and unconscious" trace is also "unfakeable."[75] Kittler and his inheritors do not include within this network the rise of ethnography,[76] yet the figure of the ethnographic, aural other is always ready to hand as a figure for the Real, the "it" that speaks in Lacan's conception of the unconscious.[77] In the shout, however, we are pursuing the trace that cannot be discerned by ethnological science, neither meaningless nor unconscious. Nor is it simply reflective (an acoustic mirror) of the listener's innermost feelings. It is critically refracting, introducing into consciousness a heterogeneous sound.

It is here that narrative theory becomes most effective as a critique of Kittlerian discourse and its memory system. The call, as a shard of colonial speech, cannot be separated from a colonial ear endowed with the power to attend to and filter sounds and voices. In the terminology afforded by Genette, it is the power to "focalize." Genette's crucial move is to distinguish a focalizer, or the agent who "sees and selects" the particularities of the world to be given over to representation, from the narrator, the one who reports the scene. In his visualism, Genette never describes at length the specificity of sound in relation to focalization, but his interest is drawn in several moments to the tension between seeing and hearing, such that what is heard by a focalizer also escapes its view.[78] We can say that to focalize (acoustically) is to choose among all audible sounds the ones to be attended to. Sounds become in this way not merely heard but listened to.

The focalizer is considered to be a selector of sensory data. It is akin in this way to the focal point of a lens.[79] Genette theorizes focalization as the accompaniment to any literary voicing—at times anonymous, at times coextensive with the narrator, at times splitting between multiple positions. Narrative space, by this logic, is an a priori selected space.[80] In one of the most enigmatic contributions to narrative theory, Maurice Blanchot writes, "the speech of narrative always *lets us feel* that what is being recounted is not being recounted by anyone: it speaks in the neutral."[81]

Blanchot does not address the question of where "it" would "speak." In this floating yet nonetheless purposive dimension of voice, there is a focalizer of what Blanchot names "the neutral space of narrative,"[82] an anonymous accompaniment to any literary voicing, available to narrative though not fully retrievable by it as its condition. Even the most neutral of spaces, one that lets me feel as though "it speaks," is a selected space.[83]

In any event, what matters most—and I say this with all the weight of trying to open for inquiry the focalizer's material reality and the issue of value—is that in Genette's narrative system, selection is ontologically and temporally prior to the narrating instance. Genette never makes any such claim, of course—quite the contrary (for example, in the case of epic, Genette argues for "zero focalization"). Does not the ontological priority of focalization support the diegetic claim to space?[84] For example, in the context of well-edited film sound that sutures the image (that is, allows us to forget that what we listen to emanates electronically from speakers), Alan Williams writes, "Transparent sound practices are 'inaudible' to the extent that the auditor accepts a surrogate listening faculty, that of the apparatus."[85] In the case of narrative, if we accept Genette's splitting of the voice and focalization (and I am suggesting we do, but with a massive proviso), then focalization is nothing less than a surrogate listening faculty. It would seem to be related to, or structurally inseparable from, the experience of reading as a "voice." As the shout calls the world into being, Conrad's narrative inverts the order of things, giving to a citation of Malay speech an audible object prior to any listening subject. In its constitution, the shout has already absorbed its subjective determination, making the object split in its being and mode of presentation. But it is as if it simply lands on the page and creates the world: That dissimulation (its veiled surrogating) is part of its power.

If the novel is a sound technology, then, in its technicity, the focalizer's "selection" is bound up with the discourse network, focalization becoming in this way a highly charged (libidinal) system of inscribing, storing, and retaining sounds and voices in readerly consciousness. After the invention of the phonograph, it becomes possible to say that to focalize is both to pick up and to record, as would a "horned mouth," or the loudspeaker of cylinder players that doubled as a microphone in what Charles Grivel deems a fundamentally androgynous event.[86] But such an analogy breaks down along the axis of readerly consciousness as listening consciousness. For Kittler, the phonograph records but does not "hear"; it picks up, but indiscriminately in a "phonographic unconscious," or the so-called Real.[87] In its technicity, the focalizer sees (or hears) but does not "say." The theory of the focalizer—latent in the case of listening—becomes important to the discourse network of 1900 in that the focalizer is delimited and determined as mode of consciousness; it perceives and *selects*.[88]

The focalizer is defined by its negating power to omit sensory data, though Genette never uses such terms. Logically, the focalizer's capacity to "select" is just as crucial as its ability to block out. But this capacity is especially important for a consideration of sounds and voices that are marginalized in texts: To some extent, they compete not only for attention but for ontological status as "voice." For Genette, voice is the overarching guarantee of narrative (despite being supported by what I am suggesting is an a priori access to something like narrative space). For example, when in Conrad's *Lord Jim* Marlow recalls first meeting Jim on a verandah in Bombay, he remarks upon "an oriental voice [that] began to whine abjectly" and other natives who argue noisily in their language (*LJ*, 70). He remembers these contingent sounds of the background when telling the story of his first encounter with Jim. This encounter not only propels the rest of the novel (its action) but also propels Marlow's narrative, his act of storytelling before a group of anonymous men, which seeks to rescue Jim for inclusion in the warm circle of "one of us." These sounds, Sanjay Krishnan observes, are not incidental but rather part and parcel of the novel's production of colonial space. "This resonance offers the first indication of a world excluded from yet operating alongside Marlow's narrative agenda."[89]

There is, in other words, a colonial focalizer, one that selects the sounds but also *deselects* them in the same instance; they are to be heard, not listened to.[90] Marlow passes through these aural others to arrive at Jim. (As I will return to in Chapter 2, Conrad physicalizes in narrative space the linguistic detritus of an idealized English voice.) But we make a mistake if we think that what is focalized in that moment is the sounds of these voices, as if they were simply available to the focalizer to be heard. What is focalized is the colonial listening consciousness that makes the novel possible, such that the focalizer is a narrative counterpart to a colonial ear. Coloniality hears itself in a technique that will prove significant for Conrad's adoption of free indirect discourse for the acoustical and linguistic production of native interiority when the colonial focalizer "overhears" Mrs. Almayer's consciousness.

The opening call is a shard of Malay (a fragment violently cut from an experience of subjugation) but also a sonic focal point. It localizes the one who shouts somewhere in colonial space. We can imagine that Mrs. Almayer shouts against a diffuse "background" of natural sound and noise. But such sound is not brought to representation; it is not focalized.

The focalizer's capacity for omission is in fact much more determinative of readerly consciousness. When the shout lands on the page, it is a direct quotation; however, this report implies an ear through which it has passed linguistically and sonically. This ear, belonging to a colonial focalizer, remains implicit in representation if only because the narration, in the third person, remains anonymous. But the quotation, qua quotation, also an optical index, marks the existence of this third set of ears (between Almayer and Mrs. Almayer). Someone, some entity, has heard the shout and "selected" it for representation. The focalizer turns immediately to the consciousness of Almayer: We can presume it is he who has focalized the shout, yet this turn establishes that Almayer won't heed the call. Almayer has heard but not listened. In other words, Conrad splits the shout's acoustic event such that it exceeds its inscription and focalization.

The colonial focalizer involves the reader in the problem of colonial consciousness as a linguistic listening consciousness. The power to begin in *Almayer's Folly* is, from its first instance, tied up with the power of selection, citation, translation, and inscription; its performative is constitutively appropriative. Though *Almayer's Folly* begins by fiat, the primacy of selection configures the possibility of its event.

As a matter of structuralist constraint, Genette does not ask the spatial questions "where does the voice come from?" or "where does it go?" That is why I claimed in the Overture that, faced with such moments, we necessarily engage not a rhetoric or a poetics but an "acoustics."

Kittler suggests that in the discourse network of 1900, the phonograph "registers acoustic events as such."[91] But what is this "as such" when it concerns colonial sound space, one harnessed by and consolidated in the presentation of a "world?" Kittler often has implicit racialized categories in mind when he writes of phonographic sound, black and non-Western sound recordings occupying the place of the "Real" in relation to the (white, European) symbolic.[92] The myth of the nonrepresentational acoustic event or of the so-called soundscape is an ideological form, and it cannot be separated from the contested spaces in which sounds and voices travel.[93] Part of that contestation involves, from the beginning, constitutive exclusions that bear profoundly on the novel as a form that registers events not recorded elsewhere.

ARCHIVING THE UNSAID

"The maternal gift is language in a nascent state, pure breath as a limit value from which the articulated speech of others begins."[94] Kittler ironizes the foundational conviction of technics in the Romantic era circa 1800: Through the apparatuses of training and memorization, Mother "creates . . . Poetry" but cannot herself "pronounce" it.[95] "Mother Nature is silent so that others can speak of and for her."[96] What kind of "silence" does Kittler indicate? He means that statements are perhaps inspired by Woman but that they cannot be fully attributed to her. With Conrad's beginning in a commanding voice of a woman, something of the "voice that keeps silence," in Derrida's phrase, or the inner voice that doesn't sound yet guarantees presence, can be routed through yet another dimension: the unsaid.

The discourse network of 1800 depends upon the figure of some "other" woman who is not Mother and haunts the scene at a distance. The *nyai*, but also "Venus," the figure whose traces Saidiya Hartman pursues in the ledgers and sentimental literature of the transatlantic slave trade, are "names for a distance." I take this phrase from Christopher Miller's invocation of the way that certain utterances "tend to be hints rather than statements, hearsay rather than direct evidence, allegory rather than realism."[97] These utterances demand a particular kind of textual practice, a reading for the implicit or tacit, which brings us to the specific inflection of "silence" that Kittler avoids.

In *Along the Archival Grain*, Stoler reads the Dutch East Indies' administrative archives against themselves to find affective artifacts that cannot be woven into national and bureaucratic narratives, artifacts that are closely related to what Stoler calls "imperial debris."[98] In engaging with colonial archives, Stoler argues, one must postulate what is not written because it "goes without saying" and what is "unwritten because it could not yet be articulated."[99] Conrad's opening shout—as what I take to be one of such traces—will prove to be a special case not only for the theory of the novel, the enunciating instance, and overhearing native interiority but for the methodological problems posed by listening to and reading for the unsaid. From another perspective, the unsaid is what is unheard or not listened to by a colonial ear. It is here that the politics of the novel as a sound technology makes itself felt.

In isolating the two words that inaugurate Conrad's first novel and seeking therein a novelistic resonance of the archive's unsaid, Stoler's archival grain is exemplary. Although the Dutch East Indies archives' primary function, like that of all archives, was to amass material, its sheaths of paper—passing through "government offices, filled with directors, assistant directors, scribes, and clerks"—are doubled, Stoler suggests, by what is "not written." Here, the antithesis to amassment takes precedence. These include the margins of archives or "what was written oblique to official prescriptions and on the ragged edges of protocol [that] produced the administrative apparatus."[100] Alongside of amassment, a plentitude of documents, we find counterproduction. In other words, it is as if incitement to discourse coproduces its negative in the tacit, from *tacere*, or verbal silence, what goes without saying (not to be confused with *silere* as the absence of noise, linked in its etymology to the silence of the dead).[101] Its activity is suspended, just before speech or a holding back, as in the *tacet* direction of a musical score indicating that an instrument should "keep quiet." Yet as Nancy Rose Hunt makes clear in confronting written documentation of "the sound of twisted laughter that convulsed around forms of sexual violence" in memories of colonial-era Congo,[102] the incitement to discourse also coproduces the opposite of discourse in sounds, shouts, and cries.

In *Almayer's Folly*, the shout of a woman carries across some distance, which begins the novel as a simple spatial marker or threshold between "here" and "there," home and outpost. The enormous weight of this distance is made sensible belatedly, when the name of the woman is given (only in part) as Mrs. Almayer. The reader grasps the relationship between the addressor and the addressee as interracial and also miscegenating. (They have a daughter, Nina, said in Almayer's reverie to be light-skinned.) Conrad's first words make sensible what in Kittler's thought is conditioned by the subjugated body of a woman in imperial and colonial memory—an unthought. These memories are necessarily incomplete, and, in the archive, they assume the form of what Hartman calls "scraps" and Stoler "debris." Kittler's concept of "discourse network" cannot address the binding agent, as it were, of debris, which links Conrad's opening shout somewhat unexpectedly to the colonial archive. How, or by what means, we can begin to think of Conrad's novel as itself an archive of sound and listening is precisely at issue.

Colonial debris does not circulate in a "network." It is not as if the discursive field could simply be expanded to include such material. The fact of resonance is what both holds and disperses. It is the form of memory and consciousness, a shape moving in time, assumed by colonial debris. We find one articulation of this fact by Hartman when she takes up the many incarnations of "Venus," or "an emblematic figure" in the Atlantic world, a woman who, despite the trappings of romance, "makes plain the convergence of terror and pleasure in the libidinal economy of slavery."[103] Though the reality of slave labor in Borneo is "excised" from Conrad's novel (along with the primitive accumulation of capital in coal, mined by kidnapped Sulus and Philippine islanders),[104] slavery's libidinal economy is not. It resonates in Conrad's early corpus.

Writing at what she calls "the limits of the unspeakable and the unknown" in the archive, Hartman finds herself "listening for the unsaid, translating miscon-

strued words."[105] In this same way, Hunt describes a methodology of working
with "sensory traces parsed from a refractory colonial archive to anchor a reading
of the immediacy of anguish and ruination and of the kinds of sounds and images people were left with."[106] Such ruination becomes, for Hunt, a countereth-
nographic field where hearing rather than the spectacular dimension of seeing
takes precedence: an "acoustic register" of violence.

If the rise of the genre of the novel cannot be thought outside of the discourse
network of 1800, animated by the breath of Mother, then it cannot be thought
outside of Venus and the *nyai* and their mode of sensorial coappearance. If the
genre of the novel persists into the discourse network of 1900, redefined by a
logic of reiteration premised upon the technological separation of the senses
("gramophone, film, typewriter"), then it follows that the novel circa 1900 is no
less defined by the "apparatuses of power, storage, transmission, training, reproduction . . . that make up the conditions of factual discursive occurrences."[107]
These conditions of (dis)appearance and separation are freighted with the unnamed woman. She is not to be confused with the Mother who breathes life into
discourse. She cannot be shown. Her (dis)appearance enjoins us to listen for the
unsaid. It is some other resonance that cannot be easily retrieved for the metaphysical warmth of idealization and inwardness.

For Hunt, Conrad contributes in *Heart of Darkness* to a hallucinatory representation of the Congo that forecloses representation of the acoustic register
of violence, a problem I return to in Chapter 3 through the fact of an entanglement between sound, mineral wealth, and sexual violence. These coordinates,
however, already inflect the Malay Archipelago of *Almayer's Folly* as a material
trace. In 1890, he carried the first draft of the novel with him to the Congo, a draft
that was tied up with Conrad assuming his identity as a writer, an English writer.
The unsaid of sexual violence inflects the novel's elliptical modes of presentation, its temporality, beginning with the shout from which Almayer turns away.
In the midst of that reverie, as the sun is setting, "blotting" the horizon, Almayer
awakens to remember he has been called and to find it has become completely
dark, missing the sunset. Twilight becomes in relation to focalization a missing
image. From the beginning, then, the elision of the sexual violence that attenu-
ates the unsaid colonial miscegenation is constitutive of the novel's modes of
elliptical presentation.

These modes include resonant delays, where hearing occurs first and understanding follows much later, a delay that actuates an acoustical dimension of what
Ian Watt famously names in Conrad "delayed decoding."[108] The reader recalls a

passing note or misconstrued word and returns to it later, at some indeterminate time. At times, however, decoding is, in Watt's term, "denied." In such moments, the sensory details lack focality; they drift and continue to drift in reading consciousness. The unsaid resounds. As I will show, however, this resonance does not make itself available to be "decoded," which is really an extension (in cognitive time) of the line that moves between signifier and signified. Neither is resonance, in Lacan's terminology, a "floating signifier" without object or referent.

For Kittler, the archive is not a positive place to be discovered and located. Colonial debris, however, is what the discourse network, as "apparatuses of power . . . that make up the conditions of factual discursive occurrences," leaves behind. The title of Genette's book, *Discours du récit*, discloses two motivating terms: discourse and recitation. If the novel is one site of the discourse network, then debris is its residuum, an aftereffect or trace of a nondiscursive occurrence: a trace of the unsaid.

The task of reading becomes a negative one—a fact of resonance. It involves asking what authoritative gestures of literary foundations exclude.[109] Drawing upon the work of Stoler, for example, Christopher GoGwilt demonstrates Conrad's familiarity with *nyai* narratives, or sentimental fiction that originated in Dutch colonial culture.[110] For readers familiar with the figure of the *nyai* (including "the not-yet-Indonesian readers of the turn of the century"),[111] the fact of colonial sexual violence, servitude, and exchange resonates from the novel's beginning. But even without such familiarity, the novel becomes sensible as having inscribed what GoGwilt calls, in relation to Gayatri Chakravorty Spivak's image of the Third World woman, "a disappearing subaltern reading effect of *nyai* narrative form." This effect is produced through both distortion and repetition to "mark a difference in a reader's sense of the *nyai* narrative pattern."[112] But such distortion and repetition mark a difference in the reader's senses more generally, as with the differentiating effect or resonance of the shout within the reader voice. As Almayer gazes over the Pantai River, "He absorbed himself in his dream," ignoring both the call and sunset to introduce into narrative the negativity of the missing response and missing image. We learn in Almayer's dream that, in exchange for agreeing to a marriage, Almayer had received a position in Lingard's company. Lingard could barely utter his proposition.[113] That the enunciating instance of *Almayer's Folly* is lined with colonial debris, with sexual coercion and violence, may be immediately sensible or perhaps becomes sensible to the reader only later, a fact of resonance that not only includes intertextual futures but demands them for its articulation.[114]

In *Lord Jim*, the third novel of the Malay trilogy, Conrad returns once again to the figure of the *nyai*. This word, however, is not said in Conrad's novels. In the part of the novel that takes place on the island of Patusan, Jewel becomes a *nyai* to Jim; she is herself the daughter of an unnamed *nyai*. At a certain moment, she tells Marlow her mother's story in confidence. Much of what she says escapes focality, the unsaid instead being indexed by tone, volume, and pitch: "'And suddenly I heard her quiet whisper again,'" Marlow recounts. "'And she added, still lower if possible. . . . [A]fter a time the strange, still whisper wandering dreamily in the air stole into my ears. . . . We subdued our tones to a mysterious pitch'" (*LJ*, 314). Marlow's recollection brings us to the threshold of narratability but also to a threshold of the audible.[115] In these gaps, the unsaid resonates. In narratives determined by coloniality, we can think of the inaudible as evading the focalizer's hegemonic audition, such that the sound is not focalized (brought to a point) but drifts. With sound's drift, we enter into a relation of escaping a certain grasp and entering into another.

In relaying the drift of her voice, reading consciousness as listening consciousness, too, atmospherically "catches" (*auffange*) a certain drift, as Freud says of the free-floating attention, recognizing while not fully understanding the enormous weight of the *nyai*'s plight. Neither wife nor concubine, domestically subservient, her story is without normative structure. Marlow remarks upon "'These few sounds wandering in the dark'" (*LJ*, 315). Such movement constitutes a circulatory memory system of the Pacific and Atlantic, sounds drifting errantly between texts, between oceanic coordinates, such that the *nyai* and her avatars appear where they are not. (To the extent that Conrad names the novel, in its formal innovation of the voice of Marlow, a "free and wandering tale," the *nyai* would seem to determine the novel's elliptical techniques, its very claim to voice [*LJ*, viii].) The sound is a paratext of the colonial archive, recording a kind of absence or charged negativity. Colonial debris includes sounds and images left behind by the descriptive function of the utterance; something of it is not a message at all. In the novel, it can appear as a shortness of breath.

What can be enunciated, articulated, and said when the speaking subject has been constituted through its occlusion? "Kaspar! Makan!" is a sonic shard of such occlusion. If we understand the archive but also decolonization to be ongoing processes, Conrad's early project is an archive of colonial sound debris, twinned by its ongoing modes of listening.[116] In its negativity, it exerts pressure on the focalizer. Like the focalizer, Kittler's model is essentially positive. By contrast, how do we seek out a world that was not yet recorded, not yet said—a negative recording?

AUDIBILITY

With the opening shout, Conrad draws our attention to how, in the Western philosophic tradition, the audible is physicalized in space and feminized as a border. A long tradition of French feminist discourse (Hélène Cixous and Julia Kristeva but also extending to such figures as the Italian philosopher Adriana Cavarero and the American poet and classicist Anne Carson) has located along this border cries, screams, crooning, chatter, and nonsense and with it a "gender of sound."[117] As I return to in Chapter 3, when Plato consolidates the meaning of the rational tradition as a transmission of the idea, he takes care to craft a scene of physical omission and banishment of feminine voice as sound.

The threshold of the audible is not simply a matter of loudness, nor is it one of pronunciation or timbre. There are sounds that do not become more or less audible through volume. Sound, as the *Oxford English Dictionary* suggests, is "that which is and may be heard."[118] I cite this definition as one that opens the recent volume *Keywords in Sound* but also because of its passive grammar, which masks the verb's subject and, with it, audibility as it is in relation to a listener. There is a spatial configuration of audibility, a "distribution of the sensible," and a distribution of sounds and points of their reflection in relation to a listener.[119] The definition in the *OED*, a project begun in the moment of the imperial expansion of English, rests upon a hypothetical space and, with it, a tautology (an "is" that "is") but also a potentiality ("that which may be").[120] Its definition is missing, to some extent, a preposition and its medial force (heard by, heard through), which thrust sound into a relational ontology and a space of coconfiguration.

"May be heard" is a modal verb, neither past nor present. Audibility is not a purely material category that can be pluralized and distributed in a series, as would be a series of things. From the moment we concern ourselves with audibility, we are concerned with sensual and somatic potentialities for recognition and transformation. As I discuss at length in Chapter 2 and the Intersonority, recognition is audiovisual in its charge. We learn from the shout at the threshold of Conrad's fiction—a demand by a woman who is not yet seen, not yet listened to—that audibility is the supportive yet occluded force of "voice" as the subject of the verb's mode of action. Tense and mood are dividers not only between inside and outside (the parent structure and its ancillary) but between what has happened and what may happen. To the extent that grammar can be wielded by the colonizer as a weapon—to posit subjects who are then deemed primitive, retrograde, or in need of civilizing—Conrad continually marks space for transformation through mood, for speaking not *for* someone else but *as if* someone else. "Perhaps it would be . . . on a verandah draped in motionless foliage. . .in the deep dusk," the unnamed narrator recalls of an event of listening to Marlow in *Lord Jim* (*LJ*, 33), the acoustical heightened and vision dampened.

"Kaspar! Makan!" as a call tantamount to an offscreen voice, is fundamentally acousmatic. Its power, the imperative mood, gathers its spatializing and temporalizing effect.

Yet something of the call-and-response relation has already been broken in the novel's first instance. "The definition of speech in colonialism, and by extension, of modern speech," Aaron Fogel argues, is "overhearing," such that dialogue is "flat," lacks "depth," and cannot adequately prepare interlocutors for the future.[121] Much later in the novel, Babalatchi will call to Almayer, receiving no verbal response. "He does not hear," Babalatchi then says to Nina. "Nina nodded to him with an uncertain smile, and was going to speak, when a sharp report from the gun mounted in the bow of the steam launch that was just then coming into view arrested the words on her parted lips. . . . From the hills far away the echo came back like a long-drawn and mournful sigh" (*AF*, 106–107).

The chapters continually end with an acousmatic sound heard on the verandah (both the mode of listening and the spatial location marking a threshold, Michael Greaney describes). But these introduce, in the failure of speech, an acute listening consciousness, one attuned to the threshold of the audible and its portents. Just after we are reminded he is "deaf" to a woman's cry, Almayer "heard a splash," followed by an "indistinct form": "His half-dead hope made his ears preternaturally acute to any sound on the river" (*AF*, 74). Someone approaches the house. Hearing sounds in the dark, Almayer first conjectures "Arabs," not yet knowing that it is Dain who approaches until he sounds his voice, addressing him as "Tuan."[122] Dain is the figure for whom Almayer is waiting. Just as we meet Almayer, he has already long been hoping for wealth owed from his allegiances, waiting for Dain Maroola ("Dain," another reference that drifts into Almayer's reveries, one that the reader has no means of understanding, not only because the character has yet to be introduced).[123] All of this suspension is held by the ambiguity of address, which drifts linguistically and politically.[124] The scene is drenched in the acousmatic, of listening for the slightest signal of sound that might reveal what cannot be seen.

The sensible is never simply or immediately such but rather regulated, censored, or organized by laws that are perhaps not fully discoverable as laws, for there is no place outside of representation from which to see them. Visibility is the perceptual condition of the object as it might present itself to vision, audibility the condition of the object as it might present itself to audition.[125] In

Conrad, we are seeking neither "light itself" nor "sound itself" but the political threshold of what is and may be heard. These determine the subjective, somatic, and political possibilities for recognition. Consequently, the moment we ask of the literary work "Who hears?" or "Who listens?" we are thrust into questions of recognition.

For example, Conrad borrows the subaltern voice to demand recognition, but for whom? If the subaltern voice is to be recognized as such, under what narrative conditions can it be heard? Spivak would perhaps suggest that there can be no such event of hearing according to the master discourse because the subaltern cannot speak.[126] "If, in the context of colonial production, the subaltern has no history and cannot speak, the subaltern as female is even more deeply in shadow."[127] Nonetheless, she sounds.[128] There are, we have already noted, traces through which subaltern consciousness may become audible in narrative despite a colonial focalizer's refusal to recognize them. The demand, then, is not to hear a "voice" but rather to hear difference and to recognize its imperative on the scene. The demand, the imperative, is also to hear transformation, a cut between what is and may be.

It is through (English) grammar that "voice" is dramatically split in its potential for representing coloniality: It subjugates the other, yet it can involve a counter-insurgency, a conjugation of differences. In other words, Conrad splits hearing and listening along a postcolonial axis, such that hearing (in which Almayer is trapped) is to be trapped in a reduced-by-half reality.

The Italian philosopher Gemma Fiumara notes, in a Heideggerian vein, that the *logos* is a "reduced-by-half concept of language," by which she means that metaphysics severs speech from its "other side," which is listening.[129] Speech (as saying) and listening are paired. What Cavarero similarly names "the devocalization of logos" is a reduction of its other side, such that the *logos* is diminished in its audibility.[130] If saying and listening are paired, then an originary part of the concept of the voice is its audibility. Nonetheless, just as we prefer to speak of vision, rather than visibility, we prefer to speak of audition rather than audibility. Audibility means that the "I" who speaks not only imputes a "you" who listens but a spatial relation, a closeness or nearness ("to speak nearby," says Trinh). Separated from the essence of the operation "I am hearing myself at the same time that I speak," Conrad's opening shout is staggered in its duration. It is differentially copresent with the reader voice without being at the same time. It resonates.

But can the crux of recognition fully come into being in Conrad's world? Mrs. Almayer's command is to hear, but if it is to hear difference, to recognize its presence on the scene, then it will involve a failure of understanding. To say "it resonates" is neither to say "it speaks" nor "it is understood." The shout is an imaginary auditory object, but in registering facts that are not recorded elsewhere, it actuates reading as historical consciousness. Resonance is a mutual struggle across some distance. In the hearing and (mis)understanding of colonial sounds, in the way that they tend to appear on the scene as if no one is there to receive them or to record their existence for history, colonial sounds are reduced by half. They are half-presented objects, and from that cut or reduction they gain in their potency.

THE HALF-PRESENTED OBJECT

Conrad understood that iteration means both separability and return. With the image of the hand organ, iterability is a formal condition of the novel's elliptical and proleptical temporality, where events are not only severed from chronology but repeated. Conrad returns to the shout and to Almayer's failure to listen across the novel, sending the narrative anachronically back to where it began, back, that is, to a sonic trace. In the final paragraph of chapter 5, for example, it is as if diegetic time has not advanced at all: "And with a gesture of abandoned discouragement Almayer . . . would abandon himself to the current of bitter thoughts, oblivious of the flight of time and the pangs of hunger, deaf to the shrill cries of his wife calling him to the evening meal" (AF, 34). In the novel's strategic ellipses, the shout is not sent and received at the same time; it is recorded and then subsequently returned to, the record in its groove. It arrives in the reader voice untranslated and difficult to pronounce. This distancing, also a deferral, in the essence of the operation of self-hearing, anatomizes the novel's presentation of the fact of decolonization. Almayer, we suspect, cannot listen to what the shout portends and still hold on to his fantasies.

Conrad's earliest mimetic concern was for an occlusive element folded into the will to representation.[131] In Almayer's Folly, this energy is tied up with the temporal determinations of decolonization that escape Almayer's focalization. For Almayer's "folly" is, at least in part, his gamble—a false, disappointed hope—that the British will take over Sambir, but it is the Dutch who formally achieve that both in the diegetic time of the novel and Conrad's own life.[132] Such folly is the novel's "disnarrated."[133] Prince's brief and radical essay posits the disnarrated as a species of elision (in French: dénarré). It refers to "alethic expressions of impossibility or unrealized possibility, deontic expressions of observed prohibition, epistemic expressions of ignorance, ontologic expressions of nonexistence, purely imagined worlds, desired worlds . . . failed attempts, crushed hopes," etc.[134] What Prince describes as the disnarrated's fundamentally alethic temporality (that is, its mood, its modal denotation of necessity, contingency, and impossibility) fractures narrative temporality. Under the sway of Almayer's consciousness, the novel cannot be narrated linearly. Its events are premised upon not only what happened but what did not happen. His folly is one determination of the sonic shards of empire, or the sound effect through which colonial and decolonial temporality first communicates itself at the novel's outset: its opening shout whose translation is delayed by reverie.

> Leaning with both his elbows on the balustrade of the verandah, he went on looking fixedly at the great river that flowed—indifferent and hurried—before his eyes. He liked to look at it about the time of sunset; perhaps because at that time the sinking sun would spread a glowing gold tinge on the waters of the Pantai, and Almayer's thoughts were often busy with gold.
>
> . . .
>
> He shivered in the night air, and suddenly became aware of the intense darkness which, on the sun's departure, had closed in upon the river, blotting out the outlines of the opposite shore. (*AF*, 3–11, *passim*)

In reciting the sun's passage, from sinking sun to intense darkness, I have passed over eight pages, populated by Almayer's reveries and fragmentary references to events, names, and places that we have no means of understanding. I have represented that passage typographically as an ellipsis.[135] It constitutes the interval between sunset and darkness, when sunlight scatters in the upper atmosphere. The image of twilight does not appear. It stands as a missing image. As he turns away from the call to "blot out" certain facts, the visible world continues without us. It is as if there is a world that is not essentially phenomenal or given to consciousness in its dependency on things as they are for it. Hasn't the Jamesian center of consciousness has been displaced by a transnational sensible? It is a marginal sensing or fringe awareness without any certainly of belonging to the here and now that anxiously senses its borders. "Setting" itself wanes. It almost misses its will to appearance. In this small and difficult-to-recuperate quantity, structure becomes weak and dissoluble, vulnerable to counterinsurgencies. On the heels of his shiver, the opening call is obliquely translated. When Almayer awakes from the reverie, it's too late; we've already lost the consolidating gaze.

Acoustically, Conrad's first words in the Malay shout come from *between* European colonial systems, between a range of European and non-European regimes of power, past and to come, a future that includes the impending presence of the United States (circa 1900) in what is now the Philippines. As I will return to, this resonance would not have been lost on William Faulkner, who writes US imperialism and maritime expansion in the Global South into the elliptical sound effects of *Sanctuary* (1931).[136] It is a Conradian strategy that decenters the narrative's claim to an enclosed region of the American South. The *English* of Conrad's novel—not only the language of Lingard but the impossible English-language event of the narrative itself—is the auditory event of acceding or receding, positive and negative, diachronic and anachronic *resonant* dominance.

For in its resonance, Conrad's novel is just as much an experiment in spatial acoustics as it is in time. Although Nina has returned, having received a colonial education from the nuns in Singapore, we never witness Nina's acculturation in the narrative except as referenced briefly in memories. In this ellipsis, there is another textual production of spatial distance. The deferred translation of the opening shout and the temporal elision of Nina's study abroad are in fact part and parcel of the narrative's spatial-acoustical production. There is a pseudo-spatial chamber in which the memory of acculturation resonates with the novel's opening, untranslated shout. Almayer is surprised when Nina suddenly speaks to him in English, likely with greater facility than his own. The novel becomes in this moment autotelic, for we suddenly wonder, in an acoustic mirror, why we read English.[137]

But in the novel's sound effects, we experience, in other words, that the novel's English-language discourse is premised upon a kind of factual impossibility. Each of its characters have been brought—by a colonial focalizer—to translation.

English is itself a half presentation, which is to say, the novel's mode of elision begins with the fact of inscribing the shout on the page, an optical displacement of Malay by the Romanized alphabet. The lingua franca of a print Malay form will later become *bahasa Indonesia*, the linguistic vehicle of anticolonial nationalism memorably described by Benedict Anderson in *Imagined Communities*. But at the time of Conrad's composition, such a moment had not yet come to pass or was still in the making. Is not Almayer's failure to listen an acoustical displacement of the fact of decolonization? He still holds out for some other false dream; he is not yet reconciled to the decolonial tilting of diegetic and world-historical events.

Over the course of his work, GoGwilt has pursued these displaced valences in Conrad in what he calls, after Conrad, "half obliterated words."[138] "Makan," GoGwilt describes, is not written in Arabic script, as Malay was traditionally, but in the Roman-letter alphabet, which, in 1895, was moving toward what would become the national, standardized, and anticolonial language Indonesian.[139]

The opening *acousmêtre* and its twin, a missing image, is a record of this now-occluded linguistic history.[140]

The print form—and the textual incitement of acoustics—is a half-presented decolonial portent. "Words are solicited only for their effacement from the page," Trinh writes of master discourses (we can include the European novel among them). "Their materiality, their glaring bodies must somehow sink and disappear from the field of visibility, to yield ground to the 'pure presence' or that which he attempts to capture and retain, which, however, always lies outside words."[141] We think of the page as detritus, a mere carrier that sheds its mediacy to transmit the idea, an essence.[142] The optical effect of the opening shout—which presents only to efface—is profoundly imaginary in its power. It is held in suspense for some time before we arrive at any exposition of her consciousness.

As presented optically on the page, the word "Makan!" is within the orbit of what Emily Apter calls the "untranslatable." Simply translating it as "eat" gives no sense of its weighty significance. Its significance is its sound effect, its optical, auditory, and durational relation to print, the act of reading, the narrative voice, and the reader voice and its conjectural sound. On the immediate (textual) surface, "Makan!" appears as a half-presented object.[143] To be sure, there is a surface effect because the word's syllabic form renders it pronounceable (Ma-kan), but again, it is in relation to an implied listener or imputed listening subject: It is audible (to me). There is, then, a mirroring effect, which is central to its translation. Audibility and legibility are here counterparts, an effect ideologically invisible to the imputed or idealized English reader, who shares an alphabet with the shout. What we introduce with the shout's half presentation, in other words, is the important distinction between translation and *transliteration*.

"The Romanized Malay form"[144] preserves—in its optics and legibility—the historical and linguistic detritus of colonial transformation, the now-eroded Arab power over the region. (These are precisely the kinds of questions that do not enter into Kittler's discussion of the rise of the typewriter.) Printed in this way, as a half-presented object that offers itself to the English reader to be sounded out, the word "Makan!" not only accommodates the reader's desire for a world at a distance but also brings it sonorously near. For a moment, the novel stands in evasive relation to the English language: The narrative voice "speaks" in an imaginary tongue of the other. Without any voiceover to locate the call in its natural "setting," the sound of the word begins as ambiguously other. In that sense, from the text's beginnings the focalization of the word "Makan" involves the problems of ethnography, for the word and its associated voice—to appear *in* and *as* text—requires description, transcription, and translation, each of which is marked by cultural power relations. We circle back, in other words, to the problem of selection, of what the focalizer mutely records while also determining it as sensible. There is a resonant conjunction of appearance and disappearance, or a surface tension. By what means can the reader say this shout or this voice "belongs" to a subject who has been articulated by a colonial narrative consciousness?

The initiating instance of the novel is direct discourse, a concept that generally demands that readers attribute voices to subjects. When this shard lands on the page, with its pseudo-three-dimensional effect, that effect can gain in reality only to the extent that the narrative apparatus, after a long hiatus in twilight, can continue to move "inside" of the colonized subject, to speak "in" her voice.

The sound effects of the novel thus require that we consider Conrad's adaption of the Flaubertian technique of free indirect discourse for coloniality. It will prove to be, in his hands, a vexed acousmatic and ventriloquizing technology. As the narrative continues, we finally receive a version of Mrs. Almayer's story presented in her consciousness. But the imputed "freedom" of free indirect discourse to move between observer and observed to create a third language between them is limited and determinate. What happens to the hermeneutic of "free" indirect discourse when it is also understood as a translation? Free indirect discourse is not an inner monologue: It is already premised upon some translation between sensibility and language, such that the language (its style) can be heterogeneous to a character's speech. But we confront with Mrs. Almayer a double and perhaps triple translation that strikes at the heart of "hearing (understanding) oneself speak."

So many names, positions, and values have been exchanged in order to produce the novel's opening call as a psychic and linguistic genealogy of coloniality and transnationality. How can this genealogy attest to its own history, speak in its own voice, the supreme Enlightenment value, if its appearance in discourse is premised upon half obliteration and half presentation?

FREE INDIRECT DISCOURSE AS FORCIBLE TRANSLATION

The shout already indicates a spatial maneuver of the colonial coordinate. For it is as if the voice is traversing the globe from the Dutch East Indies to speak ethnographically for readers at home in England. Conrad reflects in the acoustic mirror the desire to hear the aural other, brought home from afar; that is part of the colonial impulse in which the new machine is embroiled. As we have seen, the rise of new media at the turn of the last century cannot be separated from colonial administrators' desire to record, preserve, and then "salvage" cultures, even as they acted as the force of their destruction.[145] Kittler's monumental re-classification of the object of literary study is ghosted by the colonial nexus under erasure, though he claimed to have hit upon the basic, elemental fact of sonic inscription. It is as if in an acoustic inversion or mirror, we can find alongside a discourse network a sounding-out of its linguistic and paralinguistic conditions in colonial violence, including coercive linguistic acculturation. At issue is how acculturation bears upon the possibility of *Almayer's Folly*, the novel's temporality, and its claim to "voice."

The novel's narrating instance is fundamentally mediated by an act of translation, which posits a focalizing entity through which all languages seem to pass conterminously: Malay, Dutch, and Arabic are translated into English, though Almayer, the novel's central consciousness, can himself speak only in elementary English that also secures his ability to conduct business with Lingard. English, as the novel's medium (and media), is part and parcel of its production of transparency, its temporal suture. When selecting voices, the colonial focalizer hears and selects according to language and its forms of domination. What it reflects back to the reader is unambiguous: the English reader's desire for a world at a distance. In that reflection, Conrad is working through a technics that does not claim to "capture" the colonized subject's voice.

The birth of ethnographic film solved the problem of how to present the imperial auditory field while also consolidating it from afar through description and inscription, and it did so by means of what Mary-Louise Pratt calls, in relation to written practices, "the monarch-of-all-I-survey." To be sure, such a monarch sees with what Pratt calls "imperial eyes," but the monarch speaks in the consolidated voice and also hears with what Edwin C. Hill calls "imperial ears."[146]

The "murmur of the rapids below filled my ears," Paul Belloni du Chaillu writes in a late-nineteenth-century African travelogue excerpted by Pratt. I want to linger for a moment in this sound (though numerous sounds populate the documents Pratt studies, she focuses on the visual subject of ethnography). This murmur is a close companion to the abyssal experience Homi Bhabha names "colonial nonsense," an experience annotated, for example, by the narrative acoustics of the Marabar Caves that echo "Ou-Boom" to a terrified British listener in E. M. Forester's *A Passage to India*.[147] The murmur is language barely audible and words falling into phonemes, an inchoate sound, one that must be converted by the monarchic self into sense and discourse. As he stands before the valley, seeing and hearing the rapids from a summit position, Du Chaillu desires to cast the "light of Christian civilization"[148] on the Congolese. It is an "interventionist fantasy," Pratt suggests. But what does such a desire for intervention involve if not the Book, the Word, and their *fiat lux*? If that work of conversion is to be achieved, the "murmur of the rapids"—native sound—must first be converted into sense through alphabetization. The auditory setting annotates without naming the coercive fact of linguistic (re)acculturation, which mediates the scene and allows its subject and object to come into view.

To convert sound is not simply to describe it ethnographically. The work of conversion is metonymized by the sound to involve the reader—the reader voice—in a technique of converting sound into sense. Such psychic enactment in reading is the fundamental basis of a projective identification with the other. This other, the fantasy goes, can be acculturated into Western letters, that is, learn to read and to pronounce the word of God. To read of the sound becomes, in essence, an acoustic mirror that reflects back the successful work of conversion.

In this way, the imperial ear is distinct from what I've called the colonial ear. Colonial desire is not simply to intervene in and preside over but to merge with and possess (one whose libidinal economy, for the colonizer, is strategically sounded-out by Conrad but in ways that remain traumatically unthought).[149]

Emergent sound technologies, the phonograph and ethnographic writing, both simultaneously depended on the oral while superseding it through a different mode of technological mediation and order of *logos* (colonial knowledge production). But the novel, as a form, becomes a "modern" technology of voice only in its discovery of free indirect discourse. This technology depends upon techniques of listening (or what Jonathan Sterne might call "audile techniques")[150] through which voices and sounds become audible. In focalizing, an ear chooses to ignore or only hears in part. The analytic of free indirect discourse begins from the same premise as focalization: The one who is sensing is not the one who is saying. The fact that Mrs. Almayer's consciousness is focalized at all already depends upon an act of translation. Her interiority is presented to us in English, the language of the novel's master discourse. In that act of translation, something of her interiority is relayed, that is, brought "home" to the reader and into the serene region of reading. In Conrad's moment of the rise of phonograph, such a reproduction is not unlike a recording of another world that might travel and traverse a distance through sonic inscription. The possibility of translation has everything to do with transmission, with the prefix "trans-" as "carrying over across" the imagined voice of the other home to England. (These issues will become more pronounced in Chapter 3, when I consider the novel's relationship to telecommunications.) Literary theory has yet to think through the acousmatic complexities posed by free indirect discourse and its drift.[151]

Free indirect discourse, as a "voicing" of colonial consciousness, localizes the corporeal politics of Conrad's novel. It is in effect a forcible translation or coersive linguistic acculturation, a violation.[152] It reinstantiates in the space of reading—at the very threshold of text and sound—the violence inherent in the colonial encounter. If the narrative apparatus claims to "overhear" Mrs. Almayer's consciousness, then it cannot be anything but the acoustic mirror of an implied English reader. Through this technology, a reader might believe in the narrative's claim to her consciousness, to intuit who she is and what she might feel. When Mrs. Almayer finally tells her story in the novel, it is spoken putatively in her own "voice" but through the medium of free indirect discourse, put to work:

> She realised that with this vanishing gleam her old life departed too. Thenceforth there was slavery in the far countries, amongst strangers, in unknown and perhaps terrible surroundings. Being fourteen years old, she realised her position and came to that conclusion, the only one possible to a Malay girl, soon ripened under a tropical sun, and not unaware of her personal charms, of which she heard many a young brave warrior of her father's crew express an appreciative admiration. There was in her the dread of the unknown; otherwise she accepted her position calmly, after the manner of her people, and even considered it quite natural; for was she not a daughter of warriors, conquered in battle, and did she not belong rightfully to the victorious Rajah? Even the evident kindness of the terrible old man must spring, she thought, from admiration for his captive, and the flattered vanity eased for her the pangs of sorrow after such an awful calamity. Perhaps had she known of the high walls, the quiet gardens, and the silent nuns of the Samarang convent, where her destiny was leading her, she would have sought death in her dread and hate of such a restraint. But in imagination she pictured to herself the usual life of a Malay girl—the usual succession of heavy work and fierce love, of intrigues, gold ornaments, of domestic drudgery, and of that great but occult influence which is one of the few rights of half-savage womankind. But her destiny in the rough hands of the old sea-dog, acting under unreasoning impulses of the heart, took a strange and to her a terrible shape. She bore it all—the restraint and the teaching and the new faith—with calm submission, concealing her hate and contempt for all that new life. She learned the language very easily, yet understood but little of the new faith the good sisters taught her, assimilating quickly only the superstitious elements of the religion. She called Lingard father, gently and caressingly, at each of his short and noisy visits, under the clear impression that he was a great and dangerous power it was good to propitiate. Was he not now her master? And during those long four years she nourished a hope of finding favour in his eyes and ultimately becoming his wife, counsellor, and guide. (AF, 21–22)

Free indirect discourse both parallels sexual violence and naturalizes physical submission. Though we are brought "inside" Mrs. Almayer, as it were, this movement is guaranteed by what Pratt calls "the a priori relation of dominance

and distance between describer and described."[153] In the violence of translation, rape is metonymized: "short and noisy visits." Mrs. Almayer is voiced as a
primitive, natural consciousness without the liberal conception of a right to the
sanctity of the body.

In effect, Conrad writes a romance.[154] Reading this narrative as a matter of
colonial voicing and acoustics, the colonial focalizer inherent to its voicing produces both a speaking subject (an implied speaker) and a mode of listening that
makes it audible (to an implied listener). The technic of free indirect discourse
compels us to assume that implied position, or the surrogate listening faculty of
the apparatus. As I argued in relation to the colonial focalizer, "Kaspar! Makan!"
is not a neutral recording but carries with it a mode of listening, a distribution
of the sensible. Its distribution is not immediately evident in part because it has
been effaced. Such effacement (or half obliteration) begins with direct discourse
as it claims simply to cite or "report" speech, as if it were a factual unit, when it
is manifestly uncertain what kind of Malay is being spoken and inscribed (who
hears?). While Mrs. Almayer's thoughts are taken back to the moments of her
past, she is not simply speaking as "herself." Nor is she speaking as what Du Bois
calls, after Hegel, a "true self-consciousness," in which warring ideals have been
resolved.[155] Instead, the trauma of colonial violence produces a second subject
position that everywhere accompanies the voice of thought.

The very mention of Mrs. Almayer's education (like that of Nina) registers
forcible translation. Colonial education is premised upon the need for the voice
of the Third World subject to become "like" that of the West, but not too like. In
this way, the language of free indirect discourse still registers difference, such
that what is here articulated is an elected or chosen self-abnegation over and
against a freedom of the self. In other words, Conrad appears to be deferring to
readerly expectations of how one should "hear" or read the colonized speaking
subject. At the same time, we can locate in this milieu the status of English as
the lingua franca with the power to connect across difference. Phallic, it has the
emblem of mastery and individuation. "She learned the language very easily."
We can presume this language is Dutch, but since the passage is presented to us
in English, it becomes a primary medium (all other languages being under erasure). English mediates the passage in relation to the master discourse, such that
it allegorizes the fiction of monolingualism. We witness (in a kind of scopic tenor
of being forced to imagine a violent scene) what Derrida calls monolingualism's
"prosthesis of origin," origin being painfully grafted.[156] Her trafficking subtends
the novel's symbolic order.

To "have a voice" is to be individuated. It is to ward off the Mother in favor of the phallic identification with the symbolic, or the Father. But as we found with Kittler and the "mother's mouth," the ground of speaking in one's own voice is nonetheless laid in and through the maternal position, which begins as sound, breath, and what Silverman calls "the image of infantile containment."[157] By Western cultural logic, the ground of the voice, as the emblem of individuation, is laid in and through the mother, but as tectonic separation. The voice is drawn from the mother's materials, it is "of" her, but then wielded apart from her. Barthes's influential theory of the "mother tongue," a precondition of what he calls "the grain of the voice," is premised not only upon the mother as sound (rather than as *logos*) but upon the monolingual, a colonial consolidation of the mother tongue. (This issue will become more pronounced in Chapter 2 and in the Intersonority's discussion of Saidiya Hartman.) Such notions cannot fully accommodate the colonialized maternal, that is, what it is to give up forcibly one's language, one's mother tongue.

When Dain, who becomes Nina's lover, speaks—and in what language, it is unsaid—Conrad translates his voice into English in a kind of chivalric discourse. Dain's voice speaks in lost resonances of (a fantasy of) English, an older way of speaking where value, ethics, and hierarchy are clearly articulated. In this same way, Mrs. Almayer's discourse produces the fantasy of a Malay subjectivity as belonging to an older, idealized, and "primitive" structure of feeling. We have long understood modernism and primitivism as going hand in hand. But Conrad's modernism is to invert the primitive fantasy: He registers the fact of colonial education. In visual terms, we can understand quite readily that a kind of "color" has been placed over the consciousness of the other to produce the sensible effect or quality that the words are not "of" the other. It is unclear, for example, if the narrative translates Dain's words or simply the colonial affect they register. In both instances, Conrad's ironic, double-voiced presentation makes the discourse less an Orientalizing presentation than an acoustic mirror of the reader who desires and, in desiring, Orientalizes the other. In the case of Mrs. Almayer, it indicates the ways in which the victim may also be artful.

This acoustic mirror has everything to do with Conrad's vexed adaptation of the techniques of the European novel for representing coloniality. In his letters to his mistress and a writer Louise Colet, Flaubert writes of his intention to write "a book about nothing, a book dependent on nothing external, which would be held together by the internal strength of its style, just as the earth, suspended in the void, depends on nothing external for its support; a book which would have almost no subject, or at least in which the subject would be almost invisible."[158] It is from these letters that modernism gains many of the primary terms of its discourse of impersonality. Novelists "avoid amusing the public with ourselves . . . and with the personality of the writer," Flaubert writes, "which always reduces a work."[159] The book without external attachments demands a new aesthetic principle, that "you must not *write yourself*."[160] He underscores, "there is not in this book *one* movement in my name."

It is not as if the act of writing was silent for Flaubert, for he wrote to Colet of its assonances and sonorities, and sounded out his compositions in what he called his "shouting room," where he would test the efficacy of a sentence to perfection. Jameson describes *Madame Bovary* as the first "visual text," one no longer premised on rhetoric and its modes of address but on style: Sentences become "precious objects" to be fashioned.[161] But this fashioning was shouting to himself, and he crafted exquisitely sonic scenes.[162] Flaubert wrote through the pleasures of self-hearing (which were not afforded to Conrad as a "foreigner"). This sonorous trace exists in resonant relation to the shout of Conradian discourse, which adopts Flaubertian techniques in order to acoustically refract colonial consciousness.

Indeed, when Conrad remembers writing *Almayer's Folly* in his memoir, *A Personal Record*, he says that Flaubert's "thundering voice" was with him aboard ship, a merchant vessel entangled with trade and the spoils of colonization (*PR*, 3). He remembers still being aboard ship near the Seine, accompanied by "the shade of Flaubert" as he composed chapter 10 of *Almayer's Folly*. He essentially rewrites the novel and its opening shout when he recalls how his "mood of vision and words" was interrupted by the third officer.

> "What are you always scribbling there, if it's fair to ask?"
>
> It was a fair enough question, but I did not answer him, and simply turned the pad over with a movement of instinctive secrecy: I could not have told him . . . that Nina had said, "It has set at last." (*PR*, 4).

The novel's missing image of sunset, its interval, radiates across multiple moments and spaces in the text and across texts. To refuse to listen to the castrating call of the third officer is to choose to write, Conrad giving himself over to becoming a memory system, an inscriber, while also fantasizing himself to speak (inwardly) in the voice of Nina. The opening shout of coming to writing resounds the power of beginning, or, rather, the recitation of the memory of coming to writing resounds the novel's opening shout.

Conrad must write and sound out the erasure of the name: We will never know Mrs. Almayer's lost Sulu name. It becomes difficult if not impossible to "place" *Almayer's Folly* geographically, both at the level of diegesis (in narrative space and time) and text. This difficulty is related to the problem of where (textually and physically) one is to write books. ("Books may be written in all sort of places," his memoir begins, displacing exilic statelessness while also assuming, through an Oriental coordinate, the ship's community [*PR*, 3].) When scribbling aboard ship, he was still in that moment Józef Theodor Konrad Korzeniowski, such that the "K" of "Kaspar!" is a signature under erasure, a half-presented Polish name. (Conrad continually doodled elaborate letter Ks in the margins of his manuscripts, the lost or forsaken letter.)[163] But it is also a piece of colonial debris. It is not until the final exclamation of the novel that the occluded Arabic script "appears" (under erasure) on the page as a half-presented or half-obliterated object: "the beads in Abdulla's hand clicked, while in a solemn whisper he breathed out piously the name of Allah! The Merciful! The Compassionate!" (*AF*, 208).[164] This exclamation, the point of ending or closing, circles back to the beginning, an opening, while also resounding geographically.

This missing image that resonates between and within texts has significant bearing on the relationship between traumatic memory of colonial sexual violence, listening, and Conrad's negotiation of the constraints of the novel as a form. Recall, for example, that as Almayer turns back toward the sunset he's just missed, there is a "blot" on the horizon: It indexes the act of writing and, with it, a more fundamental mark of Conrad's vexed determination to become a novelist, an English novelist, which required a blotting of his identity or "voice." It is a cut, a traumatic linguistic separation.[165]

Conrad began *Almayer's Folly* in the margins and endpapers of his French-language copy of *Madame Bovary*. Ford Madox Ford recalls having seen this copy of the Flaubert: "Tormented with the curiosity of words, even at sea, on the margins of the French books, he [Conrad] made notes for the translation of phrases."[166] The writing of *Almayer's Folly*, accompanying Conrad in a trunk to the Congo, was coextensive with this work of translation into English; it began as an act of translation during oceanic passage, to be written in what James Clifford calls "awkward but powerful English."[167]

In this act, Conrad makes *Madame Bovary* a transpacific and transatlantic text, but only insofar as Flaubert's "voice" is already entangled with the spatio-temporal coordinates of empire: The modernist novel, or Flaubert as the first "visual text," begins in a colonial encounter. Flaubert had gone to Egypt just before beginning *Madame Bovary*, and Flaubert would describe the ways in which writing the novel became possible after travel to the Orient. Something of Emma Bovary, the site of the development of free indirect discourse, becomes possible, too. There is a subsumption of the Orientalized other who becomes, as it were, the invisible and inaudible ground of "a book about nothing," of impersonality, a book that sheds the plague of external attachments. In this, the external attachment is superseded by the exteriorized interiority of free indirect discourse.

That movement is essentially the "invention" of *Madame Bovary*. When Flaubert says "Madame Bovary c'est moi," he is feeling himself as a woman, desiring to be her, to speak in her voice. The freedom of free indirect discourse is the freedom to move between observer and observed and to create a third language between them.

With Nina and Mrs. Almayer, Conrad co-opts the novel as a technology of inner voice to communicate an otherwise invisible and inaudible colonial determination. This communication begins with the exchange and problem of sexual consent. Edward Said writes:

> There is very little consent to be found, for example, in the fact that Flaubert's encounter with an Egyptian courtesan produced a widely influential model of the Oriental woman; she never spoke of herself, she never represented her motions, presence, or history. *He* spoke for and represented her. He was foreign, comparatively wealthy, male, and these were historical facts of domination that allowed him not only to possess Kuchuk Hanem physically but to speak for her and tell his readers in what way she was "typically Oriental."[168]

To what extent is the freedom of "Madame Bovary c'est moi"—she never consents to being consumed in this way—premised upon the desire for and displacement of "Kuchuk Hanem c'est moi?" When Jameson argues that Flaubert wrote in "the silence and the solitude of the individual writer," in "the absence of a reading public as with some form of the absence of God,"[169] these comments are still organized by Flaubert's fantasy of autonomy and being alone with himself—fantasies that produced not only the so-called impersonal narrative voice but free indirect discourse as the impersonal, externalizing voice of interiority. Flaubert makes invisible and inaudible what Conrad makes manifest (in the scriptural remnant) and audible (in the vocal shard): the subsumption of the other, the speaking in her voice.

If Flaubert's Kuchuk Hanem is not an isolated instance and "stands for the pattern" of domination, as Said suggests, then she also stands at the birth of the modernist novel in free indirect discourse. The "impersonality" of free indirect discourse, in its technological beginnings, depends upon vocal ventriloquism. The form of the novel required an encounter with colonial difference from the outset. The vocal shard that begins *Almayer's Folly*—and the threshold of the audible that it announces—is a paradigmatic, historically foundational instance of the novel as a technology of the self.

But even here, in the most inner space of free indirect discourse, the narrator "hears" Mrs. Almayer's inner voice through the filters of coloniality: The narrative apparatus hears itself. But it is not as if a "true voice" beneath this ironically voiced discourse can be retrieved. The double voice is the only available voice.

A double consciousness speaks and hears in double ways because, if the subject and object are ontically split, then the voice that might claim to speak or narrate that condition is also split. In thinking of the possibility of interpreting Mrs. Almayer's inner thoughts, double voiced in this way, narrator and reader are coimplicated. No other critical position is possible for Conrad than that enacted as the differential and differentiating distance between vocal register and narrative register but also the differential and differentiating distance between a reader's eye and ear, the delay between hearing and listening, hearing and understanding. No voice other than a voice under erasure can narrate this story in its historicity, which is to say, in its elision, occlusion, obliteration, subtension, and marginalization, each conditioned by unspeakable grief. This "voicing" of the facts of (de)colonization can take place only in several registers at once.

In framing *Almayer's Folly* with the subaltern female voice, for a moment, Conrad merges the site of enunciation—reserved for a narrator—with that of a native woman. It is not that her voice is without meaning but that the meaning of her voice cannot be articulated within the space of narrative as circumscribed. There is no testimony available—there is no sensible witness—for such a scene of subject formation. What is the epistemic status of the focalizer as a witness when the *scene* concerns the colonial subject's emergence in exchange and cancellation? The "voice" has emerged on its other side. It can speak only under coercive and disavowed conditions. This is why I suggest that Conrad gives us Mrs. Almayer as otherwise nameless: Both "vision" and "voice"—the watchwords of novel theory—are untenable frameworks.

In relation to focalization, there remains the provocative question: In what language would Mrs. Almayer think to herself and of herself? The fact that Mrs. Almayer might speak and think to herself in a language that can only be "overheard" by the colonial focalizer is indexed more than once: The technic of free indirect discourse promotes the readerly fantasy of accessing or "overhearing" her interiority, one otherwise withheld or silent. The anatomy of such a fantasy includes an interiority purified of intervention, a pure ethnographic object. If that is the case, then she would be recalling her narrative to herself in Sulu, the language she was forcibly educated away from, marking the interior as beyond or before colonization. If so, then internal discourse is nonetheless translated into English. The reader "overhears" not the sound of a colonial interiority; what the reader hears is itself. Behind this problem is the politically vexed problem of using the discursive techniques of the European novel to represent (de)colonization. This problem is compounded by the Spivakian question of whether a subaltern interiority can be audible to these discursive techniques, namely, focalization. If so, either the focalizer or the narrator is engaged in act of translation that is not reported in the text.

Translation, Chow writes, is "the place where the oldest prejudices about origins and derivations come into play most forcefully."[170] In obscuring Mrs. Almayer's origins from the narrative, Conrad's texts capitalize on the readerly desire for derivation, of the demand that she think in a "natural" language. "Of the 'translation,'" Chow continues, "a tyrannical demand is made: the translation must perform its task of conveying the 'original' without leaving its own traces; the 'originality' of translation must lie 'in self-effacement, a vanishing act.'"[171]

It is the surrogate listening faculty. For Walter Benjamin, as Chow describes, translation is an act of complementation or putting together, but at the same time, it is "a process of 'literalness' that *displays* the way that the 'original' itself was put together—that is, in its violence."[172] What would the "original" be in the case of Mrs. Almayer, particularly if her subjectivity—and with it, the possibility of a grammatical "I" and narrating voice—was traumatically and violently instantiated? What would it mean to demand that she think in a "natural" language?

In the face of this violent obliteration of her identity, the narratological category of voice remains instructive, for, properly speaking, it is without body and a face. We can assume that Nina has been produced in nonconsensual sex, but here the word "no" cannot be recorded, repeated, or heard, because "no" cannot be heard under its social conditions of thought and utterance.[173] The conditions of audibility of the "no" of minority discourse, in the moment of writing, had not yet arisen. The question as to their having since arisen remains open.

Conrad here includes vocalities in the space of literature that cannot be framed by what Seyla Benhabib calls, after Arendt, "the political principle of consent," a politics contradicted by the very existence of coloniality.[174] The voiceover, the all-seeing voice of narrative, is no longer viable for Conrad in his project. Such a voice does not have to *materialize*—that is, its consent never has to be articulated or said aloud. The social contract is fundamentally tacit and therefore silent. Conrad begins in a woman's voice, but with the matter of its untranslateability as inaudibility. In asking after the vocal politics of refusal, its multiple registers, some of them only in the hauntings of double-voiced discourse, we again shift the question of focalization away from "Who sees?" to "Who hears?"

Conrad rarely returned to this sort of moment in which a woman narrates her story in her own voice, women being largely excluded from acts of storytelling.

Yet one doubts whether speaking in one's own voice is not itself a fantasy in the age of empire, in a novel that documents colonial consciousness in its forms of "folly," or self-delusion, fantasy, and ignorance.[175]

With Mrs. Almayer, something of the subject of narrative has been both suppressed and traumatically instantiated in the "short and noisy visits," part of the novel's colonial sound debris. My eye traces over the words "short and noisy visits"; they were almost missed, like a dropped beat. They are nothing more than a minor "detail." (I have yet to encounter an interpretation of *Almayer's Folly* that comments on the fact of Mrs. Almayer's sexual violation.)

In this midst of her discourse, there are two conflicting sounds in memory, sounds that are discordantly reconciled by the passage's tendency to minimize colonial violence: "She called Lingard father, gently and caressingly, at each of his short and noisy visits." The father's name is called, rendering the passage both incestuous and miscegenating. Even before we arrived here, this moment has already been sonically prefaced, for in Almayer's initiating reverie during forsaken twilight, he remembers Lingard saying, "Call me father, my boy. She does" (*AF*, 11). But the call, coupled with the violent sound, resonates retroactively with the opening shout that brings the novel into being. It is only much later that the shout, as a fragment, comes into sonorous conflict with the "short and noisy visits," reiterative in their event. The initiating shout, Conrad's first authorial utterance, is marred by the sonic trace of sexual violence.

What is being parabastically staged in the free indirect discourse if not the site of staging itself, the traversal of an invisible distance? The coimplicated and participatory readerly consciousness is that "stage." The word "noise" attaches to the archive of sounds in the reader's reserve of memory. The reader is enjoined by the scene, commanded to imagine sound. But in that act of imaginary sounding a canceled yet still tethered image of violence appears: It is the thin thread between the scopic and the auditory known as fantasy. The reader becomes an image machine.

In the fragment, a sonic metonym of sexual violence, there is a direct *exchange* with the opening of the novel. As an exchange, its *value* is clear. She has been trafficked by Lingard and Almayer, moved from one site to another. In that transfer she becomes the hysteric origin of narrative discourse.[176] With the shout, it's as if the narrative discourse both begins and cedes in the face of a parataxis or anacoluthon.[177] The anacoluthon is the rhetorical figure by which a periodic sentence suddenly reverses its course midspeech, failing to deliver the anticipated sense. It is, Paul de Man writes, a "foreign element that disrupts" the logic of the sentence after having been "inserted."[178] In its grammatical character, an anacoluthon is already at the threshold of sound not only because all classical rhetorical figures begin in their imagined effect on a listener but because of the temporal nature of its effect. A kind of stutter, its disruption unfolds in time, a second phrase being introduced while the other still lingers ("She called Lingard father, gently and caressingly, at each of his short and noisy visits"). The foreign element is the sound, the sound of forcible translation and transfer, a sonic anacoluthon.

Where silence or gaps relate to the spectral, a ghosting of the archive's positive function, Conrad's novel finds a companion in what Hunt calls a "nonspectral, acoustic register" of violence, which she locates in the stray sounds that populate colonial documents. But it is as if the acoustic register populates the operation of colonial memory, beginning in the listening consciousness, for the acoustic register is, Hunt writes, a "tethering to the present," but without "continuity or causality."[179] Its analytic must, then, become strategically reappropriating and decontexualizing, as I have demonstrated in relation to Kittler.[180]

Such resonance—finding the decay of a sound other than in the site of its original attack—is part and parcel of the Atlantic and Pacific as memory systems. In this way, *Almayer's Folly* resonates with the acoustic scene in Faulkner's *Sanctuary* in which Temple Drake is raped in a dark room: It never appears as a visual event; it is never shown. It is narrated only through the sonic coordinates of Temple's listening consciousness. This event takes place at Frenchman's Bend, a suspended heterotopia located between the United States and its expanded colonial regions, including the Philippines, where Lee Goodwin had been a GI. In imagining Temple's rape through its sonic metonyms, the reader becomes an image machine, cinematically implicated in the psychic penumbra of US expansion. The expropriative logic of expansion is enacted on the body of a native woman. We've found the acoustical displacement of this fact to be foundational to the modernist novel as a form. In the colonial debris through which Conrad and Faulkner touch, a white woman becomes materially bound to a Filipina, a so-called "nigger woman" that, as it is said in passing, Lee Goodwin killed a man over. (In that racist slur, a word originating in maritime pidgin, this unnamed woman doubles in consciousness as a Filipina and a black woman, both a *nyai* and Venus.)[181] That resonance announces the otherwise unsaid fact of Goodwin's Pacific exploits, for we can presume his relationship with this unnamed woman was neither consensual nor symmetrical.

The sounds of rape exist metonymically where the image is occluded. Like the imperative mood of the shout, it is at the threshold of text and sound. Yet this missing image is nonetheless coproduced by the reader as a half presentation. The very description of the sound demands from the reader a conjectural hearing—its meaning is the claim of the novel to "voice."

The novel, in its temporality as a form and in its modes of listening, is necessarily distinct from the archive. The shout is not an archival utterance but rather an acoustical displacement of the fact of colonial sexual violence. It is among the facts that have "not been recorded elsewhere." "Short and noisy visits"—as a passing sound, it radiates. It radiates as the condition of possibility of the diegesis (qua space) and narrative anachrony (qua temporality). In the latter case, such a possibility means that we cannot consider the postcolonial politics of the novel, Nina's escape with Dain, without the primary violation of the feminine body.

The plot's entanglement with the native female body is difficult to underestimate. Here, we enter into a double movement of the missing image as both the violent suppression of sexual trauma and the expression of postcolonial portent. In the former case, the double movement bears significantly on the space of narrative and, with it, the space of reading and the reader voice that is required for the missing image's articulation. The image becomes a medium for sound precisely through the way it withdraws from view. The conjectural hearing absorbs the novel's claim to a narrative "voice," to a communicative event as such. The novel's narrative voice is itself, then, a half-presented object, a record of an occluded event.

The coproduction by the reader is related to the technology of free indirect discourse as a technology of listening. Learning to read in 1800 in Europe was also learning to read, speak, think, and forget in a colonial nexus. In this regard, the acoustic mirror of the colonial nexus lies in minor sounds and partially translated words, here interpreted as the condition of possibility of colonial narrative voice and memory in its tendency to mirror the reader. Conrad's novel is a sound technology of readerly consciousness as listening consciousness. It is an acoustic mirror, one that both refracts and reflects. The violence he annotates inheres in his consciousness and thereby in ours.

CODA: CHANTAL AKERMAN AND LIP SYNC
AS POSTCOLONIAL STRATEGY

> . . . and with the very first word uttered Marlow's body, extended at rest in the seat, would become very still, as though his spirit had winged its way back into the lapse of time and were speaking through his lips from the past.
>
> Joseph Conrad, *Lord Jim*

The work of resonance, as it is elaborated across this book, is such that we continually must go elsewhere, beyond an initial inscription, to locate an object or moment's articulation. Twilight, the passage between sunset and darkness, is one such moment: Unfocalized by Almayer in text, it is a missing image. Much later in the novel, in chapter 4, the image of twilight suddenly appears, now to be focalized by Nina. The image is not missing at all, then, despite its initial negativity. It requires that we read in resonant ways, at cross purposes with the colonial focalizer. Listening appears not as an actuality of the focalized consciousness but as a political possibility. The radiation or propagation of the missing image, its resonance, means that it is to be found everywhere other than in its proper place.

A Malay song drifts in the distance.

> The sun had set, and during the short moments of twilight Nina saw the brig, aided by the evening breeze and the flowing tide, head towards Sambir under the set foresail. . . . The hum of voices, the occasional cry of a child, the rapid and abruptly interrupted roll of a wooden drum, together with some distant hailing in the darkness by the returning fishermen, reached over the broad expanse of the river. . . . *Before even she could see it she heard* the hollow bumping of a large boat against its rotten posts, and heard also the murmur of whispered conversation in that boat whose white paint and great dimensions, faintly visible on nearer approach, made her rightly guess that it belonged to the brig just anchored. (*AF*, 49–50, emphasis added)

Then "the noise of feminine laughter reached her there." The structure of the novel requires that we hold the missing image and its negativity in consciousness for four chapters, through resonance, waiting for its articulation, waiting for the missing beat. In musical syncopation, a strong beat loses its metrical articulation. Has not the hinge moment of twilight—a weak articulation between light and dark—been displaced otherwise than in its original place? The missing image cannot be subjected to "delayed decoding"; ultrasensual, it resonates.

These "short moments of twilight," nonexistent for narrative's colonial focalizer, belong to a gap or hole in the colonial distribution of the sensible. These gaps and holes nonetheless resound. Again, it is as if there is a world that is not given in advance to phenomenon and its structuration. Resonance is not phenomenal, Jean-Luc Nancy argues, for it does not "appear" or manifest in any strict sense.[182]

Emblematized by the image of the hand organ, the technology of the novel was already revealing itself to Conrad as another kind of distribution of the sensible: in the mode of lip sync, one voice speaking as through the mouth of another. His narrators are continually drawn to the sensual fact of lips hanging in the dusk, in which an idealized face presents itself, transmuting the voice imputed "beneath" or "behind" its event. From this mediation (in the space of diegesis) unfolds a second (in the space of reading). The space of reading immediately becomes dictated by the work of what we can call, in the language of film, synchronization.

In its anachrony, the novel unfolds as a problem of synchronization. Recall that after Mrs. Almayer's opening shout, we float in a space of reverie for several pages until her shout is finally, but only obliquely, translated. In this reverie, Almayer recalls the beauty of his daughter, Nina, believing that they can flee together to Europe. He fantasizes that no one will take notice of her mixed-race identity, and he anticipates her return from the convent, having learned from the nuns English and the religion. He is anticipating the arrival of Dain. One must "line up," as it were, the events that are here scattered about as shards. But the novel's opening call, I have suggested, gives rise to another register of synchronization, the work of attaching a language to a people, a sound to an image, a voice to a body, a psyche to a memory.

The Belgian filmmaker Chantal Akerman took note of the politics of the sound of Conrad's opening shout when she adapted the novel into a contemporary situation, with Malay actors speaking French. In *La folie Almayer*, it is quite some time before we hear French in the film, before we hear or see anything that might be made sense of. Akerman opens the film via the strategy of anachronic beginning. It is not a beginning in medias res, by which we understand some past moment that has not been presented but exists positively on a timeline. Rather, it is a beginning in a time and place that has no proper place in the chronology or map of events.

We are in a karaoke club in modern-day Cambodia (one coordinate of the novel—the slave girl, Taminah, is said to be Siamese).[183] A man lip-syncs on a stage to Dean Martin's bolero-mambo "Sway" (1954), written by the Mexican composer Luis Demetrio (Figure 1). Martin sings the original Spanish-language song, "¿Quién será?" in translation, its lyrics written by Norman Gimbel (most

Figure 1. Chantal Akerman, *La folie Almayer*.

famous for the English lyrics of "The Girl from Ipanema"). A row of women dance behind him in unison, their arms swaying like the ocean, and painted on the backdrop is the image of the sun. Perhaps it is the image that initiates Almayer's anxious reverie and turn away from the shout of a woman. Above the image is Khmer script,[184] which presents itself to an audience unfamiliar with the language simply as script, an optics of language that also places the scene in lieu of a voiceover or establishing shot.

The song is a relic of a moment of American exotica, mood music already premised upon Orientalized fantasies of travel and transport, entangled with expansion and domination. Exotica was one continuation of the sensuous imaginary of the French impressionist composers Claude Debussy and Maurice Ravel, a music born during their experience at the Paris Expo of 1889, which allowed them to hear Javanese gamelan for the first time. For David Toop, this moment is "the beginning of the musical twentieth century—accelerating communications and cultural confrontations became a focal point of music expression" in the West.[185] On the heels of this experience, Debussy introduced into such works as *Estampes* (1903), particularly its opening movement "Pagodes," a new use and transgressive application of the pentatonic scale and the pedals that, imitating the resonances of the gamelan, transformed the possibilities and audibility of the piano. The sound of the piano in French music, not only in rhythm and harmony, was transformed as a consequence of imperial desire. That Dain sings a Dean Martin song is not as distant from this moment as one might think, American exotica rising to prominence with the popular recordings of classically trained European émigrés.

The world, Jacques Attali writes, "is not legible, but audible."[186]

As Dain performs with the group of dancers behind him, he is suddenly and inexplicably stabbed by another man who leaps on to stage. Akerman begins with a murder, and the film that follows, as it goes back in time, will perform the feat of resuscitating the dead. After he falls to the ground, the dancers scream and scatter, but one dancer remains on the stage. Just as we have not yet heard the name "Dain" uttered, we have not yet learned that she is Nina. The music abruptly stops, and there is acute silence in the club and the scene, as if we are in the mind of someone who is not listening. She continues to dance without the music, never dropping a beat. Through her movement, we fantasize the music is still there. It echoes through the trace and trance of movement. She dances in the swaying gestures, which mimic the ocean waves (Figure 2).

An offscreen voice whispers (in French), "Nina. Nina. Dain is dead."

In this belated instance, names are attached to bodies. Akerman reproduces

Figure 2. Chantal Akerman, *La folie Almayer.*

the Malay language of the world of the novel in French. She moves, then, from foreign language to foreign language. Conrad, we have seen, writes Malay in a Romanized alphabet but also translates Malay, Dutch, and Arabic into English; Akerman stages "Malay" and "Dutch" (as optical and linguistic events) in French.

Each of these languages stands in immediate yet displaced relation to the region, each having its own colonial resonances and coordinates. In Akerman's film, the act of translation is at the level of accent, where the characters speak the French of the metropole. It is, in a way, the "wrong" accent, an accent that, to European ears, has no place in the peripheries. In other words, Akerman did not cast actors with French colonial accents nor direct her actors to shift their accents in order to derive some "feel" or "sound" of coloniality. Nonetheless, it is quite some time before we hear French in the film, as Akerman instead opens with a lounge where an as yet unnamed man lip syncs.

The first appearance of the film's elected language—central to the communication of the film's "voice"—is the offscreen whisper, a sonic shard. This delay of French is then immediately displaced. For without hearing the voice that whispers to her, she (Nina) continues to dance and then slowly drops her arms to approach the front of the stage. She hesitates but then begins to sing in Latin a Catholic song. She sings "Ave" at first quietly, then gains confidence, singing the song boldly and with pleasure, an echo of Verdi, perhaps.

The camera is fastened on her face in closeup, which in film not only gives the impression of a character's interior space but heightens identification in the *photogénie* (the third, nearly corporeal space between viewer and screen where

Figure 3. Chantal Akerman, *La folie Almayer*.

all of its psychical effects takes place). It allows a viewer to emplace herself passionately in the image (Figure 3).

What do we learn by this anachronic beginning in lip sync followed by a passionately translingual event of song? It organizes the next immediate sequence, one that is also entirely invented by Akerman: We finally arrive at the shores of Borneo, the film's withheld establishing shot. At the shore, an unnamed woman desperately moves through the marsh clutching a small girl (Nina as a child). She is a mother (Mrs. Almayer) who wishes to protect her from being sent to the convent in Singapore for acculturation; two white men (Kaspar and Lingard) shout and call to her in the distance, demanding her return.

This scene resonates with Mrs. Almayer as she is in the novel, such that resonance structures the relation between the entities, Akerman and Conrad ("in any differential system," de Man writes, "it is the assertion of the space *between* entities that matters").[187] These works touch in the sound effect, action in the one producing an effect in the other. In this resonance, it becomes undecidable which of these works is the primary, which the secondary. In the film, Kaspar discloses to Lingard directly the fact that he violates his wife in order to feel some intimacy with this creature who rejects him. Akerman names what Conrad displaces. In the contact between these voices and sounds across an invisible distance, resonance names the structure of a temporary and anachronic fulfillment.

Akerman begins *La folie Almayer* with an English lip sync and articulates the defining feature of Conrad's vocalization, a prosopopoeia whereby a voice becomes memorable as a face.[188] The opening shout of the novel is not reproduced by a sound; instead, it is rendered by the medium, by way of a technology of lip sync, which is analogous to the technology of translation. Across her films, Akerman continually desynchronizes sound and image. She is perhaps most famous for interminable durations, during which a viewer must sit with unknowing, a duration that shares in those of Conrad. In this duration, the chronological and filial (the defining logic of the racial) is disturbed in its totalizing effect. The occlusion of memory in forcible translation is registered not only by the film's fractured temporality but by its resistance to setting, its resistance to diegesis. It drifts and resonates.

In the long-drawn-out beginning, colonial miscegenation is registered by the audio-vision of Nina, a brown-skinned girl singing in archaic Latin: It is the sound and image of colonial education. Later in the film, Akerman elliptically reproduces Nina's memories of the nuns of Samarang, registered in the film by the image of another character, Jim Eng, who sits at a window, hearing the acousmatic voices of girls singing Catholic songs floating in from outside. As it is presented in the novel, I have argued, the memory of education is central to the narrative's production of a pseudo-three-dimensional space, a reality effect that works in tandem with the acoustics of the untranslated shout across distance. That is not even to speak of Akerman's own passionate attachments to Conrad's occluded Polish, the language of Akerman's mother, a survivor of Auschwitz.[189]

Among the traces in the sound space of *Almayer's Folly* is Conrad's exilic passage as a child from Poland to Russia, a journey his mother and father, agitators for Polish freedom, did not ultimately survive. The lost mother(land) is the wound from which Conrad's postcolonial and anti-imperial impulse resonates. For Freud, the sound of the mother's voice is a tether across chaotic distance when she is not visible. She calls to the infant to assert she is nearby, such that her sounds become "an aural substitute for the umbilical cord."[190] In the clearing of the early Malay tale "The Lagoon," the narrator remembers a bird's "cry discordant and feeble," skipping across the water just before it "lost itself in . . . the breathless silence of the world" (*TU*, 188). The maternal, among several valences of the feminine in Conrad, is continually excised, and its most revolutionary utterances are displaced in space and time. In displacement, however, postcolonial sound becomes a particular mode of address, or, rather, not an address in the strict sense but a resonance that presages mutuality, a sonorous bond.[191] Sound is its fragile image.

Suffice it to say, for both Conrad and Akerman, a lost maternal body is being materially reconstituted through the sound and force of the voice. The pantomime is an ur-mimetic impulse to become other, to pass, play at reality, and to bring into existence.[192] This is the power of the opening of Conrad's novel that, like the film medium, finds its origins in a pantomime and a lip sync.

But it is crucial that Nina approaches the edge of the stage to look directly at us, nearly leaping out of the film. In this moment, Akerman locates a feminist and postcolonial possibility in Conrad's acoustical strategies.

In *The Acoustic Mirror*, Silverman makes clear that in classic narrative cinema, women never rise to the status of the apparatus.[193] These classical forms privilege the frame, a traditionally masculine location that contains and controls the diegesis in which the feminine is continually "buried," unable to attain mastery over its situation. Nina very nearly escapes the diegesis where Dain, the revolutionary, is instead consigned to death. This strategy has significant bearing upon the issue of ethnography. As Trinh suggests, when the other is represented in documentary, the film is thought to be "'giving voice,' even though these 'given' voices never truly form the Voice of the film, being mostly used as strategies of legitimization" to compensate for lack.[194]

When Akerman begins her film adaptation with a lip sync, she begins with some comment about the technology of film, about the relationship (ethnographic or otherwise) between voice and body, apparatus and diegesis. At stake in any sound film is how sound and image are to become synchronized. In beginning not with Mrs. Almayer's acousmatic shout but Nina's song, voice and sound are only fantasmatically united. We cinematically emplace ourselves when we believe that the religious song now emanates not only from the screen but from Nina's mouth. We are tempted to forget that the film had already revealed to us its lack. As with the hand organ, it had revealed to us its mechanical technique just before concealing it once again.[195] After Dain's death, Nina looks out no longer at the club but at the camera; she knows she sings to us. The image is sentient. She becomes the source of the film's "voice," the locus of its mimetic reality.

Conrad begins with the shout of a woman who calls the work into being. In this anachrony, Conrad begins with a lip sync already understood, a priori, to be the condition of possibility for a narrative voice, a question we will now turn to.

A negro in a British forecastle is a lonely being. He has no chums. . . . But in the book he is nothing; he is merely the centre of the ship's collective psychology and the pivot of the action. . . . After writing the last words of that book, in the revulsion of feeling before the accomplished task, I understood that I had done with the sea, and that henceforth I had to be a writer.

—Joseph Conrad

It was pretty windy that night, and the boats rolled and creaked a-plenty. The gale roared in the mastheads. But beyond that, I heard nothing strange.

—Langston Hughes

THE ECHO OF THE OBJECT: ON THE PAIN OF SELF-HEARING IN *THE NIGGER OF THE "NARCISSUS"* AND "THE FACT OF BLACKNESS"

PRELUDE: ECHOLOCATION

Language is possible only because each speaker sets himself up as a *subject* by referring to himself as *I* in his discourse. Because of this, *I* posits another person, the one who, being, as he is, completely exterior to "me," becomes my echo to whom I say *you* and who says *you* to me.

Émile Benveniste

The proper name, unlike common names, does not designate a category of things but names the uniqueness of the one who bears the name. The proper name is in fact, first of all, the name of the call to which, in biblical language, one responds, "here I am."

Adriana Cavarero

Chapter 2 of Freud's *Beyond the Pleasure Principle* begins in a meditation on war: shell-shocked men said to return continually in dreams to the scenes whose memory they would rather suppress. Contemporary catastrophe is a textual provocation, an opening into the baffling work of repetition that touches all human relations. Freud's discussion of war abruptly breaks off, however, leaving World War I as a lesion within the text. It is a provocation whose particular historical and political charge evaporates in the face of the instincts whose fundamental quality, for Freud, is that they are *universal* in character.

As war disappears from the text, the wound of the political recedes. Freud pivots away from the "dark and dismal" topic of modern catastrophe to a nursery room far from the war front, a location that nevertheless lends the childish scene its psychic impetus and social dimension, if at a distance.[1] We know this scene well. It concerns the origins of the signifier in reiterative movement localized by Freud in a child's game and, with it, the sounds of coming to language.

> This good little boy . . . had an occasional disturbing habit of taking any small objects he could get hold of and throwing them away from him into a corner, under the bed, and so on, so that hunting for his toys and picking them up was often quite a business. As he did this he gave vent to a loud, long-drawn-out "o-o-o-o" [*ein lautes, langgezogenes o–o–o–o*], accompanied by an expression of interest and satisfaction. His mother and the writer of the present account were agreed in thinking that this was not a mere interjection but represented the German word "*fort*" ["gone"]. I eventually realized that it was a game and that the only use he made of any of his toys was to play "gone" with them. One day I made an observation which confirmed my view. The child had a wooden reel with a piece of string tied round it. . . . What he did was to hold the reel by the string and very skillfully throw it over the edge of his curtained cot, so that it disappeared into it, at the same time uttering the expressive "o-o-o-o." He then pulled the reel out of the cot again by the string and hailed its reappearance with a joy-ful "*da*" ["there"]. This, then, was the complete game—disappearance and return. As a rule one only witnessed its first act, which was repeated untiringly as a game in itself, though there is no doubt that the greater pleasure was attached to the second act.[2]

The boy transforms vocal protest against his mother's absence into a revenge otherwise "suppressed in actual life."[3] In repetition, the boy surmounts his aggressive instincts, the game simulating rather than injuring the mother and rendering the boy the "active" protagonist, not its "passive" victim. (Later, in a more advanced and differently triangulated game, the boy commands his toys to "go to the f'wont," the specter of modern war again appearing in the front that keeps his father away.) The desire to injure the mother, the first love object, has not gone away; it has been displaced. Above all, the game is a "cultural achievement"; the boy, who is on the way to language from the infancy of echolalia, has civilized himself.[4]

We find in the reflexive moment between the object and the boy a faint echo of Freud's repression of political and historical determination. But the question of civilization is there from the beginning of Freud's remarks on total war. Though he shifts away from his historical and cultural moment of the early twentieth century to posit universal perception, the theater of total war resounds in this child-ish scene in displaced ways via the unnamed specter of what Homi K. Bhabha calls "colonial nonsense," or "inscriptions of an uncertain colonial silence that mocks the social performance of language with their non-sense; that baffles the communicable verities of culture with their refusal to translate."[5] The sound of o-o-o-o is the decivilized emission, there in the "origin" of language. Though its sound is contained by articulate speech, the decivilized emission lies waiting within speech, ready to reensnare it.

What can literary criticism learn by returning to the acoustics of this scene? How does Freud's account invite a mode of reading that, attentive to its sounds, imitates his own most containing gestures? While inheritors of Freud have iso-lated the gesture of throwing as it stands in relation to a more violent one that is substituted and sublimated, we have understood less how the sound of o-o-o-o must, in his narrative, do double work. It must substitute for vocal protest, a cry or scream, while at the same time, the scene's reflexive movement condi-tions the auditory possibility of later saying "I." It is a pronunciation that leaves the self (in acoustic space) only to come back to the self. It is thus not through any sender-receiver, I-thou intersubjective dyad that the boy comes to language. There is a different structure to this scene. Virtual, it lies outside of the dyad and its elaborations by the rational tradition and the theory of the subject. Instead, the boy is passionately attached to a series of sonorous objects, objects in which his "I," his first-person voice, is mired. In his essay on the "mirror stage," Lacan famously locates the birth of the "I" as a fictional unity in the specular surface narcissistically afforded the infant by the mirror. But *fort-da* points to Narcis-sus's counterpart in Echo and, with her, a series of sonorous movements and withdrawals that spatialize, temporalize, and, above all, historicize, politicize, and deuniversalize identity.[6]

As the sound of o-o-o-o journeys toward pronouncement, which in turn jour-neys toward mental preservation, the "I" must withdraw from sound to become a purely noetic object, the kind of object that the philosopher René Descartes discovers in the act of silent meditation. "This proposition [*pronuntiatum*]: I am, I exist, is necessarily true each time that I pronounce [*profertur*] it, or that I men-tally conceive it."[7] The Latin invites the relation to an oral, vocalic pronounce-ment, an announced quotation that Descartes's silent, written event does not so much imitate as absorb via a mutually enforcing relation between hearing oneself speak aloud and thinking to oneself, as if thought is the noetic preservation of the pronouncement.[8] There is an echo between pronunciation and its silent preservation that constitutes the very birth of referral. The gesture of throwing the spool, paired with the sound of cooing, binds the object to itself and allows it to persist as itself, to maintain its identity in thought. Were it not thrown *and* sounded out, there would be no being akin, no signification or symbol for the "I" who persists as subject in relation to object. That the entirety of the scene is about sensually coming to the word "I" is emphasized by Freud's momentary suspension of his own first-person pronoun, referring to himself as "the writer." What is at stake in the coordinates of the nursery game, in this account, is the pleasure of pronouncing and hearing oneself say "I." However, its first stirring is in the sound of o-o-o-o.

Part of this work of substitution is enlivened or facilitated by Freud's powers of observation and listening. Freud is listening, and the boy is sounding for his audience; the boy is sounding and hearing himself. The scene is double not only in its "work" (or achievement), then, but, as a result of its echo, in its acoustics. The child never says "gone"—it is Freud who hears the nascent word *fort* in the child's sounds. Indeed, the scene is doubly doubled in its subjective dimensions. Freud enlists as evidence the ear of the mother, who judges the nascent word "gone" ("*das nach dem übereinstimmenden Urteil der Mutter*"). Freud's choice of words emphasizes the echo within her "accord," as *übereinstimmenden*, or the same voice or same tuning (*stimmen*, "to tune," from *Stimme*, "voice"). He calls upon many witnesses to testify to the meaning of the sound, building into the scene its own evidentiary structure.

For Adriana Cavarero, the "I," or what in linguistics is known as the "shifter," is a mere placeholder in language without physical reality. Narcissus gazing at himself in the water thus stands in for the entire semantic system as it is sustained by the fiction and "phantasm of the *subject.*"[9] By contrast, the mythic figure of Echo belongs to the interruptive order of babble that originates in the prehistory of the subject, an "originary bond [*fusione originarin*] between mother and child."[10] Echo speaks after Narcissus, uttering only the last words of his sentences, last words that, "superimposed" over the speaker's original sentence, separate it from context and distort its meaning. The sonority of the mother's voice is a relational object recognized by the infant, who in turn relates to the mother in coproducing sound, a mimetic duet of call and response. In this antiphony— which for Cavarero is the relational ground of democratic politics in general—the sound of the voice is singular and unique, recognized by a listening other in a process of self-distinction that can in no way be subsumed by the signification that constitutes philosophy's phantasm, the Cartesian subject. Breaking open the subject's self-reflexivity, an echo, through its physical reality of rhythm and phonemes, makes any voice "structurally *for* the other."[11] For Cavarero, the myth of Echo and Narcissus illustrates that when faced with "ambiguous resignifications" of babble, "the semantic system, and the subject that should sustain this system, are dissolved."[12]

However, understood in this way, as an originary bond, echo cannot compass the ontology of subordinated voices that, while itinerant, migrant, exiled, or translated, are no less relational.

When someone known to me asks me, "Who's there?" as Narcissus asks of Echo, I respond simply by sounding my voice, saying "it's me," in ways akin to saying "here I am" in response to my name. Cavarero's book pivots upon this elegant fact, lending the sound of the voice the ontological status of the proper name.[13] Nevertheless, one cannot always be so certain that the voice gains its ontology from the one who recognizes its sound or that the memory of its sound has not failed me and the listening other. Some voices indicate spacing—the spacing of difference, of geographic passage, renegotiation, passing, and survival.[14] In the deuniversalizing experience of accent, for example (one could consider the "accent tests" performed upon refugees seeking admittance into camps), one's speech makes itself felt as a compromise formation, a byproduct of historical forces to which one has been subjected or the hegemonic norms to which one has been subordinated. In such echoes, the wound of the political finds repetition.

In Chapter 1, we found that these voicings produce ambiguous resonances, where the listening other may wonder: *From where is this sound coming?* Many who speak a language with a detectable "accent," another language or nation having left its mark,[15] describe the deflating and marginalizing experience of being asked after speaking, "Where do you come from?" In such moments, as in an echo, it is as if what one had just been saying, the semantic content, matters not at all or only in distorted ways. Such resonances may be rejected or misrecognized. In any case, these voicings—as spacings—produce the double of philosophy's reflexive, self-present subject. Locked within a circuit of critical and at times painful self-hearing, one hears oneself as other, as a stranger or outcast.

The noetic preservation of the voice—its specular ideal—cannot come to itself except through the problem of echolocation. Echolocation is "the location of objects by means of the echo reflected from them by a sound-signal, as of ultrasonic sounds emitted by bats or by man-made devices."[16] Among the term's earliest contextual uses in the *OED* we find war and the use of a radar signal "so beautifully perfected that it can echolocate airplanes at great distances by sending out radio waves and picking up the reflected energy returning from the distant aircraft." The description combines perfection, completion, and presence coming back to itself through the far distance: In echolocation, one desires to overcome what is most disorienting about echo, its distancing quality of repetition and delay. Echolocation thus is not unlike *fort-da* in being twofold. It is only through the far distance that the object comes back to itself. A form of mediation (in the sense of being inseparable from a scene of recognition), echolocation becomes a way of thinking through and with postcolonial racialization in its resonant temporality.

As a methodology of reading and listening, echolocation is not unrelated to the mode of literary-critical reading that Eve Kosofsky Sedgwick famously calls "reparative," which "wants to assemble and confer plenitude on an object that will then have resources to offer to an inchoate self."[17] To read in the reparative mode is to shore up pieces and put them back together. The plenitude is not primary but arrives only later, after some feeling of disrepair, which turns out to have been primary.

Drawing from the work of the psychoanalyst Melanie Klein, Sedgwick makes it clear that repair is an affective mode first learned in the infantile relation to the "object," a term that finds perhaps its clearest definition in Freud's account of the oceanic, when the "infant at the breast does not as yet distinguish his ego from the external world."[18] The infant, later feeling himself to have aggressed the maternal object, as does Freud's nephew when he casts the spool away from himself and names it "gone," experiences guilt and longs to repair. Returning to this scene, Sedgwick effectively diagnoses a reader who feels everywhere surrounded by a shattered object that must be repaired through reading itself. But she also diagnoses a double movement: The same person who repairs is also the one who destroyed. Without this movement between destruction, guilt, and repair (also hallmarks of colonial affect), love is unthinkable.[19] Bound up in this dilemma is not only a Freud who, by Carl Schorske's account, experienced a wish to destroy his father but also Conrad's second novel, *The Nigger of the "Narcissus,"* aggressively titled through a racial slur.

In this slur, there is a postcolonial thinking that, as we will find, in its resonance with Freud, becomes audible and legible only later in and with Frantz Fanon, a Martiniquean theorist and psychiatrist who trained in France and later emigrated to Algeria. For Freud, as in the *fort-da* scene, the ego begins as a technology of reproduced voices. One such emergence is racializing, or the reproduction of a racializing voice. This is the effect of the notorious scene of "unheroic conduct" in *The Interpretation of Dreams* in which Freud recounts a story, as he heard it from his father, in which an anti-Semite shouts "Jew! get off the pavement!" and knocks the father's new fur cap into the mud, an aggression to which the father fails to respond except in silence. Listening to the story forcibly introduces into Freud's young self-consciousness (though not for the first time) an echo of a racial slur. Heard acousmatically in recitation, the memory haunts the threshold of Freud's analytic of the *fort-da* scene, formative for his modernist acoustics.[20] Echolocation will allow us to understand how Fanon, also writing of scenes of racialization in a painful aural event in "The Fact of Blackness" ("L'expérience vécue du noir"), reverses the Freudian schema to find in consciousness a particular politically and historically structured event of traumatic, auditory instantiation.

I have retained the (mis)translation of Fanon's title in what I take, across this book, to be the productive and generative moment of mishearing and misunderstanding across languages.[21] I retain the mistranslation for the threefold sense of "fact": first, as concretion (the so-called brute fact of materiality); second, as historical and biographical evidence or document; and third, as facticity, or the plural conditions of existence that must be taken up before one can even arrive on the scene or consent.

Echolocation as a form of reading, the form of reading for which I strive in this chapter, seeks to restore to narrative—to the act of writing and to Conrad's "voice"—some scarcely noted dissent, exilic voices, and sounds that Conrad's novel both designates and suppresses. As I described in Chapter 1, it often goes without saying that writing is silent. When I read, I read silently to myself. My intention here is to derive a way of echolocating the supposed silence of the grammatical voice. In contrast to the theories of voice proposed by Seymour Chatman and Gérard Genette, the aesthetic principle of echolocation derives from a wound in the physical voice, but the physical voice already understood in its traversal of distance, a spacing out from itself.[22] In echolocation, the question ceases to be one of origination or derivation whereby a primary orality leaves its sign in a silent writing. The distinction between writing and orality dissolves. In a fact of resonance, we have to go to writing to understand something about sounding and to sounding to understand something about writing. Echolocation is a method of writing as much as one of reading. It has special relevance to the concept of narrative voice.

Narrative voice, we have found, is a metaphor for an aboriginal event of orality, yet metaphor may not be the best term for what is a displacement not only of the sound of a voice but of a resonance. When I speak into a microphone—to record a greeting on my voicemail—and I hear the recording played back, I hear myself, but through a physical distance. My voice is coming to me from outside. Such an experience restores the sound of the voice to its original narcissism, the

narcissism we find in *fort-da*. For a novelist in search of a "voice," there is a cut
in the voice where it rebounds to render the speaker its object. For Conrad, there
is a wound in the writer's self-hearing, where to speak—but also to write—is to
hear oneself as exilic, a stranger in a strange land.[23]

Conrad continually and self-reflexively meditates on the question of how he
can pronounce—and hear himself say *and* be heard as saying—his own ergo
sum: I am a writer, an English writer. This assimilation involves, perennially and
at every turn, the search for what he calls, in the strange, opening remarks of
A Personal Record, Conrad's memoir of coming to writing, the "right accent."
This "right" voice will be given back to the writer from the reader's idealized perception. The right voice, the right word—the conditions under which Conrad can
rightfully take up the task of writing—are just as crucial as the conditions under
which he can be read and received.

In a section titled "A Familiar Preface," announcing its intelligibility to and
community with readers, there is a passage that is completely unfamiliar to modernist studies and novel theory as they describe the shift from telling to showing:
a meditation on sounding. He declares:

> You perceive the force of a word. He who wants to persuade should put his trust not in
> the right argument, but in the right word. The power of sound has always been greater
> than the power of sense. I don't say this by way of disparagement. It is better for
> mankind to be impressionable than reflective. Nothing humanely great—great, I mean,
> as affecting a whole mass of lives—has come from reflection. On the other hand, you
> cannot fail to see the power of mere words; such words as Glory, for instance, or Pity.
> I won't mention any more. They are not far to seek. Shouted with perseverance, with
> ardour, with conviction, these two by their sound alone have set whole nations in mo-
> tion and upheaved the dry, hard ground on which rests our whole social fabric. There's
> "virtue" for you if you like! . . . Of course the accent must be attended to. The right
> accent. That's very important. The capacious lung, the thundering or the tender vocal
> chords. . . . Give me the right word and the right accent and I will move the world.
>
> What a dream for a writer! Because written words have their accent, too. Yes! Let
> me only find the right word! Surely it must be lying somewhere among the wreckage of
> all the plaints and all the exultations poured out aloud since the first day when hope,
> the undying, came down on earth. It may be there, close by, disregarded, invisible,
> quite at hand. But it's no good. I believe there are men who can lay hold of a needle
> in a pottle of hay at the first try. For myself, I have never had such luck. And then there
> is that accent. Another difficulty. For who is going to tell whether the accent is right or
> wrong till the word is shouted, and fails to be heard, perhaps, and goes down-wind,
> leaving the world unmoved? (*PR*, xii–xiv)

In Chapter 1, we found that Kaspar Almayer could not listen to the voice that was calling to him. Both the shout and his listening operated as what I called an acoustical displacement of the fact of decolonization. This fact could not come into Almayer's consciousness except through resonance. At the same time, the novel's discourse produced its own displacement of the fact of sexual violence. Such violence was both presented and enacted by the text as a sonic trace of an event that is both real (historical) and conjectured (imagined). These displacements coproduce the opening shout of Conrad's first novel as resonance. But they also coproduce the narrative voice that "reports" the shout. We found the notion of "narrative voice" and reported speech to fail to annotate how the shout is transliterated by reading consciousness as listening consciousness. Resonance is not a report; it does not operate under the source/destination dyad. Conrad announces his modernism when he begins with a call that is ambiguous and multimodal not only in its source and destination but in its message and temporality.

As I've also described in Chapter 1, *Almayer's Folly* is addressed to a colonizer or imperial subject who seeks a fantasy of romance, an exotic escape. But in that address, Conrad encodes what I will be calling here the echo of the object.[24] Unlike the mirror, the echo returns not "me" but "not-me." "In Ovid's *Metamorphoses*," Gayatri Spivak writes, "Narcissus's madness is disclosed when he recognizes his other as his self: 'Iste ego sum [I am that].'"[25] But there are Others who cannot be rendered "self," in Spivak's view, "because the fracture of imperialism rather than the Ovidian pool intervened."[26] Mrs. Almayer calls to the colonizing reader who cannot accept or even imagine revolutionary violence: This woman, whose Sulu name we never learn, will be the one to commit the most violent act of the novel, smashing the face of a corpse that, no longer identifiable, will be confused for her daughter's insurgent, anticolonial lover and allow them to escape.

In the echo of the object, what is heard in these narratives is a companion to what Anne Cheng calls "the melancholy of race." Cheng describes the experience of being racialized, turned into an object of the other's hateful dejection. But on the other side of this experience, I propose, is the melancholy of racializing, of hearing oneself say hateful things. Hearing oneself hate is the reversal and corollary of hating hearing oneself. The racist slur is not the only domain of such melancholy, which may be accompanied by the experience of hearing oneself say things—words, phrases, but also their intonation, accent, and timbre—that may have been taken up from another whom one ambivalently loves and disavows. Disavowal marks its difference from repression through intimacy; disavowal keeps close. Ambivalence, Klein teaches, is caught up in the guilt of aggression expressed toward a love object, depression conditioning the experience of love.

Because we have not heard the auditory dimension of melancholy in the echo of the object, we have failed to interpret Conrad's most influential narrative strategies—the so-called participant-observer—as racially melancholic. Racism, Cheng suggests, is constituted through the "melancholic bind of incorporation and rejection."[27] It is not only violent rejection but "a wish to maintain the other in existing structures."[28] But is it not also a wish to maintain the other in oneself? Recall that for Freud, in melancholia, a "love escapes extinction" by housing itself in the ego as an object.[29] It is a less obvious counterpart to aggression. The melancholy of race is the other side of that event, and it is grounded in the experience of surviving objectification. This dynamic, one side in relation to the other, is what is heard in the echo of the object.

The hallmark of melancholia is that a lost object withdraws from consciousness. One cannot *hear* in one's own repetitive and painful voicing what one has lost. This displacement of a racialized loss is the primary motivation of a literary form where voices are heard but not understood and where single words are retrieved, saved, and protected by a craftsman, but not without troubling remainders. Such an internalized object is less an "entity," Kaja Silverman might suggest, than it is a gathering place of what Freud calls the "memory-traces of *things* (as contrasted with *word*-cathexes)."[30] This gathering place would be a particular kind of recording, a recording that displaces sounds and voices: The ego is both echoic and phonographic.

By contrast, narrative voice, as a concept, is logocentric, presenting itself as the center of rationality. But if the *logos,* the voice, is to be that, it must strive to become anechoic, that is, to absorb completely into itself its own reflections. It must act as if it has been transmitted directly from mind to mind, the rational tradition denigrating any trace of the body and its audible environment. Frances Dyson traces the sound-absorbing chamber of the radio voiceover, the perfectly enunciating voice in its perceived authority, objectivity, and masculinity, to the ancient fear of echo. It is to this same Platonic tradition that Cavarero traces Descartes's practice of silent meditation, which she deems a "devocalization of logos" (she describes how the *logos* as, *phone* and *semantike*, was originally paired with sound only to be radically severed from it by the rational tradition). The perfectly enunciating and anechoic voiceover of radio and the documentary is the voice of someone who knows yet speaks as if from nowhere, without physical and mortal situation—that is what it means to say that the voice has been "idealized." It is part and parcel of its neutralization. This striving for neutrality is also legible in Freud's account of *fort-da*, an account that has one foot in the historico-political conditions of war and racism that threaten his authoritative voice and another foot in the universal, which flees its conditioning moment.

The conditions of literary-critical reading are no different. Criticism adopts, designates, and sets at a distance its literary "objects." But disciplinary constraint mandates that the critic suppress the conditions of resonance, the repetitions of echo. However, according to Ovid's myth, Echo echoes the phrase "Avoid me not!" Before the narrative and the interpretative account, there was first an echo, a repetition that allowed for circling back. This echoing movement is sloughed from criticism. We will listen to it here.

SLURRED HEARING (LAST SOUNDS)

The Nigger of the "Narcissus" was Conrad's first major work and his first to tell the story of a journey to his adopted home of England. But already I have overleaped. How can one proceed after such a title, which stands as an aggressive incitement? To read further to the story is to look beyond or through the title, as though it is not a specular surface rendering a seer complicit in some act of aggression committed before she has arrived on the scene.

Perhaps a reader has already been named by this slur. In this instance, the "I" who reads is relayed through the other who is aggressively named. Perhaps a reader could never be addressed by such a slur. In that instance, the "I" who reads is relayed through the absent addresser who aggressively names. In either instance, to read is to have already participated in an imaginary twofold act: aggressed and aggressor.

Aggression against whom? The aggressed is unknown, anonymous, but so too is the aggressor. The rendering anonymous—an effacement and defacement—is the movement of the slur in its capacity to bring two positions into existence. It scratches a someone out of particularity into anonymity. By anonymity, we do not mean impersonality. Someone has become anonymous in becoming objectified.

The title of Conrad's second novel demands, like Narcissus and Echo, to be seen and to be heard. I sit with the spectral sound of the slur. The slur is spectral because it inhabits the echoic space we began to confront in Chapter 1, where Conrad's voicings brought us into stratified yet circular realms of complicity in the demand for knowledge of a colonial other's interiority. I do not say the slur; I do not utter it aloud. Yet my consciousness is suddenly "on loan," as Georges Poulet might say, to this anonymous rebuke. Someone is being injured. The title is an inscription, an act of writing. As such it immediately flits away from the "I" writing. But as a slur, there is behind it a most powerful enunciating force. Some voice persists, outside of the grammatical "I," who might take responsibility for naming a phantom other in rebuke. In reading such a title, in agreeing to proceed (by way of silent contract, the definition of the tacit), the status of my "I" in relation to the slur haunts the story as a call of relationship. In Western musical notation, a slur symbol indicates that two notes of different pitch are to be played without separation; they are slurred. (The word "nigger" itself is slurred in its origin, entering English through maritime pidgin.)[31] Whose "I" is on the scene? Who speaks? Who hears?

It is as if, from the first instance, Echo is there in Conrad's title, even though she has been displaced. Narcissus is there in the book's name, but Echo is the principle of its grammar, an acoustical displacement:

"Who is here?" and Echo, "Here!"
Replies. Amazed, he casts his eyes around,
and calls with louder voice, "Come here!" "Come here!"
She calls the youth who calls.—He turns to see
who calls him and, beholding naught exclaims,
"Avoid me not!" "Avoid me not!" returns.[32]

Who's here? In the absence of any speaker, any enunciator of the slur, the only available enunciator is me.

A title of a work announces itself to the world. It is the site along which the region of fiction first opens. It is the place of beginning and, in Conrad's tale of sea voyage, a departure. This book, in Conrad's own estimation, announced him as an "English" writer. But Conrad's title demands that the reader pass over or avoid this point of departure if she is to continue into that serene region of fiction's fantasy. The novel is often referred to in critical literature as merely *The "Narcissus."* One can comfortably read the novel as a tale of community, failed mutiny, and a vanishing world of sail. Conrad would have rejected this shortened title, just as he rejected the American publication of the novel, renamed *The Children of the Sea: A Tale of the Forecastle.* Conrad had considered this title but then cast it away. In letters, Conrad referred to the novel by the slur plus a proprietary, affectionate gesture of "my." The slur is the one word that survived for Conrad the title's possible permutations. It alone announced for Conrad the novel's identity. In his absence, it continues to announce itself as a mirror, but of whom?

Fantasy is an echo and echo a fantasy. Joan Scott writes, "retrospective identifications, after all, are imagined repetitions and repetitions of imagined resemblances."[33] In our case, the retrospection of the racial slur in the title is also retroauditive, for the word is in the midst of becoming sutured to an imaginary body. Scott's formulation of the "fantasy echo" in relation to identity and solidarity allows us to avoid the debilitating notion of imagination as purely false, as if the object imagined is readily available to one who fantasies and is, as Jean Laplanche and Jean-Bertrand Pontalis write, "caught up in the sequence of images."[34] In Freud's "A Child Is Being Beaten," fantasy has the double purpose of enacting the wish and punishing the one who wishes, punishment being reflexively enacted. Scott suggests, following Jacqueline Rose, that fantasy reconciles desire with the law and the collective, fantasy being a psychic "precondition" of social reality and its binding agent.[35]

As a space of identity, identification, and collectivity, the title of Conrad's novel is split within itself. The split functions between two nouns that visually assert their similarity by initiating the image and the sound of a single letter "N" then suddenly and radically to turn away from each other. The title acts as a mirror, as if one word looks into the other to see a strange and opposing face. The title evades the mirror function to work on the page as a "visual echo,"[36] but a distorting one—it is not AB/BA but AB/AB. This structure, not fully metrical and yet alliterative, is suddenly caught and circumvented in its negativity, for both words act as proper names. The first is a slur that substitutes a proper name (the titular black figure, named James Wait). The substitution subjugates and negates a character in his personhood, the very definition of objectification. The second is the name of a nymph's son that will be elevated to the universal. Both positions, the subjugation and the elevation, cannot be together at once: One is the universal signifier of self-love, the other a universal signifier of rebuke—unless it is the case that the one is the second face of the other, that they are two faces, locked together in ambivalence.

When we meet James Wait, like Mrs. Almayer, he shouts unseen from the margin. Mr. Baker, the chief mate, is mustering the crew:

"Can't make out that last name. It's all a smudge. . . . That will do, men. Go below."

The distinct and motionless group stirred, broke up, began to move forward.

"Wait!" cried a deep, ringing voice.

All stood still. Mr. Baker, who had turned away yawning, spun round open-mouthed. At last, furious, he blurted out:—"What's this? Who said 'Wait'? What . . ."

But he saw a tall figure standing on the rail. It came down and pushed through the crowd, marching with a heavy tread towards the light on the quarterdeck. Then again the sonorous voice said with insistence:—"Wait!" The lamplight lit up the man's body. He was tall. His head was away up in the shadows of lifeboats that stood on skids above the deck. The whites of his eyes and his teeth gleamed distinctly, but the face was indistinguishable. [. . .] The boy [Archie], amazed like the rest, raised the light to the man's face. It was black. A surprised hum—a faint hum that sounded like the suppressed mutter of the word "Nigger"—ran along the deck and escaped into the night. The nigger seemed not to hear. [. . .] After a moment, he said calmly:—"My name is Wait—James Wait." (NN, 31–32, ellipses in original)

The voice of James Wait sounds out at the fringe of the visible. It is a fundamentally acousmatic scene. The title has already hailed him, however. The title is a report of an address, its addresser only now being constituted. Sutured to the as yet still floating signifier of the novel's title, the sound of the voice is racialized in advance. Yet it is also Wait who hails, who calls out. Wait's insistent sonority reorganizes the acoustical coordinates of the deck of the ship and narrative temporality itself such that all action must for a moment cede. Though the scene unfolds objectively, that is, presenting sensations in the order of their appearance as if it were happening now, the statement "It was black" insists upon the fact of recitation: It is a return of the scene in the narrator's memory. This return in memory and narrative—a recitation—slowly renders Wait's visual and acoustical manifestation, as if in the present tense and pulling backward. The entirety of the scene passes through the memory of an unnamed narrator who has not yet said "I" and who, in later saying "I," in the novel's final paragraphs, finally discovers the condition of possibility for narration, his desire to tell the story. The scene is a fantasy echo.

Its work is the echo of the object, the work of relay that constitutes a universal. A singular being stands in for countless others, for *The Nigger of the "Narcissus"* is by all accounts an allegory of community: Disparate men aboard an English ship are being mustered and will come together as one. Their unity is tested by a powerful storm and portents of mutiny amid labor unrest.

The ship *Narcissus* disembarks from a port in Bombay with no other cited goal than to arrive home in England. Its helmsman, Singleton, is the silent image of duty and stoic reserve. Singleton stands alone at the helm during the storm that wreaks havoc upon the ship, yet he is continually watched—lovingly from afar—by the unnamed narrator, whose gaze elevates Singleton to the status of pure image, the kind of "concrete image" so lauded by Henry James and modernist discourse: "Apart, far aft, and alone by the helm, old Singleton had deliberately tucked his white beard under the top button of his glistening coat. Swaying upon the din and tumult of the seas, with the whole battered length of the ship launched forward in a rolling rush before his steady old eyes, he stood rigidly still, forgotten by all, and with an attentive face" (NN, 106).

In the narrator's reverence for Singleton's silence, he becomes a purely visible tableau. He steers the ship in unbroken steadfastness, "swaying upon" the "din" of the sea, the din of the linguistic itself. The semiotic *chora* behind the novel, behind language, is transformed by Singleton's gaze of mastery into a mirroring surface. Singleton, alone and aft, occupies a space and time that has already been vanquished by the din of new men and their values. But that lost space and time must be rendered, absorbed, and, as Conrad suggests in his preface to the novel, "held up" as a "rescued fragment" by narrative (*NN*, 14). Singleton's maternal gaze is containing, embracing. He will soon be forgotten, the narrator suggests, by this group of "forgetful men" (*NN*, 190). Profoundly reticent, Singleton is himself without any articulation of interior life; it is the narrator alone who, a new man unlike his peers, transmutes his surface into depth.[37]

From a technical perspective, the unnamed man aboard ship who narrates the story in the first-person plural and third-person plural, "we" and "they," wishes to become Singleton's mnemic substitute, to merge with his silence and solitude, to attain the place of oblivion where there is no memory trace, only pure consciousness. Singleton is the novel's avowed form of memory. What else does Singleton absorb? When it becomes clear that James Wait, "our Jimmy," is dying, "Every one stared at the nigger" (*NN*, 158). Singleton "peered at Jimmy in profound silence, as if desirous to add that black image to the crowd of Shades that peopled his old memory" (*NN*, 159). The novel, one that contemporary critics found to have little sense for action, concludes not long after Wait's death, being simply the story of group of men, a community at sea, who both love and detest their black mate. At the end of the novel, when the ship docks, the sailors disband, and the narrator alone hears the call of memory, finally saying "I." In his parting words, the figure "Shade" recurs. Hold this figure for a time. It will echo later, in the penultimate section of this chapter, "Locating the First-Person Voice," and in again in the Coda.

Here, as the ship is still in the middle of its journey, the narrator is rapt by Singleton's gaze. The novel's aesthetic impulse, as Conrad avows in the preface, is "before all, to make you *see*." Yet the place of Echo in the title of the novel is as a parenthetical remark—she stands on the margins. She is not named in the title, but she functions as its organizing structure, its condition of possibility. Echo arrives as what Cavarero describes as the subversion of semantic structure.[38] In metaphor, things can throw their voices into others. If the specular wills *Gestalt* and sameness, echo wills difference and disidentification. She is left to the side, where she will be in Ovid's account, calling out from the bushes, the margins of the clearing where Narcissus exists. So too in Freud's "On Narcissism" and Lacan's "The Mirror Stage as Formative of the I Function." Neither Freud nor

Lacan directly remark upon Echo.[39] She is nonetheless there in the work of Freud as the voice of self-condemnation (the superego) and in Lacan as both the coerciveness of the symbolic and the voice of the mother who encourages the infant to forget its discordance at the threshold of the specular image.[40]

Echo and Narcissus are locked together in a formative dance, what Spivak calls, in relation to Echo and Narcissus, "a deconstructive embrace."[41] As a series of written words, Conrad's title commands and then rebukes a certain gaze; it forces me to see a slur and then blot it out, wish that it were not there.[42] But that act of reading (no doubt a visual act) immediately folds upon an inward space where the words echo, a fact of resonance. This fact of resonance opens upon an imaginary and imagined space conjured by the force of the word, where there is a body that I cannot see except as shapeless in its blank universality, the blackness of unspecified content. The face of the deep.

Saying the title to myself, reading it, thinking it, is a sadomasochistic act. The slur injures me and inflicts injury upon an imaginary other. Without determinate content, this other becomes pure injury, not as a someone; the "someone" or the "who" is voided out by the "what." If I pronounce the title aloud, there are scare quotes around the slur that suspend it, if not tonally, then affectively, as if separating the slur from my own voice, to say "it is not 'I' but another who says this slur." At the same time, my utterance is a genesis, a performative incitement that brings that other into being. So too with reading it to myself, saying the slur in the warmth of the reader voice. This performative utterance sadistically marshals the capacity to injure this other.

Again, the mirror immediately follows from out of this echo: There is another being beaten who is "I." This movement is an acoustical displacement. Displacement, for Freud, governs the realm of representability.[43] The slur cannot be fully silenced, erased, or thrown away even as it throws away some fantasy object. In its omission or displacement, the object persists. When I write the word here in quotations, it is an act of symbolic representation that perpetuates this space—"here!"—as a suspended space.

That Conrad's work is autobiographical is an indisputable premise. Conrad took his own memories as his subject. But to say that Conrad's third novel, *The Nigger of the "Narcissus,"* is an autobiographical book, an act of self-writing and self-hearing, opens upon a transgressive racial dilemma. The book announces its subject not in a proper name but in a castigated other. *The Nigger of the "Narcissus"* is about coming to writing, about Conrad generating himself as the subject of narrative and committing to memory a period of life at sea—it is a book of autogenesis. But it is at the same time a book of dying and of inconsolable grief, which is not unrelated to what Christina Sharpe calls "wake work."[44] The man who gives the title of the novel not a proper name but its racial slur also gives the novel not only its most resonant voice but a dying man and then a corpse:

> James Wait rallied again. He lifted his head and turned bravely at Donkin, who saw a strange face, an unknown face, a fantastic and grimacing mask of despair and fury. Its lips moved rapidly; and hollow, moaning, whistling sounds filled the cabin with a vague mutter full of menace, complaint and desolation, like the far-off murmur of a rising wind. Wait shook his head; rolled his eyes; he denied, cursed, threatened—and not a word had the strength to pass beyond the sorrowful pout of those black lips. It was incomprehensible and disturbing; a gibberish of emotions, a frantic dumb show of speech pleading for impossible things, promising a shadowy vengeance. It sobered Donkin into a scrutinising watchfulness. (NN, 168)

The sound of this dying voice is a pre-echo of what Conrad later calls in his tale of the Congo, *Heart of Darkness*, "black and incomprehensible frenzy" (and in the preface to *The Nigger of the "Narcissus"* an "incomprehensible" cry that "sounds far off" and "is heard only as a whisper") (Y, 96; NN, 15). It is what Marlow—not yet fully conceived by Conrad—hears in the sound spaces of the Congo. Conrad has not yet begun writing *Heart of Darkness*, but with Wait's death, is he not hearing some echo of a memory of his journey, a pre-echo of its writing? In fact, the passage concerning the *Narcissus* at landfall could be from the pages of *Heart of Darkness*. "Nothing seems left of the whole universe but darkness, clamor, fury—and the ship. . . . No one spoke and all listened. Outside the night moaned and sobbed to the accompaniment of a continuous loud tremor as of innumerable drums beating far off. Shrieks passed through the air. Tremendous dull blows made the ship tremble while she rolled under the weight of the seas toppling on her deck" (NN, 71).

What is a pre-echo? It is, to be sure, what Conrad calls a "note of warning," a kind of premonition, from the Latin *monēre*, to advise, warn, and remind.[45] A pre-echo or preaudition is an auditory reception of a disturbance but without any monitor. In writing *The Nigger of the "Narcissus*," Conrad was perhaps hearing something in a more diminished form, something he would hear again later and in more amplified ways. A memory trace is still detached from its episteme of the Middle Passage and Conrad's personal memories of the scramble for Africa. The memory (of the Congo) has been received by literary form as a kind of signal or disturbance but has not yet come fully into form's "view." Africa in the *The Nigger of the "Narcissus"* is not an episteme (related etymologically to vision) but an echo.

The echo is a particular kind of auditory relation involving reversibility. In thinking of the literary pre-echo, or even what it is to remember acoustically having read something before, we can appeal to the cinematic sound bridge,

which David Copenhafer suggests is also defined by reversibility.[46] Though the
sound design of cinema is no doubt more intentional, it is psychically instructive
and perhaps owes its existence to the tendency to hear by echoes. For example,
the sound of a previous scene can bleed into the subsequent scene, telling the
spectator that some action or mode of relation is not yet complete. Still more
hauntingly, the sound of a scene still to come can bleed backward, as it were,
into the scene that precedes it. It is uncanny because it has not yet been seen but
allows the film spectator to sense what is to come.

Perhaps the most famous of such sound bridges is that used by the filmmaker
Alfred Hitchcock in *Psycho*, when, in the rainstorm that stops Marion's car in
front of the Bates Motel, the sound of furious rain is the same fragment of sound
that Hitchcock uses after her murder in the shower, when the water is left running, flowing down the drain.[47] In cases such as these, where we have not yet
seen the scene that is attached through the sound bridge, the sound is "both
virtual and acousmatic."[48] It can both supplement what is already at hand and
occupy the scene as its strange and indecipherable double, since it is without the
series of images that will later make sense of it.

To say that the incomprehensible sound of Wait's dying is a pre-echo is to
suggest that sounds, in some sense, can share a form. In the death of Wait, Conrad is beginning to work through some sonic trace. In the phrases "black and
incomprehensible frenzy" and "incomprehensible and disturbing; a gibberish of
emotions, a frantic dumb show of speech," Conrad repeats the words across two
texts. At the same time, there is in the words a repetition of a material, a melancholic remnant of black resonance within the space of writing.

It becomes in this way a kind of delusion or fantasy to speak of "sound itself"
or a sound in itself. What could possibly purify an audible sound of its attachments?

This incomprehensible voice emits, nonetheless, profound authority. The last
sounds of the dying man fill the cabin and command both attention and memory.
As a "dumb show," James Wait dies as if on a minstrel stage, miming and playing
at reality, even in death. Death is the moment from which, in Walter Benjamin's
view, the storyteller "has borrowed his authority."[49] "Conrad" is borrowing his
authority from a voice whose host body is being cast out. In a precise sense, a
resynchronization is at stake, the technic that is writing desiring a sonority of
what is already, if not a lip sync (sound film had not yet been invented), then
a ventriloquism, the "black lips" of Wait moving in time.[50]

The entirety of Conrad's novel occurs between the two poles of James Wait's
first and last sounds. The novel begins with mustering the crew, ordering the

men in relation to the names on the manifest, as Wait appears aboard ship to shout his own name, and "the words, spoken sonorously, with an even intonation, were heard all over the ship" (NN, 33). They are with the enunciating power to begin. The Western phenomenological tradition claims a pure possibility of listening in resonance, a claim that, paradoxically, finds a counterpart in the desonified realm of Genette's narrative voice. "Again and again we have seen this subversion of mood tied to the activity, or rather the presence, of the narrator himself, the disturbing intervention of the narrative source," Genette writes. "It is this last instance—that of *voice*—which we must now look at for its own sake, after having met it so often without wanting to."[51]

To be pure is to be heard absolutely. In a fact of resonance, however, the word—but also the sound, the inflection, timbre, accent, or intonation of voice— is "half someone else's," as Mikhail Bakhtin might say.[52] The listening that would receive these resonances is itself split by the density of its material and its affective charge. In Conrad, each representational object is the halfway point toward another impression just beyond it. The representation of reality in Conrad lies not in things but in their echo. This reality demands an acoustical criticism that takes up rather than refuses its materiality: a reading by echolocation that also listens for echoes elsewhere, not only in Freud but in the work of Fanon. For in that relay a black resonance is to be heard.

NEUTRAL VOICE: THE EGO IDEAL, MELANCHOLIA, AND RACIALIZATION

The supposed silence of writing provided Conrad with what Freud calls, in "On Narcissism," an ego ideal (*Ichideal*).[53] It refers to an inner image of oneself—who we believe we are at our best. Though he finds self-love to be a basic condition of the ego, Freud describes a narcissistic type whose love generally adheres to four object choices. Such a person loves, Freud writes:

(A) what he himself is (i.e. himself),
(B) what he himself was,
(C) what he himself would like to be,
(D) someone who was once part of himself.
                              . . . and the succession of substitutes who take their place.[54]

Such objects adhere to in voice in echo. In speaking and singing, we sound like those whom we would like to be, who we once were, or others who were once parts of ourselves—a voice ideal. But in sounding like others, some of our phrases belong to others to whom narcissistic attachment cannot be admitted except transgressively. Speech becomes the substitute for an impossible or unsanctioned intimacy across gender, sexuality, race, ethnicity, etc. To note only "imitation" in these transidentifications is to miss the dimension of loss and idealization that animates them. Whether written or spoken, the "voice" becomes—like the unified image the infant first sees in the mirror, according to Lacan—an imago, a *Gestalt* of the other person you stole from, the one whom you would like to be. Language allows one to embody for a moment the idealized but lost other. Words in this incantation are, in Édouard Glissant's phrase, "calls to relation," but in relation to others who are not only no longer available or retrievable but lost objects with whom intimacy was always partially refused or foreclosed. They demand a reading and listening by echolocation.

Read in that way, the "silence" of writing makes audible, visible, and legible a racialized psychic coordinate. In *The Nigger of the "Narcissus,"* the voice ideal is intersected in its spatial and psychic rebound with the more phantasmatic voice of the so-called black mate James Wait. Again, he is the most authoritative voice ever to speak in Conrad's fiction. "'I belong to the ship.' He enunciated distinctly, with soft precision" (*NN*, 32). As the ship docks, it is only then that an anonymous narrator, who had vacillated between the pronouns "we" and "they," finally says "I." Where Freud begins to discover in "On Narcissism" his primary theoretical contribution, the workings of *das Ich*, Conrad finally ends *The Nigger of the "Narcissus"* with a first-person voice. The "author" is discovering his mastery. The ending in the first person suggests that the narrative is structured by the egoic work of incorporation, but only to the extent that castigation and self-naming already resound before the narrative's proper beginning (in its title, a racial slur).

This resonance belongs to an ongoing movement and cannot be localized "in" Conrad, the implied author: Freud provides no vision of where disruptive psychic energy, once "bound," goes. A resonance—the echo—moves between narrative levels but also beyond the formal boundaries of the enunciating instance and the work itself. After Wait dies, his corpse is given a proper sailor's burial at sea. "'To the deep,'" Chief Baker intones, as "the ship rolled as if relieved of an unfair burden," then to complete its voyage (*NN*, 77). Wait, Albert J. Guerard once wrote, is *"something the men must get rid of before they can complete their voyage."*[55] The italics indicate some weighty topic,[56] a topic that cannot be directly disclosed without violating the principle of diegetic containment. Such a principle, or the theory of narrative levels, mandates that we not seek any determination "outside" of the text. But what is "inside" and "outside" when confronting this ongoing movement, the echo of the racial slur? Conrad calls Wait "the centre of the ship's collective psychology." He stands as the figure through which the ship's collective psychology must pass if the novel is to find completion, its form, the realization of its voice ideal of mastery.

Ivan Krielkamp, Vincent Pecora, and Bette London have each brought attention to the "disembodied voice" in Conrad, Krielkamp lending galvanizing focus to the "phonographic logic" that "separates" voices from bodies.[57] By contrast, echolocation is the methodology for seeking not a disembodied voice but a body that has been acoustically displaced. The premise of the symptom is that it can detach from experience and reattach—it is a prototechnical formation. Voices and sounds that manifest in Conrad the visual quantum of blackness—skin—have the curious quality of being both canceled out and preserved by narrative space, not unlike the melancholic object in the ego. I thus take blackness not to be an essence but a site of imaginary sonic procedures that intercalate the formal, social, psychical, and tropological.

The ideal voice of mastery is realized in a discarding that also preserves, like the structure of the ego itself. The italics in Guerard's phrase bear all the weight of this intercalation, an unspeakable. In them, the weight of Wait is both disclosed and concealed. In his dying sound, a sound that also erases or "ends" Wait, we can find a trace of a voice that powerfully seized Conrad's fantasy. It is the fantasy of a voice that, as an object, can be detached from and reattached to its host body, that could be dislocated from its source to move around a space while also containing it (a maternal fantasy, or what Eric Lott calls, in relation to blackface minstrelsy and its production of exaggerated lips, "the totalizing, and thus terrorizing, connectedness of a pre-oedipal bliss").[58] There was, in Conrad's memory, a sound he conceived as black, a black resonance for which he was writing and listening in becoming "Conrad the Author," a resonance that he desired to keep but dared not speak aloud.

Until recently, a generation of critics had not remarked upon blackness and whiteness in the novel, deriving instead an allegory of community and nationalism against failed mutiny. However, many readers have found in the novel's wayward narrative voice the first stirrings of the man who will later be named "Marlow." When referring to his greatest achievement, Conrad relished saying and writing the injurious slur among his acquaintances and in letters, and in this perspective, part of the work of coming to Marlow, his proper avatar, was the work of the slur. The slur makes this coming to Marlow a work of mourning, with Marlow the trace of a black voice that Conrad cannot fully avow; the slur makes that work audible. Like melancholia, the slur seeks out what can be preserved (brought within the full "light" of memory) and those objects—such as the body of the black mate—that are ambivalently loved, canceled out, and preserved, maintained as the "shadow of the object" under which the Conradian narrative voice lives.[59]

What does it mean for a theory of listening, for narrative, that melancholia takes on a strategically audible form? The melancholic makes himself known to Freud through his characteristic of the unending complaint, self-rebuke, and castigation of himself, and Freud finds in melancholic plaint a lost love object that has become "a loss in regard to his ego."[60] "The shadow of the object has fallen upon the ego," Freud famously writes. But if we read Freud's essay carefully, such a shadow makes itself known only by being heard (by another, and more implicitly by oneself). That the ego is a phonographic form is borne out by the melancholic, who is, as the saying goes, a broken record.[61] The melancholic does not know, and cannot hear, that in his self-rebuke he voices the experience of an object with which a relationship could not be fully realized. Melancholia's impetus is not death but "slight, disappointment," and, above all, a continual "threat of losing the object."[62] The object threatened with loss is far from abandoned; it is incorporated. The ego protects the object from rebuke while also voicing a desire for hitherto unrealized intimacy with it.

The melancholic functions under a preservative logic. Freud memorably defines the work achieved by melancholy over its object: "So by taking flight into the ego love escapes extinction [*Die Liebe hat such so durch ihre Flucht ins Ich der Aufhebung entzogen*]."[63] In *The Psychic Life of Power*, Judith Butler takes up this passage to remind us of the notorious complications that cling to *Aufhebung* in Hegelian discourse as "cancellation but not quite extinction; suspension, preservation, and overcoming."[64] It is preservation that also transforms.

What would it mean to say that the racial slur is an echo of this problematic of melancholia and racialization? From the side of those who must hear such slurs, there is commentary available on the experience of hate speech coming back to someone who has been its object.[65] It is what happens to the person in its journey toward becoming an object. Whether appearing in the shape of an object or energy, we cannot forget that the object was once a person, as spectral as he or she might become in the course being internalized. In death, the corporeal person is lost; in racialization, however, the corporeal person persists. Cheng writes:

> It is as if, for Freud, the "object" has, for all practical purposes, disappeared into the melancholic's psychical interiority. In short, one is led to ask, what happens if the object were to return—would the melancholic stop being melancholic? That scenario would seem to make sense except that, since Freud has posited melancholia as a constitutive element of the ego, the return of the object demanding to be a person of its

own would surely now be devastating. Indeed, the return of the object may not be as blessed an event as one might imagine.[66]

The return of the object—as a person—is far from the impersonating repetition that is melancholic complaint and incorporation, which both keeps and rejects. Melancholia is, in this way, not an affective state but "an elaborate identificatory system based on psychical and social consumption-and-denial."[67] Were it simply rejection, it would not be so devastating and propulsive in its effects: a being who persists in dejection, who is preserved while canceled. Racism maintains a lost love object.

That this echo of the object is one wound of the political is made clear by Frantz Fanon. If a black Caribbean immigrates to France, Fanon says, he must learn to mask the colonial overtones of his speech. From the moment he arrives at the piers of France, he will have difficulty assimilating. If speaking and communicating is a relational question of mirroring, then we might say that he is received through an acoustical misrecognition: "Ah come fom Mahtinique, it's the fuhst time Ah've eveh come to Fance."[68] In a moment of sonic textuality, Fanon ventriloquizes not the voice imputed to the Caribbean man but the mode of listening that perceives him, scorning any traces of Creole. Fanon is sounding out in text the sound of the voice that falls into the world misrecognized, occupying a zone between speaking, or hearing (understanding) oneself speak, and critical self-listening:

> The Negro arriving in France will react against the myth of R-eating man from Martinique. He will become aware of it, and he will really go to war against it. He will practice not only rolling his R but embroidering it. Furtively observing the slightest reactions of others, listening to his own speech, suspicious of his own tongue—a wretchedly lazy organ—he will lock himself into his room and read aloud for hours— desperately determined to learn *diction*.[69]

To the extent that the voice of the black Caribbean man fails to attain to the master's pronunciation, he fails to attain to the category of the human. In "Discourse in the Novel," Bakhtin notes that there are some speech types in which certain words will "sound alien," an imperfect assimilation. If every word is "half-someone else's," then to sound convincingly like oneself is to achieve a more perfect replication of the other. The origin in otherness perfectly dissolves. Sounding foreign, sounding alien: The colonized's speech is a sound-recording and -replaying apparatus. There has been some mimicry, as Bhabha might suggest, and the voice carries a trace as a copy, parroting the master's voice and presenting to it the violence of its own construction.

Fanon's "The Negro and Language" is an evocative recovery of this double voice. I say "double voice" rather than the more familiar "double-voiced discourse" of Bakhtin because Fanon returns to the *sound* of the voice in its pronunciation (it is not simply heteroglossic but heterophonic). This sound is shot through with the discursive, making the sonic linguistic and the linguistic sonic. It is not as if the sound of the voice is prior to discourse, as if discourse later arrives to "color" what had been neutral in tone. Rather, pronunciation is itself, for Fanon, a discursive formation. Sound is a racial form.

This event of self-hearing lacks what Roland Barthes once called, in relation to his famous concept of the "grain of the voice," "the voluptuous pleasure of signifier-sounds, of its letters."[70] Its pleasure "germinates from within the language and in its very materiality."[71] Barthes names this pleasure *pronunciation*, lending it "a very simple word," the one we have just confronted in Fanon: "the *diction* of language."[72] But Fanon and Barthes have inverted definitions of these key terms, for it is on the heels of this elevation of diction that Barthes denigrates styles (in the main, Germanic) that make overly clear a word's "articulation." For Barthes, articulation, in contrast to pronunciation, fails to attain to the grain of the voice, that "something" in the voice that is "not the message at all" but rather the contact between the throat, glottis, and, above all, the "mother tongue."[73]

If we bring Fanon and Barthes into a missed encounter, we find that what characterizes the postcolonial voice, the accented voice, the voice of the alien, is that it cannot attain to this lofty signifying function for Barthes. It is trapped in the expressive and communicative, without voluptuous pleasure, only self-alienation in self-hearing. Fanonian diction aspires to being heard and understood. Labored over, the signifier sound is a bad object, a rejected materiality localized in the colonized's body, that germinates not from within but from without. The colonial man articulates; he is without the good object of pronunciation, for which the materiality of the body and the materiality of the mother tongue are one. Even if the colonial man ever achieves his aim, masking colonial overtones, he incites a new aggression in his listener: "This one talks like a book."[74]

In Fanon's imaginary monologue of the black Caribbean man, the alien sound of the voice devours language, eating its phonemes. But something happens to self-hearing in turn. The colonized fails to open the space of communication with others, locked in the autocircuit of critical self-perception. To be sure, Barthes's thought of music, voice, and language is endlessly suggestive, and it opened up previously unheard and unthought spaces within the voice as object. But other spaces also determine this space within the voice, within the fact of hearing, throwing it further into remove, away from communication and the possibility of being heard. In *Black Skin, White Masks*, Fanon also gives voice, as it were, to what I argued in Chapter 1 to be the ground of narrative voice in acoustical displacement when he narrates an everyday and pedestrian encounter:

> "Look, a Negro!" It was an external stimulus that flicked over me as I passed by. I made a tight smile.
>
>   "Look, a Negro!" It was true. It amused me.
>
>   . . . It was no longer a question of being aware of my body in the third person but in a triple person. . . . I was given not one but two, three places. . . . I was responsible at the same time for my body, for my race, for my ancestors. I subjected myself to an objective examination, I discovered my blackness, my ethnic characteristics; and I was battered down by tom-toms [*et me défoncèrent le tympan*], cannibalism, intellectual deficiency, fetishism, racial defects, slave-ships, and above all else, above all: "Sho' good eatin'."[75]

"My body was given back to me sprawled out, distorted, recolored, clad in mourning in that white winter day," he continues. The French Marxist theorist Louis Althusser echoes (acoustically displaces) this scene when positing his famous formula of interpellation by which a policeman shouts, "Hey, you there!"[76] Writing of Althusser, who describes turning around to face the voice of authority, Butler writes, briefly and in passing, of "the visual rendering of an auditory scene."[77] The scene in Fanon does not concern prosopopoeia, the visual rendering of the face—Fanon calls it "epidermalization." Edwin C. Hill rejoins, describing "a specularization from sound to text—or from sound to another type of materiality: skin."[78] Some acoustic event, in its spatial parameters, yields the visual/textual. But Fanon suggests that still more occurs when consciousness is split by an internalized demand from without. In this spatial dynamic, an exterior voice interrupts him to yell not *at* him but *nearby*. I don't think we've adequately grasped that fact—what it is to hear someone nearby denigrate you.

"Below the corporeal schema" is a "historico-racial schema," a third voice in the Du Boisian dyad of double consciousness.[79] These are fragments of a historicity that are not Fanon's yet become his in the moment of interpellation, mediated also by the terms of "my race" and "my ancestors." The boy does not speak these terms, but they are imputed as part of the overall tenor of the scene, one that now collects sayings from a Bakhtinian social edifice. As written, the scene registers Fanon's regard for the power of radio, multiple and acousmatic voices drifting into the textual space.[80]

This voice from elsewhere within, as a painful example of the heteroaffection that Derrida ceaselessly pursued in the space of autoaffection, becomes his. It is absorbed into his mouth in the moment the voice of interpellation hails and brings him into being as subject.[81] He has been seen in his blackness and can no longer be heard to speak in the first person. "I took myself far off from my own presence," Fanon writes, "far indeed, and made myself an object." It is a body upon which a structural shadow has been cast.

With this shadow there is also an echo. He speaks not from self-presence but from a place of self-distance; he senses that his own voice has been cloaked, acoustically overwritten by the palimpsests of the phantasmatic and its historical layers, a devouring voice of racial stereotype, one against which his text continually sounds out in its pursuit of a "new man."[82] He cannot respond to the one who names him: It is a force that cannot be faced in the proper sense, being itself without face. The terms of communication have been suspended: He will not be "heard" and has been divested of voice as the onto-epistemological sign of presence. He has become pure body, skin, and a mouth whose appetitive function has been isolated while its verbo-symbolic function has been denied.

In his textual techniques, steeped in psychoanalytic listening practices, Fanon encourages a slippage between the spoken or interlocutory or the written or disseminated.[83] One can imagine the physical voice of Fanon shifting in its registers to "reproduce" these many voices of fantasy. This imagining is further encouraged by the fact that he dictated the essay to his wife, Marie-Josephe Dublé, as amanuensis. She remembers him "pacing back and forth in the manner of an orator," his first drafts being choreographic, shaped by "the rhythm of a body in motion."[84] (Josie was there, triangulating this already triangulated scene.) It is the written text, however, that affords virtual spacing. The palimpsests of the voice become most acute in writing because it includes and imputes, we found in Chapter 1, a hypothetical listening consciousness of the reader. Fanon's imaginary body here lends itself to be gazed at by an implied reader, who then must consider that the voice of the boy (and triangulating the ear of the mother) also animate a reader's own sense of reading, looking, and listening.

What would it mean to consider narrative voice itself as taking this form of address, one whose structure is impersonal but also articulated in the most personal zone of the interior? In Fanon, the fictional effect is the irrecuperable or unnarratable prehistory of the subject. But there is both a structural acoustics and a physical acoustics being written out. Fanon "voices" the structures of (self-)hearing. We would do well to consider fiction's entanglement with narrative voice and the irrecoverable origination of its grammatical agency and imaginary effects. It is as if apostrophe, the call to an absent or deceased other, is the fundamental figure of narrative discursivity. Fanon performatively exploits this "mask" of narrative voice as if to reproduce the fictional structure of racial formation. Fanon adopts a modernist narrativity of voices within voices and their differential effects.

"Since listening remains one of the only physical activities of the human body that occurs simultaneously inside and outside the body," Cheng writes of Fanon's scene, "we might understand listening here to condition coming-to-being."[85] But as I noted, the boy does not address Fanon. The scene is not a scene of listening but a scene of *overhearing*. At stake in it is the social value of an address, of who can be addressed. This question, I argued in Chapter 1, is never raised by Genette in his theory of the enunciating instance. Communicational theories of narrative can function only if they presume the "for me" quality of an address, which is not "enigmatic," as Jean Laplanche might say, in its signification.[86] Because the address is immediately and transcendentally for me, it never moves or resounds through some space, some duration, on the other side of which I wait.

It is the dynamic of withdrawing an address, and with it, recognition, that lends to Fanon's scene its acoustics. The voices move in multiple directions to lend the scene its spatial and imaginary proportion. In his chapter on Hegel, Fanon notes the other is *"waiting* for recognition by us."[87] Fanon writes in "The Fact of Blackness," "if I were asked for a definition of myself, I would say that I am the one who waits [*si j'avais à me définir, je dirais que j'attends*]; I investigate my surroundings, I interpret everything in terms of what I discover, I become sensitive."[88] To become sensitive is to thrust oneself into resonance; he is listening, he is waiting for a voice. He is not waiting for a voice that might address him as one worthy of being addressed, but rather, in his sensitivity, he absorbs, he reflects back like an echo. But in reflecting back (reciting the sediment of slurs and passages of text), he breaks with ontology to cease to wait for some other deferred moment of recognition where the colonial addressor will hear *himself*, will hear that he, too, is waiting in relation to another he repudiates ("I demanded an explanation. Nothing happened").[89] Instead, "I wait for me [*Je m'attends*]," Fanon writes of the moment just before a film begins.[90] (Between these two quotations, massive amounts of cited text, from poetry to fiction and to drama, vibrate with Fanon's history of reading across French, German, and American letters, passages often introduced with the command, "Listen.")[91]

The boy is incapable of addressing Fanon, who is elided in the tight circularity of the "for me" quality of the boy's shout. The boy addresses his mother, which Fanon then overhears, knowing himself to be the object of their talk. In being the third term, Fanon animates a position incalculable to the sender/receiver dyad and to the scene of interpellation as Althusser theorized it, the linear "hail." When theorizing the state apparatus, Althusser adapted Fanon's text to posit its defining force in a policeman's shout: "Hey, you!" Butler then famously turns to Althusser to find in the hail the formative aporia of the subject, the question of why we turn to an unknown voice, finding there a "certain readiness or anticipatory desire" to receive the call.[92] She writes, "The one addressed is compelled to turn toward the law prior to any possibility of asking a set of critical questions: Who is speaking? Why should I turn around? Why should I accept the terms by which I am hailed?"[93] But Althusser already misinterprets Fanon, turning the triadic into the dyadic. What would the *Fanonian* coordinates of overhearing mean for the formative aporia of the subject? No one calls to or hails Fanon. He is not a subject of listening—and that is in part where the scene gathers its most deconstituting effects.[94] He is the object of a shout. It is a third-person interpellation. The Fanonian scene of overhearing interpellation—an interpellation to the side—means that an object intercedes in such questions, an object through which the "I" must pass, or echo, before it can even pose these questions to itself.

At stake here is how racial identity, which is supposed to be evident in the blink of an eye, traverses a space and in a reiterative duration. In the shout, there is the sealing of the name (and its voice) to the image. There is an ellipsis, an echo. How does a reader differentially discover and impute to written voice a racial identity, particularly when narrative voice is a purely grammatical agency that outsources its perceptual capacities to the focalizer, as the agent who "sees and selects" what is to be represented? Mieke Bal writes, "what matters in language is not the world 'about' which subjects communicate, but the constitution of the subjectivity required to communicate in the first place."[95]

In its imaginary acoustics, Fanon's literary scene dramatizes something of the elliptical and echoing structure of constitution, or determination. The focalizer not only "sees and selects"; it also hears and selects. The archaic meaning of determinacy (*Bestimmtheit*) indicates a voice, *Stimme*. To declare *das stimmt* is to say "it is true" or "it is so." But beneath this reality is another: "It has been voiced." The meaning of declaration is to say "it is." A declarative voice is the voice in which determination speaks. To say "it is" is to assume determinative power; it is also to say of some other quantity "it is not."

Understood as determinative in this way, the audible is not neutral to the question of race; the audible is itself a racial form, and it is more determinative than vision. In racialization, a fantasy echo intercedes *as* the production of the visible. The formative aporia of the subject thus is not without foundational consequences for narrative theory, not least in the question of the formation of a voice.

LOCATING THE FIRST-PERSON VOICE

In Conrad, what is at issue is the question of the formation of the voice of a modernist writer. We learn from Fanon that the wound of the political can at times become audible. But this audibility is not limited to the event of speech. An imputed silence, I argued in Chapter 1, is the ground of both the theory of narrative voice and the modernist doxa of "showing" and "telling." Michael North employs Conrad's preface to *The Nigger of the "Narcissus"* to "inaugurate" a genealogy of modernism, racial and cultural difference becoming, in this way, both "constitutive and radically disruptive" of Conrad's aesthetic proclamations, making its preface a vexed yet "valid introduction to the rest of modern literature."[96] In the "Author's Note" to *The Rescue*, for example, Conrad writes that in addition to the "first consciousness of a certain sort of mastery," the completion of *The Nigger of the "Narcissus"* "brought to [his] troubled mind the comforting sense of an accomplished task." As I described in Chapter 1, the aesthetic ideology of the image as a means to achieve hegemony populates studies of modernism. By what kind of work, however, does the racial slur present the much-lauded virtual image of his preface—"behold!" Conrad writes of the visible world, "all the truth of life is there" (*NN*, 16)—to an otherwise spectral membership in an English collectivity and on behalf of an author who once referred to himself as "a sort of freak, an amazing bloody foreigner writing in English"?[97]

Though in memorable moments Conrad lauds the visual and imagistic ("to make you *see*"), this register takes on through the slur and its sound an entirely different valence: the achievement of a voice by the displacement of a voice. The aesthetic ideology of the image functions as the displacement of a sound.

Conrad's narrative spaces continually represent a choreographic movement where a narrative voice—at times embodied in the narrative as a character, at times disembodied in omniscience—comes to itself through the diegetic sound world, hearing sounds and remarking upon their difference. This movement is an externalization of the work of "voice" (both narrative and ideal), of what it has had to reject to become itself. The ego ideal of the neutral voice ("one of us") and the anthropological voice of someone who knows the world yet speaks as if from nowhere—each of these is for Conrad not given in advance but won. Idealization is not in advance of writing but in the act of writing and in narratological effects.

The preface to *The Nigger of the "Narcissus"* insists that the verbal artist, writing out of solitude, "shall awaken in the hearts of the beholders that feeling of unavoidable solidarity; of the solidarity in mysterious origin, in toil, in joy, in hope, in uncertain fate, which binds men to each other and all mankind to the visible world" (*NN*, 14–15). Yet behind that confident "shall," in every account of what it was like for Conrad to write, we find "blots," erasures, and defacements occurring time and again.[98] In letters to his editors and publishers, Conrad curses the poor conception of his manuscripts, manuscript pages nearly scratched out of existence, and periods of near inability to write a sentence or even make a mark on the page. And in the months following his completion of the novel, Conrad wrote to Cunninghame Graham just before he was to introduce Conrad into his circle of English literary friends: "But you know I am shy of my bad English." (His long letters to Graham "include long passages in French, and phrases from Spanish, Italian and Arabic.")[99] He continues, "At any rate prepare for a 'b—y furriner' who will talk gibberish . . . at the rate of 10 knots an hour."[100] But now, in reciting his only aesthetic maxim, the written page promises to hold the neutral image of solidarity as such.

This ambivalence is fundamental to the object that is English literature. In *A Personal Record*, as Christopher GoGwilt describes, Conrad evades the question of how he learned to speak English to tell instead the story of his first encounter with English literature in translation[101]—in exile in the Russian Empire after his father, an anti-imperialist intellectual, was reputedly apprehended and expelled when overheard uttering a dissident statement. There, as Laurence Davies describes, Conrad's linguistic formation intersected with Ukrainian, Russian ("the language of authority"), Yiddish, and Polish, but also the sacred languages of Hebrew, Latin, and Church Slavonic: "He must have experienced language as a congeries both of sounds which came gradually to make sense and of sounds which stayed mysterious,"[102] objects that were dispersed and diasporic in original ways.

Conrad had stolen into his father's office for some illicit reading of the manuscript pages of his father's Polish translation of Shakespeare's *The Two Gentlemen of Verona*. Catching him, his father commanded a young Conrad to "read it aloud!" But this beginning in a detour through sounding is, to some extent, an echo of his language acquisition, the missing story of learning English manifesting in displacement. We learn in this moment that Conrad must speak as someone else if he is to find the means of moving the world to unison. He must find an alternative accent, the right sound, the right word, the right voice, one that will become the echo of his voice. This voice can in no way be his own. Sounding out poses a risk, for there is the possibility of errancy: Sounding may be misdirected, move in a direction that the author can neither predict nor command. The word "fails to be heard." It goes "down-wind."

All of Conrad's acoustics pivot on such a primal scene of self-hearing: searching for the right voice. The drive to create the conditions of a purely self-reflexive voice comes to itself through the detour of the other. The displacement involved in speaking as someone else, in a voice that will be an echo of one's own, anatomizes Conradian narrative voices and determines the possibilities of the modernist novel. Without it, there would be no participant-observer, the kind that may be found in F. Scott Fitzgerald's *The Great Gatsby* and William Faulkner's *The Sound and the Fury*, as I will return to in the Coda of this chapter.

There is a fundamental and irreducible problem of synchronization—and as *The Nigger of the "Narcissus"* begins to draw to a close, the narrating instance is about to become host to some other voice, a problem that is technified in relation to the presentation of narrative. For, in Wait's death, "not a word had the strength to pass beyond the sorrowful pout of those black lips" (*NN*, 168). Wait's mouth—a black (w)hole of superegoic condemnation—is supreme in its rhetorical ability for "dissent": "He influenced the moral tone of our world as though he had it in his power to distribute honours, and treasures, or pain; and he could give us nothing but contempt" (*NN*, 157). This grossly audible "contempt" that cannot be silenced (he refuses the command to "shut up") is the subject of the following sentences, a summation of his wasting away into an abject materiality:

> It was immense; it seemed to grow gradually larger, as his body day by day shrank a little more, while we looked. It was the only thing about him—of him—that gave the impression of durability and vigour. It lived within him with an unquenchable life. It spoke through the eternal pout of his black lips; it looked at us through the impertinent mournfulness of his languid and enormous stare. We watched him intently.
> (*NN*, 157)

So durable is this abject trace that its figure will recur in *Heart of Darkness*, where the jungle that hosts the unseen Congolese, who sound out continuously and clamorously, is said to be "immense." *Heart of Darkness* is a melancholic remnant of *The Nigger of the "Narcissus,"* an indication that it was not yet through being written.

In echolocation, however, the echoes are not to be synchronized. When Derrida identifies in autoaffection an original, heteroaffective instance, he implies that something of hearing (understanding) oneself speak is already an *acousmêtre*, a disembodied voice, a hearing of a fragment of speech detached from its "source" or primacy instance. But in all attachment and detachment, particularly the ambivalent attachment that characterizes melancholia, something of the host body persists—otherwise, one would not feel such intimacy with the lost other in hearing oneself complain (for Lacan, the task is thus "full speech," or to become a listener in relation to one's own discourse). It is in moments of desynchronization, where the mask wears thin and the corpus becomes open to its constitutive wounds, that relations open up. It's there that relations become possible at all, both in the text and in the (white) ego.[103]

For example, the black lips of Wait hang as he issues his last sounds. The English "I" that hears these last words (still a plural "we" in this moment)—and sees the lips—frames them as the narrator, but this "I" is not grammatically available *until* Wait issues his last sounds. Conrad understood that out of blackness comes whiteness. In this moment the narrator violates what had been the prohibition of entering omnisciently into the intimate spaces of his mates. It is crucial for the participant-observer in such works as *The Great Gatsby*—Conrad invents Fitzgerald's narrator in *The Nigger of the "Narcissus"*[104]—that a character-narrator is there as a third term for what should be an intimate moment between two people. Wait's death scene is clearly a moment reserved for the detested mate Donkin, yet the narrator nearly transcends his place to be present for Wait's last moments, being so close that he hears the most minor of spaces between Wait's lips and Donkin's ear. He is somewhere between "we" and "they" as he listens to what he could not physically have heard: "'Jimmy,' he called low. There was no answer, but the rattle stopped. 'D'yer see me?' he asked, trembling. . . . Donkin, looking away, bent his ear to Jimmy's lips, and heard a sound like the rustle of a single dry leaf driven along the smooth sand of a beach. It shaped itself" (*NN*, 171).[105] It is out of this shape that the narrator's "I" becomes possible, for the novel ends:

> A gone shipmate, like any other man, is gone for ever: and I never met one of them again. But at times the spring-flood of memory sets with force up the dark River of the Nine Bends. Then on the waters of the forlorn stream drifts a ship—a shadowy ship manned by a crew of Shades. They pass and make a sign, in a shadowy hail. . . . As good a crowd as ever fisted with wild cries the beating canvas of a heavy foresail; or tossing aloft, invisible in the night, gave back yell for yell to a westerly gale. (*NN*, 190)

In synthesizing the memory of Wait on behalf of the forgetful men, the narrative voice loses its plurality to become an "I." The ship docks in England, where the "I" can now perfectly reflect a conjectured and robust "yell for yell," which gives the novel its final phrase. But the last sounds of the dying mate had to be discarded along the way. Something of his dying "hollow, moaning, whistling sounds," as a trace of the sonic more generally, is the return of the repressed of the modernist doxa of "showing." It is embodied by a marginalized figure who is then killed and discarded (by the narrative, by *its* demands for the voice ideal). But Wait becomes in this movement the condition of possibility of the novel's form, its claim to narrative voice. Wait becomes in death unnamed: "the gone shipmate," he drifts into the anonymity of the collective, but by means of a special sort of oblivion that defines not only the fungibility of figuration but the reflexive movement itself. The subject takes itself as its own object, becoming an "I" in relation to a "me"; the echo of the object relays that event. In naming Wait "gone" (*fort*), in *figuring* Wait—the only mate ever to use irony aboard ship—the narrator's "I" speaks in a misrecognized black voice. Conrad's irony originates in a black position.[106]

Conrad is discovering his modernism through the interposition of a Caribbean figure, not unlike a Jewish Al Jolson in blackface, who finds both his whiteness and modern voice through jazz. This figure dies in ambivalence, a figure who cannot be had from the beginning and who, like all melancholic objects, is lost to the disappointment of desire. Melancholia, and particularly racializing melancholia, is the framework through which we can consider a narrative voice that sublates the otherness of sound and, with it, a trace of an aggressive desire.

In Benjamin's famous remarks on the place of involuntary memory in modernist literature, he slightly misquotes Freud: "Consciousness comes into being at the site [*an der Stelle*] of a memory trace."[107] For Benjamin, wherever the memory trace evaporates, consciousness arises. The Conradian narrative voice is, in its acoustics, a psychic system in which becoming conscious and leaving behind a memory trace are compatible and copresent in the same system. It is a system that confounds the available terminology of narratology, for in it the critic must speak of voices that are there and of voices that have been discarded. They exist and persist in and as the narrating instance, which turns out to be a "crypt," as Nicolas Abraham and Maria Torok argue of melancholia and its modes of internalization. Where an experience and its object have not been sufficiently recognized, they cannot become properly past, but it is this melancholia in Conrad that also makes him so open to being taken up by and incorporated into the acoustical unconscious of his readers.

If reading is a mode of listening, then it is not the containing site where all traces become coterminous through what Barthes describes as the "double hearing" of dramatic irony. Rather, the echoes pass through some space and duration. There is a hearing *through*, for the reader is also "within" the space of echo herself. And in a doubled paradox, the involuntary memory alone becomes the "place" (*Stelle*) where Conrad's idealized voice becomes possible, the reader shoring up acoustical fragments that linger and vibrate from work to work, from reading to reading.

Gathering up the fragments of James Wait's body and voice thus is, to some degree, a reparative work in which we have been engaged, following by echolocation the words and word sounds that recur. When Conrad writes of Wait's expiring voice, his last sounds, his body becomes the alien obstacle whose residual reflection gives to Conrad the material for his "voice." He cannot let "Wait" go, and writing becomes the amalgamating space where the object both expires and accumulates, or echoes.

The repetition of words—in their accumulation—yields an inaudible idealized object toward which writing strives. In contrast with Conrad's struggles to find the right voice, the right accent, Henry James was an artist that Conrad imagined to be without a problematic relation to writing—a paradigm of the neutral voice, the idealized voice of modernism. In "Henry James: An Appreciation" (1905), the fact that James was dictating his newer works was for Conrad powerful evidence of the inwardness of his works:

> I do not know into what brand of ink Mr. Henry James dips his pen; indeed, I heard of late that he had been dictating. . . . The stream of inspiration flows brimful in a predetermined direction, unaffected by the periods of droughts, untroubled in its clearness by the storms of the land of letters . . . never running back upon itself, opening new visions at every turn of its course through that richly inhabited country its fertility has created. . . .
>
> The artistic faculty, of which each of us has a minute grain, may find its voice in some individual . . . *gifted with a power of expression*. . . . He is so much of a voice that, for him, silence is like death.[108]

The essay is dedicated to an American who embodies "fidelity," a more perfect assimilation to the literary culture of England. By 1897, the year Conrad wrote his preface to *The Nigger of the "Narcissus,"* James's critical prefaces were already beginning to ground the theory of the novel. Conrad finds in James an absolute resonance between authorial voice (which is silent, metaphysical) and physical voice—a pure voice, untouched by the outside. Conrad idealizes James's uncomplicated because unmediated relationship to speaking and writing. In this context, Conrad echoes the central tropes of his own preface. He declares that James undertakes "rescue work . . . in darkness" by "this snatching of vanishing phases of turbulence, disguised in fair words, out of the native obscurity into a light where the struggling forms may be seen" and endowed with "the permanence of memory." Language ushers the evanescent into enduring concretion.

We can hold as a pre-echo and post-echo the voice of James (Wait) in relation to the voice of (Henry) James. There is a white American idealized voice of a writer embraced by France and England; there is a black Caribbean idealized voice, whose status is ambivalent; the text never annotates whether Wait, who hails from St. Kitts, speaks Kittian dialect, and his pronunciation is never documented by a narrative ear (this novel is otherwise an archive of English sound, Conrad writing out dialect voices like Donkin's). But "Wait" could also be "White," "if pronounced with a cockney diphthong and silent 'h,'" Watt notes.[109] Like the authoritative and anechoic voices of the radio, Wait's English is standardized, profoundly idealized, and were it not for the recalcitrance of his corporeality, neutralized. He is one of the ship's men but also their scapegoat. As Conrad describes it, Henry James's voice is nation building, creating a "richly inhabited country"; it is a messianic beacon around which the mass of men "cluster" to watch the "last flicker of light." There is in these phrases an echo of Marlow's regard for Kurtz in *Heart of Darkness*, Kurtz also said to have "presented himself as a voice" and in a novel driven by Marlow's disappointed desire to hear the voice of his predecessor (Y, 113). He hears it but once, yet "the echo of his magnificient eloquence" persists in memory, "thrown to me from a soul as translucently pure as a cliff of crystal." James is "gifted with a power of expression"; Kurtz is endowed with "a gift of expression" (Y, 113). For Marlow, this gift is ambiguous, "the most exalted and the most contemptible, the pulsating stream of light," like the English language that Conrad feels chose him and drove him to write (the very act that will torture and shame him).

In an acoustical intimacy between his characters and predecessors, Conrad hears in James what Marlow hears in Kurtz, what he wishes to hear from his own body (its grain) were his reading of his father's manuscript to transform according to *le petit objet (a)* of native English: a supreme faculty of voice and an interrupted movement between mind and composition. James's language is "lit up." It is clear language, unfrustrated, neutral; "it speaks" from the inwardness of conception. The presence of dictation in this fantasy of James is difficult to ignore. Who is the transcriber, if not the pure ear with no memory, no origins? "A limitless memory would in any event be not memory but infinite self-presence," Derrida writes. Conrad "*dreams* of . . . a memory with no sign. That is, with no supplement."[110]

There is, in the midst of this dense echo, a return of the term *rescue*, the primary figure for Conrad's conception of the authorial task.[111] In August 1898, Conrad wrote to his literary advisor, David S. Meldrum, to apologize for the agonizing delay of *The Rescue*: "Nothing would induce me to lay down my pen if I *feel* a sentence—or even a word ready to my hand. The trouble is that too often—

alas!—I've to Wait for the sentence—for the word."[112] In the "Author's Note," Conrad regards the characters in the delayed completion of *The Rescue* as "They Who had Waited." This return of the trope in composition, the experience of an echo: Does it reduce the space between writing, sounding, and experience? The meaning of the word "rescue" coincides with the sound of an object that never left. Waiting, rescuing. These words populate Conrad's prose. What is the desire that animates the return? The single word, in its repetition and repletion—becoming crystalline over a corpus and a life of speaking and writing—ceases to be a signifier. It refers only to itself, eternal in its autogenesis.

"Conrad was trying to do something that his experience as a writer everywhere revealed to be impossible," Edward Said argues.[113] "For what Conrad discovered was that the chasm between words saying and words meaning was widened, not lessened, by a talent for words written."[114] But the chasm between saying and meaning was also widened by the fantasy and physical reality of sounding. When Said begins his essay with an epigraph from *Lord Jim*, "'There are no words for the sort of things I wanted to say,'" *he* cuts off Jim's immediate next sentiment: "'Just then I would have simply howled like an animal'" (*LJ*, 124).[115] If there were no words, there was nonetheless a desire for a cry, a howl, an o-o-o-o.

"Writing is that neutral, composite, oblique space where our subject slips away," writes Barthes, "the negative [*le noir-et-blanc*] where all identity is lost, starting with the very identity of the body writing."[116] We have found this oblique space to be populated by echoes. In the ideal voice of Henry James, for example, we find the reflexivity of the echo. But paired with the figure of Henry James is James Wait, a more "shadowy" lost object. In their echo, Conrad generates his "voice" as self-repetition. This echoic voice is constituted by rescued fragments, or fragments displaced and then sublimated. "Where there is sublimation there is also idealization," Kaja Silverman writes.[117] Conrad reflexively searches for his ideal voice in the acoustic mirror. We speak of an object called "my voice," but for Conrad, the gift of the voice returns back from the other to become the self. Echo courts Narcissus away from his own image.

As acoustic imagos, both James and Wait are passively idealized, that is, believed to be *"essentially* perfect," neither treated as fully separate from Conrad.[118] In both pairings, Conrad exists in what Silverman calls, after Lacan, a "state of dependence" where he hears himself through the other. (Henry) James lives, is "imperishable"; the other, James (Wait) dies, going "to the deep." But his death is temporary, resuscitated time and again in a trope, a trope whose meaning announces that the death is not final: "wait." Through repeating the name, Conrad incants a repair against an aggressed love object.

Conrad hears an ideal in (Henry) James, but we make a gross mistake if we cannot emphasize that he *also* hears an ideal in the fantasy of James (Wait).

The corporeal implications of *The Nigger of the "Narcissus"* for the psychic life of race are stunning. I have been describing a situation in which the bodily ego slips through its visual parameters in a vocal ego, a fact of resonance. If we concentrate only on the bodily ego as visually evidenced by the skin, we miss the ways in which the racial other is held in the white ego as a sound, a voice. In the Coda to this chapter, we will find that Faulkner heard clearly in Conrad the interracial implications, creating a narrative space in which a lost, black love object continually echoes within the white ego.

CODA: LITERARY HISTORY AS MISCEGENATING SOUND: *THE SOUND AND THE FURY*

The ideal name would resemble water.

Denise Riley

In interviews, Faulkner credited the fantasied image of Caddy Compson climbing up a pear tree as the origin of *The Sound and the Fury* (1929). Caddy was his "heart's darling." Faulkner avows this image and elevates it in memory and autobiographical discourse. Yet the title of the novel directs us to its neglected beginnings in "sound and fury," an echo of James Wait's sonorous "despair and fury."[119] The cry of Benjy Compson, Caddy's severely mentally disabled brother, punctuates the opening of Faulkner's first great experiment in form. "Hush up that moaning," Benjy's caregiver, Luster, says in the first paragraph of the novel's first draft, "Twilight." From the beginning, Faulkner was imagining this sound, displaced from the avowed image.

But the bellow cannot be properly credited as the origin of a form because it is the expurgation of form—Benjy's cry knows no limits, no shape, no restraint, only loss, lack, and rebuke. The task is not to instate to the cry its rightful status as an origin but to confront what in this sound is difficult to recognize, what makes every cry a beginning.

It is a sound to which Faulkner returned many times across his fiction. Benjy opens the Compson saga by gripping the fence of the pasture and moaning. The Compson saga closes in its companion novel, *Absalom, Absalom!* (1936), with the echo of such a sound in the novel's diegetic time of 1909: Jim Bond, the "idiot" and Creole descendant of the plantation master Thomas Sutpen, cries

out at the conflagration of the plantation. The sound and conflagration are imagined at a distance by the novel's protagonist Quentin Compson: "—and he, Jim
Bond, the scion, the last of his race, seeing it too now and howling with human
reason now since now even he could have known what he was howling about . . .
he (Quentin) could see . . . one last wild crimson reflection as the house col-
lapsed and roared away, and there was only the sound of the idiot negro left"
(*AA*, 300–1).

The resonance, the sonorous bond, bridges Faulkner's oeuvre between 1929
and 1936. Faulkner ends *Absalom, Absalom!* and the image of the Southern plantation dynasty in a single sound. It is one that is continuing from elsewhere. In
The Sound and the Fury, Quentin remembers Benjy's cry as it *"hammered back
and forth between the walls in waves . . . as though there were no place for it
in silence"* (*SF*, 124). In this hammering back and forth, we confront something
akin to the impossibility of genealogy and linear history after slavery.[120] The
echo of the cry is a sonorous and tenuous bond to a long, drawn-out history of
barbarism.

Between Benjy and Jim Bond there is an echo of Jimmy Wait's dying vibration
into the universal, "a hollow, moaning, whistling sound."

> Jimmy kept up a distracting row; he screamed piercingly, without drawing breath, like
> a tortured woman; he banged with hands and feet. The agony of his fear wrung our
> hearts so terribly that we longed to abandon him, to get out of that place deep as a
> well and swaying like a tree, to get out of his hearing, back on the poop where we
> could wait passively for death in incomparable repose. We shouted to him to "shut up,
> for God's sake." He redoubled his cries. (*NN*, 84)

"'Wait, then,' Shreve said. 'For God's sake, wait'" exclaims another young man
in *Absalom, Absalom!* (*AA*, 175). He is the friend to whom Quentin struggles to
narrate the story of Sutpen's dynasty one cold night in the Northeast, far from
Mississippi. In its violence, this history has not left behind monuments or testi-
monies. Though Jim Bond and Benjy Compson bear witness, they also stand at
the catastrophe's threshold in sound. That threshold is by definition annihilating
of any attempt to describe it. For it to appear in narrative, to be recited as event
at all, it involves Faulkner in the echo of the object. In Faulkner's "Mistral," a young
man will hear wind "hollowed murmurous out of chaos and the long dark fury of
time."[121] In reading *The Nigger of the "Narcissus,"* Faulkner contacts a grounding
acoustical unconscious of the formation of the Americas. Faulkner remarked that
The Nigger of the "Narcissus" was the book he wished he had written more than
any other, and he kept a copy on his nightstand.[122]

Along and through Wait, then, we encounter the resonance of Benjy and Bond, the three novels touching in what we might call *meta-acoustics* and through two racially opposed bodies.[123] As readers of the Faulknerian corpus, which is held together by resonance, we should "hear" Bond "in" Benjy. Some reality that is not totally present—not simply in the novel but in Faulkner's writerly imaginary—is concretized by the echo of a sound. Faulkner's mode of presentation, his mode of remembering and writing, participates in a sonic remaindering: It is one that must be "heard" as echo, against and through works, in order to exist.

Any direct comment on the history of slavery is missing from *The Sound and the Fury*. Yet Benjy has been castrated, his name changed, and sequestered to the "estate," at one time a plantation—he resonates with a missing slave body. A "black" sound of Wait echoes into the "white" body of Benjy.[124] Faulkner's mixed-race bodies are often threateningly ambiguous precisely because their blackness cannot be seen.

In echo, we have found, an evocative object is the halfway point toward another impression just beyond it. When the representation of reality lies not in things but in their echo, such a reality demands an acoustical criticism and, with it, a deracinating literary history that takes up its ontology. Faulkner avowed the image of a girl as the beginning of his formal conception of *The Sound and the Fury*, but we have perhaps been looking in the wrong place by adhering to the visible order. Across Faulkner's corpus, blackness often appears as a delayed epistemic revelation that quickly culminates in murderous violence (it takes nearly all of *Absalom, Absalom!* to understand that Jim Bond's father, Charles Bon, is black). If there is something of the order of a phenomenal "appearance" in these moments, then the raced body becomes schematically visible just before it is eradicated. So many of Faulkner's racially indeterminate bodies, from Charles Bon to Jim Bond to Joe Christmas (the assonances themselves testify to a mode of sonorous relation), test the visibility of racial epistemology. The order of sound for Faulkner, as it was for Conrad, is in the air—moving, vibratory, transmitting, and atmospheric—such that white and black bodies touch in resonance. We continue to lack the critical vocabulary to address such relationalities between literary sounds.

With Benjy and *The Sound and the Fury*, we are not "first" in a series, the demand of a chronological literary history. The pattern of the cry is nonidentical; it is not a leitmotif. The cry continually signals that Benjy is physically present, but he is not there in the sense of a *subject* who, through narrative, can claim to master its own persistence in time. The cry resounds from Benjy as object, in a vibrating space; the situation is also reversible, the cry resounding toward Benjy, impacting him. The cry is not what Gilles Deleuze might call a "refrain," which functions as a shelter, a comfort amid external chaos, as with the child who sings to himself in the dark. Benjy perhaps comforts himself in crying out, a kind of affective discharge that makes his interior felt by those listening, but this repetition can in no way be related to the motivic patterns of music that announce identity. In the leitmotifs of sonata form, a series of musical subjects depart and return, which produce the experience of tension and release. The motif always announces *a someone who is there*, who has aligned him- or herself with the patterning of sounds that have the capacity to reveal and name. When we recognize a leitmotif, a character announces his presence. The cry, strictly speaking, does not announce someone, or if it does, it is at one with some disappearance for which there is no voice.

With Benjy and Bond, the cry is radically exterior to what we might call "voice." It does not say, it does not communicate, though it marks an interruptive time. Benjy knows he is crying only because he feels his face begin to moisten and his eyes burn. Crying lacks the agency and intentionality of self-expression. He expresses a nothing, the radically dispossessed and expropriated.

If Wait echoes into Benjy, then, it is not in an allusion, which requires agency. Nor is the echo organized by the Bloomian "anxiety of influence," which requires the Oedipal wish to supplant the predecessor. The transatlantic acoustical unconscious moves between works. How can we describe such a structure?

The sound map from *The Psychopathology of Everyday Life* (Figure 4) is an image of echolocation. "Trafoi" is the word you cannot "remember" (or say); it is the repressed. There is, in Freud's model, a true word secreted within the sounds of the false words that function as detours and confused signals. Freud never lost the sense that the slip of the tongue and the forgetting of names concealed a positive content, that it could yield a secret of the body. Freud hears the echo of a translation. How is such a relation—an echo effect—to be linguistically and verbally represented? Where does one phoneme end and another begin?

Death and sexuality move toward the repressed thought (parenthetically contained in text), which then emits a sound. In this context, Freud mentions briefly that in the forgetting of names, words and syllables can lose their "acoustic demarcation,"[125] words effacing their boundaries in echo. There is a contamination in resemblance. To some extent, for a symptom to work, as a technic, it must be able to attach and detach. The object must lose demarcation. It is a *sound bleed* in form and content, both an injury and a sound moving beyond its allotted, permitted space.[126] The cry of Benjy is one such sound bleed, a sound emitted by an injury, moving between otherwise discrete works, a sound that seeps through walls.

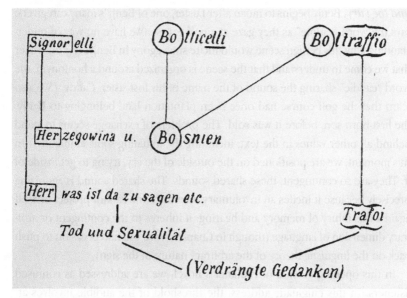

Figure 4. Sigmund Freud, "Zum psychischen Mechanismus der Vergesslichkeit [The Physical Mechanism of Forgetfulness]," *Monatsschrift für Psychiatrie und Neurologie* 4, no. 6 (December 1898).

In Freud's image, we can see an edifice or, rather, a receptacle, one that might "contain" the dispersed and multitudinous phonemes of human languages. We see, here, on the page, a Babel-like will to cohere and contain the plural in the one. We can isolate in the image the activity of sounds standing in relation or sounding as a mode of relation. It is graphically represented by Freud as lines or vectors with no center.

In the map of forgotten names, we learn that cathexis—the material yet impossible-to-evidence "ground" of Freud's conception of the libido—is sonorous. It is difficult to say if word sounds emit energy or if we ourselves do, investing energy in those sounds. If we return to the meaning of determinacy as *Bestimmtheit*, or be-voiced, then this standing in relation between the sounds of words is both thematic and overdetermined.[127] The substitutive name owes itself to a disturbing stream of thoughts whose repressed element "gains control over the desired name and take[s] it along into the repression," Freud writes.[128] In the sounds of words there are contaminations and condensations, pre-echoes and post-echoes.

Recall that when James Wait shouts his last name aboard Conrad's ship, the sound and meaning are contested. Faulkner takes up Conrad's mode of listening where words but also names begin to sound similar and take on, in that similarity, their own life: We are waiting for the voice. In the first paragraph of *The Sound and the Fury*, Benjy begins to moan after Luster, one of Benjy's many caregivers, says the word "caddie" as they gaze at a golf course. We have no way of understanding why this benign scene would incite such agony in Benjy. It is only later that we come to understand that the scene is organized around a homonym, the word "caddie" sharing the sound of the name of his lost sister, Caddy. (We also learn that the golf course had once been plantation land belonging to Benjy, the first-born son, before it was sold. The problem of exchange seems to stand behind all other values in the text, including the initiating sonic ambiguity.) In this moment, we are positioned on the outside of the cry, trying to get inside of it. They are so contingent, these shared sounds. The shared sound is agonizing precisely because it incites an involuntary memory. One cannot protect oneself against this injury of memory and hearing; it inheres to the contingent or arbitrary dimension of language (though in Chapter 3, we will find occasion to push back on the linguistic theory of the arbitrary nature of the sign).

In this opening gesture of Faulkner's novel, we are addressed as confused listeners. In this enigmatic address, the threshold of the audible involves attending to and just missing an encounter; the address indexes intimacies made structurally impossible. Luster, a young black boy tasked with caring for Benjy, a white man much older than him, at times sadistically seizes what little power he has to utter the name "Caddy" so as to wound Benjy. Yet it is remarkable that Luster, too, is insensitive, misunderstanding Benjy's cry, failing to hear "Caddy" in "caddie" at the novel's beginning. It is as if Benjy's cry cannot adhere to anyone's memory: Each time it happens, for both Benjy and those who listen, it is happening as if for the first time. It structures the novel's own formal relation to a memory of an interracial intimacy, which dissolves before it can be concretized, perhaps with the exception of maternal listening.[129] Where one cannot remember, Freud says, one repeats. In the face of Benjy's cry, there seems to be a perennial forgetting, perhaps because loss cannot be fully localized in any single event nor can race be localized in the body.

With the homonym "caddie," Faulkner interprets and adapts the first appearance of Wait aboard the *Narcissus* as an illegible "smudge" on a ship's manifest. The name Caddy is to some degree illegible in its first appearance in the echo of the word "caddie." As in Wait's shout, there is an ellipsis, an echo.

At stake in Wait's shout is how racial identity, which is supposed to be immediately evident in the blink of an eye, traverses this space in a reiterative duration. Consider how, in *The Sound and the Fury*, Quentin commits suicide, drowning himself in an effort to overtake his shadow, which he feels is pursuing and hunting him. On the day of his suicide, he wanders around Cambridge;

he's a Southern boy, a stranger in a strange land. He suddenly encounters three white boys, one of whom says to the others that Quentin "talks like a colored man" (*SF*, 120). Like Fanon, Quentin overhears someone talking about him, an interpellation to the side. One boy quickly hushes the other, saying that Quentin might hit him for the insult. This moment of audibility conditions the possibility of the novel's discourse, its claim to narrate inner consciousness. Being as we are in the space of Quentin's consciousness, we do not read of the moment in the closest point to the present (just before his death in suicide, which cannot be remembered by any consciousness). We read the scene as it is shot through with echoes of previous moments. Later in the chapter, when Quentin's suicidal desire becomes clear to the reader, he looks—like Narcissus—into the waters where he will eventually drown himself. Quentin sees his shadow in the water and thinks: "The shadow of the bridge, the tiers of railing, my shadow leaning flat upon the water, so easily had I tricked it that it would not quit me. At least fifty feet it was, and if I only had something to blot it into the water, holding it until it was drowned. . . . Niggers say a drowned man's shadow was watching for him in the water all the time" (*SF*, 90).[130]

Does not Quentin's suicide restage the appearance and disappearance of Wait? Wait is buried at sea, and in this moment, the Atlantic Ocean and the Charles River touch. When Wait appeared aboard ship, the hum of the muttered racial slur is said to run along the deck of the ship and escape into the night, but the hum has found one residual, transatlantic echo in the ear of Quentin. As Wait appears aboard ship, for a moment, "race" hangs in the air, until the epithet asserts the otherness of the figure who manifests, separating its image from that of the ego ideal. Yet in a secondary identification, I "see" Quentin's blindness but cannot also see my own. There is no place outside of double consciousness from which to see it. Quentin thinks to himself that in the Northeast, he has "to remember to think of them as colored people not niggers" and describes the black man as "a sort of obverse reflection of the white people he lives among" (*SF*, 86). Faulkner would never directly avow that he had read Du Bois, who gives us the theory of double consciousness, but in the textual echo there is a trace of the otherwise refused relation (Wait being elevated precisely along the axis where Du Bois is refused, an effect of reading and remembering through "the sonic color line"). This hearing again, later, and through determines Faulkner's most important formal achievement in *The Sound and the Fury*: his strategy of writing consciousness. For Faulkner, the act of thinking is continually an act of remembering and repeating voices.

If there is no place outside of double consciousness from which to see it, then

Faulkner cannot "represent" it; it does not appear. It resonates. The threat of miscegenation, interracial intimacy, and integration are everywhere surrounding the narrative and maintaining it as a formal condition. Quentin's consciousness originates in this threat. "Niggers say"—it is an anonymous and racialized saying that resounds as a fragment. It has no attributable or particular speaker; it is hearsay. Who speaks and who hears? Despite the saying's external manifestation, it echoes within. It is a voice that is within Quentin's speech in a real way, the sound of his own voice that he abhors, his Southern voice announcing his otherness in the Northeastern terrain. As Quentin gazes at his face in the water, the shadow does not speak but pursues him in silence. But the shadow speaks *in the voice of Quentin*, a voice that is "colored" when heard by others. Who is Quentin listening to when he listens to himself? Who am I who is reading and animating the racialized textual effects of the acoustical unconscious?

This scene calls to the supposedly neutral inner voice of reading, which must undergo a certain work of mediation even to be spontaneously recognized as such. Miscegenation, beginning in the foundational sexual terror of slavery, is neither seen nor denoted in *The Sound and the Fury* but only heard and overheard. It makes possible something like an a priori access to space. For in the midst of his associations of air carrying sounds too long, Quentin then thinks of the field holler of Louis Hatcher, among his several African American caretakers:

> And we'd sit in the dry leaves that whispered a little with the slow respiration of our
> waiting and with the slow breaking of the earth and the windless October, the rank
> smell of the lantern fouling the brittle air, listening to the dogs and to the echo of
> Louis' voice dying away. He never raised it, yet on a still night we have heard it from
> our front porch. When he called the dogs in he sounded just like the horn he car-
> ried slung on his shoulder and never used, but clearer, mellower, as though his voice
> were a part of darkness and silence, coiling out of it, coiling into it again. WhoOoooo.
> WhoOoooo. WhoOooooooooooooooo. *Got to marry somebody*
> *Have there been very many Caddy* (SF, 115)

Faulkner transcribes the echo of the object, the primordial spool of *fort-da*. We learn through the interstices of the spoken that his sister Caddy is pregnant. The italics mark dialogue being remembered or "playing back" within Quentin's consciousness, an alternative moment in the past being superimposed onto the memory of Hatcher. Faulkner omits the periods, heightening the effect of sound bleed, a place where the wounds of the past resound into the present. But the onomatopoeia brings Hatcher's voice just to the threshold of the audible, for it is as if one can "hear" it on the page (Benjy's voice will never be optically or poetically represented in this way). It tests the borders of admission. In its invisibility in Quentin's memory, the voice coils into and out of blackness, in anarchic ways, with a capacity to overtake space and Quentin's consciousness itself. For Quentin, air is inseminating, penetrating. It carries and persists. The thought of Caddy's need to marry, now pregnant, is adjacent to Hatcher's call; it is just above it as overtone while also ontologically prior as the condition of possibility of an inner voice.

Serial presentation is the only way in writing to represent what is otherwise simultaneous. There are a series of unspoken thoughts: Who has impregnated Caddy? How many men have there been? But the sound of Hatcher's voice also moves into her body as it is animated by Quentin's memory and fantasy. Hatcher's voice is for Quentin a dangerous invasion, floating at the edge of the family home, heard at the porch. Like Conrad's verandah—a tympanic space of storytelling and hearsay, "both limit and passage"—the porch marks a threshold, sounds threatening to come in. On Hatcher's shoulder is the prosthetic horn, signaling anxiety over a mediated way of listening, displaced onto the black body in imaginary ways. One cannot help but think of the horned mouth of the phonograph that, in Faulkner's childhood (before electric recording), was disseminating black voices into new and far-reaching spaces. But in his potency, Hatcher never calls upon the horn. The naturally vibrating voice of Hatcher is, Quentin remembers, "a part of darkness and silence." It is mixed up with the location of Quentin's embodied memory, determined by their shared place.

Blackness, Fred Moten argues, is the metaphysical possibility of the background as such.[131] It is the ground against which the white figure and also the white voice find relief in Faulkner. "It shaped itself." These sensations surround and condition the sanctum of Quentin's inner voice, what in Faulkner's sensorium is only ever a voice of memory, a fantasy echo.

In such moments of echo, Faulkner pauses to describe the landscape whose affect is itself racially determined. This determination remains unthought by his characters, but it is "of" the landscape and the memories it materially shapes. It marks a percussive silence in between measures of text: "*Why must you do like nigger women do in the pasture the ditches the dark woods,*" Quentin thinks to himself (*SF*, 92). Miscegenation is heard as echoic residues of voice and place; bodies are far from formed, but disaggregated in relation to fantasied sound and image.[132] "Caddy could now carry an interracial child," is the latent content of this acoustical unconscious.

When Faulkner began *The Sound and the Fury*, it was in echo of *The Nigger of the "Narcissus."* It is the misheard sound of the word "Caddy," a resonance of the fact of blackness, that opens up the possibility of the novel's formal technique of narrating by echo such that characters experience and remember at the same time.[133] Wait is "there" as an echo such that Benjy's injury takes on a transhistorical, transatlantic dimension. In echolocation, one listens both near and far, in the immediate instance and to the distant yet adjacent space that animates it by reflection.

In Conrad's discussions with his intimate friend Georges Jean-Aubrey, discussions on which Jean-Aubrey's biography of Conrad were based, Conrad reportedly had "forgotten the name of the real Nigger of the *Narcissus.*" Jean-Aubrey continues (speaking/writing in the voice of Conrad): "As a matter of fact, the name . . . James Wait . . . was the name of another nigger we had on board the *Duke of Sutherland*, and I was inspired with the first scene in the book by an episode in the embarkation of the crew at Gravesend on board the same *Duke of Sutherland.*"[134] An "able-bodied seaman," Joseph Barron died during that voyage, but there is "no evidence that Barron was black."[135] The origin of Wait disappears almost entirely from the archive, recorded only in these resonances of the fact of blackness. Reviewing the ship's manifest for evidence of his existence, Ian Watt finds no James Wait on the *Duke of Sutherland*, but he does find a first mate named Baker (whose name appears in the novel) and a George White of Barbados.[136]

Conrad retreated into the silent realm of writing, but what he found there was a world populated by sounds and voices. The act of writing promised to reflect back a purified a voice, an "English" voice. If in cockney pronunciation (James) "Wait" is also (George) "White," then something more than words loses its acoustic demarcation. In "To My Readers in America," the preface to the 1914 Doubleday edition of *The Nigger of the "Narcissus"* (owned by Faulkner), Conrad writes of James Wait: "But in the book he is nothing; he is merely the centre of the ship's collective psychology and the pivot of the action. Yet he, who in the family circle and amongst my friends is familiarly referred to as the Nigger, remains very precious to me" (*NN*, 9). Wait merges with Conrad's personhood. There is an affection for everything except for Wait, who stands out but then is rendered anonymous within the group and the general life at sea. The entirety of this pre-preface revolves around a transformation in Wait's name. But the elision cannot fully extinguish the reality of James Wait as a lost object.

This loss determines the formal existence of Yoknapatawpha County. Five years after the completion of *The Sound and the Fury*, Faulkner wrote a short essay on the composition of *Sartoris*, a novel that he began in 1926 only to be rejected by publishers; it was the first of Faulkner's attempts to take up Mississippi as his subject. In this essay, Faulkner reflects upon this novel's failure. But he newly estimates it now that he is on the other side of his formal achievement with *The Sound and the Fury*. He writes a myth of becoming a writer.

> I realised for the first time that I had done better than I knew and the long work I had
> had to create opened before me and I felt myself surrounded by the limbo in which
> the *shady* visions, the host which stretched half formed, *waiting* each with its portion
> of that verisimilitude which is to bind into a whole the world which for some reason
> I believe should not pass utterly out of the memory of man, and I contemplated those
> *shady* but ingenious *shapes*.[137]

Defining himself as an author, Faulkner rewrites the conclusion of the novel that he would have liked to have written more than any other. He echoes a memory of having read *The Nigger of the "Narcissus."* Faulkner rearticulates the event of coming to his "voice" as an author in the voice of Conrad's narrator who enunciates his "I" for the first time, both without losing the defining echo of Wait. It is a memory of reading recited, but now as the form of Yoknapatawpha. The black mate of the ship *Narcissus*, Conrad insists, "is nothing; he is merely . . . the pivot of the action." "It was nothing. Just sound," Faulkner writes of Benjy's cry. "It might have been all time and injustice and sorrow become vocal for an instant" (*SF*, 288).[138] Benjy soothes himself with a narcissus flower. "He came obediently, wailing, that slow hoarse sound that ships make, that seems to begin before the sound itself has started, seems to cease before the sound itself has stopped" (*SF*, 288).

Before there can be a "voice," there is an echo of the object.

Such an echo would seem to determine the figure of American literary history itself, its boundaries, contours, and background. In "Unspeakable Things Unspoken," Toni Morrison argues for the haunting presence of African Americans within the canonical history of American literature. The title's double negative suggests "to unspeak" is itself a historical modality. Morrison argues for "the ways in which the presence of Afro-Americans has shaped the choices, the language, the structure—the meaning of so much American literature."[139] We can extend this to English literature and the literature of empire more broadly. This is a search, Morrison suggests, "for the ghost in the machine." It is here that she asks, "What makes a work 'black'?"

We can ask in turn, what makes a sound black? We can listen to a passing moment from Faulkner's "Pantaloon in Black." Jay Watson remarks on Faulkner's phrase, "the first hour would not have passed noon when he would mount the steps and knock . . . and enter and ring the bright cascade of silver dollars onto the scrubbed table in the kitchen."[140] When writing "Pantaloon in Black," Watson describes, Faulkner had just published a short story in a magazine along with Zora Neale Hurston's "The Gilded Six-Bits." In it, Hurston writes, "There came the ring of singing metal on wood. Nine times. . . . [Missie May] knew that it was her husband throwing silver dollars in the door for her to pick up and pile beside her plate at dinner."[141] The ring of silver dollars in "Pantaloon in Black" is unacknowledged black source material—a citation, sample, or lifted voice. These sounds and words were echoing for Faulkner by way of Hurston.

Are they simply one stolen object among others? Faulkner would spend his writerly life trying to understand the difference between black voices and white voices. This moment acts as a black voice in what Faulkner had perhaps experienced spontaneously as his "own voice." The echo of Hurston came back to him in writing his story, but it was an echo he perhaps did not hear as such. The sound would be a "love and theft," as Eric Lott describes blackface, but at the same time (and constitutively so) a form of consciousness that cannot recognize the other. This theft of sounds and words demonstrates a mode of relating that conditions listening, reading, and writing. It is a crisis in remembering that defines listening as echolocation in modernism.

When Fitzgerald culminates *The Great Gatsby*, it is with an echo of the object. The participant-observer narrator, Nick, had arrived at the scene of a deadly car crash in which Gatsby will be implicated. "I became aware now of a hollow, wailing sound which issued incessantly from the garage." He continues:

> I couldn't find the source of the high, groaning words that echoed clamorously
> through the bare garage . . .
> "What's the name of this place here?" demanded the officer.
> "Hasn't got any name."
> A pale well-dressed negro stepped near.[142]

Fitzgerald reorganizes the scene, but the echo is unmistakable. The unnamed black man steps forward as the pivot of the action, ground to figure.

Wait is everywhere heard in the vicissitudes of modernism, of Conrad's and Faulkner's prose, a loved and repudiated black voice that reappears anytime there is unspeaking, an unmaking of the voice, making echo an act of reparative reading.

"Who said 'Wait?' What . . ."

"'No—nothing,'" he said, and with a slight wave of his hand motioned the boat away (*LJ*, 335).[143]

What kind of river, then, has no middle?

        —Édouard Glissant, *Poetics of Relation*

INTERSONORITY: UNCLAIMED VOICES CIRCUM-1900, OR SOUND AND SOURCELESSNESS IN *THE SOULS OF BLACK FOLK*

A moment of haunting melody will strike us as far from Conrad, though it was printed in the same period as his early works, on the other side of the Atlantic. W. E. B. Du Bois begins "Of Our Spiritual Strivings," the first chapter of *The Souls of Black Folk*, with two epigraphs that he perhaps understood as epitaphs, for "herein lie buried many things," he writes (*SBF*, 5). We return, once again, to the site of the crypt, an encrypted sound.

Beginning as they do each chapter, the epigraphs are afforded textual stature. They mark the formal beginning of a book that will claim for blackness a world-historical trajectory. Yet the first epigraphs also describe a series of voices and sounds that are, in their expression, without sanctioned venue for transmission and protection. They are floating, sourceless:

[1] O water, voice of my heart, crying in the sand,
    All night long crying with a mournful cry,
As I lie and listen, and cannot understand
    The voice of my heart in my side or the voice of the sea,
O water, crying for rest, is it I, is it I?
    All night long the water is crying to me.

Unresting water, there shall never be rest
    Till the last moon droop and the last tide fail,

115

And the fire of the end begin to burn in the west;
    And the heart shall be weary and wonder and cry like the sea,
All life long crying without avail,
    As the water all night long is crying to me.

Arthur Symons.

Figure 5

Following these epigraphs, Du Bois then begins "Of Our Spiritual Strivings" proper:

[3] Between me and the other world, there is ever an unasked question: unasked by some through feelings of delicacy; by others through the difficulty of rightly framing it. All, nevertheless, flutter round it. (*SBF*, 9)

I mark these three "voices" with numerals. The first Du Bois attributes to the British poet Arthur Symons, and the second is an unattributed fragment of song. The music quotation is the collectively authored African American spiritual "Nobody Knows the Trouble I've Seen," but I want, for a moment, to be faithful to Du Bois's mode of presentation—his mode of beginning—which withholds the title of the song, giving only the bars of music without words, title, or proper name.

How are we to understand (read, hear, interpret) this pairing of verse and music? It is followed by Du Bois's remarkable first phrase—"Between me and the other world"—that has long since resonated in American thought and letters. It echoes globally in the Black Atlantic when Frantz Fanon writes, "Between the world and me a relation of coexistence was established."[1] In this phrase, Du Bois ostensibly communicates in "his own voice," an implied authorial voice that initiates the poetic and musical epigraphs before addressing the reader.

In previous chapters, we found the audibility of a narrative "voice" to be brought into question. The speaking voice can be acoustically displaced in narrative but also phantasmatically generated by it. As a biographical person, Du Bois was known for his resonant, oratorical timbre, and its force was both recorded and broadcast on the radio. Yet we confront in *The Souls of Black Folk* an unconsolidated voice. It is caught up in the Middle Passage, in the passage of literature and music, in quotations, fragments, and their resonant lacunae. Lyrical, it is nonetheless violently unmoored from the foundational rhetorical premise of lyric: that it will reach an addressee.[2]

In Chapter 1, I noted the limitation of Wayne Booth's conception of the implied author as a site of the ethical totality of meaning. We will find that any such
totality, particularly as it might be localized in a racialized body of origin, is dispersed by Du Bois's mode of address. The phrase "Between me and the other
world" is a direct address to the reader by a narrator, one who is not fully attributable to the voice that prefaces the book in "The Forethought." Unlike these epigraphs, "The Forethought" conflates the narratorial and authorial voices there.

In the poem and song, there is an imputed speaker and singer, but they do
not address each other. Their resonance is not contained by antiphony, as if a European poem "calls" to a fragment of African American melody that "responds."
Instead, they are set in relation by a fourth position in the text reducible neither
to the two epigraphs nor to the third moment in which the "voice" of the chapter begins or announces itself. We are tempted to name this fourth position the
enunciation (*énonciation*).

According to Émile Benveniste, while any enunciation in speech or writing
includes both addressor and addressee, or "I" and "you," its condition of possibility is a silent other: a "we" or "they" (as well as a "he" or "she"). Benveniste
had recognized early on, Stéphane Mosès writes, that Saussure's "conception
of the sign as association of an acoustic image and a concept does not account
for the relation of language to external reality, that is, to what he will later call
its 'referent.'"[3] That relation, for Benveniste, is located in the enunciation. In
Chapter 1, however, we confronted the limitations of any notion of language
premised upon the unity of the speaking subject as what Julia Kristeva calls "a
logical and even metaphysical postulate which assures the permanence and full-
ness of meaning."[4] The reading of Conrad's beginnings instead emphasized not
an acoustic image and concept (classical units of structuralist linguistics) but an
acoustic register, a delay between hearing and understanding. It proved to be
constitutive not simply of the audible world but of a listening consciousness. In
Chapter 2, the relation between an "I" and "you" and a "we" and "they" was heard
in the psychic event of a fantasy echo. While any act of memory is predicated on
a distance in time and space (however minute it may be), the retroaudition to be
posited with the Du Boisian fragment underscores a self-distancing in perception itself.

As we have found throughout, something is lost, violently suppressed,
and contained by the relation of an acoustic image and concept to their reference across time and space. For Conrad, the surplus sound of that violent
suppression—a shoring up of colonial subjects by instrumental reason—is to
be heard in the last sounds issued by James Wait in death, and for Faulkner, in

Benjy's relentless bellow. In Chapter 3, the association between acoustic image and concept, word and meaning, in its materiality as association, will come under new scrutiny in the experience that Conrad named "sinister resonance." The moment we problematize this association as such, the bond between acoustic image and concept that is supposed to be arbitrary proves to be contaminated by the external world and its determinations. With Du Bois, we consider the "voice" neither in the unifying power of essence and origin (*Ursprung*) nor in the referentiality of an external world. We confront a formalizing process and desire to give shape to the sensuous experience of a not-yet-determined encounter: "change at the beginning."[5] The epigraphs arrive on the page not as structures or genres but as two aesthetic forms, lyric and hymn, in contact.

When Du Bois begins with two phrases or textual moments, one poetic and the other musical, they are not echoing, which is to say, repeating each other in a signifying chain, nor are they enunciated; they are resonating through spatial proximity on the page. At stake in this beginning is the condition of possibility of dialogue, how two or more voices can be together in the same space-time, hear one another, address themselves to one another, and change one another. The third voice, the beginning of Du Bois's essay proper, is said to be "me," yet it is accompanied by an unstated "I" who writes to a "you" and to a silent other, as well. In this relation, we are somewhere beyond any simple splitting of the subject (the "I" who takes a "me" as its object). There is a proliferation of positions, voices, and spaces—resonance.

Given the weight of the first-person pronoun, the "me" in Du Bois's opening sentences would seem to take on all the authority and identity of an autobiography, a story of immutable origin and identity. Yet Du Bois does not say "I" but "me." The dative object is prefaced by a preposition ("between me . . . there is"). The phrase strikes us as a continuation of some sentence that was already in motion. Du Bois reverses the convention of English grammar, which mandates that one begins with the givenness of things ("there is . . . between me"). He begins not with the unicity of the first-person or with the givenness of the world. He posits a kind of "pact" with the reader different from an autobiographical one, which presumes that everything has already happened.[6] This difference will return to us here in a consideration of resonance as the sonorous bond between sound and object, but a dispersive one: what it means for Du Bois, at the dawning of the twentieth century, not only to think and to write but to begin.

By resonance, we indicate a minimal site of contact but also a cut or hole in the object that awaits the quantity of the other. Readers have long understood Du Bois's pairing of verse and song as a gesture of racial amalgamation, but a Eurocentric one, slave song elevated in its status as history and culture through its proximity to European verse. Yet such a claim elides that the pairing is imme-diately bypassed or cut by a third instance: Du Bois's remarkable because initiat-ing use of the preposition, the part of grammar that shows relation. In initiating a relation between verse and melody on the page, Du Bois asks that we follow the course of the grammar that occasions the event of resonance and, with it, an imputed listening consciousness that listens in, to, and between. His formal strategies posit a threshold. From the beginning of "Of Our Spiritual Strivings," including its title in the first-person plural, the first-person voice is situated as a movement, an intermediate and dialectical site of contact that both gathers and sunders. Resonance is not a phenomenon in the strict sense or a manifestation but a productive process.[7]

In the Overture, I noted Jennifer Lynn Stoever's concept of "the sonic color line," named after Du Bois's sense that "the problem of the Twentieth Century is the problem of the color line" (*SBF*, 5). The sonic color line is within the external world, the barrier through or across which one listens to or refuses to listen to others. Heard through the sonic color line, one experiences oneself as excluded from the normative realm by a matrix of hegemonic control and auditory surveil-lance that Stoever names the "listening ear," as if in analogue to the watchful eye. The central thrust of Stoever's argument is to insist that audible sounds cannot be separated from or purified of acts of listening. In Chapter 2, we moved inward to concentrate on the pain of self-hearing and how others' acts of speaking and listening resound within to determine the self. We found the sense of hearing to constitute not a line but the porous threshold between inside and outside. The sense of hearing struck us as mediated, in turn, by this threshold's incomplete materialization: In Du Bois, we find a foundational articulation of this concept. What Du Bois calls "the Veil" is a perceptual and corporeal barrier "between me and the other world," one through which he is seen and heard. It initiates "double consciousness."

In a Hegelian turn, the Veil situates itself for Du Bois within self-consciousness such that the enunciation of *The Souls of Black Folk* is nothing less than (though it it is much more than) black *Geist*. According to Sandra Adell, when Du Bois referred to Hegel in his student notebooks, he notes "*consciousness, double-consciousness, strife, self*, and *spirit*."[8] The complex intellectual biography of Du Bois, which includes a time of studying (in German) at Berlin's Humboldt

University, mandated that he took from European philosophical interlocutors what he needed, creating a hybrid yet decidedly new theory of listening consciousness.[9] Du Bois's written techniques often trade in lyricism, adopting and reinforcing the paramount place of intuition and receptivity in his teacher William James's thought to conjoin otherwise opposed concepts that stimulate the reader's multiple senses. That hybridity is exemplified by the opening of his book. In resonance, two irrevocably severed sources are bound to each other across the Atlantic through the writer's transformative acts of aurality.

The Veil and double consciousness are in this way a transatlantic nexus of listening, spirit, world, and racialization. Du Boisian double consciousness constitutes what Hortense Spillers describes as "a dialectical movement—a double movement—between the philosopher's concept of 'consciousness' and the sociopolitical context of the formation of black subjectivity in the circumstance of national life."[10] Standing at the threshold of the twentieth century, Du Bois began writing the text from the premise of the failed project of Reconstruction that defines the era circa 1900 as an incomplete emancipation. This era is essentially caught between realities, an afterlife of slavery through which the future, the new, struggles for self-determination. *The Souls of Black Folk* commences in a world, Spillers writes, "pregnant with peril for Africanity."[11]

That is the magnitude one must bring to the threshold of the audible in *The Souls of Black Folk*. Double consciousness is not only to be seen but also to see oneself, and by this same token, the Veil is not only the matrix through which one is heard by others. It is to *hear oneself* as other through a revelation of another world. It afflicts the broader sensorium (to hear oneself through images, to see oneself through sounds).

This reflexive movement of the Veil is irreducible to the reflexivity of the phenomenological subject that always returns to itself. "Blackness exists on one side of the color line," the artist Martine Syms writes, "though on which side is often unclear."[12] In literary studies, we have understood well what Bakhtin calls "double voicing," and many critics have likened its vicissitudes to double consciousness.[13] We would do well to return to the primal scene of double consciousness in Du Bois's text, despite its being known so well, to ask what can be retrieved not for a theory of enunciation, dialogism, and speaking but for their twins, a theory of listening and a theory of resounding.[14]

With the notion of a primal scene, a scene of origination, we arrive at the most paradoxical unit of self-perceptibility in Du Bois's text. Such a scene would seem to be the most determinative of self, fixing it, as Fanon says, "in the sense in which a chemical solution is fixed by a dye."[15] By a primal scene, we mean an

injurious experience that is also formative, both severing and constituting, sundering and gathering (this double sense is also held by the etymological origins
of "critique" in *krisis*). A "scene," in the psychoanalytic lexicon, makes itself felt
through what Lacan calls the *cut*, the emblem of separation. Throughout this
book, I have taken up a series of "acoustic scenes" not only to push back upon
the overly visualistic rhetoric of the "scene" in novel theory but to invite a resonance between hearing and seeing.

In "Of Our Spiritual Strivings," Du Bois narrates a painful childhood event that
inscribed in his memory the violence of racial difference and social hierarchy.
Early works of African American literature often turn to memoir, writing elided
subjectivity into history. But Du Bois's gesture is also protopsychoanalytic:[16] He
returns to the traumatic past of the individual as a forge for self-actualization in
the present. In the middle of a sociopolitical essay, Du Bois augments this form;
he writes of the memory of a little white girl, a classmate, rejecting his visiting
card, a gift. This particular memory has significant bearing upon resonance as
it presages mutuality, for at the heart of the traumatic scene is a failed relation,
a break in mutuality. In this moment, Du Bois says, the Veil first fell before him.
As if physicalized in space, the Veil casts a "shadow," perhaps even "a shadow of
the object" in its consequences for the ego. It becomes a scene of recognition.

Any event of recognition is audiovisual. To ask "Do you recognize me?" is to
ask "Do you see and hear me?" But it is, above all, to demand that you hear me,
that you take me in, feel that I exist in consequential ways. "In its immediacy,"
Fanon writes in his essay on Hegel, "consciousness of self is simple in being-for-
itself."[17] In this way, certainty depends not upon the self but upon the other who
recognizes us, another who, simultaneously, "is waiting for recognition by us."[18]
Ultimately for Fanon, this being-for-others cannot shed light on the black man's
situation.[19] Fanon's account of reciprocity nonetheless articulates the extent to
which Hegel's ontology resonated with Du Bois's painful memory (in returning
to and writing of it, the experience retroactively gives form to Du Bois's book):

> At the foundation of Hegelian dialectic there is an absolute reciprocity which must be
> emphasized. It is in the degree to which I go beyond my own immediate being that
> I apprehend the existence of the other as a natural and more than natural reality. If I
> close [*ferme*, "shut off," "block"] the circuit, if I prevent the accomplishment of move-
> ment in two directions, I keep the other within himself. Ultimately, I deprive him even
> of this being-for-itself.[20]

We should raise some questions regarding Markmann's translation of Fanon.[21]
In American English, to close a circuit is to make the connection that makes it

function, such as turning on a light. The context seems to require that Fanon means exactly the opposite—breaking the connection, opening the circuit. The foundational premise of communicational theory, whether in narrative or linguistics, is that an addressee sends a message to a receiver. When Du Bois narrates the experience of the Veil, it is a scene of refused exchange, but it is also a foreclosed address. The effects of the foreclosure of both speaking and listening in recognition are profound, and this shadowy threshold would seem to anatomize the other senses and self-perception such that not to be heard is also not to be seen or not to be perceived in general. In his encounters with existentialism, Fanon goes further than Du Bois to underscore these thresholds as they pertain to and determine proprioception, creating a space of waiting with the bodily schema and one's own sense of sensory-motor process that the film theorist Kara Keeling has called "the interval." "To exist as one who waits is to exist in an interval."[22]

In the communicational circuit traditionally conceived, there is no interval or delay; the message arrives on time and in an instant. Instantaneity was an imperial desire foundational to telecommunications technology in the nineteenth and twentieth centuries. When Conrad began his project, the first communication over the transatlantic cable had already occurred in 1858. Queen Victoria messaged a newly elected President Buchanan to congratulate him. The cable linked world powers. Recall that in 1903, the final tract of oceanic cable completing a global communications system was laid. At the dawning of the twentieth century, Du Bois announces in the formal strategies of the epigraphs not a telegraphic space but a choreographic space. It is a space of waiting, the musical quotations not immediately cited. One has to wait for the final chapter, "The Sorrow Songs," when Du Bois finally includes lyrics and fuller transcriptions. Where Conrad writes the silent listener into narration, Du Bois writes the silent listener (who fled the moment of exchange) into the formal beginning of his text. To listen is to wait for the voice of the other. To recognize the other is to feel the other in herself who is also waiting.[23]

In the primal scene of the experience of the Veil, Du Bois seeks a listener for his message or address embodied by the visiting card as a gift. (The gift giver, we know from Marcel Mauss, seeks reciprocity.) It is paramount to a consideration of Du Bosian form that the girl's turning away is silent. She refuses him "with a glance" (*SBF*, 10). In *The Sovereignty of Quiet*, the cultural critic Kevin Quashie emphasizes the repression of feeling that overtakes Du Bois in the scene. Such silence intercedes when Du Bois continually finds himself confronted with the question that, though it is never asked directly, "is always on the minds and lips of white people when they engage a black person":[24] "How does it feel to be a problem?" (*SBF*, 9). As repression, this silence acts "under the command of rejection from the outside," its interior domain removed from "a place of surrender" to the dynamism of feelings.[25] Quashie seeks to redeem "the quiet of the interior," which has been foreclosed, he suggests, by the traumatic scene overly emblematized by both Du Bois and the history of black public resistance. The elegance and urgency of this concept is indisputable, particularly because Quashie seeks a vocabulary for a black life beyond publicness. Yet we can add to its urgency the paradigmatic act of listening. Where there is the unsaid or silence, there is nonetheless listening. Du Bois is listening for someone who will not speak to him; he desires to be listened to. But this moment is precisely that, a moment in a polyvocal and shapeshifting text that engages in a range of feelings, thoughts, and desires. Du Bois would reject the premise of "an interior that has its own sovereignty"[26] and urge instead an actualization of spirit through relation. (Not only to whiteness, for Du Bois is equally unsure of where he stands in relation to the "folk.") Du Bois's Hegelianism at the time of writing is paramount, for the interior (or, as Hegel would say, "inwardness") is merely implicit without its determinate negation.

This primal scene of foreclosed conversation and (ex)change between two entitites in their blocked capacity to change each other is substantialized into the visual and determinate reality of skin, what Fanon later calls "a racial epidermal schema."[27] But the scene, an incomplete materialization, never sheds its acoustic associations of resonance, that to be heard is also to receive a call as one would a card (a calling card). Though the primal scene is structural (it both happens once and is iterative, anatomizing, and epidermalizing), Du Bois retrieves its resonant potential. In resonance, things go beyond their immediate being. To the extent that I keep the other within himself, I deprive myself of his reality in myself. I keep him from being in me, a resonance that is irreducible to the consuming voracity of possession. In withdrawing from resonance, I hold the other at arm's length and deprive both him and myself. Particularly in Fanon's appraisal of Hegel, there is a pre-echo of Herbert Marcuse, who suggests, in an equally political vein, "The material part of a thing's reality is made up of what that thing is not, of what it excludes and repels as its opposite."[28] This (figural) thing, in our case, is resonance. Spillers recognizes this moment in Du Bois as a wound, a trauma that "splits an occurrence between the thing itself and its shadow," but as "the opening of an interior space that remains in the shade, so to speak . . . the gap, as though one suddenly felt a draft of cold air."[29]

It is this space that opens the possibility for resonance.

In resonance, the fundamental unit is two. In the primal scene of the Veil, its pain derives from the fact that the fundamental unit has been transgressed. In response, which amounts to a self-address, Du Bois splits within himself; where the young girl does not listen, he becomes two. "One ever feels his twoness," Du Bois writes (*SBF*, 11). This "two" is incomplete, however, because as yet un recognized by the other who is also two (in this solitude, Du Bois discovers an originary capacity for *self*-change). Such splitting has major repercussions for the history of modernism when in *Absalom, Absalom!* Faulkner hears and rewrites Conrad, but through Du Bois's acoustical splitting, essentially offering its missing counterpart, the double being quadrupled.[30]

In Du Bois's protopsychoanalytic gesture, we find an alternative to the origin of the listening subject in the primal scene as posited by Freud, Du Bois's contemporary, where the child listens with ears "pricked" (*aufgestellt*) to sounds he cannot understand. For Freud, listening—like the drive—is split between death and pleasure.[31] While personal, this split is also structural. It opens fantasy life as such, a universal perception. Du Boisian universality only discovers itself through the very sociopolitical conditions we found in Chapter 2 to be bracketed by Freud. Throughout his writings, Du Bois returns to the primal scene, but not in the repetition that defines the death drive. To the extent that he returns to its status as both perilous and determinative, a locus of terror, he also negates the negation: He begins his book in forethought by asking that readers receive it "in charity"—he gives away freely what the other had once refused to accept. From this moment forward, an address, also a self-address, may be imputed to the text and to reading, positioned in relation to an act of listening. The address is not given in advance by discourse but won through a textual effect of resonance. This act is oriented toward the other as much as to the self and in futural ways. It formally articulates an intellectual premise that, according to Ross Posnock, was shared by Fanon: "To live in the present demands a radical act of deracination."[32] The question for *The Souls of Black Folk* becomes one of opening the essentializing movement of the Veil, to make it sensible as open, such that the color line can be properly reinterpreted not as structural but as formal.

Already in the first essay's opening gesture of resonance between voices, Du Bois relinquishes the authoritative character of inscribing the first marks on the page. He gives up that instantiation—the will to author—to make room for the other by withdrawing, for a chorus of other voices that are not his own, to make room for the experience of sourcelessness. In Chapter 1, we found that, while the concept of a narratee is implied by Genette's and Barthes's theories of narrative voice, they never rigorously imagine how reception works, Genette in particular reproducing the phenomenological subject when he writes of the "narrating instance" such that reception—as coinstantiation—matters little, text always referring back to an ontological referent of "voice" from which it gains its reality. The notion of the narrating instance cannot annotate the ways that Du Bois writes the silent listener into his sense of beginning, one that becomes increasingly explicit as the book continues. Du Bois composes a beginning that can only become itself through an act of reciprocity. He converts the master discourse, the authoritative voice, into a slave discourse. He begins not with the given but the "between," creating an opening for whatever is to come.

This formal imperative of beginning without attribution derives from the fact that the understanding is not yet adequate to slave consciousness and its songs, which are a "message for the world."[33] When he ends his book by saying *"Hear my cry, O God the Reader,"* it is a dialectical mode of listening, one that takes in the girl's silence and sublates it as resonance (*SBF*, 164).

The experience of the Veil, in this way, exceeds the Oedipal determinations of the primal scene. The traumatic audition that instantiates double conscious- ness is no less acoustical in its event and erotic in its charge. The girl refuses to desire. There has not even been the resistance that might constitute this mo- ment as a struggle over reality in what Fanon describes as "risk." To risk desire is to be "not merely here-and-now, sealed into thingness."[34] To desire is to ask to be "considered." To ask to be desired is to ask for you to sense that without my negating activity you lack reality.

What kind of listening, then, do the epigraphs inscribe and incite? As frag- ments, they are acousmatic; they engage one, to some extent, in the practice of what the French composer Pierre Schaeffer calls "reduced listening." In pro- posing musique concrète—a tape music made up of sounds in the world that Schaeffer recorded and collaged—he hoped that one would no longer listen epistemically, asking "what" the object is that sounds out. One is listening for what Schaeffer called *l'objet sonore*, such that sonorousness itself becomes the object.[35]

What is one listening to when one listens to resonance? One listens not to a source but to a relation, a contact or touch. Not long before Du Bois, the American transcendentalist Henry David Thoreau wrote of the experience of listening to bells carried into the woods that "all sound heard at the greatest possible distance" produces the same effect, that of "the universal lyre."[36] The carried sound, he observes, "is not merely the repetition of what was worth repeating in the bell, but partly the voice of the wood."[37] Thoreau recognizes a physical fact: The space that hosts the resonance, the voice "of" the wood, is just as much in the sound "of" the bell. In this double ontology, "the echo is . . . an original sound."[38] In Schaeffer, we encounter a theory of sound that moves through a neutral space; in Thoreau the "universal lyre" is already premised upon the partial, what in one thing is dispersed in another.[39] In Du Bois, the epigraphic space recalls the universal lyre and the paradoxical orginality of the echo. In its resonance, we encounter the more than one.

In the poem that lends "Of Our Spiritual Strivings" its first epigraph, the otherwise floating, acousmatic source of sound is epistemically and expressively resolved by the pathetic fallacy. Symons's speaker both addresses the water and feels addressed by it ("O water, crying for rest, is it I, is it I?")—I hear the water, and it sounds mournful to me; surely it cries, and in crying, it sounds out me. It is from "me," as its affective source, that the water derives its personified strength; I fill it with myself. "Be thou me," says every apostrophe, Barbara Johnson suggests ("O thou, hear, oh, hear!").[40] The ancient Greek *apostrephein*, or "turning away," encourages an acoustic scene whereby the one who calls also turns away from some addressee. Yet Du Bois (through Symons) understands that in the narcissism of every self-reflection persists what I have called an echo of the object. The acoustical space posited by the grammar of Symons's poem is less tightly reflexive than it would at first appear, for we cannot forget that the sound heard by the speaker is related (relayed and replayed) through a question posed to the self: "Is it I?" This "I" is a speaker who cannot himself cry. Symons's speaker finds in natural sound a trace of the grief he cannot pronounce. In listening to alterity, "I" has become a question to itself. This is an "I" that seeks its relation to place, the site of an otherwise exilic sound.[41]

The grammatical "I" of Du Bois's text is *Geist*, but it is not purely autobiographical, as if it refers to some entity that exists before and in mere referential ways to a me. This "I," one that Cheryl Wall beautifully nominates as a "protagonist" of the book, is a "traveler, unsure of his relationship to the folk that live behind the veil,"[42] who changes shape over the course of the essays, particularly in its continued reinvocation of fragments of song and word. With each new entry— as the book traverses fiction, nonfiction, sociology, and musical anthology—the triad of voices returns, a fragment of poetry, a fragment of song, each "framing" while also prefacing a direct address, but by a subject position that is radically intervallic.

When crying, we become the water: The speaker of Symons's poem loses a sense of where his tears end and the sea must necessarily begin. In resonance, there is no source, no origin, yet we understand that some change has taken place in the apparent stability, unity, and solidity of an object or entity. That is why the resonance of the lyre must be so forcefully excluded from the theory of Form and the immortality of the soul in Platonic metaphysics.[43] When we say that a sound derives or emanates from a "source," it is not because some object genitively contains or holds it, for the sound exists in its dispersion, in a space that physically pronounces it through resonant frequencies. (That is what Thoreau means when he says that the bell is partially the "voice of the wood" through which it travels.) A genitive case—the sound "of" an object—expresses not only the genus of origin and root but possession.[44]

Each time one confronts a sound, one asks "a sound of what?" Western thought is delimited, Christian Metz argues, by "primitive substantialism."[45] But what is "primitive" in substantialism? Such an ascription cannot be thought outside of a racial object, a weighty reliance on matter. Nor can it be thought outside of primitive accumulation and its forms of extraction, a history that bears significantly on Du Bois's moment of writing the sorrow songs. The sorrow songs had already been transcribed, collected, and disseminated many times over as sheet music and performances for contesting forms of profit.[46] What Lacan calls "the *belong to me* demand so reminiscent of property" orients representation in the Western tradition to and against which Du Bois writes.[47] (In Conrad's *Heart of Darkness*, Marlow is motivated by such a demand when he pursues the voice of his predecessor, Kurtz. In turn, Kurtz's final rumination before imparting his last words is "This lot of ivory now is really mine"—"everything belonged to him," Marlow says [*Y*, 122, 156].)

The resonant opening of "Of Our Spiritual Strivings" seeks neither to possess its sounds nor supplant one voice with another. As he withholds the "I," Du Bois reminds us that the Western philosophic and literary tradition is inconceivable without a belong-to-me demand for "voice." It pertains to the voices of others as much as to the self. At least since "coon songs" and the minstrel stage, which Du Bois describes as a perversion of music by those who would desire to contain and control it, African American voice, too, has encountered this demand: the extraction of voice as the accumulation of a nascent white-owned recording industry.[48]

The final chapter, "The Sorrow Songs," is the only one of the book's essays not to have been previously published. Something of it commences. It is the only one of the book's titles to shed the genitive. Beginning with a definite article, it culminates the book to return to old songs of the slave past whose meaning "sympathetic white commentators" had commandeered from the black tradition of commentary that begins with Frederick Douglass.[49] As Eric Sundquist sets out to show in *To Wake the Nations*, Du Bois places black music at the center of writing African Americans into history, Sundquist emphasizing the once-overlooked place of the sorrow songs in Du Bois's broader philosophical project as it was at the turn of the last century. Du Bois makes use of the white anthologies of slave song, their "valuable transcriptions of lullabies, work songs, spirituals, and shouts," while also shedding their sympathetic and maudlin frame.[50] "The Sorrow Songs" chapter, Sundquist concludes, is a "critical act . . . of 'reappropriation'" that insists that "the memory of African dispossessions and life under slavery belonged first of all to those still living out its legacy."[51]

To be sure, *The Souls of Black Folk* is a literary, historical, and artistic act of reconstruction, a reparative reading and listening seeking to make good on a Reconstruction cut short and to narrate a memory of dispossession. But Du Bois never makes a claim regarding "reappropriation" and the "belonging" of tradition in any such terms. Du Bois's book effectuates its most central philosophical claim in its formal, acoustical strategies, in its apostrophic plea that ends the book: "*Hear my cry, O God the Reader.*" This "hearing" takes place as an experiential valence of reading, beginning with the epigraphs.

The minor movement of *The Souls of Black Folk* is to transform in resonance the experience of self-possessiveness, the genitive essentialism that animates the most sacred experience of autonomy, interiority, and self-belonging. It is not simply to transmit to those without direct experience the feeling of a devastating effect of exclusion, thereby transmitting self-hearing's foreclosed possibilities of listening to the other and to the self; it is to formalize a deracinated self.

That such sonorous form is also the book's content becomes apparent in the penultimate essay, "The Coming of John," the chapter immediately before and preparing "The Sorrow Songs," also the book's only fictional work. It once again begins with a fragment of verse followed by an untitled musical quotation (from the slave hymn "You May Bury Me in the East"). At the center of the story, however, is a third voice: Wagner (a crucial figure, we will find, for Conrad).

In the textual order of presentation, Du Bois asks us to hear Wagner through an epigraph, a kind of memory of sorrow song, such that the two sounds are acoustically superimposed in writing and reading. What is at stake in this hearing through, this resonance? Wagner's *Lohengrin* gives Du Bois's story its galvanizing scene when a young black man goes to the opera and experiences there a spiritual transcendence during the swan song, as if levitating out of his body. Forgetting himself, he touches the arm of a white woman and is quickly ushered out of the theater, thrown back to the schematic shores of racialized embodiment. The Du Boisian Veil becomes, in this way, Wagnerian in dimension, Wagner feeling that the full experience of music was possible only when the orchestra was acousmatic, or protected from view by a screen or veil.[52]

But any desire for spiritual transcendence is sensually rediscovered by Du Bois in its activity, the otherworldly made worldly. At the end of the story, we can assume that John is to be lynched for protecting his sister from sexual violation by a white man. As a narrative event, the moment of lynching is what I have called *half presented*, that is, it appears not as a spectacular image as seen from the outside but as experienced by the protangist's self-hearing, through sound and inwardness. In Chapter 1, we found half presentation to be the special domain of the novel as a sound technology, particularly with its free indirect discourse, which renders voices acousmatic. In half presentation, a fragment of sound recurs to a character to index another scene just beyond its immediate purview. In this moment of death, Wagner's wedding march returns to John inwardly as a melody made perceptible to us through free indirect discourse. We can't be certain of the source of the sound, nor can we be sure who hears it.[53] It is fundamentally acousmatic. Du Bois writes this moment in German, the line set apart typographically in ways that enhance its floating, sourceless quality, its resonance:

"Freudig geführt, ziehet dahin." (*SBF*, 154)

Du Bois does not misremember or mistranslate Wagner. He mixes him with a liberationist ethos, or *rehears* and *rewrites* Wagner's phrase but also consciousness and inwardness itself, such that John hears to himself not the phrase "faithfully [*treulich*] led, pass along to that place" but rather the much more sensual and worldlier "joyfully led."[54] Passing through John's consciousness, the song is remade. For the deracinated self that sings, there is no faithfulness to a "prior essence."[55] There is no grammatical "I" in this hanging, musical phrase, its space, or movement. In what we can take to be the threshold of a most violent death, the last line of "The Coming of John" is also typographically set apart: "And the *world* whistled in his ears" (*SBF*, 154, emphasis mine).

In *Heart of Darkness*, which in Chapter 3 we will find to be incomplete without *The Souls of Black Folk*, Marlow turns his ear toward what he takes to be a wilderness in a desire for recognition (he has not yet perceived it as such). Du Bois writes, in an echo of John the Baptist, "*Hear my cry, O God the Reader, vouchsafe that this my book fall not still-born into the world-wilderness*." "I am a voice shouting in the wilderness," cries John the Baptist. "An appeal to me in this fiendish row—is there?"—"I hear; I admit, but I have a voice, too, and for good or evil mine is the speech that cannot be silenced," Marlow responds (*Y*, 97). (In what airy space do these quotations touch?) Du Bois announces, "America shall rend the Veil"—each posit a voice, a cry, that seeks hearing, a hearing as yet only partial and unfulfilled.

In a project of audibility, Conrad places his English avatar as a listener in a field of sound he cannot fully understand; Conrad gives him the gift of a listener, someone to hold his sounds and voices. The silent listener in Conrad changes in relation to what he hears (as the story comes to its circular conclusion, we will find, he hears doubly, he hears as two).

Du Bois, like Fanon and Conrad, refuses to speak univocally. Conrad had spent his early years in exile; Du Bois writes from the position of the excluded class, the excluded being to whom you are not listening; his life ended in exile, with a revoked passport. (Though he chose to go to Ghana, we cannot forget that, once there, his US citizenship was essentially revoked.) Du Bois was an outlier of the nation-state as a form.

When Du Bois wrote "The Souls of White Folk" in 1912, he had lost much of the optimism for a cosmopolitan reading public that had organized *The Souls of Black Folk*. Peter Mallios notes this essay's suggestive signifying upon Conrad, its title being the echo of the object of *Heart of Darkness*, an acoustic mirror. It is just before he admits to hearing in the howl an "appeal" that Marlow says, "Well, you know, that was the worst of it—this suspicion of their not being inhuman. It would come slowly to one. They howled and leaped, and spun, and made horrid faces; but what thrilled you was just the thought of their humanity—like yours— the thought of your remote kinship with this wild and passionate uproar. Ugly" (*Y*, 96). Du Bois writes, "Yes as they [white folk] preach and strut and shout and threaten, crouching as they clutch at rags of fact and fantasies to hide their nakedness, they go twisting, flying by my tired eyes and I see them ever stripped,—ugly, human."[56] Du Bois's essay directly names the Congo and Leopold and the extraction of African resources but withholds the name "Conrad."

In the manuscript papers of Du Bois, there is what appears to be a kind of note or fragment related to this essay (Figure 6). The year is not known, but if it is from 1925, then it is not a preparation for the essay but its residue or detritus, the words "Hail Nigger!" and "Hearken Pale-face!" written in large cursive letters. The page is yelling, less a draft than a drawing or sound transcription. Both "hail" and "hearken" are commands to an addressee to listen. Is Du Bois rehearing *Heart of Darkness* through what I argued in Chapter 1 to be colonial sound

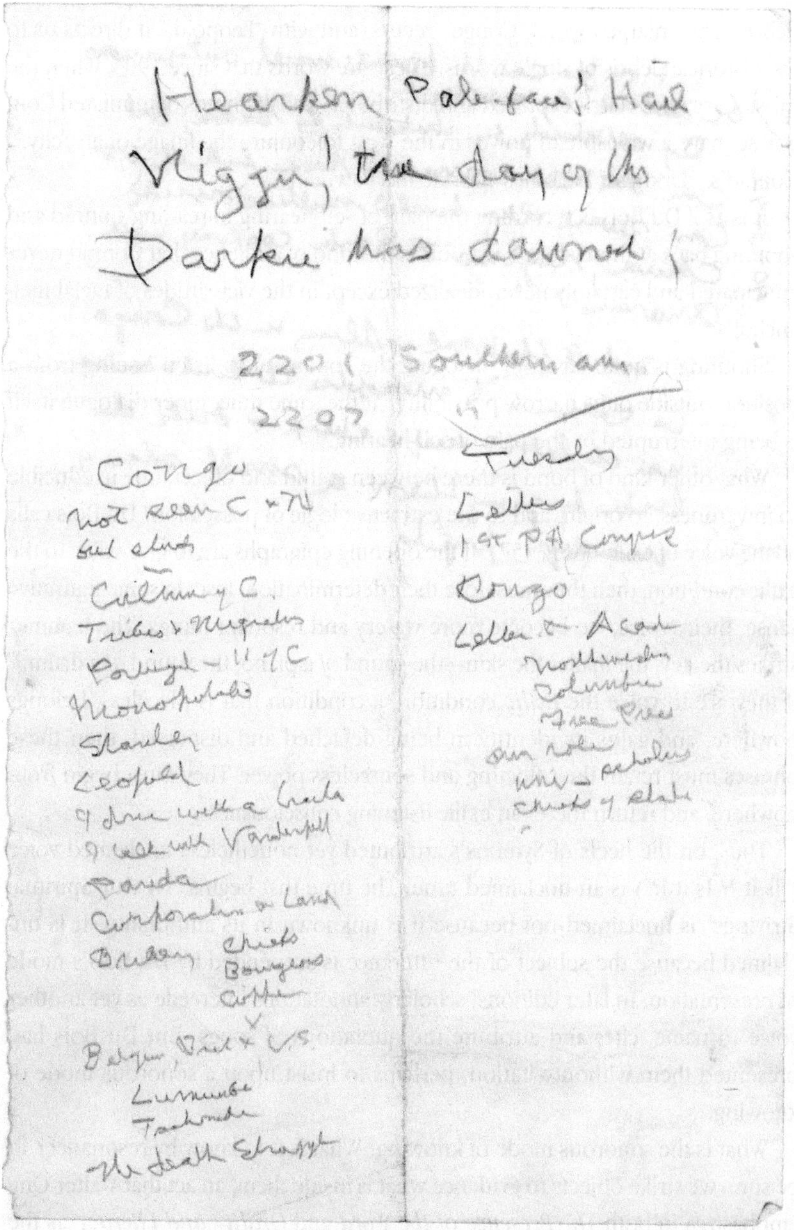

Figure 6. Congo, 1925? W. E. B. Du Bois Papers. Courtesy of the Special Collections and University Archives, University of Massachusetts–Amherst Libraries.

debris? The enlarged word "Congo" recurs, and with "Leopold," it directs us to the historical debris of single words. These are words that since 1903, when the missionary Alice Harris captured and distributed Kodak photos of mutilated Congolese, have a widespread power in the West to conjure the image of atrocity.[57] Conrad's "darkness" becomes "Darkie has dawned!"

It is as if Du Bois is recording the pain of self-hearing in reading Conrad and shouting back at these slurs.[58] Du Bois is the kind of audience that Conrad never anticipated and certainly never idealized except in the vicissitudes of racial melancholia.

Shouting is quite far from dialogue, the command to listen issuing from a position outside of its narrow possibility. At the same time, inner dialogue itself is being interrupted by the pain of self-hearing.

What other kind of bond is there between sound and object, one irreducible to inwardness, to origin, and to the extractive logic of possession? Du Bois calls it "the voice of exile" (*SBF*, 157). If the opening epigraphs are to give voice to the exilic condition, then they must lose their determination, lose, in some figurative sense, their "voice," to become more watery and resonant things. The hammer strikes the key, the mallet the skin—the sound *of* a piano, the sound *of* a drum.[59] If they are to voice the *exilic* condition, a condition that is placeless, belongs nowhere, and gains its identity in being detached and dispersed, then these phrases must retain their floating and sourceless power. They must begin from nowhere, and return there: an exilic listening consciousness.

Thus, on the heels of Symons's attributed yet nonetheless unclaimed voice ("Is it I? Is it I?") is an unclaimed tune. The tune that begins "Of Our Spiritual Strivings" is unclaimed not because it is unknown in its authorship. It is unclaimed because the subject of the utterance is suspended by Du Bois's mode of presentation. In later editions, scholarly annotations intercede as yet another voice to name, cite, and attribute the quotations of songs. But Du Bois had presented them without citation, perhaps to insist upon a sonorous mode of knowing.

What is the sonorous mode of knowing? What is it to know by resonance? To be sure, we strike objects to evidence what is inside them, an act that Walter Ong emphasizes in both *The Presence of the Word* and *Orality and Literacy* as the orienting spatial concept of interiority. Du Bois's essay is titled "*Of* Our Spiritual Strivings." What is the sound *of* such strivings? When struck, what kind of interior will such a sound portend?[60] These initiating questions open Du Bois's subject, but not reflexively to itself, in the circle that defines the phenomenological subject, but open it to another, who is reading but also potentially listening.

For, in this moment, shortly before the rise of mass-produced recordings will make it possible, the only way to hear music at home, for oneself, was to sing and play it. In relation to the "folk," with which Du Bois struggles yet out of which he makes so much, is a simple historical question of what it means to write about black music, of what a recording was in this moment and will later come to be. Du Bois invites the addressee—who is perhaps the folk or, later, the mass or collective—to sound out the tune. In a moment when musical performance in public concert was still rare, the invitation is to sing, play on the piano or the harmonium, or otherwise sound out (with mass-produced piano rolls, the mechanical means of sound reproduction that existed before recordings).[61] He invites touch, wood, vocal instrument, sense, and domestic practice. In this way, the materiality of resonance is not in conflict with Du Bois's disarticulation of the subject and reracination of the self. For the melodies, as they are without immediate attribution or the name of an individual subject, address and incite "the other side of language," which is listening. This other side is among the many thresholds of Du Bois's book that are both perilous and pleasurable, sundering and conjoining.

When Du Bois included the songs as what he calls "some echo of a haunting melody from the only American music which welled up from the black souls in the dark past," he does not presume some song that is immediately known or recalled (*SBF*, 6). It is an echo of a haunting, a doubly distant sound. In this moment, the Fisk Jubilee Singers were returning to old songs that already were, in Du Bois's phrase, "persistently mistaken and misunderstood," but also "half forgotten" and "half despised" among many African Americans (*SB*, 151)."[62] This form, to some extent, had begun to pass away because the original circumstances that gave rise to them had. Yet he could presume in his readers (of a certain class) a wider musical facility. To name the song in a scholarly annotation, as the original printed version does not, is to eliminate the sonorous mode of knowing that Du Bois calls upon by printing the musical bars without title and without name.

In inviting "you" to play, sing, and hear the melody (if you can), there is in the space of reading a moment of *musica practica*.[63] To "read" the melodies is to open an extradiegetic possibility of a sound, an act of sounding and self-listening, but acoustic and in physical space. This space is not circular and self-reflexive, nor is it presence. It is an elliptical opening. It is to play and then recognize the tune or perhaps to hear it for the first time.

Today, the recorded songs are readily available, and the tune that begins "Of Our Spiritual Strivings" is most likely one you have heard before. Nevertheless, one can imagine a reader who goes to the piano and plays or sings the tune, having never heard it before, as an unknown tune. Du Bois leaves it for a moment—and for those who cannot or will not sing or play, an interminable one—unattributed, unknown, and unsounded. The resonance is waiting. To me, someone with rather weak sight-reading ability, it is nothing more than a bare shape. As my eyes follow it, that quick movement into the lower frequencies and a slow creeping back up, the end of the line circling back to the first tone, it becomes unmistakable:

"No-body knows the trou-ble I see."

Even if the tune is known or recognized, it remains indeterminate. It is indeterminate, or has lost determinacy (*Bestimmtheit*: be-voicedness), for the simple fact that Du Bois's text is *with no single mode of address*. He eschews completely what, in previous chapters, I have argued to be the metaphysics of narrative voice. The nobody has claimed the space of the subject. Where there should be a "you" of the apostrophe, there is the nobody. This position—one no longer occupied or occupiable by the subject—is opened by the silence of the optical presentation. The musical bars have been denigrated by critics alternately as "mute ciphers" and "hieroglyphs," claiming that notation confronts the reader, optically and acoustically, merely with silence.

There indeed is a silence at the heart of Du Bois's text, a place where the immediate physical surface of the page meets a negative historical trajectory. This silence at the heart is borne out by the initiating muteness of the page. But if the "tactile content" of the page is "followed," there is a direction, an invitation—hospitality.[64] The melodies introduce in the reader's praxis of playing, singing, or imaginary listening a "follow sound" and "follow voice," or if one prefers the spatial metaphor, an "alongside sound" or "alongside voice."[65]

These are not echoes as they were defined in Chapter 2, but resonances that actualize what had not been there before and cannot exist in isolation. "The music functions antiphonally with respect to Du Bois's written text," Sundquist writes, "such that one must 'hear' sounds that are not on the page."[66] We can take this being of the page seriously in materiality. This quasi-hearing points to a larger problem of ethical encounter—the possibility of receiving or "hearing" the other—for which audition is both medium and metaphor.

Sorrow song is premised not upon the individual performer but a collective singing toward emancipation.[67] Slave song was not performed before an audience, since to hear the song was to be singing, a participant, or, as Douglass says, "in the circle" that also defined the ring shout.[68] This means that early white transcribers were overhearers, not receivers or participants. Douglass makes this autobiographical statement of memory, on the other side of his escape; he also implies that to be "in the circle" is not yet to know how to write. To learn to write is to become split in relation to the song. One does not write of the song; one sings the song. Douglass is split by the memory of song while writing of it, which is both to lose and regain the sound. He says that a teardrop has fallen on the page's ink while writing of the song—it is a trace that we, as readers of the printed book, cannot see. It is another distance within the sonic trace of slave song.

When Angela Davis suggests that "the spirituals, as they survived and were transformed during the post-slavery era, were both intensely religious and aesthetic bearers of the slaves' collective aspirations for worldly freedom," her phrasing indicates a dual ontology.[69] Collective, a sound both survives *and* is transformed. Du Bois no doubt wishes to indicate that African American culture "was worthy of preservation," "that it spoke identifiably in a language of its own."[70] For white anthologists, the project of inscribing black song had been enacted through what Sundquist describes as nostalgia for a "fading world" of the Old South, with racist norms continually framing the work of cultural preservation.[71] For Du Bois, in contrast, something transformative is at stake in listening. Listening, inscribing, and recording—these are transformative acts of reception. Du Bois brings sociological and aesthetic acumen to the post-Reconstruction landscape, asking not how to document what is fading (the preservative impulse) but how to retrieve in the present what is still left of striving within a black structure of feeling.[72]

This question of transformation begins in and as the most minor activity of resonance. Is not the contact between worldly survival and transformation in sounding one way of defining resonance?[73]

When we say that a thing resonates, we say that a thing survives yet has been transformed, that it has been made to sound out in amplifying ways, and that it is no longer simply itself. In this, Du Bois begins quite far from an essential sound "of" an immutable source for and to which he claims belonging. He begins with a sound that is a trace in its first instance, a song that would not be were not something else violently torn away.

He begins, in other words, with a sound that is already *writing*. When the Jubilee Singers arranged these slaves' songs circa 1900, their return to sorrow song was in fact radical; in moments of "political disappointment," Sara Marcus suggests, communities return to old songs to rehear and transform them: a "migration of form."[74] It is an act of rehearing but also rewriting (see Figure 7).

Du Bois made this remarkable work of art just after the publication of *The Souls of Black Folk*, and it continues on to include each essay of the book. Du Bois took his own printed book and, in an act of décollage, cut up its original image. He omitted the essays of the book to leave only its opening epigraphs. Du Bois had recently assembled photos and other displays for the "The Exhibit of American Negroes" at the Paris Expo of 1900. It is as if he takes the photographic and curatorial sensibility back to the printed book to (re)present, as a visual artifact, the quoted matter of the book, its songs and verse. It is as if, were the book to be reduced (to listening), it would leave only this material.

Throughout this book, we've been preoccupied with a sonic trace or residue on the page. Du Bois's cut-ups are a different kind of remainder.[75] In another image from the archive, in preparation for compiling *The Souls of Black Folk* Du Bois simply lists the titles of individual sorrow songs that will later open the essays. He is thinking of these melodic openings independently of these essays. To be sure, the archival images suggest a songbook, an anthology, but in Du Bois's nascent moment of sound recording, *The Souls of Black Folk* reaches us as an experiment in a record album compilation.

Of course, I make an anachronistic claim, since circa 1900 recordings had not yet been put to such use and the long-playing record had not yet been invented. But Du Bois's modernism announces what Alexander Weheliye calls "phonographies."[76] As such, it is also a sound technology avant la lettre; Du Bois receives and writes sounds in imaginative excess of available technology. For example, in *Mules and Men*, the novelist and anthropologist Zora Neale Hurston imagines walking with the singer who awakens workers in the turpentine mill, following him and writing of his song moving in space ("listen as he is singing," she writes), as if she imagines the possibility of a field recorder, which had not yet been invented. The earliest music recordings, before the invention of the electric microphone and multitracking, were of single performances, captured acoustically by a single microphone, the phonograph's horned mouth. But in his approach to his text, Du Bois, like Hurston, was already thinking beyond his technological moment: The compilation stretches across moments in time, both in performance and in reproduction.

In "The Sorrow Songs," Du Bois announces his ignorance regarding music "in the technical phrase." (In the first page of the original manuscript of "The Coming of John," Du Bois notates by hand the melody from "You May Bury Me in the East," numbers being visible above the notes, as if Du Bois was counting

The Souls of Black Folk

I

OF OUR SPIRITUAL STRIVINGS

O water, voice of my heart, crying in the sand,
All night long crying with a mournful cry,
As I lie and listen and cannot understand
The voice of my heart in my side or the voice of the sea;
O water crying for rest, is it I, is it I?
All night long the water is crying to me.

Unresting water, there shall never be rest
Till the last moon droop and the last tide fail,
And the fire of the end begin to burn in the west;
And the heart shall be weary, and wonder and cry like the sea,
All life long crying without avail,
As the water all night long is crying for me.

ARTHUR SYMONS.

II

OF THE DAWN OF FREEDOM

Careless seems the great Avenger;
History's lessons but record
One death-grapple in the darkness
'Twixt old systems and the Word;
Truth forever on the scaffold,
Wrong forever on the throne;
Yet that scaffold sways the future,
And behind the dim unknown
Standeth God within the shadow
Keeping watch above his own.

LOWELL.

III

OF MR. BOOKER T. WASHINGTON
AND OTHERS

From birth till death enslaved; in word, in deed, unmanned!

Hereditary bondsmen! Know ye not
Who would be free themselves must strike the blow?

BYRON

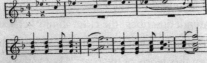

Figure 7. Poems and music from *The Souls of Black Folk*, c. 1903. W. E. B. Du Bois Papers. Courtesy of the Special Collections and University Archives, University of Massachusetts–Amherst Libraries.

the beats while writing, twinned by hearing.) The optical presentation on the page suggests a correlate to a recording, as if anticipating that one could move a needle in the groove to hear sudden, fragmentary, and exemplary sounds:

> The monotonous toil and exposure is painted in many words. One sees the plough-men in the hot, moist furrow, singing:

> "Dere's no rain to wet you,
> Dere's no sun to burn you,
> Oh, push along, believer,
> I want to go home."

> The bowed and bent old man cries, with thrice-repeated wail:

> "O Lord, keep me from sinking down,"

> and he rebukes the devil of doubt who can whisper:
> > "Jesus is dead and God's gone away."
> > Yet the soul-hunger is there, the restlessness of the savage, the wail of the wanderer, and the plaint is put in one little phrase:
> > "My soul wants something that's new, that's new."[77] (*SBF*, 159–60)

Du Bois is sorting through the songs, categorizing and typologizing them (love songs, but also songs of the motherless). "The songs are indeed the sift-ings of centuries; the music is far more ancient than the words, and in it we can trace here and there signs of development" (*SBF*, 157). This "sifting" reproduces itself in the mode of textual presentation, the songs again presented without at-tribution. It is as if an ear is turning away (*apostrephein*) from the individual and toward centuries of collective articulation. Du Bois transcribes and inscribes from these collective waves of sound single phrases that stand in for a multiplicity of songs, waves of sound being what we will find in *Heart of Darkness* to be the sonorous condition of linguistic community. He is not simply writing the words but their pronunciation (eye-dialect, in Hurston's famous phrase), along with the whispers, wails, plaints, cries, "eloquent silences and omissions" (*SBF*, 160).

Du Bois was, in a manner of speaking, a record collector. Writing of Walter Benjamin, Hannah Arendt describes "the close affinity between the break in tra-dition and the seemingly whimsical figure of the collector who gathers his frag-ments and scraps from the debris of the past."[78] But gathers where? To be sure, on the page. Yet in Du Bois's manipulation of passages, as optical and acoustical entities, the page becomes not a merely accumulative site. In the postpublica-tion décollage of the verse and song (see Figure 7), made not long after the book appeared as a book, Du Bois lends the document the same title, "The Souls of Black Folk," as if the soul *itself* is a collection of sounds, songs, silences, verses, and voices (just as we will find the heart to be in Conrad). The word "of" is underscored twice, as if it is the active, agential component of the title. The direct object of the title, however, "black folk," loses in that resounding its status as source: The title visualizes and grammaticizes the recordings of transformation in striving. When the cultural critic Kodwo Eshun indicts "soul" as an essentializing, metaphysical figure in discourses of black music, to uphold instead an Afrofuturist figure of the postsoul, he elides these palimpsests in the sound and in the voice—the soul as phonographies, or both *phone* and *graphe*.[79]

Sorrow song calls out to writing and to rewriting, to citation and recitation. In this, Du Bois writes and listens somewhere outside of the metaphysical tradition of the Word that sheds its earthly dependence on the body.[80] The soul becomes instead a medium or, better, mixed *media*, an inscriptive site "'in and on' which impressions can be made."[81] Du Bois rushes headlong into the Western philosophical tradition to echolocate for it the implications for black song. But this version of soul—a soul that "versions," in the reggae sense, giving an alternative cut of a song—is not merely an inscriptive copy of prior impressions. As an entity, particularly as it is elaborated in "Of Our Spiritual Strivings," soul exists for Du Bois in clear relation to the sublimating activities of *Geist* in *Aufhebung*, the cancellation that preserves. The soul is not merely a transcription of the past but a transformation of the index. In other words, the soul in Du Bois is the medium where inscription transforms.

This split in a soul that must remember and transform aligns with Paul Gilroy's sense of a defining tension in Du Bois "between a politics of fulfillment and a politics of transfiguration" in the creation of the Black Atlantic. "These movements allow us to see manifestations of the restless black political sensibility that was forced to move to and fro across the Atlantic and crisscross the boundaries of nation states if it was to be at all effective," Gilroy writes.[82] Du Bois's strategy of rewriting and relistening to song and sound is one manifestation of this political and oceanic sensibility. When Du Bois writes that the songs "welled up from blank souls in the dark past," it is not as if there is a well in which essence languishes, but in its welling up, its striving, there is a restlessness, a movement.[83]

Here, I suggest, our domain is not echo, which I argued in Chapter 2 dealt with the repetitive formation of the self in fantasy. Instead, we confront the fundamental unit of being, which is two.

Sound, Hegel writes, "relinquishes the element of an external form" such that "every part of the cohering body not only changes its place but also struggles to replace itself in its former position."[84] In resonance, we find restlessness but also the most minute material basis of Hegel's premise that *the smallest unit of being is two.* Vibration exists as oscillation and self-annihilation, but in that struggle against itself, vibration mediates a transformation in listening consciousness, in inwardness. The sound presupposes a listener, even if that listener is not yet available. In its struggle to replace itself in a former position, the vibratory character of resonance is both physical (in its being as sound) and political (in its being as listening). The object of the listening to come is "some echo of haunting melody from the only American music which welled up from black souls in the dark past" (*SBF*, 6). In Chapter 2, we found the echo to be partial; it is a memory of listening many times removed from the "source." Here, such echo, a faint trance, is hardly a fantasy but a political demand; it perhaps begins in consciousness as an echo of the object, as when the Veil falls for Du Bois to return his body to him clad in mourning, but does not end there.

"Of Our Spiritual Strivings" is a dialectical assessment, a historical "outline," as Du Bois calls it, not only of the book that follows but of the affective movements in black life, art, politics, and thought in America, each moment textually punctuated by a sensuous modality and its attendant failures in seeing and, above all, listening.[85] If the title, "The Forethought," had indicated the page's place in consciousness, the historico-political outline of the first chapter culminates in the future tense; it proffers a follow voice or alongside voice that exists in a fundamentally *asymptotic* relation to text. It is a writing that would sound out if it could: "And now what I have briefly sketched in large outline let me on the coming pages tell again in many ways, with loving emphasis and deeper detail, that men may listen to the striving in the souls of black folk" (*SBF*, 16). "On the page," "in the soul"—these prepositions are indications. The famous sentence punctuates "Of Our Spiritual Strivings" as a codicil and opens upon the body of the text as it moves toward "The Afterthought." Its grammar proposes a methodology of reading and listening that is transhistorical. In writing it again, and in you reading it again, there is some striving toward audibility. It is an acousticality that shares in sound without sounding. If not simply "heard" but "listened to," Du Bois suggests, this cry might set a reader free. The cry resonates beyond the Veil and at the threshold of the audible to become the text's most unifying figure.[86]

In relation to this auditory future, "that men may listen," Benjamin's theory of the storyteller is instructive. The novel is defined not principally by the evacuation of listening—its form still bears a trace—but by a historical task. The novelist takes up what Benjamin calls, after Pascal, memories that "do not always find an heir."[87] The novelist, he continues, "takes charge of this bequest" and not without profound melancholy, which is to say, the novel is a site of *heirless memories*, of things that have been left behind. It is the residue of form that, in Chapter 3, I will pursue in "sinister resonance." These heirless memories occupy at times no more than an acoustic register, an echo of a haunting, or a shadow of a sound.

With the fragments of unattributed melody of slave song that populate the openings of each chapter of his book, Du Bois nominates himself not as "heir," for these songs are not a patrimony in the traditional sense, descended not only from a people who were themselves property and who, in the words of Toni Morrison, "never owned anything." But at least one song—the song at the core of Du Bois's memory—is transmitted along the maternal line. This maternal voicing is the unspoken wound of Du Bois's text. He recalls "Do ba-na co-ba," sung by his grandfather's grandmother, a Bantu woman seized by Dutch traders. Du Bois transcribes both the melodic line on the treble clef—notating it perhaps for the first time—and these lyrics:

> Do ba-na co-ba, ge-ne me, ge-ne me!
> Do ba-na co-ba, ge-ne me, ge-ne me!
> Ben d' nu-li, nu-li, nu-li, nu-li, ben d' le.

He continues:

> The child sang it to his children and they to their children's children, and so two hundred years it has travelled down to us and we sing it to our children, knowing as little as our fathers what its words may mean, but knowing well the meaning of its music.
>
> This was primitive African music; it may be seen in larger form in the strange chant which heralds "The Coming of John":

> "You may bury me in the East,
> You may bury me in the West,
> But I'll hear the trumpet sound in that morning,"

> —the voice of exile. (*SBF*, 157)

While the opening epigraphs of Du Bois's book and the subsequent chapters provide musical fragments offered without comment, his final chapter is a sustained protomusicological analysis of African American song. The one amplifies silence, heightening the gap between reading, hearing, and understanding; the other produces cultural knowledge.

Du Bois was writing just as music studies was becoming a discipline and *Wissenschaft* in Germany circa 1900. These discussions could not have escaped him while involved in the intellectual milieu of Humboldt University.[88] "One of the most urgent tasks of the young discipline," the musicologist Alexander Rehding writes, "was to establish an archeology with which to reconstruct music history from its very first beginnings."[89] Archeology too was being established in this moment, Freud attending lectures on which he modeled his early theory of the psyche as a sedimented, layered site.[90] "Being perceived as fundamental to any *wissenschaftlich* enterprise," Rehding writes, "a study of origins" mired musicology in evolutionary thinking about race.

It is here, poised between the beginnings of psychoanalysis and music studies, that Du Bois's monumental work is interposed. At the core of "The Sorrow Songs" is a memory of an African song (Hegel's philosophy of history had instead denied Africans world-historical status). While in Berlin, Du Bois perhaps heard or participated in discussions about the "origins" of music; perhaps the memory of the Bantu song, drifting from the other side of the Atlantic, returned to him. In the circum-Atlantic moment, "circum-" becomes, in this way, a key modifier of "circa," constituting a chronotope of world-historical proportion.[91] *The Souls of Black Folk* galvanizes a theory of (black) consciousness but also an alternative theory of music, one that takes up not origins but, like the text itself, beginnings.[92]

"Do ba-na co-ba" is perhaps his earliest memory of song, though we cannot be sure, and its place, while autobiographical, is also allobiographical, or a writing of the self through the other; it cannot be localized within the individual life.[93]

With Du Bois, then, we exceed the limits of ego psychology. The memories are not entirely personal but instead transpersonal. It is being there in the world alongside others that we can isolate song's political locus, not simply through relating narratives but sounds.[94] When Du Bois writes of a transgenerational memory of the Bantu woman, he transliterates the phonemes held by childhood memory into adulthood. These phonemes are heard not as words but as sounds. It is a contact between orality and writing through retroaudition.

This hearing again later politicizes childhood listening through a return. "Do ba-na co-ba" has yet to be translated (in what language she sings, we don't know), but Du Bois's sonic memory of these Bantu beginnings touches *Heart of Darkness* via the Niger-Congo family of languages, including Kongo, which we will find, in Chapter 3, to be occluded from the semantic body of Conrad's novel. In locating not an origin but an intersoronous relation—a resonance—between Du Bois and Conrad, one simply cannot follow the traditional route afforded by either philology or even polysemy. The words of Édouard Glissant are suitable: "The call of Relation is heard, but it is not yet a fully present experience."[95]

The impossible memory of the Bantu woman lends the song, its sound, the same kind of dimension afforded the acousmatic, in which one hears something one does not understand and from a distance. Du Bois never sees this woman, nor could he have, yet he imagines her. There is in "Do ba-na co-ba" a transmission from the mother, but what kind of transmission? Certainly not a narrative transmission. "There is not one extant autobiographical narrative of a female captive who survived the Middle Passage," Saidiya Hartman writes.[96] History becomes, she continues, a project of "listening for the unsaid, translating misconstrued words" that we encountered in Chapter 1.

Here, traditional psychoanalytic modes of listening are both instructive and limited. Across a number of works, Freud's student Theodor Reik privileges the atmosphere of a session and a musical tune's affective valences, noting the unbidden resurgence of "haunting melodies" (the same phrase used by Du Bois to describe the resonance of sorrow songs on the other side of the Middle Passage and Emancipation). These atmospheres must be listened to with what Reik calls, after Nietzsche, a "third ear." However, insisting that two ears are already too many, Lacan resists Reik's emphasis upon listening for meaning to suggest that an analyst instead "listen for sounds and phonemes, words, locutions, and . . . not forgetting pauses, scansions, cuts."[97] Even transcriptions of patient speech, Lacan says, must include these as the basis of "analytic intuition." A haunting melody is nonepistemic, but ultimately for Reik, it can be retrieved for the order of meaning. In Chapter 2, however, we found that Freud and Lacan bracket history, politics, and the social—"Do ba-na co-ba" sounds in excess of these modalities.

The word-sounds or phonemes "Do ba-na co-ba" are not the translation of a misconstrued word, but they do bolster a song of survival, of living on. I've been arguing that a sound that survives in transformation is one way of thinking about resonance. "Do ba-na co-ba," in a manner of speaking, survives the Middle Passage and reopens it as a primary channel of listening and receiving.

Who hears such a transmission?

The song cannot be heard as such, or rather, it necessarily involves the forms of hearing that attend partial memory. It is as if Du Bois "overhears" this woman, but not because he stands at a clandestine threshold where the message is not intended for him, as in the Freudian primal scene. He overhears because to receive the song in the New World is already to be on the outside of some possibility of full transmission. It is unclear if the song itself is partial or rather the forms of hearing that afford their subject a historical consciousness. Since

Melanie Klein, we think of the "part-object," or unattainable objects that cause desire (Lacan includes among them not only the breast but also the gaze and the voice); they are, from their first instance, cut off from the source. Du Bois's protagonist listens, to some extent, to a part-object, but its partiality—and the partialness that sustains the temporal movement of his text—is not simply structural, related to the cut that is language and to the lacuna of the unconscious. It is related to a history that, Spillers describes, was dramatically cut short by the Middle Passage.

The locus of Du Bois's book in the final chapter is the missing image of the mother's place of birth and, with it, her original transport. It is what Rizvana Bradley might call a formal "vestige of motherhood" in the Black Atlantic.[98] In ways that are consequential for my thinking of this missing image, Bradley turns to Hartman's lyrical memoir of her experience traveling along the former routes of the Atlantic slave trade in Ghana—a memoir defined by the feeling of what it is to "lose your mother," losing a motherland, a mother tongue.[99] The missing image, I suggested in Chapter 1, becomes sound precisely through the way it withdraws from view. "Do ba-na co-ba" is sung in a mother tongue but one that is unknowable, unretrievable. The words "do ba-na co-ba" are phonemes, part of a lost because extracted and stolen mother tongue (while also being evocative of the future of jazz).[100] Melody provides, in this way, what Aaron Carter-Ényì calls "an alternate theory" of orality and literacy, one that privileges not a spoken oral tradition but a survival of music, an *aural* tradition in which melodies hold fast when language is "violently submerged."[101]

I want to fasten upon a different but related aural affect, not one of immediate recognition (through which the song is passed down) but rather its attendant ambivalence and gaps. The crooning voice of the Bantu woman—the voice of the black maternal vestige—is the encrypted philosophical locus of Du Bois's narrative form. To remember this song is to transmit into new form its strange and deterritorizalizing chant.

From its beginning in Symons's "The Crying of Water," Du Bois's text finds its enunciation in the wound of the missing maternal. But this wound is only articulated as a wound in the final chapter, making it something of a displaced center. It's there that Du Bois positions himself as a receiver and singer of song whose words he cannot understand. In this moment of writing circa 1900, there is a trace of an oral/aural transmission where some source, as in Benjamin's thought of the storyteller, actuates itself in slow release—some substance as what has traveled down. Writing in the age of the phonograph and telegraph, Benjamin notes that information, unlike the story, travels "without losing any time."[102] This nonloss of time is not merely physical, that is, owing to the experience of instantaneousness, the wires' ability to transmit an event during and immediately after its unfolding. In contrast to information, the story loses time because it is fundamentally ambiguous: It is not understood now but later, and it continues to emit an affective potency, a "continuation" (*Fortsetzung*, an episodic installment) that Benjamin calls "germinative."[103]

To listen for the black maternal in Du Bois involves returning to the story of the white girl's rejection of his young self in the opening chapter—the scene that cuts him to initiate his subjectivity. But we receive its significance only in resonance, in a delay on the other side of the closing chapter and its most traumatic memory of song that links him via the maternal to the generations. We have to read forward to read back. Du Bois gives us the pedagogical clue—teaching us how to read and how to listen—from his first sentence ("Between me . . . there is"). Du Bois does not begin the book with this memory of a Bantu woman's crooning but rather ends with it. By relocating the (personal) primal scene at the end, he redefines the epistemological rupture of its linguistic cut as political.

The genesis of writing is the maternal song. This end that is also a natal beginning releases the reader back into the world of praxis, as a listener whose ears are now "pricked," alert to sounds that in their uncanniness widen the gap between hearing and understanding.[104] Here, however, Du Bois's formulations exceed Freud's: The listener's ears are pricked to the historical injury (rather than a purely developmental one) that sustains subject formation (in the Reprise, we will find the same to be true of Faulkner). The *formal* elision of the song animates the autobiographical locus of the book, its subject and its self. In other words, it is a locus that has to be displaced in order to be represented.

The kidnapped mother is the silence at the heart of Du Bois's quotations. Through her, we enter into an alternate set of implications for the primal scene. In "Of Our Spiritual Strivings," the opening chapter, Du Bois elliptically notes "the red stain of bastardy," that is, the rape of black women by white men. But is not the trauma of this "stain" registered by Du Bois when listening as a child to "Do ba-na co-ba," a song that emanates from the kidnapped woman? The meaning of its sound is "well understood" but never put into words by Du Bois. Barthes says the "grain" is "the body in the voice" and "the materiality of the body speaking its mother tongue,"[105] but he remarks upon the grain's fundamentally phallic status. The grain is the sound of an "erect" voice that stands at the threshold of the entry into language and the symbolic.

When Spillers takes up the lexicon of psychoanalysis for African American life, she insists not on crimes against the body (a central category for psychoanalysis) but on the "flesh" in its capacity to be harmed. Flesh forms the basis of a central distinction between captive and liberated subject positions, more recently theorized by Weheliye as the crux of biopower.[106] By the "primary narrative" of flesh, Spillers writes, "we mean its seared, divided, ripped-apartness, riveted to the ship's hole, fallen, or 'escaped' overboard."[107] By "materiality," Barthes does not mean the "flesh," thus denoting the limitations of his theory for transatlantic resonance (the transatlantic as resonance). For what is the mother tongue or the semiotic *chora*, the nurse of the world's forms that sustains Barthes's theory, in the face of a transmitted memory of a kidnapped mother and her crooning?[108] This unnamed Bantu woman's crooning is a song of becoming violently undifferentiated, "ungendered," a thing, alienated, and forced out of language—a song of the flesh, not of the body. In this way, Du Bois's political subject position cannot be fully separated from the flesh of the past, whose searing and ripping also "transfers," Spillers suggests, across generations. According to Spillers's monumental paradigm shift, then, the textual displacement of the Bantu song cannot merely be symbolic, owing to the cut that is language: It also owes itself to the real displacement of exile, the forcible entry into an imperial or colonizing language.

There is a scant place for black women in the political and social imaginary of *The Souls of Black Folk*, Wall notes. This suppression, and with it a black maternal vestige, already begins in the memory of the white girl who appears under the sign of the feminine and sexual difference. It has gone largely unnoticed that to the extent that the scene of the calling card is structured by the master-slave dialectic, it is also structured by desire. This scene of trauma is shattering for both boy and girl. The desire coursing through the scene is suppressed in Du Bois's adult memory in favor of its meaning for him as a political subject. What would it mean to recollect, on both sides, the trace of sexual (and interracial) desire? The fact that she is white, however, casts a different taboo over the scene and allows for a suppression of sexuality in his memory that is more easily retrieved; it is speakable in social terms.

The circuit of desire is foreclosed by the girl, and to the extent that this moment instills in Du Bois the first self-consciousness of racial difference vis-à-vis sexual difference, we can sense that interracial desire already courses through the scene. Her desire mandates that she not speak. Such an exchange operates at some other level not fully fathomed by Hegel, yet its structural acoustics, we've found, are narrated loudly by Fanon in "L'expérience vécue du Noir," an essay whose mistranslated title, I've noted, in part provides the title of my book. Mistranslation (of Fanon) is, for Fred Moten, an act of recovering optimism such that "the non-attainment of meaning or ontology, of source or origin, is the only

way to approach the thing in its informal . . . material totality"—"the object vibrates against its frame like a resonator."[109] If for Heidegger being with others in
the world "is a condition of facticity into which one is thrown and in which one
loses oneself,"[110] then for Du Bois it is only with others in the world that we discover ourselves. In refusing to be addressed, the girl gives to the young Du Bois
his body, as Fanon might say, "clad in mourning." He surfaces, quite literally, on
the other side of the failed exchange as a racial object, as "fact." But in writing
sound, he transmutes this scene and resonates.

Nonetheless, we can note with Wall that Du Bois emerges from the scene as
a political agent disentangled from black women—with one notable exception,
the maternal vestige, and this exception demands that we listen with ears pricked
to "The Sorrow Songs," as Du Bois's early contribution to the psychoanalytic
theory of listening. Such a claim involves intervening in the racially neutral terrain of the so-called sound object (a kind of part-object) to insist that it emanates
in Du Bois's memory from a black maternal position. This position makes the
epigraphic space not so much an otherworldly union but a violently charged,
historical space that listens for the traces of miscegenation and forced migration but also transformation and self-migration. It desires a place for the black
maternal that could be articulated without also being repressed. We began with
the simple notion of an amalgamation of verse and melody. But where there is
amalgamation, there is sexuality. Du Bois's formal strategies are radical: They
indicate potential for a theory of listening derived from or animated by a black
feminine position.

In his epigraphs, Du Bois omits from the anthologized transcriptions the bass
clef, where the bass and tenor (traditionally male) voices reside, to leave only the
soprano and alto (traditionally feminine) voices. "The Sorrow Songs" restores the
severed clef. The notation is gendered. However, it is more overtly a performative
reflection on writing and sound in relation to world history, literacy, and consciousness. The Jubilee Singers were revitalizing songs that had been, Du Bois
makes clear, "half forgotten," and not simply by the exclusionary dictates of the
nineteenth-century repertory but by the black folk who were desiring for various
reasons to forget. The notation animates questions of inclusion and inscription
in national and cultural memory making.

The mode of address in Du Bois's melodic fragments is unstable: They are
addressed to sight reading as a "hearing" of the feminine melody or harmony
to oneself. They are addressed to practice, to a musically literate audience. But
the fragments do not lose their quality of address before those of us who look
mutely at the page as one would at "hieroglyphs,"[111] deaf or otherwise unable to

hear, play, or discern anything more than a *shape*. The listening consciousness does not attain the meaning, and even to play or sing the bar of music is to sound it but once. In each of these instances, it is a transformative sound addressed to reading consciousness become open, mutable. The italics in Du Bois's last pronouncement to the reader, "*Hear my cry, O God the Reader*," register some sense that the written word is striving for a transformation into another register. They vibrate.

"My soul wants something that's new, that's new."

Cocoxochitl was no longer the name of that flower. It had become the dahlia. . . . At what moment is the germ of possession lodged in the heart? . . . And so the dahlia: Who first saw it and longed for it so deeply that it was removed from the place where it had always been, and transformed (hybridized), and renamed?

> —Jamaica Kincaid

Neither the formula from Parmenides, "Being never changes," nor the related view by Heraclitus, "All is in a state of flux," through which Western metaphysics were conceived, but a transphysical poetics that could be briefly expressed as—that which is (that which exists in a total way) is open to change.

> —Édouard Glissant

3

A SINISTER RESONANCE: ON THE EXTRACTION OF SOUND AND LANGUAGE IN *HEART OF DARKNESS*

PRELUDE: SINISTER RESONANCE AND THE DREAM OF COMMUNICATION

> Of all the writer's inventions, none has commanded such profound and earnest attention throughout the civilized world as has the phonograph. This fact he attributes largely to that peculiarity of the invention which brings its possibilities within range of the speculative imaginations of all thinking people, as well as to the almost universal application of the foundation principle, namely, the gathering up and retaining of sounds hitherto fugitive, and their reproduction at will.
>
> —Thomas Edison, "The Phonograph and Its Future"

In 2018, an electronic message circulated on the social media website Twitter, wishing users "good morning"—an echo of among Thomas Edison's first recordings—and disseminating an image: the "cursed orb."[1] Ground down to a fine dust, it is the particulate matter of a broken iPhone, encased in glass as if it might wield some toxic power. From dust to dust. Niobium, tin, tantalum, and tungsten—anaphoric, rolling off the tongue: the 3Ts. Invisible, they nonetheless resonate with the voices and sounds that pass through the passive electronic circuits they create. In the lexicon of humanitarian struggle, these are "conflict minerals." Because the supply chain works precisely to cloak their origins in political unrest, child labor, and sexual violence, we cannot be certain of any particle's proximity to or origin in the killing fields of eastern Congo.[2]

It is from coltan, a dull black metallic ore, that the elements niobium and tantalum are extracted. One already hears within these words the rustling of language, an etymological content of mythological origin: Niobe, daughter of Tantalus and, according to the *OED*, "an inconsolably bereaved woman, a weeping woman."[3] In her grief, it is said, Niobe was forcibly transformed into stone, so excessive were her cries. Niobe is not unlike Echo, who dissolved into bone, leaving only the reflective surfaces against which our voices still reverberate.

We hear the geological filiations, from woman's voice to stone, from mineral and back into voice. If we are careful not to forget, which is, after all, the lesson of etymology (the study of the sediment of words), we also hear a genealogical filiation: Tantalus, "wretched" and cursed to unfulfillable desire.[4] The circuit is part media, part linguistic. We know from Marx's conception of the fetish that violent encounters are secreted within things that carry the ghosts of human relations. But violent encounters are also secreted within words. These sinister resonances are proper to the foundation principle of philology, or "love of literature and learning."[5] They are also proper to the foundation principle of phonographic modernity, that sounds may be captured, stored, and transmitted.

Heart of Darkness is a primal scene of global modernism, irrevocable, like a scar, yet procreant, like an opening.[6] Yet if it were to be cleared away (healed beyond all memory), a form and subjectivity would be cleared away with it. *Heart of Darkness* becomes a primal scene only by way of the event that Paul Gilroy and Édouard Glissant argue constitutes modernity as such: *Heart of Darkness* is written and received through the Middle Passage as a memory system, its systole and diastole. ("Memory system"—one name Freud introduces for the psyche in *Beyond the Pleasure Principle*.) This event is circulatory, not unlike the heart.

In 1975, the Nigerian novelist Chinua Achebe argued that *Heart of Darkness* should no longer be read. His unstated wish is that this novel had never been written. This wish perhaps discloses another: to undo the injury to which *Heart of Darkness* owes its existence. When Achebe titled his essay "An Image of Africa: Racism in *Heart of Darkness*," he attempted to say as directly as possible that "darkness" stands in for "Africa." He makes it clear that when he looks at (sees and reads) the word "darkness," he sees (beneath or shining through it) two missing words, both "Africa" and "blackness," but also a third, the authorial name "Conrad."

Achebe's essay is organized around the problem of the image, beginning with the title. But for evidence that the novel's principal narrator, Marlow, stands in for Conrad, Achebe turns to the author's diaries, where he writes of a fascination with dark skin and of seeing an "enormous buck nigger" in Haiti.[7] What makes it possible for this image of Haiti to abound as a signifier, a signifier then bound to an image of Africa?[8] There is something in Achebe's essay that is not an image at all but a fact of resonance: the black diaspora, which goes unnamed in his essay, except through this passing invocation of Haiti.

To say that *Heart of Darkness* is a primal scene of global modernism, of the Black Atlantic, and of the fact of (black) diaspora is to render uncertain the genitive coordinates that a title, as a kind of name, are supposed to make intelligible. The meaning of "diaspora" takes root in the ancient Greek "to disperse" (διασπορά) but also "to scatter and sow." Nadia Ellis argues in *Territories of the Soul* that the meaning of diaspora lies in its nonphysical existence—it cannot be actualized as a location. The problem of naming introduced by Conrad's title is underscored by the fact that the locations "Congo" or "Africa" are never written in the novel. A so-called frame narrative, the novel's event of storytelling takes place aboard a cruising yawl, the *Nellie*, at rest in the River Thames (also unnamed in text). There was nothing left to do but "wait for the turn of the tide," an anonymous narrator remembers, and so Marlow began to tell a story late into the night (*Y*, 45). This narrator looks upon the river and recalls the ghosts of Roman conquerors: "It had borne all the ships whose names are like jewels flashing in the night of time, from the *Golden Hind* returning with her rotund flanks full of treasure . . . to the *Erebus* and *Terror*." Marlow interrupts this placid space to recount his journey along another unnamed river: "'And this also,' said Marlow suddenly, 'has been one of the dark places of the earth'" (*Y*, 48). Marlow had pursued his forebear in the trading company, Kurtz, who had formed a rampart of disciples in the Inner Station and refused to return to Europe. Marlow had gone to retrieve Kurtz, but instead became enthralled by a pure, vibrating voice whose "folds of a gorgeous eloquence" he longed to hear (*Y*, 155).

In Chapter 2, I relayed this desire for a pure voice through the melancholy of race and, with it, the idealization of a black resonance whose loss could not be mourned. Here, Conrad's omission of the words "Thames" and "England" stand in relation to the omission of "Congo" and "Africa," the imputed location of Marlow's journey. These are not an involuntary forgetting but an erasure, both an overwriting and a cutting out. But they are also an elision (in linguistics, to delete a word sound). In the Intersonority, I suggested that W. E. B. Du Bois's memory of a Bantu woman's song transmits the trace of an original tongue not to be retrieved in positivist ways. It transmits the memory of a making of a lacuna, a blank yet resonant space. Christopher Miller turns to early manuscript pages of Conrad's novel to note that he had at first included geographic references, which would have located Marlow's story in "Africa." This erasure is, for Miller, an allegory of the problems that inhere in the name of the continent. "It was relatively recently that 'Africa' came to be the sole representative of a single continent, differentiated and circumscribed."[9] The word, Latin in derivation, first applied only to a small area around Carthage but became in its adoption by other Western languages a synecdoche, at the core of which is the problem of the trope, the part in relation to the whole.[10] Conrad's erasure of names invokes the trauma of naming places, colonization as a trauma of renaming.

When Achebe argues that *Heart of Darkness* denies Africans indigenous languages, he elides a moment whose displacement is central to this chapter and to the thesis of *The Fact of Resonance*: Conrad's corpus and, with it, a theory of modernism can be unfolded from its acoustical beginning, the shout of an ignored, subaltern woman. "'She came abreast of the steamer, stood still, and faced us,'" says Marlow in recollection of a "wild and gorgeous apparition" of a black woman (*Y*, 83). Among Kurtz's disciples present at the scene was the "harlequin," or "man in patches." (His colorful garb reminds us of the root of "text" in *texere*, from the Latin "to knit or weave," but also of the map of the unnamed continent that Marlow says has become overwritten with colors, insignia of colonization.) The harlequin remembers that this same woman had "'talked like a fury to Kurtz for an hour, pointing at me now and then. I don't understand the dialect of this tribe'" (*Y*, 85).[11] Conrad does not quote, transcribe, transliterate, or translate this "dialect" but includes within the text the fact of its existence in the voice of a woman: It is a language the harlequin hears but does not understand or recognize as language.

Before Marlow meets the Russian harlequin, he had encountered a remnant of him en route to the Inner Station, an abandoned book of English seafaring with notes scribbled in what he took to be "cipher" (we later understand them to be Cyrillic). The book further incites his desire to hear Kurtz's voice, a wraith educated partly in England: "'This was because it could speak English to me,'" Marlow muses (*Y*, 117).[12] When Marlow finally reaches Kurtz, Kurtz is nearing death, and this "real presence" of voice—a pure voice—is at its weakest, "'a cry that was no more than a breath'" (*Y*, 113, 149). Marlow will hear its fullest (English) resonance only in fantasy. The famous last words of Kurtz, who is both English and French, are uttered in English: "'The horror! The horror!'" (*Y*, 149).

In Marlow's pursuit of a master's voice through the vector or tangent of an unheard woman, we are reminded of the framed tale upon which Conrad, trained in the classics, likely modeled *Heart of Darkness*.[13] Plato's *Phaedo* documents the death and last words of Socrates, in which he confirms his theory of the soul's immortality and the claim that philosophy is the practice of dying. It is framed as Phaedo repeating the story of Socrates's final hours and, with it, his last argument concerning knowledge as recollection of what the soul gleaned before embodiment. An incantation, Phaedo repeats the story to Echecrates, who was not present. The structure of the dialogue raises the dead and gives the words of Socrates out of the mouth of Phaedo. When Echecrates asks who else was present in those final hours, Phaedo somewhat astonishingly remarks that Plato, if he remembers correctly, was not there; he was "not strong enough to attend." As a written text, *Phaedo* essentially bears witness to the complete transference of the dying voice of Socrates via Phaedo to Echecrates, who speaks perfectly in Socrates's place, transmitting the story and the doctrine of philosophy to Phaedo (and implicitly, to Plato), his listener.

But the *Phaedo* includes a passing moment that resonates with the "wild and gorgeous apparition" of a black woman. As Phaedo tells the story, he remembers that Socrates's wife had entered the deathbed chamber where Socrates was detained as a prisoner of the state. Enter Xanthippe:

> We hadn't waited for a long time when he came and told us to go in. So we went in and caught Socrates just freed from his bonds and Xanthippe—you know her—holding his little boy and seated beside him. Now when Xanthippe saw us, she cried out and then said just the sort of thing women usually say: "Socrates, now's the last your companions will talk to you and you to them!" And Socrates gave Crito a look and said: "Crito, have somebody take her home."[14]

The entry and exit dramatize the disambiguation of hearing as what Plutarch takes to be both the most logical and the pathetic of the senses; it is the separation of *logos* from *pathos*, the soul from sonorousness, or the "devocalization of logos." They banish Xanthippe as the trace of the grief they cannot express if they are to occupy the realm of philosophy, constructed by the space of talk, or *muthos*. Women talk but do not speak.[15] She was there, but not as a disciple in the space of dialogue—she remains embedded in the margins of fiction, as it were, margins described and then displaced. Where does Xanthippe go?

Here, we enter into a new relation, one that returns to my claim in Chapter 1 regarding acoustical displacement. Xanthippe is not a lost object but an ignored object adjacent to the master scene. Frederic Jameson famously argues that in the "symptomatic" reading of a text, the master code may be revealed. But this woman is neither concealed nor revealed. Like Bertha's creole "noise" in *Jane Eyre*, she is sounding off in the next room. She is escorted off the stage. In a final gesture before returning at the end of the dialogue, as if a shell to its kernel, she

beats her breast. The gesture localizes, figures, and gives form to what is otherwise abstract. The gesture figures all that Socrates will go on to discard from the
theory of the soul. Of the woman who complains, Sara Ahmed writes, "She makes
an announcement. She is an announcement."[16] Ahmed here gestures toward the
root of "complaint," which is shared by "plague": "*compleinen*, 'lament, bewail,
grieve,' also 'find fault, express dissatisfaction, criticize,' also 'make a formal ac-
cusation or charge to an authority,' from stem of Old French *complaindre* 'to
lament' (12c.), from Vulgar Latin **complangere*, originally 'to beat the breast,'
from Latin *com-*, here probably an intensive prefix + *plangere* 'to strike, beat
the breast.'"[17] The woman who complains is a percussive, sounding instrument.

We know that we must attend to Plato's props, the dramaturgy of scenes as
they are elaborated, just before the props disappear to become the site of dialogue, where words alone manifest. It is there that Derrida finds the *pharmakon*,
hiding in the offhand remark about playing with Pharmacia or the winds of
Boreas. It is there we find the cicadas, which sing a droning song and spy or listen in on Socrates in the *Phaedrus*. What's more, such banishment, as a structural
configuration of the scene of talk, must be externally visualized, taking the visible
shape of scenography as such—in this case, a physical border around the space
of masculine dialogue. It is in the process of appearing in order to disappear that
the dialogue conducts its ultimate sleight of hand, transferring the dying master's
discourse to Phaedo, Socrates standing in for the body of Plato, the writer. As if assisting that transference, Xanthippe's cry is banished from the space of dialogue.

The work of banishment functions centrally in the theory of contraries as laid
out by Plato in the *Phaedo* and the *Republic*. In ways that are foundational for
Genette, these contraries include that between *haplé diégésis*, or "pure narrative," and mimesis in its mixing of voices and realities. (The degrees of mimesis
and diegesis distinguish quotation from narrative summary.) One proof for the
immortality of the soul is that it is contrary to death and that opposites will not
"admit" their opposite. Socrates explains through the concept of enumeration,
whereby the Even will not admit the Odd, that "contraries would never be willing to receive a coming-to-be from one another."[18] "Will not admit" is the common translation across many of Plato's texts for this form of demonstration that
proves exact contraries. But Socrates's theory of admittance must be related here
to a physical border. To admit, or *dechomai* (δέχομαι), is to accept, but in the
manner of receiving or giving warm welcome, as in a home—to welcome, but in
the middle voice, so highly related to the self that is acting upon itself. Indeed,
"auto" appears in Plato's original phrasing: what will not admit into itself. The

force of keeping out is not outside of it but within it and maintains itself without any other support. *Dechomai* thus includes both the active and passive states: to give and to receive hospitality.[19] In the Overture, I noted that in its semantic field, we find *chōreō*, of which one derivative is choreography—to make space, to make room for another by withdrawing.[20] It orients the physical and ethical boundary, no less a cut, that constitutes the act of listening. *Dechomai* is "to give ear to." We will find it is to be the essential work conducted by *Heart of Darkness* as a tale of foreclosed listening.

In meditating on the sonorous entrance and exit of a subaltern woman, we should recall a different border in the *Republic*, one that establishes the *polis* as homologous to the soul. In book 3, Socrates distinguishes showing and telling to describe a man who could imitate anything, a charmer and musician, a player of the many-stringed instrument who could bend his voice in the most dazzling and deceptive ways. What if he were to appear in the city? Socrates describes a scene of sanctification. They would kneel down before and garland this man just before saying that that there is no room for such a man in the city. It is not, then, that such a man does not exist but that he cannot be admitted. There is a fault line in the figure of music: It reveals that the soul, which is eternal, is also porous; it is like an ear into which adverse influence pours to (re)shape its borders. It desubstantiates, converts identity into warning. In what the classicist Ramona Naddaff calls "exiling the poets," the poet is turned away, as if at the borders of the city. In the same semantic field of *dechomai*, we find the masculine-gendered *chorus* and the feminine-gendered *chōra*, originally the name of a district of Lower Egypt, a territory, remarkably enough, also outside of the city walls. Its name was mobilized by Plato as the word for a maternal receptacle or "nurse," the anterior matrix space that allows for but cannot retain Forms. This choric space is lent in Julia Kristeva's monumental reading of Plato's *Timaeus* the feminine status of rhythm and pure semiosis.[21]

In Chapter 1, I argued that Conrad hears otherwise—he hears through a feminine principle. But now, in *Heart of Darkness*, Conrad returns to a series of scenes that populate the history of Western recitation to rewrite the dream of communication. This dream is the "foundation principle," in Edison's phrase that serves as the epigraph to this Prelude, not only of the phonograph as a *capture* of sound but of colonialism's extraction of indigenous language and names. When Achebe reads *Heart of Darkness*, he elides the complaint of a woman to take issue with a different instance of black speech, a shard of broken English spoken by a Congolese man who announces to Marlow, "Mistah Kurtz—he dead"

(*Y*, 150). This moment resonates with the languages visually imposed on a map in names, which include palimpsests—other ways of conceiving, dividing, and inscribing place, both African and Arabic, that have been displaced.

To confront the Black Atlantic as a memory system, circulating past, present, and future, once again involves proceeding through acoustical displacement. The problem of naming James Wait in *The Nigger of the "Narcissus"* (he is first a slur, then a smudge on a manifest) returns to name *Heart of Darkness*, the slur standing in relation to darkness qua the image of skin. As a "smudge" on the ship's manifest, however, Wait's name metonymizes the many other manifests that, as Christina Sharpe describes in *In the Wake*, unnamed its passengers as cargo, objects of insurance through which human futurity is valuated, traded, and guarded against. "The loss of the indigenous name/land provides a metaphor of displacement for other human and cultural features and relations," Hortense Spillers writes of the slave ship, "including the displacement of the genitalia, the female's and the male's desire that engenders future."[22]

The smudge on the manifest of the *Narcissus* names in displacement the loss of proper name and filiation. But it also names a geopolitical extraction by empire that, in mapping and remapping, overwrites again and again in colonizing languages, sounds, and scripts the indigenous names of places and languages. Marlow recalls being a young boy and looking at a map of Africa, its "blank spaces" being overwritten by colors to become "dark," which echoes the visual phenomena of a blank (*blanc*) page written with ink. Recall that Saidiya Hartman's memoir of her experience traveling along the former routes of the Atlantic slave trade in Ghana is defined by the feeling of what it is to "lose your mother," including a phantasmatic "mother tongue," longing for "a new naming of things."[23] At the same time, Hartman suggests, the African American subject— whose surname is often derived from the slave owner—is "born with a blank space where a father's name should be." (I don't know whether Hartman intends to echo Conrad, but to the extent that *Heart of Darkness* is a primal scene of global modernism, she could hardly have escaped reading it.) This blank space makes an imputed maternal inheritance of the black subject in the American cultural imaginary nothing less than a "monstrosity":[24] Culturally and in psychanalytic theory, it is the father who gives the name.

In the *OED*, under "genitive," we find the following citation from 1955: "W. L. Westermann *Slave Syst. Greek & Rom. Antiq*. xiv. 92/1 The names of their owners appear in the genitive case after the slave names." The slave name is not the name of the father but names a possession, being in the possessive case. The genitive case: "n. (in inflected languages) a case of nouns and pronouns, and of words in grammatical agreement with them, the typical function of which is to indicate that the person or thing denoted by the word is related to another as source, possessor, or the like; (also in uninflected languages) a word or word form having a similar possessive function." It is conditioned by an ontological and biological meaning of "source" but quickly understood through the logic of property, the proper, and possession. The genitive rests on the possibility that things might belong to each other, that one might possess another.

To be sure, in the title *Heart of Darkness* something of *The Nigger of the "Narcissus"* is repeating, including the genitive case in English grammar (intensified by the fact that Conrad now sheds the article). But it is not an echo, a slapback where the first term comes back to itself through a second. Instead, there is a multiplication without series. With *Heart of Darkness*, Conrad again returns to and rewrites the problem of naming, but the two novels do not echo (repeat) so much as indicate a hole or cut in the object, fillable by the quantity of another: the fact of resonance.

Resonance involves annihilation. That an object can resonate at all means its primary openness to the vibration of other objects. But what constitutes this openness, in the case of *Heart of Darkness* resonating with *The Nigger of the "Narcissus,"* is a cut or wound. Recall that resonance is a sympathetic vibration, "the condition in which an oscillating or periodic force acting on an object or system has a frequency close to that of a natural vibration of the object." Its etymology borrows from the French to become "the reinforcement or prolongation of sound by reflection or by the synchronous vibration of a surrounding space or a neighbouring object (c1365), property of an object of giving rise to this phenomenon (1532)."[25] Resonance does not create closeness; its fact is posited on closeness but here understood as the "neighbor" and, with it, a parceled out space to be rejoined. The *OED*, we have seen, was an "eminently colonial undertaking." Linguistically, then, it becomes difficult to separate "resonance" from a relationship of subjection where one object becomes occupied and occupiable by another. The aesthetic and psychological task in *Heart of Darkness* was how to represent the cut that constitutes the colonial violence of naming.

The split subject, or the "cut" between the "I" and the "me," defines for Lacan the entry into language (and it later makes autobiography possible, when "I" takes "me" as its reflexive subject). Though imaginary, the cut is nonetheless literal, localized in genital fantasies. Lacan borrows from the Freudian primal scene, which is a threshold scene in which the child is listening in. It is an acoustical point of entry upon an event not fully understood. ("Children, in such circumstances, divine something sexual in the uncanny sounds that reach their ears,"

Freud writes in *Dora*, an uncanny sound that persists into Marlow's fantasy of the chattering black woman.)[26] For the boy who listens, this scene is triangulated by the threat of castration that underwrites his entry into language.[27]

For Spillers, however, the "black woman" is "a particular figuration of the split subject that psychoanalytic theory posits."[28] Slavery's displacement of genitalia is not merely symbolic. It owes not only to the structure of language but to the displacement of exile, the forcible entry into an imperial or colonizing language while one's "mother tongue" is extracted, stolen, or erased. The New World, she writes, is "written in blood." There is not a fantasy of castration but "a scene of *actual* mutilation, dismemberment, and exile," a "*theft* of the body" that severs it from its motive, will, and desire.[29] These attributes of the "human," Alexander Weheliye argues, are grafted onto black flesh in its always present yet receding corporeality. Lacan's move is to deliteralize castration in favor of structure; Spillers's (poststructuralist) move is to reliteralize it without losing the insight that the cut is language, the separation between word and thing.

In "The Question of Lay Analysis," Freud writes, "We know less about the sexual life of little girls than of boys. But we need not feel ashamed of this distinction; after all, the sexual life of adult women is a 'dark continent' for psychology. But we have learnt that girls feel deeply their lack of a sexual organ that is equal in value to the male one . . . and this 'envy for the penis' is the origin of a whole number of characteristic feminine reactions."[30] Barbara Johnson writes of Freud's theory, "The dream of psychoanalysis is of course to represent sexual difference as a recursive figure, a figure in which both figure and ground, male and female, are recognizable, complementary forms. This dream articulates itself through the geometry of castration in Freud in which the penis is the figure, or positive space, and the vagina the ground, or negative space."[31] But the figure of the recursive figure, Mary Ann Doane was among the first to observe,[32] is the phrase "dark continent," which appears in Freud's original text in English. This phrase marks the presence of the same text that Conrad references in titling his novel: Henry M. Stanley's nineteenth-century imperial travelogue *Through the Dark Continent*.

Both *Heart of Darkness* and *The Nigger of the "Narcissus"* are narrated by anonymous men aboard ship, but through the revelation of the figure of the black woman—who gives form or figure to the abjection of total abstraction— we enter into a precise distinction between an anonymous narrator (who is implicitly universal) and an unnamed narrator. The latter carries the resonance of the vertiginous loss of self and name. Who is the speaker of the title, *Heart of Darkness*, and what does it designate?[33] It names not a place but the violence of sexual (de)differentiation and the extraction of the name: the cut that constitutes not only language but the difference between the sexes, between the human and inhuman, and between captured and liberated subject positions, localized in (displaced to) an encrypted black feminine body. The title names a permanent and vertiginous suspension between the figural and literal, the Middle Passage through which "Europe," "America," and "Africa" were born as inextricable coordinates connected through human traffic understood as a primary sexual violence.

Recall that for Roland Barthes, "Writing is that neutral, composite, oblique space where our subject slips away, the negative [*le noir-et-blanc*] where all identity is lost, starting with the very identity of the body writing." This famous sentence is one fulfillment of the modernist dictum that the author not "tell," that he become impersonal to his text. Spillers allows us to hear another kind of resonance, a subject position in the making through another vertiginous experience of loss of identity and body where an indigenous name becomes a mark in the manifest, a book of accounting. What makes Barthes's phrase "le noir-et-blanc" translatable as "negative" is opaque, though the contrast bears within itself a dialectical and thus negating relation, a preface to Barthes's thinking on photography. Barthes's original sense might have been the blank (white) page and black ink, the blank space become filled, not unlike the map of "Africa."[34]

Historically, the "Congo" had already been renamed and reterritorialized many times over in Conrad's moment, such that it becomes impossible to cite its name properly. The year is never cited in the novel, making its moment floating to some extent. Should one then say "Congo Free State," "Belgian Congo," or "The Democratic Republic of Congo," "Léopoldville" or "Kinshasa"? Should one write "Kongo" or "Congo"? In this second question, there is an echo of the forsaken letter "K" in Conrad's Polish name, making his elision of the name Congo/Kongo a kind of signature under erasure.

For Achebe, the voice that says the racist slur between the diaries and the fiction is the voice of Conrad. Achebe grounds the voice of Conrad in the diary, which then functions as a kind of control that allows Achebe's argument to move between fiction's narrative levels, the voice of Conrad attributable to and speaking through Marlow, the sailor who tells a story aboard ship, then reported by a second man, an anonymous "frame" narrator who listens to Marlow. For Achebe, he and the anonymous narrator each speak in *one voice*; there is not a "frame" but what Achebe calls a *cordon sanitaire* that protects Conrad from articulating in his own voice Marlow's worst, racist, and diseased sentiments.

In Chapter 2, however, we confronted the difficulty of locating the first-person voice except through *echolocation*. We followed the echo of the racist slur as an audiovisual shard of a disavowed melancholic desire for a black, male object, an echo whose origins were not only impossible to locate but structural in proportion. In this chapter, we are interested instead in how resonance and vibration relate not only to the *cut*, where a sound is in the middle of becoming a word, but the transatlantic memory of the flesh, where a body is in the middle of becoming a thing, a sexually undifferentiated object to be possessed. What kind of literary form can become *proper* to this fact of expropriation?

SINISTER RESONANCE

In the "Author's Note" to *Heart of Darkness*, the kind of text that is supposed to channel and verify an authorial voice, Conrad indicates that something of the novel's form is not conceivable at all as a "voice" but as a sound. He concludes the note just after evading any direct account of the beginnings of Marlow as the fictitious sailor who narrates *Heart of Darkness* and his earlier short story "Youth." We can approach this "Author's Note" as what Freud might call a "screen memory," where one memory (in this case, the birth of Marlow) protects consciousness from another memory—a different kind of impetus than a *cordon sanitaire*. Conrad asserts a kind of "autobiographical pact," as Philippe Lejeune might say, in which, as Tonya Blowers helpfully summarizes it, "the author's name," attributed to "both protagonist and narrator," posits the "truth, sincerity and intention" of the text.[35] But then Conrad undoes it:

> "Youth" is a feat of memory. It is a *record* of experience: but that experience, in its *facts*, in its inwardness and in its outward colouring, begins and ends in myself. "Heart of Darkness" is experience, too; but it is experience pushed a little (and only a little) beyond the actual *facts* of the case for the perfectly legitimate, I believe, purpose of *bringing it home* to the minds and bosoms of the readers. There was no longer a matter of sincere colouring. It was like another art altogether. That sombre theme had to be given a sinister resonance, a tonality of its own, a continued vibration that, I hoped, would hang in the air and dwell on the ear after the last note had been struck. (*Y*, xi)[36]

In the preface to *The Nigger of the "Narcissus,"* Conrad argues that the genre of the novel strives toward the "magic suggestiveness of music." Here, however, he becomes interested in a single musical quantum: the note. Across the philosophical tradition, melody is the "supreme example," Katherine Bergeron writes, of "a substance capable of preserving itself in decay," being both *nota* and *vox*, both inscriptive and sounding.[37] What kind of substance, then, is a sinister resonance? Conrad indicates something of music, but he does not name it "counterpoint" (the term that gives Edward Said his famous notion of contrapuntal analysis). Nor does he name it "melody." He names it a "note" but also some sonic space and duration that is *not* the note and instead its decay, its vibratory aftereffect, "a continued vibration that, I hoped, would hang in the air and dwell on the ear after the last note had been struck."[38]

In music studies, Michael Gallope writes, "the English word 'note,' the German *die Note*, the Italian *nota*, or the French *note* generally prescribes the execution of a single musical sound, and implies a normative medium of musical notion."[39] Gallope continues:

> As a condition for its intelligibility, then, the musical note relies upon a metaphysical structure: tones that are played—physically stretched and sustained—are taken, understood, and even ontologically reified as being identical with their discrete visual insignia. Because English translations of "tone" were written during the past half century, one might speculate that, by then, the medium of musical notation was so naturalized as a musical a priori in ordinary language that a tone could not be thought of otherwise than as a note.[40]

Conrad's note places him somewhat unexpectedly in the history of modern physics as it was intersecting with modern European discourses of music (for example, in Herman von Helmholtz's *Tonempfindungen*, based on his experiments with the resonator through which he discovered that sonic phenomena are materially outside of the ear and that the ear is tympanic, which is to say, resonant).[41] Conrad's "Author's Note" articulates the lost meanings of tone as what Gallope calls "a living dialectical practice, as a term with a range of meanings, with the *range* being essential to its meaning."[42]

Conrad rephrases himself three times, naming "a sinister resonance," "a tonality of its own," "a continued vibration." Conrad's "Note" articulates meaning as range. In that range of meaning, he communicates his linguistic project. It breaks from "the philological presumption of a connection between language and the people."[43] The sinister resonance is not a word, voice, or name. It is a phonic substance caught between meanings, traditions, lands, and languages. The "note" begins to figure words that share its root: annotation, denotation, and connotation. In naming "another art altogether," Conrad points toward connotation itself, or the work by which, through figures, one quantity stands in for another or is brought into existence by another: in sum, the figurative work of language.[44]

The shouting black woman aboard the steamer points and gesticulates. In pointing, she points to herself. What is Conrad's phrase "sombre theme" meant to remember, figure, point toward, and eulogize? On the face of things, it is human atrocity. This atrocity will not be laid bare or made visible. This atrocity will be encapsulated by—or communicated through—the most intimate material there is, an "inner ear sound." For Toni Morrison, the inner ear sound of a novel is a sense of rhythm mandated by sentence structure. Yet what Conrad describes is closer to what the anonymous narrator of *Lord Jim* calls "less than a sound, hardly more than a vibration" when he recounts the disaster at sea that vibrates the ship, just before he disappears into the novel's structure, handing the narrative over to Marlow (*LJ*, 32).[45] He listens where the men eager for juridical "facts" cannot; the event is "open to the senses," visible and "something else besides, something invisible" (*LJ*, 30–31).

The memory of atrocity cannot be communicated directly as a "record of experience," a phrase that, in Conrad's moment, already had phonographic implications. It maintains its double valence as the surface onto which marks are inscribed and the document that evidences. Yet sinister resonance and continued vibration are indications that something has been recorded but not yet registered—they are not aspects of a recording of experience. Could the story become an object of memory or remembrance in the proper sense, it could be told and sequestered. The critical theorist Cathy Caruth makes clear in *Unclaimed Experiences* that trauma's mode of communicating, its "voice," is the wound. It speaks through a wound.[46] *Heart of Darkness* is a text that communicates its wound by wounding. The status of the wound as what we might call a *resonator* will have profound bearing upon the aurality of *Heart of Darkness*. Resonance and vibration are objects that, by definition, take time. Conrad came to this definition of his novel and its art in a much-delayed way, writing the preface long after completing the novel. It is as if the writing of the novel was not, for him, totally complete, as if some act of hearing was still ongoing and would yet continue. A vibration continues; a note hangs. Where (in what kind of space) and for how long?

In describing *Heart of Darkness* as a sound dwelling "on the ear," Conrad recognizes that the novel is something other than form as traditionally conceived, that it operates within the structure of communication that, with Saussure, is universalized: the circuit between phonation and audition. The sinister resonance is nothing like the "noise" that a signal must overcome or be shielded from if it is to be communicated. The sinister resonance presupposes some remainder of the informational field. In describing form through the qualities of sounds that "hang . . . long after," Conrad begins from that premise. It is not secondary to the novel but primary. It assumes for itself its own leftover as form, but that assumption is in no way a subsumption: The *sinister* resonance persists in its status as other; it cannot be fully internalized as a story. If it did not, the work would merely be said to "resonate."

There is in the word "sinister," then, both a connotation and a displacement. There is some avoidance of pronouncing another word.[47] Ethnocentric, it figures without directly naming a racialized content but also some libidinal experience in memory. But as it displaces, it connotes the left side, something left aside. Writing by hand, the writer was limited, one hand lying limp, flaccid, and useless. (As a piano player, Kurtz would have been endowed with "sinister dexterity," as Herman Melville might say, a two-handedness.) Cutting across languages and cultures, the left or sinister hand conjures evil. Notions of the left side proliferate words in their wake, for "even words with happy meanings, when applied by antiphrasis to the left, are quickly contaminated by what they express and acquire a 'sinister' quality which soon forbids their use."[48] More recent words, such as the English *droit* (from the Latin *directum*), expresses "the idea of a force which goes straight to its object."[49] The continued vibration is a force, but its movement is indirect; it does not go straight to the object; it contaminates, proliferates, and returns after having been gone. The sinister resonance is "torturous, oblique, and abortive," it is "the *outside*, the infinite, hostile."[50] In drumming, among the Wulwanga tribe of Australia, the right hand holds the stick that strikes (the man), the left being the stick (the woman) that receives blows. The right hand receives benediction in Genesis, while the left both annuls and propagates death.[51] In English culture, the left hand is put under the right in polite embrace—the left hand is therefore "underhanded," both being underneath but threatening return and dominance.

Sinister resonance and continued vibration name not a repetition but a sub-aural movement of a *substance*, its continued, transhistorical action at a distance: blackness understood as vertiginously constituted in relation to what Rizvana Bradley calls "the violent racing of sexual difference," the black woman as an uncanny because absent figure and body whose force is the means of the "fleshing out of form."[52] That is why I suggested in the Intersonority that *Heart of Darkness* is incomplete without *The Souls of Black Folk*, a work whose form is inconceivable without the black feminine. The sinister resonance is dual, split: it both hangs in the air and dwells on the ear. It announces and subtends. It is undecidable whether it is inside or outside, in or on, neighboring or dwelling.

Here, we are in a domain quite different from that posited by the conception of communication in the rational tradition, whereby the voice communicates and transmits itself in unidirectional ways and in neutral space to the listening subject, who absorbs it. The familiar ur-image of "the dream of communication," as Geoffrey Hartman and many others have named it,[53] may be stated according to a theorem: "The ADDRESSER sends a MESSAGE to the ADDRESSEE."[54] It travels through without losing any time. The sinister resonance exists in the domain that Saussure's theory of language names as "impossible" with regard to what fundamentally constitutes language. Saussure writes: "In any case, it is impossible that sound, as a material element, should in itself be part of the language. Sound is merely something ancillary, a material the language uses. [*D'ailleurs il est impossible que le son, élément matériel appartienne lui-même à la langue. Il n'est pour elle qu'une chose secondaire, une matière qu'elle met un œuvre.*] . . . Linguistic signals are not in essence phonetic. They are not physical in any way. They are constituted solely by differences which distinguish one such sound pattern [*image acoustique*] from another."[55]

In his seminal pursuit of a theory of black sound in the radical tradition, Freud Moten returns to Saussure to retrieve the exclusion in a captured woman's shriek: "the resistance of the object."[56] This exclusion has special bearing on the split character of the sinister resonance. Black sound in *Heart of Darkness* is, first, the material envelope of Marlow's discoursing voice—the formal womb through which it is born (*Geburt*) in narrative time—and, second, the residue of its dialogic form and narrative voice—the containment of accent, of what the neutral voice must shed to become itself.

Of the circuit of communication between two speakers (Figure 8), Saussure says that we must distinguish "the sound patterns of words and the concepts," which are psychological, from "actual sounds," which he does not render for the simple reason that the diagram has "included only those elements considered essential."[57] The circuit is nonetheless thought to encompass an unrepresented outer rim of "sound vibrations passing from mouth to ear."[58]

Communication takes what it needs. It is not that the circuit disposes of the waves and vibrations in a word's "material envelope." The linguistic signal sheds its material dependency. Sound (in pronunciation and accent) is carried along with it and remains in a kind of indisposed state; it is "irrelevant."[59] We can include in this irrelevance the acoustic space through which the signal travels.

That is how it becomes possible to conceive of the autonomous field of inner "speech." In the adequation between the inner and its mode of expression, nothing, no errant vibration, is left behind; the resonance is total and pure. When I say "that resonates with me," I say that your words have become for a moment adequate to my inner life. Sinister resonance appropriates this adequation to become a sign of the outside: the hanging in the air and dwelling on the ear.

The metaphors "continued vibration" and "sinister resonance" thus posit a figure of transmission that is itself a sinisterly resonant formation of the rational tradition. This is why I suggest that *Heart of Darkness* is something other than a story, "voice," or message, the idealized image held by Conrad's narrator who still believes in the epic journey—when the story begins—of the possibility of leaving home and returning fully, unchanged, in a circle. Instead, the narration of the journey opens the circuit to some other tangent and movement.

Yet there is, beyond this outer rim, a series of errant vibrations irreducible to the word's equally occluded material "envelope" (another name, Luce Irigaray suggests, for "womb").[60] One thing is clear: In such schema, nothing can be recuperated of what falls errantly or fugitively outside of the circuit. In hanging "in the air" and dwelling "on the ear," the sinister resonance lives in this outer rim. The content of *Heart of Darkness* is the extraction of language and the name. What is left behind is waste, the waste of signifying in a so-called brute materiality (what is brute about the leftover material if not that it is improper—not only cries, howls, and shrieks, but the materiality of conveyance itself?). The sinister resonance is a voice that has lost determination to become an acoustic register.

Marlow is tasked with being the hearer and bearer of Kurtz's last words in death. He is continually haunted by a distance in the assumption of Kurtz's voice; he can never make the voice his own. Marlow ventriloquizes and recognizes that he is outside the voice that, through the medium of the last words, is inside him. It is here that Conrad communicates his most forceful critique of autocracy and empire. In the autonomous is the sonic trace of the heteronomous, what cannot become "my voice," what cannot be captured within the sphere of speaking as myself. There is something of listening that is, by definition, subject to the erotic tie. The autoaffective begins as the desire to take in, to consume (but twinned by the desire to be consumed).[61] In Marlow's desire to hear Kurtz, he experiences

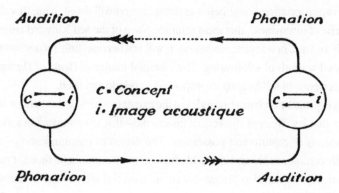

Figure 8

the belong-to-me desire for a voice. It is a desire that, in the Western tradition, begins with Homer and Odysseus's desire to preserve the sound of the Sirens. In Conrad's acoustical imaginary, the Sirens sang "in the darkness," the night "full of strange murmurs, bidding him go and tell all men."[62]

As Marlow recedes into the preoedipal dark aboard the ship to tell the story of Kurtz to the other men who are listening, something is happening to structure itself as it affords narrative levels. Their fundamental quality, for Genette, is that they stay in place. Genette gets to the heart of the structuralist project when he describes levels (narrating, narrative, story) as "a shifting but sacred frontier between two worlds."[63] In *Heart of Darkness*, narrative levels resonate; they resonate from "there" and "then" to "here" and "now." What Conrad perhaps felt—writing in a moment of technological adaptation to the wireless imagination—is that the form of his novel must be an open and incomplete one if it is to interrupt the imperial dream of communication. This dream is not only of transmission but of reproduction, the dream of what Edison, in "The Phonograph and Its Future," called "the almost universal application of the foundation principle, namely, the gathering up and retaining of sounds hitherto fugitive, and their reproduction at will."[64] This foundational principle is the extraction of sound and language.

As a sinister resonance and continued vibration, *Heart of Darkness* takes up and appropriates for itself—between itself as resonance—the condition of possibility of reading conceived as an inward experience. It appropriates self-hearing. In resonance and vibration, form gives way to a *structure of occurrence*. A structure of occurrence relates to the experience of reading understood as a form of quasi-audition and self-audition. A sinister resonance is a duration, or a dwelling and hanging of a residue of a sound for some indeterminate, long time. In a negative aesthetic, that it takes time (*langweilig*) is boring.[65] In the time it takes, the form is appropriative: Some heterogeneous sound will dwell, hang. It will take the shape of inwardness, that most intimate place of the self's inward animation of itself. But as a heterogeneous sound, it will not become fully reconciled to the contained warmth of self-hearing. The essential matter of *Heart of Darkness* is the experience of self-hearing expropriated in relation to itself.

This expropriation is just one index of the extent to which Conrad understood—in ways that few Western thinkers of his era did—that communication's motivating dream is of capture and possession. The dream of communication—of the perfectly communicable and indexable fugitive voice—cannot be thought outside of coloniality in general as primitive accumulation and the extraction of material.

For colonialism to operate, that is, to develop its protocols, it must steal material and land but also sounds, voices, and languages. If communication is to operate, it must radically reduce the scope and meaning of the sound of the voice in its claim to "humanity."

But if the content of *Heart of Darkness* is extracted language, in the infinite adaptability of extraction, then this content still continues into while also absorbing, extracting, and adapting to our moment. It is as yet incomplete. One need only remember that, today, minerals are extracted from the Congo to produce the smartphone, coltan mined by bare hands, in order for the truth of *Heart of Darkness* to be brought home as the resonating and vibrating "center" of a still-continuing history of telecommunication as the extraction of material and captured speech. The title names the impossible genitive coordinate that is the Middle Passage: not a place but an ongoing, world-constituting displacement of voices, sounds, scripts, and languages.

Again, Hegel has something to tell us about the vibration upon which communication depends. (The significance of invoking Hegel in this context rests upon the Intersonority and its discussion of W. E. B. Du Bois, who notes that Hegel denied Africa a world-historical trajectory, which Du Bois restores through the matrix of sorrow song.) Vibration, as invoked by Hegel's *Lectures on Aesthetics*, is fundamentally violent. Sound exists in the "cancellation of space," unlike painting, which is "peaceful and undesiring" in its spatiality. Hegel writes: "The cancellation [*Aufhebung*] of space therefore consists here only in the fact that a specific sensuous material sacrifices its peaceful separatedness, turns to movement, yet so vibrates in itself that every part of the cohering body not only changes its place but also struggles to replace itself in its former position. The result of this oscillating vibration is a sound or note [*Ton*], the material of music."[66]

In its struggle to replace itself in a former position, vibration mediates a transformation in listening consciousness, in inwardness.[67] The result of this struggle is *Ton*, the most well-ordered, Pythagorean, and suggestive of moments.[68] That is why it is misleading for T. M. Knox to translate it as "sound or note."

What Hegel calls the "heavy matter" of sound (as *Klang*)—the sensual origins of tone—cannot be fully absorbed by the ideal. "At no point could the tone leave behind the raw material of its sensual origins," writes Gallope.[69] Music requires the heterogeneous material of sound for its instantiation, and though what one "feels" is Spirit, it never sheds its vibratory and oscillatory character, its violent "inner trembling" in the cancellation of space.[70] When Conrad posits the novel as a "continued vibration," he posits a form that does not leave behind its sensual origin. The novel that vibrates is a cohering body that is also oscillatory. It is a physical fact that the page carries an infrasound, some inaudible, but palpable vibration and frequency that makes contact through touch, and an acousticality, which shares in sound without sounding.

NARRATIVE, METAPHOR, TRANSDUCTION

Conrad's concept of novelistic form as sinister resonance absents itself from two key figures of listening in the Western tradition while also leaving them in the space of the novel as empty husks: the voice of the storyteller and the voice of the pedagogical master. In "The Storyteller," Walter Benjamin describes at length the communication of "mouth to mouth" tales whose strength is nonexpendable. Unlike information, the story "does not aim to convey the pure essence of the thing," but is preserved, concentrated, and released in its potency after a long time.[71] Through the gift of listening, these stories return to us, after having been received in moments of boredom and lulled attention; they carry the propensity to be repeated, and retelling "comes . . . all by itself."[72] Central to their ontology is "counsel" (*Rat*) as a form of internationalization. I take in what the storyteller says and it later returns to me when needed as a precept for action. Benjamin laments not only the loss of stories in modernity, then, but a limitation in and destruction of lived experience that might become an object of storytelling and counsel. He invokes men returning from modern warfare shattered and mute, unable to communicate their experiences except as traumatic repetition (a "profound perplexity," or *tiefe Ratslösigkeit*). "After all, counsel is less an answer to a question than a proposal concerning the continuation [*Fortsetzung*] of a story which is just unfolding. To seek this counsel, one would first have to be able to tell the story. (Quite apart from the fact that a man is receptive to counsel only to the extent that he allows his situation to speak)."[73]

Before anything that might be called a "story," there is a material transmutation of an empirical situation into a voice, either an audible or legible event.[74] The raw material of experience is converted. That one "be able to tell" is a first condition, a kind of capacity for the conversion of experience into language. This conversion grounds storytelling as ethos. (Even in solitude, one tells stories to oneself in soliloquy.)

Benjamin's conception of the story, in this way, does not depart greatly from foundational conceptions of vocal transmission in the rational tradition explored in this book. In the Western philosophical tradition, if you are *in my ear*, you are inside me in the most idealized sense; you are there even when you are not.

This is why Plato says thought is internal dialogue: Thought continually gives the impression we are answering to someone.[75] For the Stoics, Michel Foucault writes, "listening is the first moment of the process by which the truth which has been heard, listened to, and properly taken in, sinks into the subject so to speak, becomes embedded in him and begins to become *suus* (to become his own) and thus forms the matrix for *ēthos*."[76] It resonates, for it is now "in" me. All hearing, according to Plutarch, is ambiguous, being both the most *pathetikos* and *logikos* of the senses. It demands that the ear be trained not to admit the adverse, such that hearing is split.[77] Benjamin also retrieves an ambiguity within the historical origin of the novel in epic memory, thought to be divided between voluntary and involuntary impulses: the dedicative, or "remembrance," and the diffuse, or "reminiscence." It is through this split that novels may touch ambiguity through an anonymous voice, which "resounds."[78] Such resonance is to be distinguished from the genitive (*suus*, one's own) movement of counsel.

The narrative structure of *Heart of Darkness* is essentially Platonic: Marlow sits aboard the *Nellie* and posits to his listeners the memory of another voice, authoritative and pedagogical. (Marlow continually describes his desire to hear Kurtz speak in the way one desires to hear a master.) Across the dialogues, Plato teaches that to transform the master's speech into one's own, particularly in the development of ethos, is the work of idealization. This self-subjectivation (to the master's voice that becomes one's own) is nothing but the reduction of the space of the outside: to be able to hear oneself think and speak.

However, Kurtz's last words and dying anaphora resist sinking in; they may be recorded and repeated but not embedded or internalized as the basis of ethos, that is, idealized. In narrating his situation, in telling his story, Marlow neither seeks nor provides counsel. Yet the baseline condition of the concept of the written *récit*, or recitation, is that someone, anonymous or named, remembers.[79] As the men sit at the threshold of the Thames, where the river touches the sea, the Atlantic here being also the Black Atlantic, we are not given names or any sense of specificity. There is already an act of censure, a remembering that is also a forgetting, as if the journey is not willing to be totally converted whatsoever into a story. Someone is making himself empty for listening. He is changing, the insensible becoming sensible. The sinister resonance is not a storytelling voice. It is an acoustic register, a voice that has lost its determination. It is the leftover of the work of internalization as such.

Heidegger, for whom conscience is above all a "call," helps us clarify *Heart of Darkness* as a nodal, transformative point in the long tradition and history of inner speech in the West when he writes of the deep connection between hearing and understanding: "Hearing even constitutes the primary and authentic openness of Da-sein for its ownmost possibility of being, as in hearing the voice of the friend that whom Da-sein carries with it [*als Hören der Stimme des Freundes, den jedes Dasein bei sich trägt*]."[80] Conscience is a soundless inner voice whose call is intimately known and heard only by me. When Heidegger invokes existence as it "carries" (*tragen*) the voice of a friend, however, he invokes the archaic meaning of "metaphor" in Greek, "meta" (between) + "phero" (to carry or *transfer*). Some quantity of the "inner" has been carried and transferred across a distance. In the root of metaphor itself is transmission, a vibration. Even the voice that is most intimately mine includes some sense of self-distancing. Such an experience Kaja Silverman might name, after Benjamin's concept of the aura, "identity-at-a-distance."[81]

In carrying the last words of Kurtz, Marlow is carrying home something other than this "voice of a friend." As he begins to tell his story, this inner distance becomes sensible as distance. The very narrow gap that the self requires to relate to itself, in the tight circle of "hearing (understanding) oneself speak," now becomes a chasm. In the "Author's Note," Conrad calls Marlow a "personator" and "whispering daemon" (*Y*, ix). The aural implications of the classical figure of the daimon could not have been lost on him when he writes that Marlow "haunts my hours of solitude, when, in silence, we lay our heads together in great comfort and in harmony; but as we part at the end of a tale I am never sure that it may not be for the last time. Yet I don't think either of us would care much to survive the other" (*Y*, x). Plato suggests across multiple works that Socrates's daimon, his companion and "strange god," is heard, but never seen, and that this voice, though experienced inwardly, has the curious quality of coming from the outside: "A sort of voice (*phonê*) comes, which, whenever it does come, always holds me back from what I am about to do but never urges me forward."[82] The daimon is phonetic but not semantic, less a voice than a sound. One wonders if this voice "speaks" at all or if it is not instead an activity suspended just before speech, a holding back, as in the *tacet* direction of a musical score indicating that an instrument should "keep quiet" (the direction made famous by John Cage's silent work for piano). In calling Marlow a whispering daimon, Conrad does not mark Marlow as a version of the self[83] but rather marks the paradoxical intimacy between him and a voice that is also coming to him through a distance. The etymology of daimon is uncertain, but the philosopher Giorgio Agamben considers it according to a root in the verb *daiomai*, "to divide, lacerate."[84] The daimon, according to the classicist Robert Laynton, is the distribution or allotment of destinies, which is all important to our sense in *The Fact of Resonance* that the acousmatic carries a political potency in its quality of not yet being seen.[85]

This voice cannot be commanded or mastered: Marlow for Conrad is a call of existential proportions, even though Marlow himself has missed the call, Conrad recreating the pairing in the text through the narrator. But to the extent that the narrator registers Marlow's insensitivity, the reader now mirrors or echoes that pairing. The sinister resonance is the continuation of that sense that some indeterminate counterpart to my consciousness exists outside of me, outside of the tight enclosure of the autoaffection suddenly become resonant and open.

But from the beginning of the novel (and into its circular conclusion, which takes us back to the beginning, the men still waiting for the turn of the tide), Conrad makes it clear that to carry and transmit across distance is also necessary to the commodity form under colonialism and global capital. These two epistemologies, existential and colonial, define the split event of listening in *Heart of Darkness*. The narrator—who is also a listener—becomes aware that Marlow carries back not simply a story but a heterogeneous quantity of voice, a voice whose reception makes sensible in his own consciousness the fact of social reproduction at a distance: the cultural, economic, sentimental, and domestic dependency on the subjugated other he cannot see.

For there to be understanding and, with it, the "someone" who can hear, there first must be a "resonance," as an event of self-hearing, consciousness being-for-itself in its immediacy.[86] The *sinister* resonance lies in the secondary sense that, as Fanon might say, "the other is waiting for recognition by us."[87] This is perhaps why one has the feeling that the narrative ends in a circle that just misses its touching point, becoming a spiral.

The recitation aboard the *Nellie* takes place in a transitional dimension of metaphor. The prefix "trans-"—in "transition" but also "transmission" and "translation"—means "to carry over across." It is no longer appropriate to speak, then, of what Genette and Barthes both call narrative "levels." This is a fundamentally optical figure. The unnamed narrator is perhaps less a voice (he speaks but three times after the introduction of Marlow) than he is *resonator*. An acoustic resonator is the hollow part of the musical instrument that "reinforces and amplifies sounds."[88] As "another art altogether," sinister resonance involves the traversal across distance of a profane sound as *the condition of a colonial consciousness becoming a postcolonial consciousness*. The novel cannot become fully reconciled to its own movement. It becomes formalizable only in its aftereffect—the note that "hangs" in the air long after.

In Chapter 1, I argued that this resonance is there in the opening shout across a river of a subaltern woman. In Chapter 2, we found it in the interruptive shout of a black mate across the ship's deck. In both instances, Conrad introduces profanity, a heterogeneous movement and propagation of verbal sound in space. Propagation is to be contrasted with transmission as a unidirectional and authoritative transmission. It could be so wide as to be a matter of hundreds of miles or so minute as to be "the space of a breath" (*NN*, 16). It is carrying, vibrating. "Continued vibration" and "sinister resonance"—these are simply metaphors. The printed text emits no physical sound (though all matter, being waves, vibrates). But in metaphorizing *Heart of Darkness* in this way, Conrad redefines the form of the European novel and returns to its materiality in the archaic meaning of metaphor as transfer, bringing over across, but bringing over across a self-consciousness that, in the course of bearing this form as an aftereffect—in listening and reading—will become changed in relation to itself: identity-at-a-distance.

Perhaps, then, this profane sound is in fact a physical activity, beginning with its erotic charge (Eros, neither a god nor mortal but a "mediator" between the two).[89] The electric potential of coltan also brings us into a translative space. The capacitor it creates is, in simple terms, a holder of capacity; it is what a device requires to retain its charge. (Consider, for example, the kind of affective substance designated when the Kenyan novelist Ngugi wa Thiong'o says that he had stopped reading Conrad, whose "image of Africa" repelled him before it once again recalled him; Conrad's work, he writes, "still has strong resonance today.")[90] In relation to resonance, we can also consider transduction, which the media theorist Stefan Helmreich describes as the qualitative transformation of sound in its energetic substrate "as it traverses media" (in microphones and telephones). Transduction originates in the Latin *transducere*, "'to lead across, transfer,' out of *trans*, 'across to or on the farther side of, beyond, over' + *ducere*, 'to lead.'"[91] At its base, "sound is a form of energy transmitted through a medium."[92] Transduction involves a quantity and its qualitative conversion, at times bringing the inaudible into the audible realm, or infrasound (as vibration) above the threshold of human hearing. But in our case this medium is consciousness itself. At stake is how narrative becomes both a (h)ear(t) and a resonator (at the heart of "heart" is "ear," an optical slippage)[93] and how, in becoming a resonator, the insensible becomes sensible. The heart is heard.

Historically, this novel is situated between the decline of storytelling and the rise of telecommunication: a "proto-telephony."[94] There is some fundamental confusion, then, between resonance and transduction, between an acoustic amplification and the conversion of energy. Marlow's silent listener is, as transducer, a medium situated between being and nonbeing.

MINIMAL DIEGESIS

Heart of Darkness begins in twilight, a transformative hinge. "The sea-reach of the Thames stretched before us like the beginning of an interminable waterway. In the offing the sea and the sky were welded together without a joint" (*Y*, 45). The narrative begins in relation to an unseen coordinate: imperial space as it stretches out in the sea reaches to touch the site of beginning—the site of the sovereign voice of narrative genesis. The River Thames is the site of the production of discourse, the closest point to the "here" of the diegetic present, and it touches the river that goes unnamed in the novel, the Congo River, as the site of the production of the story, or "there," the point farthest from the location of the diegetic present. The entirety of the discourse transpires at the threshold of here and there, waiting and acting, speaking and listening, seeing and receding, as the sun traces its course from east to west. An unnamed narrator recalls having listened to Marlow tell a story of another imperial journey, its river and ship, and the pursuit of another man, Kurtz. As the scene grows dark, Marlow returns to the space and time of storytelling to address his listeners directly, saying to them, "'you see me, whom you know'."

Situated on the other side of this address (the "other side of language"), the narrator remembers having listened in the dark:

> It had become so pitch dark that we listeners could hardly see one another. For a long time already he, sitting apart, had been no more to us than a voice. There was not a word from anybody. The others might have been asleep, but I was awake. I listened, I listened on the watch for the sentence, for the word, that would give me the clue to the faint uneasiness inspired by this narrative that seemed to shape itself without human lips in the heavy night-air of the river. (*Y*, 43)

Conrad places a speaker and listener in the scene, and they become nearly invisible to each other. Once again, he makes space for an aesthetic principle for which "impersonality" has no descriptive power. It is not an oral event in the strict sense, nor is it visual. It neither shows nor tells but sounds. It is aural. Here, as elsewhere, the essential content of *Heart of Darkness* is its form: the experience of self-hearing, confronted, changed, and, above all, expropriated in relation to itself. The anonymous listener begins as being content with the narratives of conquest handed down to him, recalling Sir Francis Drake and Sir John Franklin, "knights all," as they once moved along the same waters that "had borne all the ships whose names are like jewels" (*Y*, 47). He believes himself to be autonomous and, though he goes unnamed, to be proper to himself, with a self-enclosed identity that participates only in the long order of things and rightful domination.

Heart of Darkness is a tale of self-hearing's alternative destiny, of its foreclosed possibilities of listening to the other and to the self. This possibility involves what it means to listen to oneself and to another as something more than a relic of a loss, where in the other one is only finding and listening to a narcissistic version of oneself.

A narrative voice that neither shows nor tells demands that we revise the concepts of a narrative voice and of diegesis. In its purest diegetic function, narrative voice regulates time. It produces an invisible barrier between the time of the story and the time of the discourse. Here, as Marlow speaks in the dark to the unnamed other who is listening, the barrier itself becomes the object of narration, which is striving for some opening in its own discursiveness. In twilight and darkness, the edges of visible bodies dissolve. The narrator's "we" is held together by some fragile mode of address; through the anonymous narrator not as a point of view but as a point of audition, we are placed in the scene.

We find ourselves "there" in a written but also acoustical correlate of anamorphosis. Lacan developed the psychic concept of anamorphosis when commenting upon the skull that sits in the corner of Holbein's painting *The Ambassadors*, the skull being an anamorphic object visible only from a certain angle.[95] After Marlow has spoken for nearly 11,000 words, lulling the reader into a mimetic illusion, the unnamed narrator suddenly interrupts to remind us that he was there, listening and mediating the scene. In such moments, Conrad deals in an acoustical counterpart to the skull as it localizes an object gaze by which it is possible to feel "seen" by looking. In this acoustical counterpart (which was already implied by Jean-Paul Sartre's original formulation of the gaze),[96] we are emplaced so as to listen to listening—to hear someone hearing someone hearing. Painting's anamorphotic object spatially implicates the viewer in the presented scene and its visibility, but the acoustical counterpart instead locates the hearer in what Anne Cheng calls "one of the only physical activities of the human body that occurs simultaneously inside and outside the body," as we found in Chapter 2.

My premise in this book has been that reading is a resonant event, one that implies various modes of listening and sensation. My concern here is with an object of audition, one that, if it exists, would always be partially inward, presenting itself in the subject's self-hearing, implicated more fully in self-consciousness as it relates to acoustic self-perception.

In speaking, I experience directly or indirectly a demand for voice. For Derrida, consciousness forgets or fails to sense the heterogeneous beginnings of the seductive, closed-circuit autonomy he named "hearing (understanding) oneself speak." "It produces a signifier which seems not to fall into the world, outside the ideality of the signified, but to remain sheltered—even in the moment that it attains the audiophonic system of the other—within the pure interiority of auto-affection. It does not fall into the exteriority of space, into what one calls the world, which is nothing but the outside of speech."[97] To be sure, Marlow is a "storyteller" and spins a yarn for the men who listen to him. But something of the *scene* of storytelling—its physical situation—is unseen. It is the charge of the primal scene as it was understood by Freud, a traumatic and paradigmatic inflection and induction of the senses. Unseen sounds forever introduce into hearing oneself the memory of the outside.

Such is the case in one of the most famous dreams analyzed by Freud, one whose contours I have suggested we confront in Du Bois. Sergei Pankejeff (the "Wolf Man") recalls dreaming as a young boy that he was lying in bed at night near a window that slowly opened to reveal a tree of white wolves. Silent and staring, they sat with ears "pricked" (*aufgestellt*). Pricked toward what? The young boy couldn't hear, but he sensed the wolves must have been responding to some sound in the distance, perhaps a cry.[98] In the Wolf Man's case, it is impossible, Freud writes, for "a deferred revision of the impressions so received to penetrate the understanding."[99] The critical theorist Mladen Dolar pursues the implications of such an unclosed gap or temporal lag between hearing and understanding. In Dolar's estimation, this gap in impressions cannot be closed or healed, and for Lacan, it also orients the failure of the symbolic order to bring the imaginary order to language. From this moment forward, the subject is split, listening in a dual posture for the threat of danger and the promise of pleasure.[100]

Speaking aboard ship, Marlow becomes not, as Dolar might say, "a voice and nothing more," the so-called object voice that, in its absence, is essentially mute.[101] He becomes for his listener aboard ship a vibration and a sound, a faint uneasiness, an atmosphere: "Forthwith a change came over the waters" just before he speaks (*Y*, 46). In French, *acousmatique* simply designates "listening to sounds whose origin one cannot see, the acoustic equivalent of indirect lighting."[102] To be sure, the acoustics aboard the *Nellie* have this merely sensory or less weighty inflection. There has been much commentary on the anonymous narrator's sense that Marlow's tale is akin to the "a glow [that] brings out a haze"

(Y, 48). But with the sounding of his voice aboard ship first in the twilight air and then in dusk and darkness, Marlow becomes also the "acoustic equivalent" of this glow. With the disappearance of Marlow's body and face, some fragile substance persists, the narrator concentrating on its minimal appearance in the diegesis, which is usually reserved for the space of action, description, and dialogue. In the weightiness of the minor inflection, of mere atmosphere, neither dialogue nor monologue are at issue but rather what Lacoue-Labarthe suggestively names, without exploring in detail, a "minimal diegesis."[103] What makes it minimal? To what is the diegesis reduced?

It is reduced to listening and to the implications of that reduction for the narrative it produces. In the Intersonority, I described how, recording the concrete sounds of things in the world and editing them on tape, Pierre Schaeffer theorized acousmatic acts of "reduced listening." Defamiliarized and severed from its visual source, sound becomes an object in its own right, *l'objet sonore*. In relation to the sonorous object, Schaeffer suggests, the subject is no longer listening to preconceived objects but is listening to listening. The sonorous object allows a listener to bracket the world in order to be able to concentrate solely on sonorous properties.[104] Through this object, the listener perceives not the sound itself but "the perception itself," such that I perceive that I am perceiving. The acousmatic, then, is to be differentiated from the acoustic, which is a purely physical event.[105]

But Schaefferian "reduction," localized in consciousness in this way, is also phenomenological.[106] Schaeffer's theory is not entirely applicable to a theory of the novel's object audition, in part because it further consolidates the place of what Adriana Cavarero calls "the phantasm of the *subject*," a "fictitious entity" generated by signification.[107] It is the entity shared by narrative theory in its grounding presupposition of a disembodied "voice" and its reflexive instance. Ultimately, the phantasm of the subject, which Cavarero traces to the silence of the Cartesian *cogito*, cannot be separated from what we found in Chapter 1 to be, in Mary Louise Pratt's phrase, the "monarch-of-all-I-survey."

Conrad's concern in *Heart of Darkness* is the subject's *minimalization*, where the fictitious entity that supports Marlow in his initial enterprise—his imperial "I" and imperial ear—are diminished.

His subjectivity, his sense of autonomy, is reduced by listening. Aboard the *Nellie*, the men gather, to some extent, in an acousmatic situation: They hear Marlow, but his face is diminished in the dark. There are no sounds of the space of telling in *Heart of Darkness*, only changes in light that indicate duration, the passage of time. The sound space of the *Nellie*, at rest and at a distance from

London, is nearly reduced to the voice of Marlow, perhaps with the exception of the single "grunt" issued by one of his auditors just after Marlow remembers the "fiendish howl" that "appeal[s] to me" (*Y*, 97)—in this echolocation, a paralinguistic sound resonates with the kinds of sounds otherwise located by Marlow in the Congo. We seem far from the city noise of London. But we can imagine, as Orson Welles did in his 1938 radio adaptation of the novel, some baseline rhythm of lapping, signaling that the boat is at rest against a minimal motion that is not enough to propel it forward ("'The voice of the surf heard now and then was a positive pleasure,'" Marlow recalls, "'like the speech of a brother'" [*Y*, 61]).[108]

But we can only presume the *Nellie*'s spatial silence if we omit from perception a minor and anamorphic detail. Just before announcing the presence of Marlow, the unnamed narrator recalls a company man playing dominoes aboard ship. He toys "architecturally with the bones," ivory reshaped into this other form, without having lost completely its sense of being a residue of colonial extraction (*Y*, 46). These silent shards of ivory litter the ship where an event of oral storytelling takes place. A dialectical image of extraction thus begins the novel in the dominoes, as they are, at the same time, a deconstituted image of the piano, its ivory keys. The audiovision of the ivory is not total and cannot be sustained; it "flits by," as Benjamin once wrote of the dialectical image.[109] The spatial coordinates of the dialectical image are fundamentally anachronic, a constellation and optical illusion by which the past and present touch in relation to an impending afterlife.[110] In the "bones," akin to the anamorphic skull, there is a simultaneity but also a muted sound, an acoustic equivalent of the dialectical image.

The shards have been shaped into dominoes, but as an image—or a "symbol," in the sense upheld by Paul Valéry and other French Symbolists—it resonates with a structural condition in extraction, the elastic material of the commodity form. In the piano key, ivory is acculturated into European music. The modernist symbol, as Northrop Frye once defined it, is "something material" that means, "by virtue of association, something *more* or something *else* (. . . something immaterial)."[111] But here, the symbol is already beginning to shift in its register, where this something material refers to its displaced or forgotten material, that is, social reproduction that cannot, by definition, enter fully into consciousness except as a ghost of human relations.

Attending to this minor detail, the narrator registers, without fully sensing, that a shard of the Congo is within European aesthetic production, as its silent material condition. A determination is "silent" to the extent that, according to Marx, the commodity fetish cannot speak.[112] In Chapter 2, I noted that the archaic meaning of determinacy (*Bestimmtheit*) indicates a voice, *Stimme*. "*Bestimmen* is to *be-voice*, to *vocify*, to *voculate*, render, *articulate*, to *define*, to *determine*, or *distinguish into the implied constitutive variety*: even to *accentuate* will be seen to involve the same function; or we may say *modulate*, then, *modify*."[113] In determination, things become tangible and recognizable. They find their qualities and features such that to be determinate is to be this and no other thing and to have gained in distinction and organization amid abstraction. To declare *"das stimmt"* is to say "it is true" or "it is so." But beneath this epistemic reality of voice and its naming—as we already learned in Chapter 2 from Fanon—is the echo of the object.

When *Heart of Darkness* ends, the object—disavowed black life—echoes in Marlow's claim to a storytelling voice and in his sense of bodily morphology. Having returned from his journey, Marlow meets with the Intended, who asks him to repeat Kurtz's last words. Marlow famously withholds them to say "your name"—a name that we never learn. This moment occurs along some axis of a scriptural impossibility of inscribing her name that touches the impossibility of inscribing the unnamed black woman's "dialect." Two objects split his voice: repeating Kurtz's last words (for us and for the men) and silencing them (for her). He recounts to his fellows aboard ship what it meant to approach the Intended's door and prepare for the encounter:

> "And the memory of what I had heard him say afar there, with the horned shapes stirring at my back, in the glow of fires, within the patient woods, those broken phrases came back to me, were heard again in their ominous and terrifying simplicity. I remembered his abject pleading, his abject threats, the colossal scale of his vile desires, the meanness, the torment, the tempestuous anguish of his soul. And later on I seemed to see his collected languid manner, when he said one day, 'This lot of ivory now is really mine. The Company did not pay for it. I collected it myself at a very great personal risk.' [. . .] I rang the bell before a mahogany door on the first floor, and while I waited he seemed to stare at me out of the glassy panel—stare with that wide and immense stare embracing, condemning, loathing all the universe. I seemed to hear the whispered cry, 'The horror! The horror!'
>
> ". . . I saw her and him in the same instant of time—his death and her sorrow— I saw her sorrow in the very moment of his death. Do you understand? I saw them together—I heard them together. She had said, with a deep catch of the breath, 'I have survived' while my strained ears seemed to hear distinctly, mingled with her tone of despairing regret, the summing up whisper of his eternal condemnation." (*Y*, 156–57)

Marlow in this moment essentially syncopates the narrating instance, suggesting to his reader that he is hearing between times and spaces, hearing in two realities at once, a simultaneity marked by the absent presence of the double,

Marlow once again repeating the last words in the narrative. His listeners aboard the *Nellie*, in other words, hear that quotation twice. Marlow hears in the double. Kurtz's broken phrases "were heard again," but against or through the present-tense sound of the Intended's voice. "I heard them together . . . my strained ears seem to hear distinctly." The space of memory, occupied by his listening body, affords an acoustical superimposition (one that the advent of the recording studio will later realize with multitracking). The Intended and unnamed African woman resonate, like the white and black female pairings to be found in Du Bois and Faulkner.

In the syncopation, a timing at odds with itself, we can recognize a trace of the polyrhythmic African music, a music whose memory Marlow otherwise suppresses when in the Intended's drawing room. There, Marlow does not recall, except in metonym, the African music that, in other moments, he continually brings to the acoustical space of memory aboard ship. He protects the drawing room from its resonance. There is something of the space of the drawing room that must be shielded, as it were, from both the last words of Kurtz and the racialized and eroticized sound of the Congo.

LISTENING TO RECORDS

The phonograph nowhere appears in *Heart of Darkness* and is missing from Conrad's corpus (it appears only in the earlier technological form of the hand organ in *Almayer's Folly*). As Ivan Krielkamp was among the first to observe, *Heart of Darkness* adopts the technological sensibility of the voice as a "part-object" loosened from its source: "not an expressive trace of the fully human, but a material sign" that incites an acute metaphysical anxiety.[114] But some of these objects—colonial sounds—are partial because they are vulnerable to dispossession. Such a relation unsettles the *l'objet sonore*, or "sound object" in its orthodox conception. Vulnerability cuts both ways in Conrad's sensibility. It is not that colonial sound—in drumming, shouts, cries, and moans—contaminates the European *logos* in an interracial encounter. Instead, in the moment that Conrad was most seeking to possess an authorial voice purified of linguistic attachments—a desire reenacted, to some extent, in Marlow's desire for the mysteriously powerful voice of his predecessor, Kurtz—Conrad is acutely aware of the extraction on which such bounty is premised. The missing image of the phonograph is the form assumed by this ambiguous recognition.

The missing image, we found in Chapter 1, turns upon a dual logic, presenting through omission; it becomes in this way free floating, intensifying its displaced effect. What is made concrete in the phonograph's omission? We learn in Marlow's story that a visit to a European drawing room provided both landfall and departure to his journey to the Congo. Before leaving, he sits with his aunt there, believing it to be a feminine space shielded from reality. This space is what the literary critic Adrian Daub might call a "sonic hearth," an intimate space of stories and music that defined bourgeois listening in the nineteenth and early twentieth centuries, first through the piano, then the phonograph, and finally the radio.[115] The sound theorist Jonathan Sterne shows how, in the nineteenth century, the phonograph was ruled by a desire not simply to share intimacy but to preserve, making the machine a "resonant tomb." It was one preservative technology among others. For a culture in which death was still "everywhere," a wider ethos of preservation, from canning to embalming, offered a way both to describe and to prescribe the sound technology's primary use value: a keeper of the dead.[116] Other sound technologies were conceptually entangled in this poetics, for while "the telephone facilitated the hearing of a voice physically *absent* to the listener," the phonograph, as a tympanic machine, further facilitated "the audition of voices absent to themselves."[117] A keeper of the voices of the dead, the resonant tomb is a reversal and corollary of the sonic hearth (this phonographic space did not escape Adorno's critique of its participation in "herbaria of artificial life").[118] We can say, then, that a life instinct and a death instinct splits the drawing room and, as Peter Szendy might suggest, listening itself.[119]

The piano manifests as an image in *Heart of Darkness*, yet it never resounds. It is *a pure image* from which the potential for sound has ostensibly been expunged. Its appearance is delayed until the novel's end, when we return to the drawing-room space—a domestic space, where women sit, listen, and play music—from which Marlow had also launched his journey.[120] Conrad takes the material of the image to displace and reshape it into nearly corporeal form:

> "The dusk was falling. I had to wait in a lofty drawing-room with three long windows from floor to ceiling that were like three luminous and bedraped columns. The bent gilt legs and backs of the furniture shone in indistinct curves. The tall marble fireplace had a cold and monumental whiteness. A grand piano stood massively in a corner; with dark gleams on the flat surfaces like a sombre and polished sarcophagus. A high door opened—closed. I rose." (*Y*, 156)

The piano does not sound, but as a dialectical image it strikes "*the resonant strings of remembering*," as Faulkner might say (*AA*, 172). The image is calling back to the beginning of the novel to create a circular form that is not so much phonographic (in the turn and return) as it is sonorously containing; it is the narrative equivalent of simultaneity. Such resonance is not localized in anything that might concretely produce and hold sound but rather in the formal quality of elliptical return and touch. Yet the piano is never fulfilled: There is never a moment of playing, of sounding its sarcophagal body; it remains incomplete. The formal resonance is, itself, nontotalizing. The resonance is not an analogy, that is, the yielding of a "likeness" between two images. It is analog, however, for in it, we recognize a resonant body, an amplification by vibration, as a string against wood. The dialectical image of the piano is, at the same time, technological, protophonographic and prototelephonic, the novel straddling two discourse networks circa 1900.

In the drawing room, Marlow confronts what Said calls a "consolidated vision." The consolidated vision, I argued in the Overture, posits a "here and now" against a background—a sensorium—of imperial possessions and self-possession sensing itself. The consolidated vision struggles against the presence of some other scene that is simultaneous with this one, in the periphery and at an extreme distance, that cannot be omitted from Marlow's thought and memory. Life in the peripheries—whose unrest guarantees the serenity of the sonic hearth—goes on unseen. Paired with the consolidated narrative vision is a *consolidated voice* of Marlow's narrative and, with it, the sound of European classical music. In the consolidated scene of the drawing room, there appears to be no fugitive vibration, no trace of mediation. The space of the drawing room is secured by extreme brutality. Its moment is without any apparent determination, worldliness, and simultaneity.

In thinking of reduced listening, of the so-called sound object—twinned by the concept of audibility—we must consider what it is for things to become objects. For Lacan, such a transformation (from thing into part-object) is always partially determined by loss and separation, which does not enter into Schaeffer's lexicon in his commitment to phenomenology and resistance to the psychical. But we also must consider what it means for persons to be reduced to and racialized as objects.[121]

Though the commodity cannot speak, the speaking and screaming enslaved woman reveals for Moten, in "The Resistance of the Object," a secret hidden in Marx's theory of the commodity fetish, which mutes the resonance of disavowed black life. The enslaved woman, for Moten, is the commodity that screams. The dialectical image of the domino "bones" aboard ship is a sonorous object not because, if tapped, it might issue a sound but because the bones lose their determination in narrative space, bleeding into the piano keys and back. It is a dialectical sound, which is to say, a resonance. As a thing, it's lost its voice, its definiteness.

As we've seen, the sinister resonance is a voice that has lost determination to become an acoustic register. If the silent piano were to "speak," it would be in the form of European music. But that music is presupposed by the violent extraction of ivory. The piano would "speak" in Western classical music, but already in a metamorphosis akin to what I argued in Chapter 1 to be forcible translation. The music's condition is the extraction of ivory in one shape and its manifestation in another place and as another shape, its sound muted but nonetheless resonant in the image.

In *Culture and Imperialism*, Said turns to Western classical music forms in order to theorize how the metropole both acknowledges and obscures its distant rule over the periphery, imperial spaces rendering colonized spaces suprasensible. It demands we read "contrapuntally."[122] Calling upon this symphonic metaphor, Said describes an "*organized* interplay that derives from the *themes*" in the English novel—not a "rigorous melodic or formal principle" but still a principle of what Said calls (after Nietzsche's return to Greek tragedy) *melos*, which is the classical origins of melodic and harmonic order.[123] The contrapuntal, then, is no less a figure of containment and forcible translation. Describing the Elizabethan origins of blackface in New World colonialism, Michael Rogin writes of illumination in the classical and Neoplatonist imaginary. In blackface, it was thought, night and substrate yield, and "Apollo gives form to the Dionysiac African, making art from his nature."[124] In Conrad, it is not that the discursive space contains an acoustic resonance but that *melos* already appears as a "haunting melody," that is, under the sign of afterwardness and return—an earworm.

In the Intersonority, we encountered this concept in Du Bois as the material return of what does not have origins in the individual life. For Theodor Reik, Freud's famous but overlooked and at times denigrated student, the haunting melody returns in involuntary ways: "an unknown self sings."[125] The earworm for Reik is essentially orchestral. A single melody divorces itself from the larger work to attach itself to memory as a part-object of some other unnamed experience of grief. In *The Congo Diary*, one basis of the novel and a journal that Conrad kept in English, his not-yet-mastered tongue, he does not describe music—it took writing the novel for music to return. He spells many words phonetically; his experiences there were fundamentally mediated by the desire for English. When Conrad returns to his aural experience of the Congo, then, it is a kind of proto *field recording* whose apparatus for inscription is not notation or performance but memory and recitation. Listening to such a record links us powerfully to the notion that the sinister resonance appropriates self-hearing. For this field recording was paired in Conrad's memory with the act of coming to writing (in English) and a haunting melody, a single memory of having heard Wagner, such that the sound of the Congo in Conrad is a translative space. Sounds, memories, languages, and musical traditions abound.

Conrad claimed that he knew "absolutely nothing" about Wagner's legends "mis en musique." "I don't even know them by way of opera-books, as the only Wagnerian production I've ever seen is his Tristan—24 years ago in Brussels" (the city that gives to Marlow his site of departure).[126] Marlow remembers hearing drumming and cries at a distance, the bodies of its makers seen but once in the story, when he arrives in the Inner Station, their genders being opaque in what is tantamount to a primal scene. In Conrad's descriptions of visual occlusion and the "curtain of trees" that conceals the makers of music, we can recognize something of what Brian Kane describes as Wagner's acousmatic aesthetic of the "invisible orchestra" at Bayreuth.[127] In the Intersonority, I noted Wagner in relation to Du Bois's acousmatic figure of the Veil. Wagner felt, Kane writes, that "the fully absorptive experience of music's spiritual content" could be consummated only when the orchestra was unseen. Wagner designed a series of architectural occlusions, protective mechanisms Kane suggestively links to Marx's thinking of the phantasmagoria of commodity form.[128]

This erotic fantasy is heightened by the mode of recording that supports it. With the field recording and the memory of opera, their appeal is increased by retrospection, or what really is a case of *retroaudition*. It is the mode of memory first opened by the mother and her absence, an absence that allows for the space of the object as such, an inner presence retained through "the evocative power of memory that allows us to hold on."[129] All haunting melodies are maternal in their charge. We found this charge to be the case with Du Bois, and it is no less the case with Conrad. The substrate of night is sounded such that "a *being maternal* . . . is indistinguishable from *a being material*," Moten writes, recitation being a rematerialization of a missing, black feminine body.[130]

Conrad was among the last generation of writers who did not live long enough to hear opera emanate from the long-playing record.[131] What held the music close could only have been the persistence of a long-form mode of musical memory, a decade-long memory. The retroaudition of the opera—in some form, as a residue or outlining shape of musical experience—was perhaps ringing in his ears as he wrote. "One of the essential properties of operas, particularly such as those from the later period by Wagner and Strauss, is long temporal duration,"

Adorno writes. "They are sea voyages."[132] But we make a mistake if we fail to note that Conrad wrote from the reserve of two singular musical memories, divided and acoustically superimposed. In the drawing room where he encounters the European woman, there are two sound spaces at once, simultaneous with each other but missing each other, the one sounding in memory, the other its disavowed condition.

In a kind of counterpart to anamorphosis, Conrad's retroaudition involves the sound of the Congo, which both intrudes upon and is entangled with the space opened by the maternal object (the "oceanic" feeling that Freud links to the unboundedness of infancy before differentiation). Is such disavowal because, as Cheng asks of European modernism more generally, "the specter of the Middle Passage . . . ties the dream of freedom [upon the oceans] eerily close to dreams of profound constraint?"[133] When a haunting melody is without a recording or score against which to check itself, it incites the sense of Reik's "unknown self [that] sings." For Reik, this unknown self is ultimately retrievable through the talking cure, though he felt that Freud made a mistake in listening only to the words of melodies that occurred to an analysand during a session, rather than to the melodic content or the atmospheric "tone" of the session itself. Recall, however, that Lacan resists Reik to emphasize "pauses, scansions, cuts."

The haunting memory of *sound*—above all, a music that Marlow could not understand—is further unmoored and difficult to reconstruct textually. It is the memory of a cut. In the figure of vibration, a material substratum, Marlow recalls embodied aural practices that Nidesh Lawtoo traces to Fang ritual-possession trance (from Latin *transire*: to pass), though it is never named as such in the text.[134] "'The monotonous beating of a big drum filled the air with muffled shocks and a lingering vibration. A steady droning sound of many men chanting'" (*Y*, 140). In the lull of recitation aboard ship, is there not a sonic trace of the oceanic feeling resonating with the rhythm of trance? It is noncontrapuntal. The *Nellie* becomes a close companion to Congo sound space, floating upon the vertiginous waters of the Black Atlantic and touching it in vibration. It is a scene of seduction but also a politically potent anachrony. Female prophets of the Lower Congo—perhaps among them the unnamed black woman who displays "inscrutable purpose"—later resisted Belgian colonial authority with their trembling bodies (in Kongo: *zakama*, or "vibration," "shaking," and "spirit-induced trembling") (*Y*, 136).[135] The vibration exceeds its inscription and transcription.

Writing sound in Conrad is a technology of listening. It is as if Conrad writes of the sound of the Congo in order to try to hear and feel again, yet the memory vibration also tears at the memory of containment. As I will return to, we can echolocate here some of Conrad's most destructive writing habits of scratching out, blotting, and rendering text illegible.

The voice of Kurtz is the avowed symbol of the most operatic strain of Marlow's memory, and though Wagner's music had not yet been recorded, it is technified in relation to the story of Marlow's search for this voice. Kurtz's last words, Krielkamp observes, are iterated and repeated. (The entirety of the dialogue in the drawing room is freighted with graphic iteration, "'Forgive me. I—I—have mourned so long in silence—in silence,'" the Intended says [*Y*, 161].) These words include the question of their sound: If Kurtz is part French, perhaps his last words (in English) would be pronounced "or' or' . . . or' or.'" This voice is the *proper* object of the story's exchange value in remembrance (in Benjamin's sense of epic memory, or *Gedächtnis*, which is "dedicated to *one* hero, *one* odyssey").[136] Kurtz is Marlow's voluntary memory. Marlow uses the technology of direct discourse to "play back," as it were, the words of Kurtz: In repeating Kurtz's last utterance, Marlow is "bringing it home," as Conrad says of the novel's form, the needle in its groove.

Music in the Congo but also extramusical sound in vibration, groans, and cries are *improper* objects in relation to Marlow's memory, which has been shaped by Eurocentric and colonial protocols. Except through the powers of description, these sounds cannot be brought back home. Marlow describes a music that, not yet recorded, his silent listeners have never heard. Conrad wrote just before ethnographic sound was disseminated globally[137] and decades before African American music would become the primary accumulation of a nascent white-owned recording industry. Conrad published *Heart of Darkness* in the same year that Scott Joplin composed "Maple Leaf Rag" (1899) (a recording of the song played by Joplin survives on a pianola roll). In 1912, James Weldon Johnson wrote of a Du Boisian protagonist who travels to European clubs to play ragtime, an international music. Writing in 1898, Conrad remembers the Congo in the moment that ragtime was becoming itself in the United States and Europe. (He would have been familiar, too, with the imitations of black song on the minstrel stages of England.)[138] In 1900, London hosted the anti-imperial Pan African conference, organized by Du Bois. It is not that Marlow hears in the Congo a pure "origin" of this African American classical music; rather, he hears what is coeval to the Victorian culture of the piano. In this way, the sound he hears "in" or "from" the Congo (resonance destabilizes all such genitive coordinates) is split or divided by the existence of the Black Atlantic. Possibility and impossibility converge upon this drawing-room space that brings an end to Marlow's memory of the journey. The diegetic space of the drawing room resounds with the extradiegetic

sound space that it repels as its opposite, making its existence essentially negative. "'Incidentally he gave me to understand that Kurtz had been essentially a
great musician. "There was the making of an immense success," said the man,
who was an organist. . . . I had no reason to doubt his statement; and to this day
I am unable to say what was Kurtz's profession'" (*Y*, 153).

When Marlow returns to the space of the drawing room, confronting the silent
image of piano, he carries with him the memory of a not-yet-recorded music of
the Congo. The image and sound touch in this missed encounter under the impending aegis of the phonograph. In his story, he avows that the last words of
Kurtz ring in his ears. Marlow claims to his fellows that he could not repeat them
to the Intended, saying them for the first time aboard the *Nellie* and in the closest point to the reader's present. But in that moment of withholding the words
(keeping them not to himself but *for* himself, stealing the last words, as it were,
from their rightful *destinataire*, the Intended), Marlow also carried the memory
of indigenous music. The inner field recording was silent in that instance, or it
ceased for a time to resound. Its sound nonetheless surrounds the possibility of
a diegesis as such—if not narrating consciousness itself—as a bifurcated space of
speaking, listening, and remembering.

Conrad takes this private and domestic space of storytelling and Western classical music—one that is also, ostensibly, the scene of the contemporary reader's
own enjoyment of reading novels for pleasure—and racializes its scene through
the injection, as if of some hypothetical substance thought to be carried by distant sounds and voices from Africa to Europe. Though the black (feminine) coordinate of Marlow's voice is less articulated, less heard, and less understood by
Conrad himself, it is no doubt acoustically "there" in the resonance of Central
African music, its return in narrative not only in stories of music but in the temporality of narrative.

Were Marlow not hearing in the double, then narrative time and space could
take on the character of a pure essence or medium, relaying the events of his
memory (the past) without also, at the same time, being forced to relay their
own condition, the violence of their construction. It is as if the silent listener
senses that narrative holds together through an invisible yet sustaining sensibility of empire.

In the story he tells, Marlow's own act of listening splits between the desire for
a voice ("envy," we might say in a Freudian lexicon) that never occurred except in
fantasy, a paternal voice that, if it could have been heard, would have answered
all questions,[139] and a sonorousness of music in the Congo experienced as both

prior to and outside of speech, its extreme void into which speech might fall (castration). The event aboard the *Nellie* is fundamentally androgynous, but it is also transracial. Marlow desires to hear "Africa" just as strongly as he desires to hear Kurtz. Only, sound and music is on the way to Kurtz—he must go through the space of sound and music to get to the voice of Kurtz, whose last words he will carry with him home. The first object, the master's voice, is an authoritarian and unidirectional transmission; the second is a sonorous and feminine propagation:

> "[A] cry, a very loud cry, as of infinite desolation, soared slowly in the opaque air. It ceased. A complaining clamour, modulated in savage discords, filled our ears. The sheer unexpectedness of it made my hair stir under my cap. I don't know how it struck the others: to me it seemed as though the mist itself had screamed, so suddenly, and apparently from all sides at once, did this tumultuous and mournful uproar arise. It culminated in a hurried outbreak of almost intolerably excessive shrieking, which stopped short, leaving us stiffened in a variety of silly attitudes, and obstinately listening to the nearly as appalling and excessive silence. 'Good God! What is the meaning——' stammered at my elbow one of the pilgrims . . ." (*Y*, 101–2).

What Marlow hears is a relational sound, not an object that he observes. Yet in this sonorous propagation, coloniality is hearing *itself*. The colonial sound occupies the place of the nonrelational in colonial consciousness, what in selfconsciousness remains nonrelational to *itself*. He hears nonethnographically. There is a sound that Marlow cannot accumulate. While the story concerns ivory, rubber, and coal (the unnamed mineral that energizes Marlow's ship in the moment that sail is giving way to steam), he concentrates on sounds as the thing he cannot bring back, as what will continually exceed the site of its inscription. Conrad positions Marlow as a listener who cannot "domesticate" the music, that is, make it his own.

Marlow continually hears sounds that he feels to be not sounding in proximity to him but addressing him. He is never fully able to go beyond his being-initself and in a way that would involve attributing to the African being language, a lacuna that Achebe condemns in "An Image of Africa." Achebe does not comment on this pronounced place of extralinguistic sound in the novel, which is to say, music (though music also plays a profound role in his fictional writing). What we can hear (in what Marlow hears) in such sounds is the interruption of an imperial linguistic consciousness that only begins to feel the other within itself. The shrieks of the jungle, as they are heard by Marlow, are "colonial nonsense," Bhabha suggests, but they are nevertheless preserved in what is a long-duration memory, a memory of a sound in consciousness that is supposed to be committed to carrying home only the epistemic voice of Kurtz. Produced not only by voluminous calls but by drums, this music that Marlow carries in memory is long-distance music. It is a signal that assumes space. In the fact of being heard, it demands his recognition. He reiterates several times that what he hears is *music*, though he doesn't understand it. He repeats the fact of its existence to his silent listeners aboard ship, and he indicates time and again that he knows nothing of what it means, except that it mourns. But he is, from the beginning, convinced that what he hears is music. It becomes in this way a transatlantic conjuncture—a resonance—of sorrow song.

The novel both reveals and conceals its mechanically reproduced form. Sinister resonance makes near a distance in self-consciousness. At the same time, Conrad understands that the phonograph can separate—at times violently—the voice from the human body. Coloniality, as a technological and modernizing project, begins with the extraction of language and, with it, gesture, habitus, and voice. To capture a people for capital is to capture their sounds and language, to make it functional for the *image*, as what I argued in Chapter 2 to be racially schematic. The formal problem for *Heart of Darkness* was how to "speak" this reality that is asignifying, to bring "home," transmit, or carry this reality of this extraction. Conrad knew that to carry this reality to the innermost space of hearing (understanding) oneself he must to some extent surpass language in appealing to its auditory substratum. There is a split in the narrative voice—it is other from itself at its fundamental or material level. It is split not simply between a phonic substance and the linguistic but by a spatial acoustic tasked with carrying both sounds and voices.

RESONANCE AS *LINGUA FRANCA*

In the "Preface" to *The Nigger of the "Narcissus,"* Conrad states that his task as a novelist is

> to hold up unquestioningly, without choice and without fear, the rescued fragment
> ["a passing phase of life"] before all eyes in the light of a sincere mood. It is to show its
> vibration, its colour, its form; and through its movement, its form, and its colour, reveal
> the substance of its truth—disclose its inspiring secret: the stress and passion within
> the core of each convincing moment. (*NN*, 29)

The sensory conditions that support this vision in its desired social immediacy invoke a larger aesthetic and psychic bind, one irreducible to the distinction between showing and telling. It is a history in which seeing and hearing blend, registering subtle motions that touch the reading subject as a sensing subject.

> All art, therefore, appeals primarily to the senses, and the artistic aim when express-
> ing itself in written words must also make its appeal through the senses, if its highest
> desire is to reach the secret spring of responsive emotions. It must strenuously aspire
> to the plasticity of sculpture, to the colour of painting, and to the magic suggestiveness
> of music—which is the art of arts. And it is only through complete, unswerving devo-
> tion to the perfect blending of form and substance; it is only through an unremitting
> never-discouraged care for the shape and ring of sentences that an approach can be
> made to plasticity, to colour, and that the light of magic suggestiveness may be brought
> to play for an evanescent instant over the commonplace surface of words: of the old,
> old words, worn thin, defaced by ages of careless usage. (*NN*, 31)

"I cannot make coherent sense of it," one contemporary critic wrote of Con-rad's "Preface." "I do find repeated statements of faith in visualization, embod-ied in a hodgepodge of platonic, positivistic, and romantic sentiments. And when those are shaken out, there remains, I suppose, a credo of impressionis-tic realism—in Henry James's phrase, solidity of specification—qualified by the somewhat obsessive emphasis on the optical process."[140] Since then, critics have lauded Conrad's "Preface" as testament to his visual impressionism, which has shaped prevailing discussions not simply of Conrad but modernism as a project.

It was Michael North who, in *The Dialect of Modernism*, returned to the "Preface" as a "valid introduction to the rest of modernism," but by doing some-thing that other critics before him had mostly avoided: refusing to sequester the "Preface" from the novel and its title as a racial slur. For North, it is central that Conrad came to English as an outsider, and the racial slur was a technique of announcing and demonstrating Conrad's potential for inclusion in the English tradition. North concentrates on the sensual totality of Conrad's ascendant claim for the novel, "My task which I am trying to achieve is, by the power of the writ-ten word, to make you hear, to make you feel—it is, before all, to make you *see*." Conrad believes in the "natural conversion of written symbols into aural sensa-tions and finally into things themselves," North writes, invoking the resonance of the English idiom "the ring of truth" in relation to Conrad's "shape and ring of sentences."[141] The "ring," a kind of pure sound, cannot be separated from the fact of the slur in relation to Conrad's dialect English.

Recall the formative scene of Conrad being commanded to read aloud the Pol-ish text of his father's translation of Shakespeare: "If I do not remember where, how and when I learned to read," Conrad writes, "I am not likely to forget the process of being trained in the art of reading aloud." In Chapter 2, we found in this moment the primal scene of the "right voice," neutral and ideal in its tones, a memory not unburdened by the echo of a racialized object. The young Conrad experienced himself as being doubly tested by his father, Christopher GoGwilt suggests, tested not only in his skills of reading aloud but in what GoGwilt calls, after James Russell Lowell (the poet and second president of the Modern Language Association), "the spiritual *lingua franca* that abolishes all alienage of race."[142] (Lowell provides the poetic epigraph to Du Bois's "Of the Dawn of Freedom.") This citation appears in the *OED* under the figurative uses of *lingua franca*, or "any mixed jargon formed as a medium of intercourse between people speaking different languages."[143] "It was a form of English *lingua franca* on board the ships of the British merchant marine," GoGwilt writes, that provided Conrad "with his first sustained exposure to spoken English." He learned English by overhearing it, but in *A Personal Record*, GoGwilt notes, Conrad displaces this memory to emphasize instead his encounter with English *literature*.

Where there is a dialect English, there is a displaced linguistic register. Polish and French languages resonate throughout the "Preface" as a condition of Conrad's authorial expression through (physical and psychical) displacement. Ian Watt notes, for example, the trace of French within several of the key and motivating terms in the "Preface," including "solidarity."[144] When North finds the English idiom hidden in Conrad's diction, however, he ignores that Conrad also *misuses* it—by the idiom's logic, it is truth and not the sentence that would ring. In other words, there is a differential and displacing movement between "ring of truth" and "ring of sentences," the kind of displacement that occurs when one has heard an idiom and misremembered it, filling in the blanks in memory, in part because it does not appeal to logic. (Like other figures, catachresis begins in dislogic.)[145] In losing its originary, sensual truth, the idiom is among those "old words, worn thin by careless usage."[146] In Conrad's misuse of the figure, one imagines a series of sentences that form a communing circle, "shape and ring" becoming a double entendre, a double understanding and hearing. The ring is both vibration and formal containment.

By what means is the written converted into the aural, its "power"? Conrad asks after the substance that carries the words on the page, making the novel not only intelligible in its Englishness but communicable. To be sure, the slur functions through disavowal, providing a site of otherness that might contain and localize the hated voice. Throughout the "Preface," however, Conrad continually isolates a concern not just for the "shape" of sentences but for the "form" of the novel, which, though it cannot be seen, can be *figured* as emitting a "light of

magic suggestiveness" akin to music. The spiritual power of the novel is to convert the raw material of sensation, "to show its vibration, its *colour*, its *form*; and
through its movement, its *form*, and its *colour*, reveal the *substance* of its truth
[emphasis mine]." In the "art of fiction" debates of the late nineteenth century,
initiated by Walter Besant and Henry James, writers insisted that the novel is an
"art," that it bears a "form." To what extent is the body of the black mate—and in
a more displaced way, the black feminine body—part of the process of figuring,
shaping, and forming, and what kind of displacement, if not simply linguistic, is
at stake in declaring the novel to be a *form* akin to painting, music, and sculpture? Conrad introduces into that debate what the others do not and perhaps
cannot: the displacement of the corporeality of the colonial body, the form of the
novel and the form of the body being impossible to separate.

European modernism was founded, Cheng has shown of Le Corbusier's
desire for the performer Josephine Baker, on an unacknowledged, primitivizing attachment to the black maternal that, "more a medium than a source,"
contains the ego precisely because it disembodies it. Longing for dedifferentiation, racial appropriation allows the European male "to break out of his own
skin" into another.[147] With the "ring" (a "sonorous envelope" in psychoanalytic
terms, the infant contained by sound before birth, hearing before seeing), Conrad posits the space of reading as an inward space, but he both believes in and
doubts inwardness as a total adequacy between signifier and signified, word
and receiver.

To receive is a maternal gesture, to provide a resonating chamber for the ring.
Conrad never loses the sense that the space of reading might, in its facticity, be a
physical space of touch in resonance, that is, an embracing because sympathetic
vibration. This vibration, color, form, and substance shares in the Wagnerian
sense of the total work of art that "is consummated only when present 'fully to
the senses'" in live performance.[148] But it also shares in the music and ritual of
the Congo, in its vibrant performativity. Recall that resonance, as sympathetic
vibration, allows Jean-Luc Nancy to ground his ethics in its physical, dialectical
event when he writes, "To sound . . . is not only to emit a sound, but it is also
to stretch out, to carry itself and be resolved into vibrations that both return it
to itself and place it outside itself"—the constitutive motility (*Bewegtheit*) of
Dasein, such that being is always being-moved. This (black) maternal resolution
and, with it, the return of vibration as a unifying figure of the corpus, both recalls
and elides the direct problem Conrad raises in the "Preface" to *The Nigger of the
"Narcissus"*—not simply the *physical* means by which the literary work of art
can become the basis of "solidarity" and "kinship" among men across time and

space but the *corporeal* medium, the novel and the body of the reader cohering into a "shape and ring."

The passionate ideality of vibration found Conrad on September 9, 1898, just before beginning *Heart of Darkness*. Krielkamp recalls a letter Conrad wrote to Edward Garnett to describe his astonishment after meeting with a radiologist who had showed Conrad an X-ray of his own hand and played for him a recording of a Polish pianist:

> The secret of the universe is in the existence of horizontal waves whose varied vibrations are at the bottom of all states of consciousness. . . . And, note, *all* (the universe) composed of the same matter, *all matter* being only that thing of inconceivable tenuity through which the various vibrations of waves (electricity, heat, sound, light etc.) are propagated, thus giving birth to our sensations—then emotions—then thought. Is that so?[149]

Tenuity, weakness of barrier, dedifferentiation, and birth.

The phonograph had been invented by Cros and Edison in 1877, gramophone discs first being used in 1887. The X-ray machine had been invented just two years before this meeting. In this encounter in Glasgow, however, when Conrad was still seeking a post at sea and not yet resolved to enter a writing life, he received a lesson in physics, extrapolating from it a new ontology not only of consciousness but of writing. Krielkamp cites this letter to Garnett in order to open up a remarkable insight concerning *Heart of Darkness*'s turning upon the haunting voice of Kurtz, a voice obeying a "phonographic logic."[150] Yet we should take the letter as a whole, which speculates beneath the phonograph and X-ray machine a shared, almost invisible stratum, a tie that binds any physical body to the world of matter. In vibration, Conrad finds *the* "spiritual *lingua franca*" he had been already seeking in the "Preface" to *The Nigger of the "Narcissus"* and in English literature.

When Conrad describes the "vibration" of the novel in the "Preface," one can recognize a literary theme that would have been reinforced and empirically demonstrated by the physicist: the essential theme of vibration in the *vers libre* of the French Symbolists Paul Valéry, Stéphane Mallarmé, and their younger colleague Gustave Kahn.[151] For Kahn, in particular, the artist is "a nervous system that senses the rhythm, realizes it virtually as an idea, and produces it externally."[152] Such a notion completely reframes Conrad's sense that the task of the novel is to make you hear, feel, and see such that hearing is no longer localized in the ear: To "hear" would be akin to a physiological sensation of rhythm, less an audible sound than an infrasound, a subaural vibration. When Conrad seeks the novel's communicability as written words, then, what he seeks is its vibration, an acousticality.[153] As the Polish audio recording sounds out a lost location and motherland, Conrad values not the sound of the music but its propagation of waves, though that mournful sound of the loss of nation is no doubt folded into the desire to idealize vibration as absolute touch across distance.

In the moment Conrad most wishes to demonstrate a prelinguistic fact of community, the racial slur makes itself felt as a corporeal intrusion upon form. Blackness is form's restless and featureless outside. Yes, the radiologist asserts, even the Whistler painting on the wall and Conrad's recently published novel "your Nigger" are nothing but vibrations. In resonance, Nancy upholds a pure possibility of listening prior to any content. Conrad, however, allows us to recognize in that pure possibility a colonial displacement. The sonorous condition of the audible—of prelinguistic and linguistic community—is in Conrad a violent and racialized form. When Conrad writes of "waves," his ear, always attuned to the homonym, likely heard a double meaning that would not have been lost on him as a sailor: the voyage and tumult of the sea.[154] Conrad then returns nearly two decades later to write the "Author's Note" to the Doubleday edition of *Heart of Darkness*, and the thinking of "vibration" has not left him but it is now cut by the residual. He posits the "*continued* vibration" as the afterlife of form's idealization. The work begins in but also leaves, it being a vibration as a remainder. We make a mistake if we posit a "fall" of vibration away from ideality, which is fantasized to be an originary physical connection that supersedes the outward trappings of corporeal difference.[155] There is a phonographic logic but also an X-ray logic, a vibratory logic of permeation of the visible boundaries the individual body but also some stopping of permeation, a hypervisibility within these most invisible movements. There is opening but also some threshold, the visibility of the skin, through which vibration cannot fully pass to universalize and anonymize matter. Conrad believes in the sonorous condition of language as a pure, material condition. But if this sonorousness acts upon Conrad's imaginary as a positive pole, it is nonetheless split by a constant negativity of the body's *Gestalt* and the cut that constitutes it, a vertiginous formlessness that pulls at his theory of sympathetic vibration.

The sinister resonance and continued vibration are not immediately conceivable as a spoken word or a symbol, even at its most vibratory (as the symbol was for Válery and others). It becomes difficult to say—to theorize and silently contemplate, that is, take up as an object of the episteme—if resonance and vibration are figures for an atrocious content or its *medium*. To be sure, Conrad indicates something that is no longer a "story" in the formal sense. He indicates that something of the totality of the novel's form is being routed through its material, such that the reading consciousness is "afflicted" with the burden of matter that, as Marx and Engels write in *The German Ideology*, "makes its appearance in the form of agitated layers of air, sound, in short, of language."[156]

WRITING, SCREAMING, CRYING

In *The Nigger of the "Narcissus"* Conrad is already hearing some memory of these "agitated layers of air, sound," for which he seeks a form. It is heard as a cry: "Nothing seems left of the whole universe but darkness, clamour, fury—and the ship. . . . No one spoke and all listened. Outside the night moaned and sobbed to the accompaniment of a continuous loud tremor as of innumerable drums beating far off.[157] Shrieks passed through the air. Tremendous dull blows made the ship tremble while she rolled under the weight of the seas toppling on her deck" (*NN*, 63).

It is some long reverberation of a passage whose memory, Conrad suggests time and again, is inscribed in the sea as a surface for retaining memories. For Conrad, the sea is both mirror and memory system, the sea remembering when men will not (it is imperative that James Wait is buried there). In the cries of night, there is an irrecoverable memory of the Middle Passage, the ur-voyage that to some extent obliterates the referential power of any voyage that came before or after it. How does this nonmemory resonate nonetheless? A crying and sobbing gale is a fantasized retroaudition of the Middle Passage, but its status as mere "fantasy" is uncertain, particularly if we are to take Édouard Glissant at his word when he begins *Poetics of Relation* by writing that the cry of the open boat of the Middle Passage "still reverberates today."[158] Conrad wrote of Africa only twice, but in the missing image, he was always writing of Africa, never not writing of Africa, his Atlantic and Pacific being at one in the suspension of the open boat.

With Glissant and Conrad taken together, this cry—its continued vibration—becomes intelligible as the ground of English literature and its consciousness, the ground of the European novel. It is the sonorous condition of possibility and not simply because language originates in the cry. In the belly of the slave ship, Glissant writes, there is a total confrontation "between the powers of the written word and the impulses of orality."[159] There is a cry of stolen, extracted, and disappeared languages. With Conrad and Du Bois taken together, this cry is sorrow song. Writing through an exilic listening consciousness, "the voice of exile," Conrad understood this confrontation to be a condition of the novel as an imperial form. When contemporary narrative theory, exemplified by Anne Banfield, rejects the notion that narrative is an act of "communication," positing instead pure writing and "unspeakable sentences" without reference to an aural or oral event, it elides a phonic substance in the novel's history. The novel, as a modern form, comes to itself historically through flesh. The cry in Conrad's acoustical imaginary is the violent origin of the European novel.[160] By "origin" we understand not the genesis of an object, or what Nietzsche calls tragedy's "birth" (*Geburt*), but what Eli Friedlander calls, in a Benjaminian vein, "the traces it has left in the course of its history."[161] With *Heart of Darkness*, Conrad communicates the novel's communicability in extraction. What is left behind is waste, the waste of signifying in a so-called brute materiality or noise (in French: *bruit*).

In vibration, Conrad experienced the sonorous condition of community prior to speech: The "all" makes itself felt not in speaking but in listening and shared acoustics. Yet the figure of material as "brute" and "brutal" will return in racialized sound. *Vibration and sound are a racial form*, both unifying and violently differentiating. Recall that when James Wait appears aboard ship, "He put his hand to his side and coughed twice, a cough metallic, hollow, and tremendously loud; it resounded like two explosions in a vault . . . and the iron plates of the ship's bulwarks seemed to vibrate in unison" (*NN*, 11). The space of narrative and the space of a ship are often coextensive in Conrad's imaginary, narrative discourse becoming susceptible to the fluxes of feeling and sensation aboard ship. Narrative space becomes a strategy of containment, but in an *atmospherics*, written narrative "catches," as it were, both the logic and voice of its object.[162]

The racial form as it unifies and violently differentiates defines Conrad's relationship not only to the novel but to the written page that mediates its voices. In Chapter 2, I described Freud's thinking of melancholia, which remains instructive in this case. In Judith Butler's account of Freud's figures, she highlights the ego as a "place" (*die Stelle des Ichs*) into which love objects are withdrawn and preserved, taking "flight" and escaping "extinction" (*Aufhebung*). Recall, though, how Butler describes the notorious complications that cling to *Aufhebung* in Hegelian discourse, "cancellation but not quite extinction; suspension, preservation, and overcoming." The word *Stelle* in German also indicates a passage, a passage of literature, a figure whose double meaning is central to GoGwilt's thinking of transnational literary modernism.[163] Conrad's tendency to return to passages across *The Nigger of the "Narcissus"* and *Heart of Darkness* resonates these multiple registers, the passage of the ship, the passage of literature, and the passage of the lost object, each of which mutually constitute vibration as a racial form and its "wake work," as Sharpe might say. We have already echolocated the passage of the *Narcissus* as a premonition of *Heart of Darkness*, one that we took in Chapter 2 to be quite literal, as a hearing without monitor, a *preaudition* where a signal disturbance is received but not yet formalized. The premonition is a kind of hearing before hearing (or "fore-hearing," in Gaston Bachelard's phrase, which hears a weak but indicative sound just before catastrophe):[164] It moves fitfully through form as sonic disturbance. I introduced the possibility of hearing in memory a sound that will later be amplified or presented more fully; it finds not only its sustained attention—listening—but a form.

In the vibration of the ship *Narcissus*, its violent and tumultuous passage, Conrad is beginning to hear the sound memory that finds in *Heart of Darkness* a more determinate shape. But Conrad posits shape—the sinister resonance—as a leftover of form. Beginning with Wait's cough, a black resonance that vibrates the ship "in unison," the sinister resonance is the vibratory surplus of bodily morphology. As image, localized not only in sexual difference but racial difference as the visual sign of skin, morphology delineates where the single body begins and ends. As Spillers demonstrates, however, racial differentiation always already refers to sexual differentiation, it being impossible to separate the two (a racialized sexual difference, a sexualized racial difference).

The figure becomes all important to the work of homology by which the novel, the ship, and the human body may partake of one another. A night that "moans" and "sobs" is an extreme example of the pathetic fallacy, that is, one of the crucial techniques of anthropomorphism made available to literature as it converts things into human shapes. These sounds are "of" the sea, yet, through the pathetic fallacy, they also belong to an unnamed human source. The fallacy to which Conrad gives voice, as it were, is more profound than anthropomorphism, which fills up an inert nature with human attributes. The tremulous night through which the ship passes gives voice to the inhuman difference upon which any anthropomorphism turns: Conrad hears that the "human" is, in its first instance, an anthropomorphism, a tenuous formalization that begins in and returns to heavy matter. Freud's theory of the death drive in *Beyond the Pleasure Principle* rests upon this sense that the human being as matter longs to return to an inert state.

Consider Conrad's presentation of *Narcissus* in landfall not as a containing embrace whereby land gives "ground" to the ship's "figure" but as a violent dedifferentiation, a fall into formlessness:

A low cloud hung before her—a great opalescent and tremulous cloud, that seemed to rise from the steaming brows of millions of men. Long drifts of smoky vapours soiled it with livid trails; it throbbed to the beat of millions of hearts, and from it came an immense and lamentable murmur—the murmur of millions of lips praying, cursing, sighing, jeering—the undying murmur of folly, regret, and hope exhaled by the crowds of the anxious earth. The *Narcissus* entered the cloud; the shadows deepened; on all sides there was the clang of iron, the sound of mighty blows, shrieks, yells. (*NN*, 181)

Conrad returns to this passage in *Heart of Darkness* when Marlow recalls that "'the memory of that time itself lingers around me, impalpable, like a dying vibration of one immense jabber, silly, atrocious, sordid, or simply mean, without any kind of sense'" (*Y*, 115). Shortly after, the narrator will look toward the *Nellie*'s landfall and see "an immense heart of darkness." The formless murmur resonates still further. Faulkner writes this passage in the final sentence of "Carcassonne" and again in *As I Lay Dying*, as if the Atlantic waters could touch the Mississippi (they perhaps do, via the Caribbean): "Before us the thick dark current runs. It talks up to us in a murmur become ceaseless and myriad. . . . Above the ceaseless surface they stand—trees, cane, vines—rootless, severed from the earth, spectral above a scene of immense yet circumscribed desolation filled with the voice of the wave and the mournful water."[165] Du Bois resounds here, too.

The Middle Passage is a nonmemory; it is the "abyss" of forgetfulness from which memory arises.[166] It is where, as Maurice Blanchot might say, "forgetting speaks." Forgetting speaks as a cry. When Marlow remembers the sounds "of" the Congo aboard the *Nellie*, his memory touches its sublime limit: He remembers the experience that cuts memory into two. These sounds, the shrieks and tremors that *pass through* both *The Nigger of the "Narcissus"* and *Heart of Darkness*, share in a racial form. Yet to the extent that the Middle Passage is a nonmemory, its vibratory corporeality exceeds the site of its inscription. This is why I claimed in the Coda to Chapter 1 that resonance names the structure of an anachronic and temporary fulfillment.

Conrad understood that the ship's *place* of beginning and return, the abyss, is racialized in its first instance: Blackness as a figure holds the terrifying anxiety of bodily morphology, its condition in formlessness. In this way, Conrad gives voice to a historical truth. The ship *Narcissus* is near the Atlantic waters that touch Africa (traveling from Bombay to England, the ship is said to pass by Madagascar, which places it in the Indian Ocean). But in that watery distance, the chasm of the black body as the slave body, its fungiblity in Saidiya Hartman's sense, still radiates and vibrates. In *Heart of Darkness*, the passing moment of sound finds its form, as it were. Music, sound, and lament are no longer passing moments but the surrounding condition of each action along Marlow's route. If the infant cry, as Cavarero argues, "establishes the first communication of all communicability,"[167] then the cries of the tumultuous sea communicate communicability. When engaged in the at times quite torturous act of writing, Conrad heard and understood that without the cry as a sonorous condition, there can be no language, form, or symbol.[168] But in this form, Conrad approximating music in the novel, he maximizes sound as the unformalizable: A continued vibration and resonance pass through the textual corpus.

Conrad never stopped hearing this sound of formlessness, writing in his memoir of seafaring *The Mirror of the Sea* (1920) what will strike us as a retroaudition of *Heart of Darkness*, the center from which formless sound and the inhuman difference radiates:

> For, after all, a gale of wind, the thing of mighty sound, is inarticulate. It is a man who, in a chance phrase, interprets the elemental passion of his enemy. Thus there is another gale in my memory, a thing of endless, deep, humming roar, moonlight, and a spoken sentence. . . .
>
> There is infinite variety in the gales of wind at sea, and except for the peculiar, terrible, and mysterious moaning that may be heard sometimes passing through the roar of a hurricane—except for that unforgettable sound, as if the soul of the universe had been goaded into a mournful groan—it is, after all, the human voice that stamps the mark of human consciousness upon the character of a gale.[169]

"The monotonous and vibrating note was destined to grow into the immediacy of the heart, pass into blood and bone, . . . remain to haunt like a reproach."[170] There is some sense that for the wind to be heard, it must be translated into words. But there is also the (displaced) sense that "humanity" might rest upon this same act of translation, that the human might be translation at its core and through a single figure: the figure of prosopopoeia by which, Paul de Man writes, "voice assumes mouth, eye, and finally face, a chain that is manifest in the etymology of the trope's name, *prosopon, poien,* to confer a mask or a face (*prosopon*)." It names for de Man an autobiographical activity "by which one's name . . . is made intelligible and memorable as a face."[171] In Chapter 2, we understood Conrad to be searching for his voice, but through the melancholic intermediary of a black resonance, such that the act of autobiography is a "heterothanatography," or the memoir of a dead other.[172] Here, we understand that with *Heart of Darkness*, Conrad gives form to his placelessness and namelessness in the English tradition of the novel. Writing from an exilic consciousness, he gives form to the terrifying sense that prosopopoeia, as the figuring of a voice into a face and name, might in fact be the determining figure of the human as such. (Violence, Barbara Johnson suggests, is encoded in rhetorical figures as such.) His exilic memories and consciousness open a space for the unrecordable memory of the Middle Passage, the inhuman difference, such that inscribing that memory, writing it, must also be at the same time an unwriting, an uninscribing.

In 1894, Conrad wrote to Marguerite Poradowska to lament the difficulties of composing *Almayer's Folly*. He included in the letter a marred manuscript page, overwritten with blots and crossings out ("to give you the look of the thing"). He wrote to her in French, the language they shared in letters; Conrad's letters at times revert from English into French, when they are most urgently expressive. He writes in 1903, "La solitude me gagne: elle m'absorbe. Je ne vois rien, je ne lis rien. C'est comme une espèce de tombe, qui serait en même temps un enfer, ou il faut écrire, écrire, écrire."[173] Conrad reverses the modernist dictum in an acoustic mirror. He does not write of absorbing the object, as in Flaubert's famous sense of impersonality ("Let us absorb the objective; let it circulate in us, until it is externalized in such a way that no one can understand this marvelous chemistry [*absorbons l'objectif et qu'il circule en nous, qu'il se reproduise au dehors sans qu'on puissse riene comprende à cette chimie merveilleuse*]").[174] In a reverse echo,[175] Conrad writes of the agonizing solitude of writing that absorbs him. The modernist doxa insists that the writer be impersonal, and impersonality in composition is thought to yield a "visual" text from which the "voice" of the writer had been purged. In Chapter 2, we found Conrad wanted the impossible: to create an "I" that was ideal and to become an avatar of modernist principles. To create a writerly "I" that is ideal and to be an avatar of modernist impersonality—these two are opposed to each other, resolved only through resonance. What Conrad calls the "shape and ring of sentences" takes on an essential life, purified of contaminating, deuniversalizing accent.

If one sounds out the repetition of *écrire*, it becomes possible to hear a sound designated but also withheld by the infinite form of *écrire* (to write)—the infinitive form of the verb *écrier* (to cry out or to scream):[176] to write, write, write, but to write through the fact of repetition in some optical and auditory proximity to screaming or crying.

SOUND BLEEDS AND CONTAGION: ILLEGIBILITY, SEXUAL DIFFERENCE, AND ASIGNIFYING SOUNDS

In "vision and resonance," as John Hollander might say, the sounds of the words fuse in their patterns on the page.[177] *The Fact of Resonance* is a claim on behalf of a close reading as close listening, but there is a surplus that is not entirely known to me; I can't close the gap: It is where words bleed, moving beyond themselves to the prelinguistic, to the sounds issued by an injury.

What is the injury? It is overdetermined. But among its resonances is bodily morphology. Conrad wrote a letter after Poradowska had shared a bit of her own writing in progress. He sent in return this marred manuscript page of *Almayer's Folly* (Figure 9), recovered and remarked upon at length by Michael Fried as one fragment of what he calls "a particular fantasmatic relation to the blank page [that] lies at the heart of Conrad's fiction generally."[178] Through Fried's reading of the "face" of Conrad's manuscript pages, we are able to *see* this page (rather than simply read it). We have seen it now more than once.[179]

This page, for Fried, is grounds for thinking through impressionism as it pertains not only to the images presented by the text but by the *look* of writing itself (and not as symbols but as marks on the page, which he encourages us to distinguish). Indeed, I re-present the page here for its illegibility. It is not meant to be read. Fried begins his remarkable project by reminding us of the culmination of Conrad's famous phrase "to make you *see*." In concert, I want to "hear" this page and its phonic substance. Michael North regards Conrad as believing in the "aural conversion" of the written word into image and finally the thing itself. Here, we behold not a conversion but an aural struggle of the mark itself.

This aural struggle begins in the marred manuscript page as it is paired in Conrad's imaginary with blankness, an inability to write.[180] "I *never mean* to be slow. . . . I am always ready to put it down; nothing would induce me to lay down my pen if I *feel* a sentence—or even a word ready to my hand. The trouble is that too often—alas!—I've to Wait—for the sentence—for the word."[181] In Chapter 2, we followed the echoes of the words "wait" and "nothing." Conrad capitalizes "Wait" in this August 1898 letter to his literary advisor, David S. Meldrum. The blankness of the page and "the long blank hours" of writing resound with Wait's lost body, beginning to anthropomorphize the page itself as a physical form, but one whose corporeality also recedes, a *corps perdu*. The blank page, GoGwilt suggests, always carries for Conrad the French resonance of *blanc*, or white. When Marlow gazes at the map of Africa to remark on what had once been "blank spaces," filled in by colonization, the phrase takes on the resonance of the page but also of a white body.

In the image he sends to Poradowska, the page is marred, illegible, crossed out, and nearly destroyed: Writing here bears no essential relation to the inward unless it is self-annihilation, making the page a particular kind of gathering place of withdrawal and preservation. The page is far from being a vanishing mediator, one that in Conrad's early imaginary of "the shape and ring of sentences" promises to convert written symbol into aural sensation and the thing itself. The page as mediator contains the capacity to mar and decimate (visually) what it

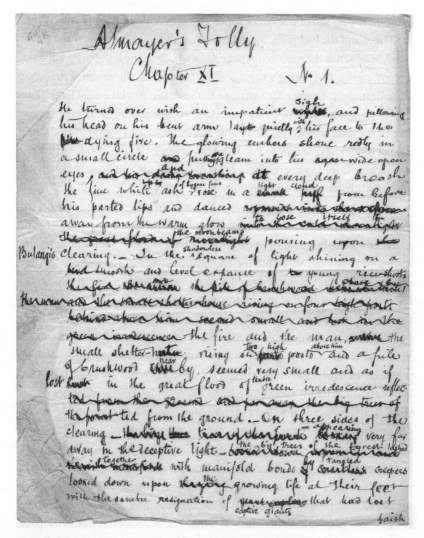

Figure 9. First page, first version, of chapter 11 of the manuscript of *Almayer's Folly*, written in late March or early April 1894. The Rosenbach Museum and Library, Philadelphia.

records, interrupting the aural conversion. Words, as they pass through Conrad's mind (not silently but aurally, I've been insisting in this book), are an artifact of inwardness. Yet the conversion into written marks shatters them in aggressive affect, for the visual register is more corporeal than Fried suspects: If Conrad does not intend Poradowska to read the page but to look at it, then he is also asking her to *witness* it in the scopic tenor of masochistic fantasy, a child being beaten.[182]

Inwardness (the site of resonance for Hegel) is here divided in its objects—the good page and the bad page, the beloved page and the hated, aggressed page.

When he sends the manuscript page, Conrad begins the letter to Poradowska, "Forgive me for not having written sooner, but I am in the midst of struggling to the death with Chapter XI; a struggle to the death, you know! If I let go, I am lost!"[183] He sends Poradowska the first page "to give you an idea of the appearance of my manuscript. This I owe you, since I have seen yours."[184] Both Fried and Bill Brown, responding to Fried, displace a genital fantasy that is at the heart of the scene. Conrad presents himself, his physical body, but as castrated. In this rivalry with Poradowska (also an author), he insists "this is yours" and "this is mine," as it were, the page speaking to the castrating experience of sexual difference, making the manuscript a fetish that conceals lack, but mediated by the desire for a black body (to be in that body or with that body, it is unclear). This castration orients and subsumes the act and art of writing. The manuscript page is an aggressive "gift" that presents not an injured autobiographical face but an injured genital wound that sounds forth the artifact of marred or hated voice, a counterpart to what I called in Chapter 2 the right voice.[185] The page, in other words, visualizes the dejected sound of the voice ideal. But it also visualizes the sound of extracted language, the cry. For in the moment of this epistolary exchange, he is still deciding whether to write in French or English, aggressively proposing that Poradowska publish his novel in French under her name, which would render him a kind of ventriloquist, writing (fantasmatically speaking) through her. This page is an artifact of the primal scene of Conrad's decision to write in English, a rivalry between the two languages, but also a third: Polish.

Remarkably, a draft of a March 1890 letter from Conrad to Poland survives on a verso page of what became chapter 4 of *Almayer's Folly* (Figure 10).[186] We can *see*, as a visual palimpsest, the English language bleeding through into the surface of the page in Polish. In this way, Fried's claim about the look of the page is precise. But the look of the page is twinned by a resonance, an audibility—a sound bleed. It is the palimpsest of the voice. For the immigrant, Wendy Xu suggests, writing a letter home is always both imagining and remembering.[187] Conrad writes to a family friend, and who is likely quite ill with the awareness that he may not see this friend again, recalling old times. A line in the final draft, reads: "but apparently out of a yearning [*potrzeby* or need] of my heart [*serca*] which has not forgotten the old times. And were they really so long ago? My later life has been so completely different from my childhood years, that those first impressions, feelings and memories have not in any way been erased [*nie zatarly sie wcale*]."[188] *Zatarly* can mean "disappear," "fade," "smudge out," but also "erased" (its use being both intransitive and transitive).[189] He writes this letter as he does in English, with many clauses, and by the end of the sentence, it is clear that it is the *heart* that has not forgotten, Conrad writing of it in reflexive ways. The heart is the subject of the sentence, a site of memory, inscription, translation, and resonance. This heart is the medium from which the sound of memory radiates.

The "heart" in Conrad is among the most recursive figures. The phrase "heart of darkness" will itself be loosed to echo across literary scenes across modernism (it appears, for example, in the conclusion of Ralph Ellison's *Invisible Man*, just before the narrator wonders why he tortures himself with the act of writing). The heart in Conrad's imaginary has inscriptive capacities, as a phonographic surface and medium for retaining. J. Hillis Miller notes that as a prosopopoeia, "heart of darkness" is a catachresis (from *kata* or "down" + *khresthai* or "use," a "misuse"), and, as with the English idiom the "ring of truth" that Conrad mishears or misremembers, it does not appeal to logic. The motility and tenuity of such a phrase is one quality that drew Conrad to English in the first place. The phrase's capacity to be stretched—to resonate across meanings, places, and contexts— counteracts "the commonplace surface of words . . . old words, [being] worn thin, defaced by ages of careless usage."[190] Catachresis is a misuse of words that is fundamentally *proper* to English. (It is a property of impropriety, we might say.) This very misuse, however, is also what allows for the eliding of blackness in the title, an eliding that is also a turning back and forth between blackness and darkness. "Heart of darkness" as prosopopoeia is catachrestic, but the moment darkness becomes blackness, it is with a (feminine) body. When is this moment? It is so overdetermined to have always already happened, as I noted in the Coda to Chapter 2 when we found Quentin Compson looking in the water at his "shadow," carrying "Negro resonances in his mind." In either case, this body is unseen, making *the figure as such* a fundamentally acousmatic event.

In the phonic substance of languages and between languages, words return to their beginnings in vibration and resonance. Yet this resonance still elicits affective attachment when discerned. The sound effects of Conrad's sentence to Poradowska echo across two languages (and perhaps more). "C'est comme une éspèce de tombe" is rhythmic and incantatory. The edges of written words lose what Freud calls their "acoustic demarcation." It is along this vibrating edge of the resonant tomb where I begin to hear my own memory of reading Conrad:

> We had a glimpse of the towering multitude of trees, of the immense matted jungle, with the blazing little ball of the sun hanging over it—all perfectly still—and then the white shutter came down again, smoothly, as if sliding in greased grooves. I ordered

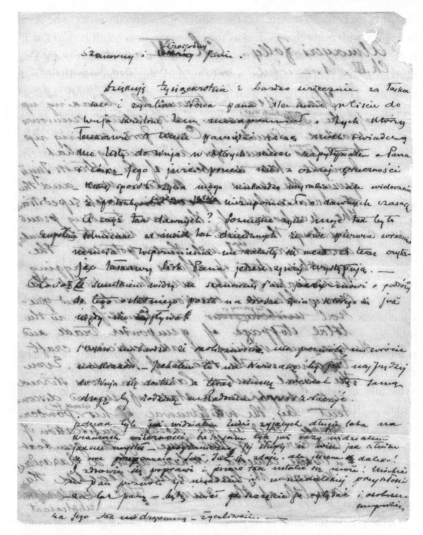

Figure 10. Draft of Polish letter of March 17/29, 1890, on the verso of a manuscript page of *Almayer's Folly.* The Rosenbach Museum and Library, Philadelphia.

the chain, which we had begun to heave in, to be paid out again. Before it stopped running with a muffled rattle, a cry, a very loud cry, as of infinite desolation, soared slowly in the opaque air. It ceased.

Conrad rewrites (I rehear) his letter to Poradowska again in *Heart of Darkness*: "a cry, a very loud cry." A cry, a . . . cry, *écrire* . . . *écrire.* Music, Conrad says in the "Preface" to *The Nigger of the "Narcissus,"* is "the art of arts." Here, Conrad—like Henry James and Walter Pater before him—seeks to define the novel as "art." But it seems impossible that music might grow out of writing unless this music is a scream or cry. "The supreme cry of Art for Art itself . . . sounds far off," Conrad continues. "It has ceased to be a cry, and is heard only as a whisper, often incomprehensible, but at times and faintly encouraging" (*NN*, 15)—echoes of the words Marlow uses to describe Kurtz's last sounds. It is not a cry of passion but of extraction and trauma. For Jean-Jacques Rousseau, the cry is central to his humanism; it is *the* way that humans make themselves known to one another as human. "How could I suffer when I see another suffer if I do not even know that he suffers, if I do not know what he and I have in common?"[191] The social for Rousseau is first incited by the sonority of the cry. "By transporting ourselves outside ourselves; by identifying with the suffering being. We suffer only to the extent that we judge it to suffer; we suffer not in ourselves, but in it [*lui*]"[192]—in listening, a form of transport, community is born. Conrad suggests, however, there is no pure "human" cry or aesthetic form on the other side of the Middle Passage.

At times it seems that Marlow is addressed directly by the music, accompanied by cries, shouts, and moans, but in other moments, he overhears it. Marlow knows nothing about what the sounds mean, except that they mourn. The "source" of this mourning, however, is highly unstable in its genitive coordinates. Marlow never himself cries out when communicating the story: *Heart of Darkness* is, in a manner of speaking, a text that cannot cry, that cannot mourn or does so only through the imaginary proxy of black sound as its affective substitute. In melancholia, as unfulfilled mourning, it keeps its lost objects close. As Derrida makes clear, to hear oneself cry violates autoaffection, the sense of hearing (understanding) oneself speak.[193] In Marlow's foreclosure of crying, he only hears his own voice telling the story through the autoaffection, thus separating himself from the crying sounds he describes and communicates in language.

Conrad far exceeds the epistemic claims of ethnology in presenting a man who, in listening, hears the otherness of his own voice projected back to him but also represses that self-awareness: It is ultimately the anonymous listener—and the reader—who hears that Marlow cannot hear himself.

"Western nations were established on the basis of linguistic intransigence," Glissant writes, "and the exile readily admits that he suffers most from the impossibility of communicating in his language." He continues: "The root is monolingual. For the troubadour and for Rimbaud errantry is a vocation only told via detour. The call of Relation is heard, but it is not yet a fully present experience."[194] When Conrad writes of "old words, worn thin," we cannot mistake this statement as proposing to restore the root philologically in any monolingualism. He invokes what it is to live, listen, and write in what Glissant calls *écho-monde*, the world of things resonating with one another, in contrast with the *toute-monde*, the world in its entirety, and the *chaos-monde*, a world that cannot be systematized. It is where words begin to sound like one another across multiple languages. The call of relation is a troping of sounding, of words becoming alike in sound.

The sound of extracted language is the cry, and its remainder in groans, sighs, and other asignifying sounds amid exchangeable goods:

"Everything else in the station was in a muddle—heads, things, buildings. Strings of dusty niggers with splay feet arrived and departed; a stream of manufactured goods, rubbishy cottons, beads, and brass-wire sent into the depths of darkness, and in return came a precious trickle of ivory.

"I had to wait in the station for ten days—an eternity. I lived in a hut in the yard, but to be out of the chaos I would sometimes get into the accountant's office. It was built of horizontal planks, and so badly put together that, as he bent over his high desk, he was barred from neck to heels with narrow strips of sunlight. . . . When a truckle-bed with a sick man (some invalid agent from upcountry) was put in there, he exhibited a gentle annoyance. 'The groans of this sick person,' he said, 'distract my attention. And without that it is extremely difficult to guard against clerical errors in this climate'" (*Y*, 68–69)

The accountant had just come outside "'to get a breath of fresh air'" and hears a dying man. Marlow is split in this moment: He is not the one "focalizing" the groan; the manager is hearing, and we (over)hear this violent hearing. Marlow speaks of such sounds but does not imitate them. But we would be mistaken if we did not recognize that *Heart of Darkness*, as a circulatory system, takes on a mimetic, communicative, contagious valence. The sounds Marlow describes have no verbal or alphabetic counterpart. He does not reproduce such a sound with his own mouth. The paradox of extraction, of the attempt to possess resources, involves a "fear of what that possession will mean" for the one who desires to possess.[195] The possessor, in this way, becomes the possessed, both penetrated and infected.

The form of *Heart of Darkness* as mediumship, a "possessed" work, circulates within this libidinal economy of extraction. Both Friedrich Kittler and Avital Ronell have traced how the earliest desires circulating within the telephonic and phonographic imaginary were telepathic desires. But where there is conveyance (in vibration), there is the possibility for infection, that the thing transmitted will be absorbed into the channel that hopes to carry it. All of the air in *Heart of Darkness*, we must recall, is *infected* air, with "the groans of this sick person" distracting attention and with Kurtz himself exhaling a breath just before issuing his last words. In revising his text, Conrad added a hyphen to the moment of Kurtz's last words, "'a cry that was no more than a breath—'" as if to create a visual break that is also a pause for readerly breath, an infectious inhalation (*Y*, 149).

The groan (and other sounds across the text, such as "'the hurt nigger [who] moaned feebly somewhere nearby, and then fetched a deep sigh'") is of a person who has outlasted his use (*Y*, 80). Marlow cannot stray too far or tarry too long into the sound space of the needy stranger. It is the sound of exhausted and extracted being. These sounds are inconsequential to the narrative except in being the trace of a memory that cuts the neutrality of space in its rational abstraction, an acoustic exterior traced around or within Marlow's episteme. Marlow attends to yet withdraws from what is an adjacent or tangential space traced by his sounds—adjacent to the path of his journey, adjacent to the central narrative.

To the extent that unmourned loss determines the sounds of *Heart of Darkness*, a more profound trauma of sexual difference opens up the primary possibility of its diegesis—its narrative space—as such. When Marlow suppresses Kurtz's last words before the Intended, it is a double suppression, an acoustical displacement of the fact of colonial sexual violence. Marlow cannot narrate this fact, a missing image in relation to *Heart of Darkness*. It determines not only his temporal presentation but his representations of the jungle as a feminine body that is to be penetrated. It is a "body of touch, a nocturnal blackness that could not be seen . . . associated with . . . the invisible female genitalia."[196] (On a textual level, displacement populates the typography of the novel whenever Marlow trails off, punctuated by Conrad as ellipses, which abound in the text, a record released from its groove. In the gendered language of musical form and tonal harmony, these are "feminine endings," or metrically weak cadences that refuse the containment of the barline.)[197] Such concrete absence confronts the black woman who appears but twice in *Heart of Darkness*, described in the critical literature invariably as a "concubine" or "mistress," phrases that romanticize domination. The moment we listen across the spaces of the text, its enfolding regions of darkness, with their cries and shouts, cannot be separated from violation; it is the novel's disnarrated.

As resonance, *Heart of Darkness* is fundamentally anachronic, determined by the future of the Congo, including its displaced place in Western telecommunications. At stake everywhere in *Heart of Darkness* is the reproduction of a voice that might communicate. Marlow sequesters in memory the sound of the

Congo when confronting the Intended, when he makes himself known as the one who will carry the story that is the condition of possibility of this narrative qua narrative: What he sequesters is the black feminine body. She is encrypted in the diegetic sound space, as the sinister resonance of what Nancy Hunt calls, in relation to colonial rape and its continued afterlife, "twisted sounds." Rape was already a technique of violence in the Congo when Conrad was there and it continues to be a technique today. "Listening for twisted sounds," Hunt writes of archival records and testimony, "allows concentrating on nonnarrativity . . . the convulsive, frenzied quality of sadistic violence in process, the hidden, the shameful"—what Roger Casement, in a 1904 report on abuses in the Congo, simply described as "unfit for repetition."[198] These fragile acoustic memories demand a contrasting archival technic, one that Hunt names, after Benjamin, "a technique of nearness." Hunt explicitly contrasts this technique with Conrad's hallucinatory evasions. But perhaps that is because we, as critics, have not been listening to Conrad. Though in the immediate years after the publication of *Heart of Darkness* Alice Harris's Kodak photos of mutilated hands in the Congo would circulate spectacularly, genital mutilation and other sexual abuses went unphotographed, Hunt describes, leaving only inward scars. (Such scars meant that the reproductive capacity of the Congo was to be cut from itself in the body of the black woman.) We speak of "reproducing" voices with "fidelity." *Heart of Darkness* is obsessed with reproducing voices and sounds. This obsession is cut by the formless figure of a violated woman. The music both cancels and preserves its nonmemory.

In this sonic trace, the central figures of Conrad's "another art altogether" become physicalized (a sinister resonance, a continued vibration). In the intimate space of reading, the index of atrocity itself is physicalized. The sinister resonance and continued vibration stimulate and agitate some invisible part of the body usually reserved for "warmth." The form of the novel is autoerotic; it becomes apparent in the shape of the desires it stimulates. No one, strictly speaking, will appear in such a shape. It is anonymous. There is nothing except the desire to "see" on the other side of a sound.

Heart of Darkness, in being both a system of transmission and a system of storage, both carries and encrypts a sound with contagious portent for imperial listening consciousness. How is Marlow, as the idealized English voice through which Conrad wrote, to be understood in relation to the voices that Marlow hears, casts off, yet *re-members* while also re-calling and re-citing? What does it mean for Conrad's project—the search for the right voice, the spiritual *lingua franca* that might reach his reader—that Marlow confronts voices that he must oppose to his own? The condition of hearing the sound is the recitation such that it has already happened: Marlow carries it, brings it back to England. The continued vibration dwells not "in the ear" but "on the ear," hanging at its door, neither inside nor outside.

"I am lost!" shouts Conrad in his letter to Poradowska. Here, there is a failed antiphony, where the groan or moan, overheard, is a cry or call that is not synthesized or received as an address. Nor is it synthesized into the musical memory that haunts the margins of Marlow's journey: This groan and moan is, then, a margin of the margin, in the furthest reaches of the outer rim of Saussure's circuit. We found the slur in Conrad's experience of vibration and the sonorous substratum of thought. It is a symbol that has lost all determination to become an acoustic register. When Marlow announces himself in twilight, his voice begins to lose its determination, no longer to "speak" in any precise sense but to vibrate. The storytelling voice loses its determination not because something is unspeakable but because the symbol has been scratched out.

Conrad never heard his own voice recorded, though he heard a recording of Polish piano music and saw an X-ray of his hand. The hand that defaces the page where the voice and sound expire: This is the matrix in which all of Conrad's "Africa" is concentrated.

So that at last, as though out of some trivial and unimportant region beyond even distance, the sound of it seems to come slow and terrific and without meaning, as though it were a ghost travelling a half mile ahead of its own shape. "That far within my hearing before my seeing," Lena thinks.

—William Faulkner, *Light in August*

A philosophy of the event must move in what *at first glance* appears to be a paradoxical direction: towards a materialism of the incorporeal.

—Michel Foucault, "Return to History"

REPRISE: REVERBERATION, CIRCUMAMBIENCE, AND FORM-SEEKING SOUND (*ABSALOM, ABSALOM!*)

FORM-SEEKING SOUND

A sonority is the product of physical action on physical materials. . . . An energy field, certain to vanish completely once the musicians put down their instruments.

Charles Curtis

I conclude by engaging an experience that cannot be fully retrieved or pragmatically narrated, though it will have bearing on the historical. Theodor Adorno writes of a passing phrase in Beethoven's piano sonata *Les Adieux* that "this most transient of things, the ineffable sound of disappearance, holds more hope of return than could ever be disclosed to a reflection on the origin and essence of the form-seeking sound."[1] This statement covers a long duration of sound, one that exceeds, on an empirical level, attack and decay. The hope of return opens upon the historicity of a single sound—a sonority that, like weather, hangs on too long or disappears too soon. If an inquiry into the "origin and essence" (*Ursprung*) of the form-seeking sound discloses so little, it is because Adorno suggests in place of an ontology of sound a mode of listening. This mode of reception cannot be fully outlined but indicates an attention to what is almost missed, to what is barely articulated as meaning in the highly narrativized and orchestrated space of the sonata form, constituting both the sonata's granular fabric and its residual surplus.

It disappears but not completely. The form-seeking sound, a reverberation, clings to memory and the space that hosts it to indicate some other possibility of praxis in return.

Literary sound studies must work at this threshold, pursuing sounds that cannot, as graphemes on the page, be empirically heard yet still register ways of hearing. There is something minor, within the history of feeling, wherein a reverberative literary history might take shape. We have experienced aspects of this resonance in Conrad and Du Bois. I reprise with another instance: reverberation in Faulkner—with Conrad and Du Bois.

REVERBERATION AND CIRCUMAMBIENCE

A chronicler who recites events without distinguishing between major and minor ones acts in accordance with the following truth: nothing that has ever happened should be regarded as lost for history.

Walter Benjamin, "Theses on the Philosophy of History"

Faulkner's *Absalom, Absalom!* begins with a meditation on listening as it has shaped things past and to come. Minor sensations have composed an invisible reality behind immediately available voice and visible action, the basis of drama and choreography, of all *poiesis*. There is in this beginning not simply a poetics but an acoustics among a broader sensorium of moving air wherein sounds, scents, and light rays intertwine before having been forcefully separated by thought.

The unnamed and anonymous narrative voice of *Absalom, Absalom!* speaks— and listens—from out of a profound forgetting: the creation of collective memory through its partial suppression. We are told that the Sutpen plantation and its formal gardens seem simply to have appeared out of nothing and nowhere, its origins concealed in the invocation that also brings it into being, *"Be Sutpen's Hundred*, like the olden time *Be Light."* The "soundless Nothing" of fiat generates Sutpen's Hundred but is not without physical substance, for the plantation is said to have been "torn violently" out of the earth by slaves speaking a "strange tongue" (*AA*, 4). This tongue is never heard fully by the narrative, perhaps because it is never comprehended by its auditors in the moment. It is later attached, in residual ways, to the knowledge that Sutpen gains his wealth, his slaves, and a mixed-race son in Haiti.

When the word "Haiti" is finally uttered, it resonates in the acoustics of narrative space, in the reader's space of cognition and reception. This space is, in a precise sense, reverberating with the past of reading. The occluded opening of the diegesis touches the present of reading in its residuum. Readers of the novel often comment that it is difficult to remember when "knowledge" of an event first manifested or how that knowledge came to be. "Memory believes before knowing remembers," Faulkner writes.[2]

The sensory and linguistic memory of Native American dispossession, slavery, and the historical present of US imperial expansion in Haiti are invoked by the narrative beginning, only to be quickly displaced by a missing image and a missing sound. But slavery and conquest have, nonetheless, been called to the space, or summoned from out of it, in an evocation that vanishes to define the unfolding of the novel. It demands reading for resonance: a "recalling."[3] Words vanish but later strike what Faulkner calls *"the resonant strings of remembering."*

Although Faulkner is tempted to share in the command by which a novelistic world also tends toward authoritatively appearing out of nothingness, he begins in medias res, in a room where two people have already been sitting, talking, for how long we don't know. It begins on the precipice of negating the long-existing pronouncements that delimit action and perception, residual to their core. The novel begins in the temporality that Walter Benjamin also invokes in "The Storyteller" as "coming to end,"[4] within what is the verge of the object tending toward transformation, the as yet incomplete or form-seeking dimension within any ossified formation. Faulkner named this fourth dimension—from out of which narrative voice is no longer an "it speaks" but an "it listens"—*"the circumambient air"* (AA, 119).

Quentin Compson, who is bound for Harvard, had been hailed by Rosa Coldfield for a "day of listening" (AA, 23). She recognizes that there is little left in the South for such a young man and wishes, before he leaves, to tell him a story. Here we are somewhere in the vicinity of Conrad's drawing room, its sonic hearth now transported to Yoknapatawpha (from the Chickasaw *yocona petopha*, or "split land"—it is a name held by the "Chuck. Chuck. Chuck." of the adze that opens narrative acoustics and the sound of place in *As I Lay Dying*):

> From a little after two until almost sundown of the long still hot weary dead September afternoon they sat in what Miss Coldfield still called the office because her father had called it that—a dim hot airless room with the blinds all closed and fastened for forty-three summers because when she was a girl someone had believed that light and moving air carried heat and that dark was always cooler, and which (as the sun shone fuller and fuller on that side of the house) became latticed with yellow slashes full of dust motes which Quentin thought of as being flecks of the dead old dried paint itself blown inward from the scaling blinds ... There was a wistaria vine blooming for the second time that summer on a wooden trellis before one window into which sparrows came now and then in random gusts, making a dry vivid dusty sound before going away.... (AA, 3)

The day moves toward its repository to lose particularity and join the longer thread of what Nietzsche calls the "so it was" out of which the spirit of revenge emerges. Things seem to speak their own constitution and hardening. Words accumulate without pause or comma, as if narrative voice is holding its breath in this suffocating room, the consequences of breathing here being quite dire. This room is defined by the accumulation of authoritative names and words, defined not simply by endurance but by restless preservation. Time, Faulkner knew, does not "pass" but gathers in things.[5] Before the reader has even arrived, all motion has already been cut by an intransigence: The voice of an absent yet continuing and fixed authority clings to objects in the room, as if it would take new air to circulate new names, names derived not from knowing but a childlike, unwavering belief. The air is heavy with thingness, the "dust motes" offering evidence that air carries more than air. Dust, nothing more than dead skin, carries something of those who have breathed there before. While a sparrow song arrives with a gust through Rosa's window, it makes a "dry vivid dusty sound," but the blooming world it carries is dried as if upon entry, becoming too an agent of dust. This natural sound, which should be for the first time, is already old in its fiat.

The people of Jefferson are waiting for a relief more profound than rain.

The South, as the national "other" alterior within American consciousness, is doing a constitutive work for a nation that would deem slavery and empire a sin of some other place, American consciousness drawing the *cordon sanitaire* between the South and itself but also between itself and the occupation of other lands. As narrated through that Veil, one that Faulkner recognized fundamentally as American double consciousness, it is undecidable whether the novel takes place in 1833, 1909, or 1936.[6]

In *Absalom*, Faulkner turns his attention to what has been lost to the historical present, missed chances for feeling among four generations of black and white brothers and sisters who cannot fully acknowledge their own blood relation. The central crux of the storytelling voices in 1909 is an account of why Henry Sutpen shot his closest friend, Charles Bon, at the threshold of Sutpen's Hundred at the end of the Civil War. This murder, we only later discover, is not committed on the threat of incest (Bon is his half-brother and intends to marry their sister, Judith) but the threat of miscegenation (Bon is the partially black child of Sutpen's first marriage in Haiti). The echo of the shot is said to hang in the air of Jefferson for a phonographic duration of four decades. An experience of the sound reaches Quentin through the account of Rosa, the novel's first narrator and one of the few living witnesses of the Civil War remaining, in the narrating present of 1909.

But even here, among such stagnation and reproduction of the same, there is the possibility that will come to define the unfolding of the narrative as it moves backward in an act of reparative recovery, a "rescue," in Benjamin and Conrad's lexicon. What is to be rescued is not for a limitless future but an aggrieved past: the seat of transformation.[7] The room has been hollowed out by the naming function as memorialization and reimpression. As she sits, Rosa guards not only town memories but an "implacable unforgiving," which, in its tenacity, has acquired the status of a thing (AA, 9). Faulkner insists upon this space as one of both mediation and reproduction, having added as a marginal note and codicil to the original manuscript that the wisteria, the scent of the South itself, is "blooming for a second time"—something has already taken place here before, but a second bloom is an uncanny and uncommon occurrence; something more than what has already happened, a rift in unfolding (AA, 3). Something is happening here by way of listening amid so much apparent reproduction of the same.

Yoknapatawpha, as Faulkner's epic without resolution, "would be an unsuspected and unpredictable opening," Édouard Glissant writes after his journey to Faulkner's Mississippi, "not at all systematic; it would be fragile, ambiguous, and ephemeral."[8] In this opening, there is a poetics of relation, an échos-monde. During Faulkner's time in residence at the University of Virginia, a student perhaps sensed this acoustics when he asked if Faulkner had "got something in the way of arrangement of words from Conrad."[9] He notes in Faulkner similar "arrangements of cadence, rhythm": "I'm thinking of a passage in 'Youth,' an arrangement of adjectives, 'resplendent yet somber, full of danger, yet promising,' the description of the East when the young boy comes upon it. There's something of the same kind of use of—kind of heavy arrangement of adjectives I've noticed in your writing."[10] "Full of danger, yet promising"—what might happen cannot be positively deduced from what has already happened. Conrad makes an encounter with the fantasy of the East palpable at the level of the sentence, one that, though it desires this object, also knows it to be irreducible to possession. Faulkner responds to the student, "Quite true. I got quite a lot from Conrad."

Faulkner says no more, but in a later seminar, a second student returns to the specter of Conrad in Faulkner: "I was thinking of the particular thing of Conrad's effort to surround an event by throwing light on it from past and future as well as present. He seems to stop at a particular event and throw light . . . from the front and the rear and the side, in a way I don't remember other novelists doing before his time."[11] Faulkner's responds that Conrad's "cleverness" in this regard "was because he deliberately taught himself a foreign language to write in." He continues, "And mine may be because I never went to school enough to save myself the short cuts of learning English."

In Chapter 1, we found a politics of anachrony in the doubled sense of what Christopher GoGwilt calls the "passage of literature." This politics of anachrony—as a materialist potential in literary language—became audible in the sound space of an untranslated shout. In the first student's example, "resplendent yet somber, full of danger, yet promising," Conrad again revels in the ambiguity afforded by the English language, words accumulating in Conrad's desire for presence mediated by a desire for the image of the East. But that desire willingly admits a split sensibility, where one does not cancel out the other but touches it and holds it in mutual vibration. The tension between what is and what might be ceases to be a contradiction. Words are heavy with a desire for a presence, but one that is not given in advance. It is horizonal, in the philosopher Hans-Georg Gadamer's sense, or more precisely *circumspective*.

I draw this phrase from section 29 of *Being and Time*, where Heidegger concentrates on facticity and mood (*Stimmung*, or attunement), the metaphors becoming decidedly auralistic. Mood is an "attunement" to what is there. Heidegger meditates on the call of conscience as one modality through which the existence of otherness makes itself felt. However, he describes the circumspective (*Umsicht*) as another way to approach facticity. A translation, *um-* (as aroundness, but also in order to) + *sicht* (seeing), implies the referentiality of things to their larger worldliness. Yet the visualism of the metaphor is a limit. To do an *Umsicht* would be impossible; one would have to see all in an instant. It would be something like an act of listening, which becomes in *Being and Time* the paradigm for the experience that would disclose facticity.[12]

One does not "have" a *Stimmung*; one is in a *Stimmung*. "From this we can already see that attunement is far removed from anything like finding a physical condition. Far from having the character of an apprehension which first turns itself around and then turns back, all immanent reflection can find 'experiences' only because the there is already disclosed in attunement."[13] He writes, "disclosed, as such, does not mean to be known."[14]

It is in such disclosure that *Absalom, Absalom!* begins, in the form-seeking dimension that Faulkner names circumambience. The narrative's mode of attention to an event circles around it in a simultaneous effort and refusal to seize it. To the extent that the event is seized by the narrative, it will become past. But to the extent that it escapes, as did the missing image of twilight when Conrad's Almayer gazes over the Pantai River, its unfulfilled and postcolonial dimension will return, and in some residual form. Faulkner makes it clear that for him, these qualities of perception and disclosure cannot be heard outside of Conrad's relationship to English as an idealized, cathected object. The "kind of light" thrown on the event drifts into the aural.

Faulkner's circumambience—a way of hearing around things as they were and as they are yet to be, which for Conrad begins with translation—developed amid a series of unlikely sources in which the givenness of mood and listening intertwine, placing Faulkner's modernism somewhere both within and without the Southern region that defines his fictional world. The language (of) atmosphere is beyond the strictly American sources that would seem most naturally to frame it.[15] Faulkner writes, of completing *The Sound and the Fury*, "I wrote this book and learned to read. . . . [A]nd in a series of delayed repercussions like summer thunder, I discovered the Flauberts and Conrads and Dostoievskys whose books I had read ten years ago."[16] In another version of the preface to *The Sound and the Fury*, Faulkner writes "James, Conrad, and Joyce" (and there are still more iterations of the sentiment, recursive in his own thinking about writing). In each triplet, it is only Conrad who recurs, and it becomes impossible to decide what comes first, reading or writing. Conrad is a repercussion that arrives later than it should have, not with the writing of Faulkner's own text but after it, as part of its return and reappraisal in memory.

It is Conrad, we found in Chapter 2, who provides Faulkner the materials for confronting the conflicted feelings surrounding miscegenation as slavery's own delayed psychic repercussion. The "delayed repercussion" becomes, at the same time, Faulkner's suggestive aural metaphor for remembering having read after having written. In its event, region and the specificity of place, its modes of forgetting and wish for amnesty (a kind of amnesia), begin to resonate with the outside. They resonate with what Quentin Anderson calls "temporalized thought."[17] As Michael Milgate beautifully describes in *Faulkner's Place*, temporalized thought exerts pressure upon American ahistoricism, and, with it, the mythology of Southern innocence and a self-created world. Temporalized thought gives time where there had only been reification and genesis. "It is late," Conrad begins the Malay tale, "The Lagoon." Temporalized and temporalizing thought calls to Yoknapatawpha from across the Pacific, the Atlantic and, in more anachronic ways, the Black Atlantic. In this way, it becomes impossible to think of Faulkner purely as a writer of the American South, as Mallios makes clear in the final chapter of his stunning book *Our Conrad*, as does Glissant, who turns to Faulkner as an echo of the Caribbean sensibility in his opus *Faulkner, Mississippi*.

The aural specificity of the figure of summer thunder, its delayed repercussion, is resonant in its geographical coordinates and temporal(izing) effects. It is the sound for which the people of Yoknapatawpha, stifled by air laden with both heat and time, wait. It is a figure that gives time. In this thunder, we recognize the summer sound of a *place*—a specific region and locale—that had inscribed itself in Faulkner's memory; the memory records this sound and knows it well. But in its temporality, it holds within two conflicting tendencies, the will to forget and the counterwish to remember (anew). Faulkner once wrote that he preferred reading to listening to music, because "the thunder of the prose takes place in silence."[18] This *taking place* in Faulkner is never quite complete, and the site of sound, "where" it takes place, becomes just as open or irresolute. It is not that symbols lose their determinacy, as we found in *Heart of Darkness*, but rather that they gain in their determination by what would seem to be outside them.

This placeless place of resonance returns us again to Conrad. When at the end of chapter 4 of *Lord Jim* Marlow is evoked on the verandah, "the ear of Conrad's buildings," there is a single dangling passage concerning dusk. It is a "space of appearance," as Hannah Arendt might say, that supports storytelling, where *physis* becomes palpable as the necessary condition of speech and action.[19] Dusk is indicated just before dissipating into darkness. It is not to be more fully elaborated or returned to. It is merely a surplus hinge between the first part of the novel, narrated in third-person omniscience (which too never returns, as if it has been sublated into some new modality), and the second part of the novel, narrated by the directly discoursing voice of Marlow. Whatever voice this "is" that evokes Marlow on the verandah speaks but once before disappearing, after never having become fully substantialized.

> And later on, many times, in distant parts of the world, Marlow showed himself willing to remember Jim, to remember him at length, in detail and audibly.
>
> Perhaps it would be after dinner, on a verandah draped in motionless foliage and crowned with flowers, in the deep dusk speckled by fiery cigar-ends. The elongated bulk of each cane-chair harboured a silent listener . . . and with the very first word uttered Marlow's body, extended at rest in the seat, would become very still, as though his spirit had winged its way back into the lapse of time and were speaking through his lips from the past. (*LJ*, 33)

Neither revealing nor concealing, dusk finds no psychic aim to obey. Internal forces have not yet crept in upon the armature of the day, the motive of sleep whose complete withdrawal from world into self returns us to the night of memory. Dusk is a creaturely time and space, not simply for the metamorphosis it brings but in rescinding, arresting, and withdrawing (death and decay on its immediate other side), the interval immeasurably negative.

"Perhaps it would be." In this nearly subjunctive mood, it is undecidable whether it has happened or not, the "would be" seated somewhere between past and future. (Faulkner rewrites this passage time and again in *Absalom, Absalom!*, the circulation of light, sound, and scent: "It was a summer of wistaria. The twilight was full of it and of the smell of his father's cigar as they sat on the front gallery after supper until it would be time for Quentin to start" to return to meet with Rosa again; "even now the only alteration toward darkness was in the soft and fuller random of the fireflies" [*AA*, 23, 71]. The circumambience of the verandah, "both limit and passage," is transferred to Mississippi and back; the Southern porch is not contained but globally comported in time and space.) Yet "Marlow showed himself." In that moment, Conrad *translates* from Henry James's dusk what would become the quintessential watchword of novel theory: "showing." The art of fiction, Percy Lubbock famously insists after James, "shows" and does not "tell," a dictum that continues to orient novel theory and the study of modernism. But Marlow's speaking body surfaces in a moment of national and lingual passing. The mask is quite thin. Marlow does not show; he shows *himself*. There is a foreign resonance: *pokazał się*. The "*się*," or self upon which an action is performed in the Polish language, is not the itself to which the phenomenological subject returns.[20] Conrad's tense is ultrasensual, ultrahistorical.

There is a voice, but one that lurks within grammar without wielding it. The "free and wandering voice" of the minimal diegesis makes palpable another register, transatlantic and transpacific in contour, transphysical in aim, seeking to overcome distance between self and other and to initiate a heterogeneous experience of the other in the self (*IJ*, viii). Recall from Chapter 3 of this present book that this distance "could be so wide as to be a matter of thousands of miles or so minute as to be 'the space of a breath.'"

Tense itself resonates. In the Overture, we found the resonant subject for Jean-Luc Nancy to go back from "an intensive spacing of a rebound that does not end in any return to self." Not "posed in itself to its *point of view*," he continues, "the subject of listening is always still yet to come, spaced, traversed, and called by itself, *sounded* by itself."[21] The subject of listening—distinct from the hearing-as-understanding of the philosophical tradition—is "suspended and straining between arrival and departure." Conrad's "voice" is this straining. Where does it come from? What are its coordinates? Marlow showed himself willing to remember, audibly. Someone is showing himself willing to listen.

As Marlow shows himself willing to remember audibly, there is no focalizer, because there is no focal *point*. The technical form of the focalizer loses itself: It loses itself in an *evocator* proper to circumambience as an anachronic and transitional object, the seeming to shape, coming to shape, but always reflexively toward the one who is shaping as he is also shaped. "It shaped itself," Conrad writes of James Wait's final breath. Conrad's reflexive tense and subjunctive mood of change is encoded with a desire for English, an approximation of or nearing and transfer of English. In speaking, friends recall, he often misconjugated verbs, if he conjugated them at all. Conrad "heard" himself as misspeaking, not ignorant of this critical valence that was given to the listening other (his voice was never recorded, an object we long to hear). His English is separating itself from Polish and French and stretching out English itself, making it resonate. This form of reflexive expression continually recurs around a passage, a movement, that is an event of textual listening: "I listened, I listened on the watch for the sentence, for the word, that would give me the clue to the faint uneasiness inspired by this narrative that seemed to shape itself without human lips in the heavy night-air of the river."

This word doesn't exist. The scene is premised upon a loss of language and a grammar of change. There is no way to put into English words what is in Polish a poetic valence that can be spoken ("There are no words for the sort of things I wanted to say," Conrad's Jim says). The Polish reflexive "self" says, above all, that there are distances, poetic and transfigurative states (*szukam siebie*, one might say, "I look for self" or "I am in search of self" because I feel lost). In those distances within itself, there is a resonance: The minimal value of resonance is not the one but *two*, the more than one. Polish is the lost or relinquished language, the "mother tongue," but Conrad is returning it to English in a broken offering. "He wrote a beautiful hand," Conrad writes, "became soon perfect in English."[22] The reflexive tense is an artifact of a reflexive act of self-translating. It is a sonic trace. As I have used it throughout this book, by that catechesis, I indicate what is caught between writing and sounding, caught between writing English and speaking in Polish and French.

In this spacing out on the verandah and the porch, as resonance, relay, broadcast, and traversal, there will be a speaker and a listener. Nothing appears, nothing manifests, except the possibility of listening. "Perhaps it would be on a verandah." But for the novel to exist, "it" already must have been. Marlow speaks from the transnational sensible, one that we found in Chapter 1 to open Conrad to the postcolonial; its narrative instance has the quality both of having happened and not yet having happened.

It is not as if there is merely some latent quality beneath what is manifest, where the manifest expresses a quantity that cannot be seen in itself. This quantity is insurgent; it is not yet itself. Nor is there an impersonal someone (who sees) upon which modernist discourse is premised. There is a nameless someone who, like Marlow, is making himself vacant, emptying himself out in order to listen; he is not yet known to himself, for even though the sensible of the *récit* is first incarnated in a memory of a someone who is the speaker of the phrases "And later on" and "Perhaps it would be," the mood hypostatizes the subject of the verb's mode of action. The subjunctive mood, the mood of change, is paradoxically given the weight and reality of a substance. The subjunctive is materialized into or by the dusk itself. The entirety of the scene is premised upon a leap into faith. Within its weight, vertical, crowned, and elongated, two men are evoked, the first a "silent listener," an anonymous figure unseen and then multiplied into the many. A second man, Marlow, is the destining of the story's voice—but only to the extent that one of these silent men on the verandah will have become a listener, or the one who can receive and will be the one to have carried and transferred over (to us) Marlow's event of sounding. The narrative is narrating itself, narrating its condition of possibility.

There is still in the scene, hanging over it as a remnant, a third voice, the presence of a watcher who Jim thinks "looks at me as though he could see somebody or something behind my back" (*LJ*, 33). But even this watcher is in the midst of diffusing and disappearing into the possibility of Marlow's embodied voice. There is a place—a verandah at twilight at its darkest phase of dusk (among Du Bois's most recursive figures and in close proximity to dawn). But even here, in this hypothetical because purely subjunctive moment, Marlow's lips hang in the dark, on an immobile and transforming surface that, inhuman, belong to no one body.

In this grammar, the weakness of structure makes itself felt, its holding together of a "we" who is addressed at its most permeable. There is some minimal substance through which things, as Conrad continually remarked, "shape themselves." In the English turn of phrase, one would say passively "was shaped" or actively "that he shaped." This shaping is without a watcher. Though we begin from the premise of the dusk in Henry James's *The Portrait of a Lady*, that there are no persons, only the textual effect of the verb's mode of action, Conrad's twilight orients a translingual and transnational verb. It is a reflexive tense—drawn from Conrad's still-evident being in French and Polish—that refuses subject and object to open upon a mood of transformativity. On the witness stand, as Jim's voice "rang startlingly in his own ears," his words "came to shape themselves with pain and anguish in his breast" (*LJ*, 32). The duration of transition is otherwise foreclosed by the simple past. It is then that he thinks that he might never speak again. Then someone shows himself willing to listen ("that men may listen to the striving," says Du Bois).

"Then hearing would reconcile and he would seem to listen to two separate Quentins now"—as if separated by a Veil (*AA*, 4). If we return to where Rosa has called Quentin for a "day of listening," it is here, in this room, that something occurs that does not occur in any other space of Faulkner's novel: The "demon" ghost of Thomas Sutpen appears, a specter often likened to a kind of early cinema in a projection, a *photogénie* in the lexicon of the early film theorist Jean Epstein. The *photogénie* is cinema's fourth dimension, the affective, enlivened, and "overtonal" space between screen and spectator localized in neither but resonantly coresident.[23] This specter remains tethered to the incantatory voice of Rosa: The ghost is "itself circumambient and enclosed by its effluvium of hell," taking on solidity in the room "as Miss Coldfield's voice went on, resolved out of itself" the invoked scene (*AA*, 8). One must imagine the sonic hearth in its high-ceilinged drawing rooms and wooden floors by which voices reverberate. This room is metaphysically caught between two acoustical realities. It is an echo chamber, filled with "sonorous defeated names" (*AA*, 7), but at the same time, some residual sound seeks a new form.

Faulknerian temporality is defined by repercussion, by which we understand, according to the *OED*, "repulse or recoil of a thing after impact" and "the fact of being driven back by a resisting force or body." In music, the figure of repercussion relates to "the repetition of the subject of a fugue after the exposition," and in acoustics, simply "reflection of a sound; echo, reverberation" or "recurring sounds or vibrations."

Under this acoustic sense of the word, literary examples begin to populate the *OED*, as with Edith Wharton, who writes, "The repetition of the name seemed to carry it to the farther corners of the room and send it back to them in long repercussions of sound." With reverberation, we begin to sense we are in some arena defined by the trope. Faulknerian characters and events are continually driven back into themselves after an often-brutalizing force. This otherwise difficult-to-represent experience of force requires the fictional to make itself known in its effects.[24] In *The Sound and the Fury*, Quentin's memory is continually punctuated by Benjy's crying: "*he was pulling at her dress and bellowing his voice hammered back and forth between the walls in waves and she shrinking against the wall getting smaller and smaller . . . until he pushed her out of the room his voice hammering back and forth as though its own momentum would not let it stop as though there were no place for it in silence bellowing*" (*SF*, 124). The intensity of reverberation diminishes the distinction between inwardness and outwardness, physical place and psychical space. This sound is a part-object of an experience that has nowhere to go or be yet continues, violently exteriorizing its demand for containment.

Denise Riley distinguishes between echo and reverberation precisely along this axis. Reverberation is a striking or beating back. An echo is "self-repeating," whereas reverberation, though it resembles an echo in its effect, requires an impact, the action of one striking against the other. It is beyond Echo's "ironic recuperations."[25] We might say that the distinction is rendered in the subject and object: If I say "it is being echoed," I presume the object is continuing beyond the object; if I say "it is being reverberated," I presume an action has come upon an object. In Chapter 2, we pursued resonance by way of echo, which we understood to be the structural dimension of the call-and-response relation. In reverberation, the space and time of the recurrence is elongated. With it, we understand what Emily Thompson calls "the acoustic signature of a place" through "the lingering over time of residual sound in a space, . . . a function of both the size of a room and the materials that constituted its surfaces."[26]

In Faulkner, we are once again outside of the "soundscape," which naturalizes the relation between sound and place. What I have called "sound space" is the nonlocalizable structure of resonance's occurrence; it is transpacific, transatlantic, diasporic, heterochronic, and anachronic in dimension. To be sure, Faulkner *localizes* the memory of a sound—such as with summer thunder, a Southern sound—only to open up that place radically to some other kind of memory of reading. But the peculiar being of resonance is to be both localized and an array. He wishes to re-produce that experience in the space of reading. In narrative space, sound originates in place only to become highly charged by other geographic and temporal coordinates.

We return, once again, to Rosa's room, but now as if on the precipice of world. There is genuine opening—echo will become reverberation.

As the sun "shone fuller and fuller on that side of the house" it also carries the sensuous condition that is succession. Light, air, heat. If Sutpen's Hundred conceals its origins behind fiat, these are the immediate materials out of which *Absalom, Absalom!* makes itself; they are the base materials of perception and the sensuous appearance of the object. So many of Faulkner's novels begin in this way, by isolating the materials out of which the literary world and its figures might appear.[27] But the earliest appearance of objects in this novel also instructs us as to the sensuous condition that is time, the succession of sensations that governs appearance. The novel begins by interrogating air as the condition of human experience as well as sound and voice, primary to Faulkner's novel in its content and form.

Far from ever being gone, this air settles into permanence, "as if there were prisoned in it like a tomb all the suspiration of slow head-laden time" (*AA*, 6). The weight of Faulknerian atmosphere is historically derived. These are Balzacian walls that "speak," the margins of space in which action might even take place being registered in exhausting detail, as in a passing moment in *Père Goriot* when the narrator notes that typhoid is passed by coughs retained in hospital walls. The walls of Rosa's office retain the fixed and haunting names of Father, something of an air heavy with sounds and voices, which constitute an atmosphere long before one arrives on the scene—the forgotten material history of air. Rosa will later say, "*Once there was—Do you mark how the wistaria, sun-impacted on this wall here, distills and penetrates this room as though (light-unimpeded) by secret and attritive progress from mote to mote of obscurity's myriad components? That is the substance of remembering—sense, sight, smell*" (*AA*, 115). This is no anacoluthon but a pointed tutorial on the material reality of the "once there was": the beginning of any story, any *récit*.

We learn in Rosa's carefully guarded sanctuary that feelings do not simply vanish. Nor does the space of possibility amid so much reproduction of the same. Feeling clings to its material contexts. These walls retain and transpersonally communicate not only the names of the Father but also the possibility of desire never fully reckoned, lived, or bereaved. "*There is a might-have-been which is more true than truth*" (*AA*, 115).

This tension in history suggested by Rosa's room remains inaccessible, without positive knowledge, since who or what will redeem these lost chances cannot be fully deduced from what has already happened. Mr. Compson will later suggest that Rosa has called Quentin in particular ("why tell me," he asks) because he is partially responsible "through heredity"—his grandfather had lent the first cotton seeds to Sutpen. Here, the past and present are "irreducibly connected—without being causally determined in an external way."[28] Faulkner's unnamed narrator remarks, "It was a part of his twenty years' heritage of breathing the same air and hearing his father talk about the man . . . eighty years' heritage of the same air which the man himself had breathed" (*AA*, 7). Circumambient, this air has origins far beyond Yoknapatawpha.

Faulkner continually notes the air through which sounds and voices move, and in this, it is fundamentally reverberative. There is little language for these textual atmospherics because they are unempirical. They cannot be shown or demonstrated (*apodeixis*), yet they govern (re)appearance. Air in Faulkner—between people and works—is the principal force of feeling's transmission toward release. It is the point of contact between necessity and contingency. We are rarely allowed to forget that air is the carrier of sound and scent—but also speech, which becomes in this way one material artifact among others. In it, we are so far afield from Aristotle's *pneume* as the Western seat of vocality that it is as if some long trajectory of thought has expired in the formal exhaustion of Faulkner's own prose in *Absalom, Absalom!*—in the words of Quentin in *The Sound and the Fury,* "the air was worn out with carrying sounds so long" (*SF*, 114). Narrative voice has positioned itself as a recording device in relation to the diegesis—as if a phonograph in which both ear and mouth are united in the horn—but one so sensitive, so discreet, that it captures the past conditions that cling to any present-tense unfolding without casual determination. Faulkner begins in 1909 resonating into 1833. This resonance—as reverberation—tips the stagnant room toward its ownmost precipice of difference. As potential, what will have been actualized cannot be extrapolated from what is now.

This air is thoroughly mediatized via Faulkner's moment of writing in 1936, the echo of the shot that kills Bon radiating for over forty years. It is a phonographic temporality, transmitted across an unnatural, radiophonic distance, but unnatural because it is the only way to represent what is always untimely in listening. The echo of the shot is a form-seeking sound. What is it to hear through disappearance, by a reverberation of an event?

In tracing sound technology's impact on literature, discourses of disembodiment, or the separation of sound from image, tend toward neutralizing these affective dimensions of sound and the concomitant problem of historicity and collective determination. To be sure, the shot is an acousmatic sound, a sound whose source is not seen.[29] But reverberation—the "echo" of the shot—structures the temporal layers of Faulkner's novel between 1833 and 1909, also moving between bodies, memories, and selves in a *transembodiment.*

Were Bon's racial identity and familial heredity not under question, the sound would have been sealed and forgotten long ago. Miscegenation and interracial desire, as it has structured the Sutpen family, is the foundational repression of the world of *Absalom.* It will also determine the way voices apprehend the past through an ever-moving circumlocution—it takes nearly the entire novel to state the fact of Bon's racial heredity directly. Quentin and Shreve's rehearsal of the story in Cambridge, decades after the Civil War, slowly compounds a first version rife with occlusions, as told by Rosa one stifling hot summer afternoon in Mississippi earlier that year. That indirection drives the shape of the narrative forward, and with it a series of residual sounds more powerful in their echo. "*I heard an echo, but not the shot,*" Rosa will repeatedly say (*AA*, 121). "*I saw a closed door but did not enter it,*" a door beyond which lay Bon's unseen corpse.

Rosa continually indicates that she knows more of Bon's racial identity and desires more of his body than she will ever directly assert. Rosa has very little by which to organize her own belated sexual awakening, foreclosed before fully articulated or embraced. Fantasy intervenes before an understanding that comes too late.[30] Her sense of knowing and desiring has been structured by acts of residual hearing, *"that unrational hearing sense."* She learned everything she knows in her "Cassandra-like solitude" of listening in on a series of closed doors (*AA*, 47). These are unsanctioned, erotic events of overhearing—but also painful events that we found in Chapter 2 to be hearing too much, hearing just beyond what can be acoustically and socially heard, as in *"the dim upper hallway where an echo spoke which was not mine but rather that of the lost irrevocable might-have-been which haunts all houses"* (*AA*, 109).[31]

Here, in chapter 5, the novel doubles back to Rosa's room where the novel first began. But she now speaks in a new voice rendered in italics. It is among the most enigmatic voices in the history of literature, being what Nietzsche might call "unheard of" (*unerhört*, both inaudible and outlandish). It is the form of inaudible content and finds its ground in residual auditory acts. For Judith never says Bon's racial identity out loud. As with Clytie, a biracial child of Sutpen and an unnamed slave, Bon's racial and hereditary status is communicated in delayed ways that strike *"the resonant strings of remembering."* The reader moves forward remembering words that are never fully named but only imply identity in ways that haunt a deferred, resonant understanding. New words fuse with old ones in the resonant penumbra of cognition. The whole of the novel's techniques of listening are determined by Rosa's sexual experiences, a refusal of intimacy shared and actualized merely at the level of sound and its attendant fantasies.

In being blocked at the threshold of desire and experience, Rosa is profoundly bonded to Sutpen, the man she demonizes. Before arriving for a day of listening, Quentin has already learned part of the story of Sutpen from his father and grandfather, who heard it from the man himself one night by a campfire. We learn that Sutpen's will toward a plantation, a dynasty, emanates from a wound. He was once a young, poor boy, and he came to the closed door of the Planter's house on the land where his family members were sharecroppers. He came with a message from his father. He expected "to be listened to because he had come" (*AA*, 189). Opening the door is not the Planter but a black servant. He is told to go around back, prevented from handing over the message.

In the Intersonority, we encountered a young Du Bois who had desired to give a card to a young girl but is refused. On the heels of this refusal, the Veil falls and consciousness is split. Though he refused to meet Du Bois in public debate, Faulkner likely learned of the problem of Hegelian recognition through reading Du Bois's internalization of it.[32] Fixed at the moment before transmission, Sutpen's message is not repeated—his own father is left suspended, unauthorized. In what Jean-François Lyotard calls "the pragmatics of narrative knowledge" (*pragma*, or fact and event), the speaking voice must encounter a receptive other so that the addressee might then go on to occupy the post of addressor. This acoustic and epistemic interval must constantly be in the process of reorienting itself to new pairings. Sutpen is suspended in the interval between listening and speaking, at what Lyotard calls the "ephemeral temporality inhabiting the space between the 'I have heard' and 'you will hear.'"[33] *Absalom, Absalom!* takes place almost entirely in this ephemeral, vibratory, and airy space, elongating the temporal moment that is supposed to bind addressor and addressee through the message. For it is in that moment that all of the violence of the name of the Father is propagated. It must be elongated, made reverberant, to change.

We can recall the ancient sense of category (*kategoria*) as it organizes Aristotle's theory of predication. To categorize is not simply to assert but to accuse or call another citizen publicly in the agora.[34] It is a vocal act that names. Let us not forget that the scene Fanon invokes in "The Fact of Blackness" also circles around the call and *kategoria*. It is an auditory event of naming that, though the call claims to identify a body posited as actual, *brings that body into being accusatively* as what Fanon calls the "crushing objecthood" of the "racial epidermal schema" that replaces the corporeal.[35] The auditory event, in near simultaneity, seals in vision the body now "clad in mourning."[36] Nearly coincidental—but not completely. The event can never quite cover over the nonidentity at the heart of the scene masquerading as nominalization. It is there in the space, as the spoken call wraps around the body to make it visible, a distance of perhaps no more than several seconds, that the fact of resonance still vibrates with potential. Faulkner's *Absalom, Absalom!* is crafted entirely around this space, brought to narrative.

In a certain moment of listening, after having taken in Rosa for what seems like an eternity (her story passes in one evening), Quentin rewrites to himself the myth of Narcissus, the thought itself vibratory, italicized on the page:

> *Maybe nothing ever happens once and is finished. Maybe happen is never once but like ripples maybe on water after the pebble sinks, the ripples moving on, spreading, the pool attached by a narrow umbilical water-cord to the next pool which the first pool feeds, has fed, did feed, let this second pool contain a different temperature of water, a different molecularity of having seen, felt, remembered, reflect in a different tone the infinite unchanging sky, it doesn't matter: that pebble's watery echo whose*

fall it did not even see moves across its surface too at the original ripple-space, to the
old ineradicable rhythm thinking Yes, we are both Father. Or maybe Father and I are
both Shreve, maybe it took Father and me to make Shreve or Shreve and me both to
make Father or maybe Thomas Sutpen to make all of us. (AA, 210)

The "original ripple space" renders in the water what is invisible in the air: rings of sound, an original event maternally attached to its aftereffects that nurture and feed it. Quentin discerns an instant making material contact with a past becoming present. The ripples seem to move out, yet, most paradoxically, in a repressed direction: It is not a forward movement but a circumambient one.

Rosa calls Quentin because he is the one. The paradox to which he is attuned allows Quentin to access how voices are moving into voices. It no longer matters who did what or why, for the egregious and phantom act around which the novel revolves—one grounded in the sin of slavery—seems to have been done by all agents feeding into one another. Quentin posits a self that is nonidentical, and it is precisely such a theory of self that will allow him, with his friend Shreve, to tell another, deracinated story that rescues the demon's narrative in its traumatic dimension. It wrests the past for history in its openness to change.

Faulkner was born one year after the *Plessy v. Ferguson* case upheld the doctrine of de jure racial segregation in the United States, a year on the cusp of rapid technological change. This was a change whose own doctrine was, as an advertisement for the telephone suggested, "time and distance overcome." Recall that Faulkner's avowed purpose was to remember a disappearing Southern landscape and way of life, to "bind into a whole the world which for some reason I believe should not pass utterly out of the memory of man." He was determined to capture in prose voices and ways of talking in the Deep South that have since passed away, no longer audible to us except through the indices of writing.[37] It was a period of aural dissemination and preservation.

When in *The Audible Past* Jonathan Sterne proposed the possibility of a "history of sound," his project was grounded in a desire to pursue the history of "sound culture as such."[38] But what, strictly speaking, separates the history of sound from the history of literature, sound disciplinarity from literary disciplinarity? Who is the subject of the history of sound, or, more precisely, what subject might "voice" this diachrony in the grammatical sense, and would it be in the singular or the plural? Who has this subject been, and what might it become? These are the questions inevitably posed when the literary enters the scene. The question invited by Faulkner is not what the place of the history of media and sound technology is in literature, but rather: What is the sound of history? What technology might record and transmit it? Such questions presume that literature and sound technology are coformations, that literature is a form of sound technology and sound technology a form of literature, that each take up—simultaneously in mutual inflections—the task of recording history. If the sound of history is a reverberation, then it cannot be linearly reconstructed.

ACKNOWLEDGMENTS

Because I began this book nearly two decades ago, there are many people to thank.

Eugene Lang College supported this book from its first draft to its completion. I am grateful to each of my colleagues in the programs in the Arts, Culture and Media, and Literary Studies, as well as to Dean Stephanie Browner. This project was also supported by a number of fellowships and grants at the New School, including a Mellon Fellowship in 2014–2015 at the Graduate Institute for Design, Ethnography, and Social Thought; a Mellon Grant in 2015–2016 through the Civic Liberal Arts Program; several mentoring grants through the Provost's Office; and the Lang Faculty Opportunity Award. The final stages of the book were supported by a Mellon Fellowship at the Price Lab for Digital Humanities at the University of Pennsylvania. Thank you to those communities.

I am lucky to have been embraced and supported by the American Comparative Literature Association, the Joseph Conrad Society of America, the Modernism Studies Association, and the William Faulkner Society. There I owe a special debt to Chris GoGwilt, who read the manuscript several times and offered invaluable feedback, and to Peter Mallios and Jay Watson, who helped shepherd my work from thoughts and intuitions to a completed book. Their generosity, compassion, and scholarship continue to be a source of striving. My development editor, Bud Bynack, is the ghost in this machine. Thank you to Tom Lay, Jacques Lezra, and Paul North at Fordham for seeing something in this project and making a home for it. Thank you to Dori Hale, whose encouragement and insight were crucial to overcoming many hurdles.

I am extremely grateful to a cohort of interlocuters who provided feedback on chapters at various stages over the years, also being sounding boards and champions: Todd Barnes, Nathan Brown, Amy Cimini, Emily Farrell, Seb Frankin, Michael Gillespie, Clara Latham, Joe Lemelin, Ben Lempert, Paul Nadal, Benjamin Steege, Naomi Waltham-Smith, and Soyoung Yoon. Special thanks to David Copenhafer, whose infinite conversation resounds in these pages, and to Niki Shelley for her friendship and beautiful cover art. Thank you to Dale Napolin-Bratter, Warren Bratter, Lee and Vichai Chinalai, Barbara Murphy, and the Starke family for their warmth and kindness. I am especially thankful for the life, writing, and wit of Leah Napolin and for my mother, whose bookshelves were a site of wonder and desire and who asked me in the morning what I dreamed. The empathetic ears of Brenda Bauer and Louis Roussel; my bandmate, Trevor Healey; and my sister, Rachel Napolin, helped sustain my writing and voice.

At The New School, thank you to Jay Bernstein, Juan de Castro, Stefania deKenessey, Laura Frost, Danielle Goldman, Mark Greif, Orit Halpern, Carin Kuoni, Orville Lee, Lana Lin, Ricardo Montez, Dominic Pettman, Hugh Raffles, John Roach, Ivan Raykoff, Zisan Ugurlu, and Jennifer Wilson. Essential support and feedback were provided by members of the Junior Women's Mentoring Group at Lang: Carolyn Berman, David Bering-Porter, Deborah Levitt, Inessa Medzhibovskaya, and Genevieve Yue, advocates all.

Beyond The New School, thank you to the American Studies working group organized by Jennie Kassanoff at Barnard, and to Noa Bar, Alex Benson, James Clifford, Debra Rae Cohen, Liisa Cohen, Rachel Corkle, Jonathan Cayer, Laurence Davies, Jed Esty, Sarah Gleeson-White, Felipe Gutierrez, Liz Hillie, Marta Figlerowicz, Taylor Hagood, Audrey Hawkins, David Kazanjian, Homay King, Erica Levin, Julia Li, Sara Marcus, Carter Mathes, Jack Matthews, Petar Milat, Adam Newton, Rochelle Rives, Paul Saint-Amour, Anna Snaith, Gustavus Stadler, Noah Wall, Cecilia Wee, and Damon Young. Thank you to *Philosophy Talk* at KALW in San Francisco, especially Ken Taylor, whose memory will live on in acts of listening. I thank the show for bringing me back on the air to discuss this book over a decade after finishing my dissertation. At Penn, special thanks to Jim English, Gerald Prince, and Stewart Varner, as well as the Departments of Music and English and the Mods and Latitudes research groups.

At Lang, a number of remarkable students provided research assistance and intellectual support: Thank you to Eric Bayless-Hall, Chris Howard-Woods, Elisa Muthig, Nicole Story, and to the members of the Faulkner Research Group, Brendan Heldenfels, Allegra Isenberg, and Griffin Sherbert. They inspire me.

Thank you to Justin Raden for help with the bibliography.

The community surrounding the *Sounding Out!* blog has been essential to my development as a thinker, writer, and listener. Thank you to Jennifer Stoever for welcoming me into that forum. Thank you also to the Black Sound and the Archive Working Group at Yale University, organized by Daphne Brooks and Brian Kane, whose warm community was a crucial site of the book's completion.

Brian in particular has been a long-standing supporter, hosting me at a number of formative events.

This book's core concepts were presented at "Anachronic Now" in 2013 at the May Faculty Colloquium at Fordham University organized by Chris GoGwilt; in 2016 at Fordham's Sound Studies Working Group; and in 2017 in Penn's Department of Music speaker series organized by Naomi Waltham-Smith. Sections of Chapter 1 were presented in 2014 at the ACLA, in 2015 at the "Sonic Shadows" symposium organized by Dominic Pettman and Pooja Rangan at the New School; in 2016 at the "Techniques of the Listener" symposium organized by J. D. Connor, Ben Glaser, and Brian Kane at the Whitney Humanities Center at Yale; in 2017 at the "Theorizing Literary Sound" symposium organized by Carter Mathes at Rutgers University; and in 2018 at the MSA panel organized by Elicia Clements. Portions of Chapter 2 were presented in 2017 on a panel that I co-organized with Catherine Flynn at ACLA. Portions of Chapter 3 were presented in 2008 on a panel organized by Rochelle Rives for the International Society for the Study of Narrative Literature conference; in 2012 on the Conrad and Faulkner Societies joint panel at MLA; in 2015 on the panel organized by Fred Solers at the MSA; in 2016 at the Centre for Expanded Poetics at Concordia University; and in 2018 at "Conjecture: 21st Century Philosophy, Aesthetics, and Politics," a symposium organized by Nathan Brown and Petar Milat at the University of Dubrovnik. Portions of the Intersonority were presented in 2012 at the American Literature Association's panel on Du Bois. In 2019, the Haverford Faculty Colloquium generously read and provided feedback on the full chapter. Portions of the Reprise were presented in 2012 at the Faulkner and Yoknapatawpha conference and in 2015 at the Department of English at the University of Mississippi. Thank you to these many auditors and respondents and to the organizers for their invitations.

A number of libraries and museums assisted my research. Thank you to Allen Jones at The New School Libraries, to Special Collections and University Archives at the University of Massachusetts for assistance with the Du Bois Papers, to Research Services at the Rosenbach Museum and Library, and to the Freud Museum.

The book's earliest experiment was at Hampshire College with my advisors Christoph Cox and Josh Kun. They first taught me how to hear texts; some sentences from my Div III, "Data Thieves: Imaginary Musics of the Future World," remain in these pages. The book found its strongest intellectual animation in the Department of Rhetoric at the University of California, Berkeley. I was lucky enough to be there at a moment when Dwinelle Hall seemed like the center of the world. I owe an incalculable debt to my advisor and mentor Ramona Naddaff, and I cherish my time studying with Judith Butler, Adriana Cavarero, Shannon Jackson, Catherine Malabou, Trinh T. Minh-ha, Carolyn Porter, Denise Riley, and Kaja Silverman; if I could stay in seminar always, listening to these women, I would. Each of their voices comes back to me in different intervals, and in some ways this book is an effort to sustain them.

Behind everything is the gift of Ben Williams, whose love holds me together.

NOTES

OVERTURE: THE SOUND OF A NOVEL

1. Samuel Beckett, *Nohow On: Company, Ill Seen Ill Said, Worstward Ho: Three Novels* (New York: Grove, 1996), 3.

2. Beckett's sentence is also scrutinized by Namwali Serpell in *Seven Modes of Uncertainty* (Cambridge, MA: Harvard University Press, 2014), when she describes a "capacity" of literature "to make readers do things, imagine things," noting "the fact that fictions work on us—*work* us" (2). The second sentence is more crucial for Serpell's analysis of the ethical dimension of literature, Beckett's text stating directly an otherwise implicit demand of fiction: "Imagine."

3. Gérard Genette, *Narrative Discourse: An Essay in Method*, trans. J. E. Lewin (Ithaca, NY: Cornell University Press, 1972), 27.

4. This point chimes with the work of Tom McEnaney's *Acoustic Properties: Radio, Narrative, and the New Neighborhood of the Americas* (Evanston, IL: Northwestern University Press, 2017), which also seeks "narrative acoustics." Also see my "The Acoustics of Narrative Involvement: Modernism, Subjectivity, Voice," PhD diss., UC Berkeley, 2010, https://escholarship.org/uc/item/1ws2f1tr. Of course, the study of poetry is wonderfully sonic. Here, I simply mean the traditional Aristotelian definition of poetics as units of narrative structure.

5. Percy Lubbock, *The Craft of Fiction*, Project Gutenberg, https://www.gutenberg.org/files/18961/18961-h/18961-h.htm.

6. Henry James, *The Portrait of a Lady*, 2nd Norton Critical ed. (New York: Norton, 1995), 7.

7. James, *The Portrait of a Lady*, 17.

8. Transformation, Prince notes, is the sine qua non of narrative: One state of affairs is transformed into another and without any logical presupposition. Gerald Prince, "On a Postcolonial Narratology," in *A Companion to Narrative Theory*, ed. James Phelan and Peter J. Rabinowitz (Malden, MA: Blackwell, 2005), 373.

9. Genette, qtd. in Sylvie Patron, "Homonymy, Polysemy, and Synonymy: Reflections on the Notion of Voice," in *Strange Voices in Narrative Fiction*, ed. Krogh Hansen et al. (Berlin: Walter de Gruyter, 2011), 18.

10. "While the dyadic structure of interpersonal relation (especially between representer and represented) that is so crucial to James and Lubbock remains in force for Booth, Genette, and Barthes, the second wave theorists seek to identify a transpersonal agent—language—that conditions the possibility of these personal relations"—these are, respectively, "rhetoric," "discourse," and "writing." Dorothy J. Hale, *Social Formalism: The Novel in Theory from Henry James to the Present* (Stanford, CA: Stanford University Press, 1998), 68.

11. Said describes the consolidated vision as "a codified, if only marginally visible, presence in fiction, very much like the servants in grand households and in novels, whose work is taken for granted but scarcely ever more than named, rarely studied . . . or given destiny." Edward W. Said, *Culture and Imperialism* (New York: Vintage, 1994), 63. James famously asserts that "relations stop nowhere"—the task of the novelist was to make the novel's world *seem* delimited. But relations do in fact stop somewhere for James. Jamaica Kincaid writes of the opening scene of *The Portrait of a Lady*, "The quotation could have only been written by a person who comes from a place where the wealth of the world is like skin, a natural part of the body." "Flowers of Evil," *New Yorker*, October 5, 1992, 154. Thank you to Melissa Zeiger for sharing this essay with me.

12. This space of the "hour . . . known as afternoon tea" could be brought under the analytic elaborated by Lisa Lowe's reading of silk and chintz in Thackeray's *Vanity Fair*. There, empire's peripheries exist in narrative only through its commodity traces, but they produce what Lowe calls a sense of "intimacy" between continents. Lisa Lowe, *The Intimacies of Four Continents* (Durham, NC: Duke University Press, 2015), 73–100. In *Culture and Imperialism*, Said notes that Ralph Touchett travels in *The Portrait of a Lady* to Algeria and Egypt, although the narrative never follows him there (63).

13. Lukács argues that the "inner action of the novel," as a fundamentally modern form, "is nothing but a struggle against the power of time [*nichts als ein Kampf gegen die Macht der Zeit*]." Georg Lukács, *The Theory of the Novel: A Historico-Philosophical Essay on the Forms of Great Epic Literature*, trans. Anna Bostock (Cambridge, MA: MIT Press, 1971), 122. This quotation is central to Walter Benjamin's elaboration of the distinction between storytelling and the novel.

14. See, for example, Frederic Jameson's "Criticism in History," in *Weapons of Criticism: Marxism in America and the Literary Tradition*, ed. Norman Rudich (Palo Alto, CA: Stanford University Press, 1976), 31–50; and *The Political Unconscious: Narrative as a Socially Symbolic Act* (Ithaca, NY: Cornell University Press, 1981). In the first text, Jameson argues that Conrad could not relinquish rhetoric and its class attachments, and in the second text, sound becomes an element of Conrad's repression of labor and history. Through resonance, I retrieve another potential, a companion to the remarkable work of Michael Greaney, who describes how oral community in Conrad

is tested by hearsay and "linguistic instability." Michael Greaney, *Conrad, Language, and Narrative* (Cambridge: Cambridge University Press, 2005), 26.

15. I use the term as given to us by Conrad in the profoundly decolonial statement that opens the Malay tale "The Lagoon": "'We will pass the night in Arsat's clearing. It is late'" (*IV*, 187). By definition, the enunciating instance can only arrive on time. When "it speaks," it always the time when it is speaking. By "clearing," I also amplify the Heideggerian resonance (see his *On the Way to Language*, trans. Peter D. Hertz [New York: Harper & Row, 1971]). This latter resonance is central for Jean-Luc Nancy, in what he calls narrative's "clearing the way" [*frayage*], because of which a narrator's subjectivity can never fully merge with his narrative (see his "Récit Recitation Recitative," in *Speaking of Music: Addressing the Sonorous*, ed. Keith Chapin and Andrew H. Clark, trans. Charlotte Mandell [New York: Fordham University Press, 2013], 243–55, 248).

16. In a foundational feminist critique, Julia Kristeva interrogates the matrix space (*chōra*) through which Plato argues the *logos* appears but also through which form adheres to matter. Sounds and the space of sounding are mere material hosts for Plato, who makes it clear across the dialogues that to eliminate the acoustical is to eliminate the problem of a gap between or around realities. See Julia Kristeva, *Revolution in Poetic Language*, trans. Margaret Waller (New York: Columbia University Press, 1984). Also see Jacques Derrida, "*Khōra*," in *On the Name*, ed. Thomas Dutoit, trans. David Wood, John P. Leavey Jr., and Ian McLeod (Palo Alto, CA: Stanford University Press, 1995), 89–130. I shall return to these issues in Chapter 3, and a related discussion of Plato's ear and choric space can be found in my "On Banishing Socrates' Wife: The Interiority of the Ear in *Phaedo*," in *Poiesis*, ed. Nathan Brown and Petar Milat (Zagreb: Multimedijalni Institute, 2017), 156–75.

17. John Llewelyn, *Margins of Religion: Between Kierkegaard and Derrida* (Bloomington: Indiana University Press, 2008), 278.

18. Llewelyn, *Margins of Religion*, 278.

19. Greaney, *Conrad, Language, and Narrative*, 26. Greaney draws from Jacques Derrida, *Margins of Philosophy*, trans. Alan Bass (Chicago: University of Chicago Press, 1982), 154, who suggests that philosophy become sensitive to the membrane of the tympanum, as it is "stretched obliquely (*loxos*)," being a "thin and transparent partition separating the auditory canal from the middle ear."

20. "resonance, n.," *OED* Online.

21. Christopher L. GoGwilt, *The Passage of Literature: Genealogies of Modernism in Conrad, Rhys, and Pramoedya* (New York: Oxford University Press, 2011), 217.

22. See, for example, GoGwilt's beautiful reading of the "dialogic force" of the title of Chinua Achebe's *Things Fall Apart* in *The Passage of Literature: Genealogies of Modernism in Conrad, Rhys, and Pramoedya* (New York: Oxford University Press, 2011), 228. Allusion (to Yeats's "The Second Coming") cannot encompass this force.

23. Lucier says in the piece, "I regard this activity not so much as a demonstration of a physical fact, but more as a way to smooth out any irregularities my speech might have." As written here, his lyrics do not disclose the irregularity of Lucier's speech—his lifelong stutter.

24. Jean-Luc Nancy, *Listening*, trans. Charlotte Mandell (New York: Fordham University Press, 2007), 21.

25. Nancy, *Listening*, 21.

26. Nancy, *Listening*, 21. Nancy's translator reminds us of the play within the French word, *sonner*, or to deafen, to play a musical instrument, to summon, and to pronounce a word (75n43).

27. Nancy, *Listening*, 8.

28. Nancy, "Recít Recitation Recitative," 254.

29. Brian Kane, "Jean-Luc Nancy and the Listening Subject," *Contemporary Music Review* 31, nos. 5–6 (2012): 439.

30. Yet the door is opened within Nancy's own oeuvre. Not only has his thinking of plurality been central to transnational literary studies, but in 2002, Nancy explicitly took up globalization in *The Creation of the World, or Globalization*, trans. François Raffoul and David Pettigrew (Albany: SUNY Press, 2007). What demands that listening be a separate consideration?

31. See Jennifer Lynn Stoever, *The Sonic Color Line: Race and the Cultural Politics of Listening* (New York: New York University Press, 2016).

32. Roland Barthes, *Image, Music, Text*, trans. Stephen Heath (New York: Hill and Wang, 1977), 142.

33. Barthes, *Image, Music, Text*, 147.

34. In one of few reflections on the question of sonorousness in the event of reading, Garrett Stewart, *Reading Voices: Literature and the Phonotext* (Berkeley: University of California Press, 1990), asks, "Where do we read?" Such a question, he suggests, leads us immediately to the "reading body" as the "somatic locus of sound-less reception" (1). What he calls the "phonotext" is in part "a somatic *effect* as the site of reception" (9). What kinds of audible traces of racial and sexual difference are carried over across—i.e., transmitted—in this somatic event?

35. Barthes, *Image, Music, Text*, 148

36. When Banfield proposed to sidestep the problem posed by the metaphor of "voice" and to double down on fiction's linguistic effects, she argued that there is no oral event of which written sentences are an imputed copy. Fiction renders the majority of its sentences, at best, grammatically erroneous if spoken aloud; the flexibility of tense, she argues, is at odds with the grammatical mandates of speaking in person. To burrow into the linguistic is not to be freed from the problems posed by conjectural sound. See Ann Banfield, *Unspeakable Sentences: Narration and Representation in the Language of Fiction* (Boston: Routledge & Kegan Paul, 1992).

37. Naomi Schor, *Reading in Detail: Aesthetics and the Feminine* (New York: Routledge, 2007), xliv–xlv.

38. Rodolphe Gasché, *Of Minimal Things: Studies on the Notion of Relation* (Stanford, CA: Stanford University Press, 1999), 6.

39. Gasché, *Of Minimal Things*, 6.

40. Emily J. Lordi, *Black Resonance: Iconic Women Singers and African American Literature* (New Brunswick, NJ: Rutgers University Press, 2013), 6.

41. Wai Chee Dimock, "A Theory of Resonance," *PMLA* 112, no. 5 (1997): 1066. Dimock's remarks celebrate "semantic life at the moment of reading" (1062). They also rebut the new historicism of Stephen Greenblatt, "Resonance and Wonder," *Bulletin of the American Academy of Arts and Sciences* 43, no. 4 (1990): 11–34. Greenblatt argues that resonance is the confusion of the object with what is circumambiently outside of it (the reader's present), as opposed to "wonder," a visual paradigm in which "everything but the object is excluded" (28). The object comes to be known as possessing an essence or integrity that endures. Dimock's sense of resonance is contiguous with Derridean dissemination, except that it is, above all, the becoming apparent of historical change in the object.

42. For Prince, "postcolonial narratology" cannot be thought outside the heterochronic and anachronic. In this book, my use of *acoustical* prevails over *acoustic*. The distinction is not simply euphonic. According to F. V. Hunt, "Acoustic vs. Acoustical," *Journal of the Acoustical Society of America* 27 (1955): 975, "*acoustic* is used when the term being qualified designates something that has the properties, dimensions, or physical characteristics associated with sound waves; *acoustical* is used when the term being qualified does *not* designate explicitly something which has such properties, dimensions, or characteristics." Of course, my book is meant to trouble this distinction. Walter Benjamin, *Illuminations*, ed. Hannah Arendt, trans. Harry Zohn (New York: Schocken, 1968), theorizes translation as resonance when he metaphorizes the totality of a language as a forest; translation "calls into it without entering it, aiming at that single spot where the echo is able to give, in its own language, the reverberation of the work in the alien one" (172). It is an acousticality that shares in sound without sounding.

43. In this same vein, John Mowitt, *Sounds: The Ambient Humanities* (Berkeley: University of California Press, 2015), uses the term "audit" for the way it involves both listening and textuality.

44. Sigmund Freud, "Two Encyclopedia Articles," in *The Standard Edition of the Complete Works of Sigmund Freud*, ed. James Strachey (London: Hogarth, 1975), 238 (*Gesammelte Werke* XIII, 215).

45. Ian Baucom, *Specters of the Atlantic: Finance Capital, Slavery, and the Philosophy of History* (Durham, NC: Duke University Press, 2005), 312.

46. See Edward W. Said, *Beginnings: Intention and Method* (New York: Columbia University Press, 1985).

47. Benjamin obliquely proposes a counterpart to his famous theory of the "optical unconscious" when he writes, "Shouldn't we rather speak of events which affect us like an echo—one awakened by a sound that seems to have issued from somewhere in the darkness of a past life?" See my "The Fact of Resonance: An Acoustics of Determination in Faulkner and Benjamin," *Symploke* 24, nos. 1–2 (2016): 180. There is a fold between matter and metaphor—events affect us "like" an echo and are awakened "by" a sound. Unlike the famous "political unconscious" of Frederic Jameson, these relations are noncausal, and their field underdetermined.

48. Fred Moten begins his monumental *In the Break: The Aesthetics of the Black Radical Tradition* (Minneapolis: University of Minnesota Press, 2003) with an intertextual exchange with two intellectual forebears, Saidiya Hartman and Frederick Douglass. Moten is interested in the ways that Hartman refrains from citing a violent passage from Douglass's text. Creating in text a space for their coexistence and intertextual encounter, Moten suggests that texts pass on not simply passages but their constitutive repressions.

1. VOICE AT THE THRESHOLD OF THE AUDIBLE

1. Drawing upon the work of Tessel Pollmann, Stoler writes, "the term *nyai* glossed several functions [in Java and Sumatra]: household manager, servant, housewife, wife, and prostitute," which "depended on a complex economic, social, and affective equation." Ann Laura Stoler, *Carnal Knowledge and Imperial Power: Race and the Intimate in Colonial Rule* (Berkeley, CA: University of California Press, 2002), 240n50.

2. In classic narrative fiction cinema but also certain strains of ethnographic and documentary filmmaking, an anonymous and implicitly universal voice—what I called in the Overture a "neutral" voice—occupies an omniscient position, an authoritative and symbolic one, which immediately engenders the voice, particularly the male voice, with the authority to grant access.

3. Mark McGurl, *The Program Era: Postwar Fiction and the Rise of Creative Writing* (Cambridge, MA: Harvard University Press, 2009), 228. In relation to this ideal, my use of the word "doxa" is precise. Doxa, Barbara Cassin writes, is "one of the most polysemic Greek words." Cassin notes its derivation from *dokeó*, "to appear," but also that it is in the same family as *dechomai* (to admit), a word I noted in the Overture in relation to listening, choreography, and space. We are confronting in this chapter what can and cannot appear in the space of the novel and how narrative and novel theory delimit their objects. Barbara Cassin et al., eds., *Dictionary of Untranslateables: A Philosophical Lexicon* (Princeton, NJ: Princeton University Press, 2014), 228.

4. Henry James, *The Art of Fiction and Other Essays* (Oxford: Oxford University Press, 1948), 11.

5. McGurl, *The Program Era*, 230. McGurl notes, for example, the new intrusion of a "soaring spasm of exclamation" on the page (227). The demand in 1940s creative

writing programs to "find your voice," McGurl describes, took on vexed meaning for minority and women writers. Such a demand, McGurl reiterates in concert with Dorothy Hale, sends us back to the metaphysics of "voice" and to the "implied author" as influentially defined by Wayne Booth in *The Rhetoric of Fiction* (1961): the site of an ethical totality of meaning.

6. The phrase "aesthetic principle" is central to work of Yael Levin, who argues for "the otherwise present" in Conrad. Such an "otherwise," neither this nor that, makes itself felt in Conrad's ambiguous opening. See Yael Levin, *Tracing the Aesthetic Principle in Conrad's Novels* (New York: Palgrave Macmillan, 2002), 1–22.

7. Gérard Genette says we suspect mood to be a priori irrelevant to narrative. "Since the function of narrative is not to give an order, express a wish, state a condition, etc., but simply to tell a story and therefore to 'report' facts (real or fictive), its one mood, or at least its characteristic mood, strictly speaking can be only the indicative." Gérard Genette, *Narrative Discourse: An Essay in Method*, trans. J. E. Lewin (Ithaca, NY: Cornell University Press, 1972), 161.

8. Plato, qtd. in Genette, *Narrative Discourse*, 166. These terms are *haplé diēgēsis* and "mimesis." Genette suggests we translate *haplé diēgēsis* not as "simple narrative" but rather "pure" or "not mixed" (161n2).

9. Genette, *Narrative Discourse*, 166.

10. Genette, *Narrative Discourse*, 166.

11. See Dorothy J. Hale, *Social Formalism: The Novel in Theory from Henry James to the Present* (Stanford, CA: Stanford University Press, 1998), 64–112. As I noted in the Overture, where James and Lubbock locate the organizing principle of fiction *outside* the novel in the "artist," later theorists simply relocate that principle *inside* the novel as "language."

12. Michael North, *The Dialect of Modernism: Race, Language, and Twentieth-Century Literature* (New York: Oxford University Press, 1998), 42.

13. Mieke Bal, *Narratology: Introduction to the Theory of Narrative*, 3rd ed. (Toronto: University of Toronto Press, 2009), argues that when direct speech occurs in narrative, the narrator ceases to relate as a fictitious spokesman: "It is as if the narrator temporarily transfers this function to one of the actors" (9). Bal does not ask by what means—and in what physical space—the transfer may occur and what kind of residue it leaves.

14. See Anne Carson, "The Gender of Sound," in *Audio Culture: Readings in Modern Music*, rev. ed., ed. Christoph Cox and Daniel Warner (New York: Bloomsbury, 2017), 43–60. Carson describes the ways in which "shrill" is continually attributed to women, a denigrated because castrating sound.

15. See Trinh T. Minh-ha, *Woman, Native, Other: Writing Postcoloniality and Feminism* (Bloomington: Indiana University Press, 1989).

16. Friedrich A. Kittler, *Discourse Networks, 1800/1900*, trans. Michael Metteer and Chris Cullens (Stanford, CA: Stanford University Press, 1992), 25.

17. Hale, *Social Formalism*, 68.

18. Ruth Nadelhaft, *Joseph Conrad: A Feminist Reading* (Atlantic Highlands, NJ: Humanities Press International, 1991), 14. Nadelhaft's book is one of few to recuperate the women of Conrad's fiction: "It is they who grope to envision and articulate another sort of reality which would transcend or at least deny the struggle between white and native which absorbs energies needed (and lost) for resistance" (14).

19. Nadelhaft, *Joseph Conrad*, 14.

20. Peter Brooks, *Reading for the Plot: Design and Intention in Narrative* (Cambridge, MA: Harvard University Press, 1992), 11, also notes that the dictionary definition of the word "plot" includes "A measured area of land." These "heterogenous meanings," I would suggest, are held together by the logic of empire.

21. In the classical sense of parabasis, the actors leave the stage for the chorus to take over and speak directly to the audience. It is for de Man a central figure for the failure of narrative closure. Paul de Man, *Allegories of Reading: Figural Language in Rousseau, Nietzsche, Rilke, and Proust* (New Haven, CT: Yale University Press, 1979), 301. In what Spivak calls, in a postcolonial vein, "permanent parabasis, persistent interruption," a master discourse never returns after having been ushered off the stage. Gayatri Chakravorty Spivak, *The Critique of Postcolonial Reason: Toward a History of the Vanishing Present* (Cambridge, MA: Harvard University Press, 1999), 157n65.

22. Conrad, qtd. in Geoffrey Galt Harpham, *One of Us: The Mastery of Joseph Conrad* (Chicago: University of Chicago Press, 1996), 121. Harpham (121) finds in this phrase an annotation of queer desire. He is especially interested in the ways that the exchange of women solves the problem of homosociality in *Almayer's Folly*.

23. Michel Chion, *The Voice in Cinema*, trans. Claudia Gorbman (New York: Columbia University Press, 1999), 23, 22.

24. Chion's discourse is burdened, Kaja Silverman argues, by contradictory fictions of the feminine body. For example, Chion describes the *acousmêtre* not only in relation to a castrating and devouring maternal but also to "virginity, derived from the simple fact that the body that's supposed to emit it [the voice] has not yet been inscribed in the visual field." Chion, *The Voice in Cinema*, 23. Showing the body, he continues, is a "deflowering." See Kaja Silverman, *The Acoustic Mirror: The Female Voice in Psychoanalysis and Cinema* (Bloomington: Indiana University Press, 1988. In Chapter 3, I shall discuss the racializing rhetoric of Chion's *acousmêtre*, which does not factor into Silverman's seminal critique.

25. Jacques Lacan, *Écrits: The First Complete Edition in English*, trans. Bruce Fink (New York: Norton, 2006), 96.

26. Lacan, *Écrits*, 95.

27. See Joan Copjec, *Read My Desire: Lacan Against the Historicists* (Brooklyn, NY: Verso, 2015), 15.

28. See Sigmund Freud, *The Interpretation of Dreams*, trans. James Strachey (New

York: Avon, 1998), 340–44, where he describes displacement as a series of psychical intensities assisting one another in being ushered into the dream space, weaker intensities (i.e., more repressed) latching on to stronger intensities. To some extent, what I describe here is simply the work of displacement.

29. Silverman, *The Acoustic Mirror*, 43.

30. Christian Metz, *The Imaginary Signifier: Psychoanalysis and the Cinema*, trans. Celia Britton et al. (Bloomington: Indiana University Press, 1982), 45.

31. Metz, *The Imaginary Signifier*, 45. In *Read My Desire*, Copjec argues that film theory misconstrues the screen as mirror and suggests in contrast the more radically Lacanian notion that the mirror is a screen, one related to the "intercalation" of the apparatus and gaze (14). Also see her discussion of Metz (22).

32. Wolfgang Iser, *The Act of Reading: A Theory of Aesthetic Response* (Baltimore, MD: Johns Hopkins University Press, 1980), 141.

33. Iser, *The Act of Reading*, 141. Emphasis added.

34. Jacques Derrida, in *Speech and Phenomena, and Other Essays on Husserl's Theory of Signs*, trans. David Allison (Chicago: Northwestern University Press, 1973), 11–13, writes of "the invisible distance held out between the two acts" of phenomenological reduction, one also held out between the transcendental and the world that requires it to appear.

35. Thank you to Mara Mills, who made this point during the question-and-answer segment of my presentation of an early version of this chapter at the Whitney Humanities Center symposium "Techniques of the Listener," organized by J. D. Connor, Ben Glaser, and Brian Kane (April 2016).

36. McGurl, *The Program Era*, 232.

37. Marc E. Blanchard, "The Sound of Songs: The Voice in the Text," in *Hermeneutics and Deconstruction*, ed. Hugh J. Silverman and Don Ihde (Albany: State University of New York Press, 1985), 123. Blanchard is rightly confused that, after the intense *textual* analysis offered by Genette, his book's study nonetheless concludes with "Voice" (*Voix*). Thank you to Dorothy Hale for suggesting this essay.

38. For example, Seymour Chatman, *Story and Discourse: Narrative Structure in Fiction and Film* (Ithaca, NY: Cornell University Press, 1980) argues that a "voice" of a narrator may be "covert or effaced" and that the covert voice "occupies the middle ground between 'nonnarration' and conspicuously audible narration" (197).

39. Émile Benveniste, *Problems in General Linguistics* (University of Miami Press, 1971), 226.

40. Derrida, *Speech and Phenomena*, 76.

41. Derrida, *Speech and Phenomena*, 77.

42. Derrida, *Speech and Phenomena*, 77.

43. Derrida, *Speech and Phenomena*, 77. Derrida elaborates this phrase across numerous works and evokes the double sense of the French verb *écouter*, both "to hear" and "to understand."

44. Jacques Derrida, *Of Grammatology*, corrected ed., trans. Gayatri Chakravorty Spivak (Baltimore, MD: Johns Hopkins University Press, 1997), 166.

45. Derrida, *Speech and Phenomena*, 77.

46. When Genette says "voice" he does not mean to invoke the object that invites Derrida's poststructuralist critique. I am claiming, however, that what Derrida calls "the voice that keeps silence," as a metaphysical presumption, sustains Genette's entire theory. It is because of this idealized operation that the physical silence of Genettian "voice" can exist comfortably as a quasi-metaphor for a spoken event. Genette never proposes a typology of such qualities because it would undermine the fundamental nature of the enunciating instance, its *es gibt*. Recall that he writes, "*There is an enunciating instance . . . always present*" (emphasis added). Gérard Genette, qtd. in Sylvie Patron, "Homonymy, Polysemy, and Synonymy: Reflections on the Notion of Voice," in *Strange Voices in Narrative Fiction*, ed. Krogh Hansen et al. (Berlin: Walter de Gruyter, 2011), 18. According to Derrida, such presence is "the power of the voice" as a concept (*Speech and Phenomena*, 75). Genette's oral paradigm (narrative as reporting) is essential to his structuralism. For further discussion of the relation between Genette and deconstruction, see Dorothy J. Hale, "Structuralism, Narratology, Deconstruction," in *The Novel: An Anthology of Criticism and Theory, 1900–2000*, ed. Dorothy J. Hale (Malden, MA: Blackwell, 2006), 186–204.

47. Roman Ingarden, *The Literary Work of Art: An Investigation on the Borderlines of Ontology, Logic, and the Theory of Literature*, trans. George G. Grabowicz (Evanston, IL: Northwestern University Press, 1973), 34–35.

48. Eudora Welty, *One Writer's Beginnings* (Boston: Faber and Faber, 1983), 11–12. Welty's origin story is prefaced by an account of listening not only to her mother read aloud but also to recorded music. Also see Toni Morrison, *Tar Baby*, 1st Vintage International ed. (New York, Vintage International, 2004). Morrison prefaces the novel with a remarkably similar account of writing as listening intimately to parental voices and recorded music: "All narrative begins for me as listening. When I read, I listen. When I write, I listen—for silence, inflection, rhythm, rest. Then comes the image" (*Tar Baby*, xi).

49. Denise Riley, "'The Voice without a Mouth': Inner Speech," *Qui Parle* 14, no. 2 (2002): 58.

50. Riley is incredibly attuned in her poetry and criticism to this "silent sound" as it is nonetheless heterogeneous to the self. It includes words that do not, as it were, "ring true" to the person who thinks or utters them. For Riley, as for Bakhtin, the linguistic conditions of selfhood (which are also partly sonic) mean that its origins are alterior. Denise Riley, *The Words of Selves: Identification, Solidarity, Irony* (Stanford, CA: Stanford University Press, 2000).

51. Georges Poulet, "The Phenomenology of Reading," *New Literary History* 1, no. 1 (1969): 56.

52. The notion of timbre, Emily Dolan, *The Orchestral Revolution: Haydn and*

Technologies of Timbre (New York: Cambridge University Press, 2013), describes, is premised upon a descriptive desire in relation to the "eachness" of sounds (88). But how is particularity to be resolved with an attention to the structural levels that support the gendering and racialization of timbre—the claim to (mis)recognize the gender, race, ethnicity, or nationality of a voice not only in listening but in reading? For further discussion of these issues of writing and reading racialized timbre in literary modernism, see my "Elliptical Sound: Audibility and the Space of Reading," in *Sounding Modernism: Rhythm and Sonic Mediation in Modern Literature and Film*, ed. Helen Groth, Julian Murphet, and Penelope Hone (Edinburgh: Edinburgh University Press, 2017). For a related discussion of racialized timbre in African American music, see Nina Sun Eidsheim, *The Race of Sound: Listening, Timbre, and Vocality in African American Music* (Durham, NC: Duke University Press, 2019), who argues that singing voices and "the race of sound" are best understood through genre. Throughout this book, I insist instead on structure and form.

53. Poulet, "The Phenomenology of Reading," 56.

54. If in the Western ontological tradition, "hearing (understanding) oneself speak" is a basic experience of self-awareness, then this tradition excludes the deaf. Derrida did not take the deconstruction of phonocentrism so far that he made an adequate place for deafness within grammatology, his broader project, which H-Dirksen Bauman, "Listening to Phonocentrism with Deaf Eyes: Derrida's Mute Philosophy of (Sign) Language," *Essays in Philosophy* 9, no. 1 (2008): 2, describes as "an exploration of a mute language outside of speech." However, throughout the various recapitulations of Rousseau's account of sign language, Derrida incites what Bauman calls a "deaf-mute philosophy" (2).

55. Barthes does not deviate from the phenomenological subject when he writes, "Language knows a 'subject,' not a person, and this subject, empty outside of the very enunciation which defines it, suffices to make language 'hold together.'" Roland Barthes, *Image, Music, Text*, trans. Stephen Heath (New York: Hill and Wang, 1977), 145.

56. Adriana Cavarero, *For More Than One Voice: Toward a Philosophy of Vocal Expression*, trans. Paul A. Kottman (Stanford, CA: Stanford University Press, 2005), 43.

57. Silverman, *The Acoustic Mirror*, 44.

58. See Aaron Fogel, *The Coercion to Speech: Conrad's Poetics of Dialogue* (Cambridge, MA: Harvard University Press, 1985). Fogel both adopts and critiques Bakhtin's theory of discourse in light of the aesthetic ramifications of Lacan's theory of language, showing how, in Conrad, the decision to speak or write is never simply willed.

59. Also see Rey Chow, *Not Like a Native Speaker: On Languaging as a Postcolonial Experience* (New York: Columbia University Press, 2014). Chow strikes against linguistic melancholia over "irretrievable origin" to comment on Derrida's relationship to French as an Algerian-Jew, language becoming "something that no one," Chow writes, "not even the master and the colonizer, can possess" (29). One could go

further to conjecture that Derrida's prime intervention into Western metaphysics—the concept of *s'entendre parler*—was grounded in the aural sensitivity of one who was not like a native speaker.

60. See Roland Barthes, *The Rustle of Language*, trans. Richard Howard (Berkeley: University of California Press, 1989).

61. Fidelity, Chow argues, is the passion most intimately tied to the event of translation between cultures. Rey Chow, *Primitive Passions: Visuality, Sexuality, Ethnography, and Contemporary Chinese Cinema* (New York: Columbia University Press, 1995), x.

62. Modern media technology cannot be separated from its origins in ethnographic practice, what Brian Hochman, *Savage Preservation: The Ethnographic Origins of Modern Media Technology* (Minneapolis: University of Minnesota Press, 2014), calls "savage preservation." According to Erika Brady, *A Spiral Way: How the Phonograph Changed Ethnography* (Jackson: University Press of Mississippi, 1999), ethnographic phonography begins in the spring/summer of 1890 with Jesse Walter Fewkes's fieldwork with the Zuni, Fewkes later trying out these ideas in Maine with the Passamaquoddy.

63. Homi K. Bhabha, *The Location of Culture* (New York: Routledge, 1994), would perhaps locate colonial mimicry in this scene. But the novel does not position a site of natural or original sound that is free from such technological resonances of iteration. For a discussion of how Conrad's form itself is contrapuntally related to an emergent form of popular Malay opera, see Christopher GoGwilt, *The Passage of Literature: Genealogies of Modernism in Conrad, Rhys, and Pramoedya* (New York: Oxford University Press, 2011), 39–60. For a related discussion of the first trial against mechanical music as launched by Verdi's music publisher, see Peter Szendy, *Listen: A History of Our Ears* (New York: Fordham University Press, 2008), 72–76.

64. See Mark Goble, *Beautiful Circuits: Modernism and the Mediated Life* (New York: Columbia University Press, 2010).

65. See Roshanak Kheshti, *Modernity's Ear: Listening to Race and Gender in World Music* (New York: NYU Press, 2015). For Kheshti, modernity's ear is indisputably colonial in its drive. Her feminist account of the beginnings of ethnography is exceptional in being psychoanalytically inflected. Jonathan Sterne, *Audible Past: Cultural Origins of Sound Reproduction* (Chapel Hill, NC: Duke University Press, 2003), 287–334, shows how "preservation" was a nineteenth-century rhetorical shift entangled with the ethnographic desire to capture "disappearing" cultures but also new techniques like canning and embalming.

66. Pramoedya, qtd. in GoGwilt, *The Passage of Literature*, 53. Far from being a neutral repository of historical facts, the literary work exists in "counterpoint" to the archive, composed of the political and cultural questions that "haunt the historical record" (*The Passage of Literature*, 53).

67. Jacques Derrida, *Archive Fever: A Freudian Impression*, trans. Eric Prenowitz (Chicago: University of Chicago Press, 1998), 7, 3.

68. Kittler, *Discourse Networks*, 27.

69. This point is an analogue to Ann Laura Stoler's *Race and the Education of Desire: Foucault's History of Sexuality and the Colonial Order of Things* (Durham, NC: Duke University Press, 1995), which argues that Michel Foucault's *The History of Sexuality* deals with the European sexual imaginary but never touches on imperial incitements to discourse and desire.

70. "There at the back of the house . . . did that astute negotiator carry on long conversations in Sulu language with Almayer's wife. What the subject of their discourses was might have been guessed from the subsequent domestic scenes by Almayer's hearthstone" (*AF*, 38).

71. Gerald Prince, *A Dictionary of Narratology*, rev. ed. (Lincoln: University of Nebraska Press, 2003), 1.

72. In *A Personal Record*, Conrad's memoir of becoming a writer, he claims that the desire to write suddenly possessed him as if from nowhere, and he found himself ringing the bell to have his table cleared of afternoon tea, so that it could become a surface for writing. "I . . . rang the bell violently, or perhaps I should say resolutely, or perhaps I should say eagerly—I do not know. But manifestly it must have been a special ring of the bell . . ., like the ringing of a bell for the raising of the curtain upon a new scene" (*PR* 69).

73. Foucault, qtd. in Kittler, *Discourse Networks*, 43. This notion underscores Hale's critique: Genette invests in language a materializing power but never explains this power or what is meant by materiality. His claim, it would seem, rests in part on the metaphysical logic of the fiat.

74. Kittler, *Discourse Networks*, 237.

75. Kittler, *Discourse Networks*, 237.

76. In the case of photography, Roland Barthes, *Camera Lucida: Reflections on Photography*, trans. Richard Howard (New York: Macmillan, 1981), 28, writes of details that exist in service of the photograph's message, composing its *studium*. These details "constitute the very raw material of ethnological knowledge."

77. Consider this exemplary remark: "Freud listens for things no one has noted before. . . . It's no coincidence that one of the first uses for the microphone equipment is field recordings, hermetic coils and dials used in the service of an opening distance. . . . Songs once considered below the belt, beyond the pale, grey room, black night songs. Itinerant blue shamans. Haitian ceremony. Hawaiian unheimlich." Ian Penman, *On the Mic: How Amplification Changed the Voice for Good* (New York: Continuum, 2002), 26–27.

78. For example, Genette discusses "visual and auditory restriction" in narrative, when Proust's Swann believes himself to be at Odette's window and is "able to see

nothing . . . only to hear, 'in the silence of the night, the murmur of conversation.'" On the heels of this moment, Genette discusses what is "reduced . . . to a purely auditory perception" (*Narrative Discourse*, 204).

79. Bal, *Narratology*, 146, prefers "focalizer" over something like "perspectivizer" for its technical and subject-oriented associations, and she frequently turns to the language of film and photography. Perspective, Bal maintains, "covers both the physical and the psychological points of perception," but it has come traditionally to mean both the narrator and the "vision." The examples that anchor Bal's theory of the focalizer are drawn from spectatorship; that is, they are fundamentally specular.

80. For Genette, selection at times coincides with the person narrating and at times does not. He topologized, for example, focalizers that are "internal" and "external" to the diegesis (*Narrative Discourse*, 189–94). He does not investigate the givenness of space and time to narrative, which I'm suggesting amounts to an a priori focalization.

81. Maurice Blanchot, *The Infinite Conversation*, trans. Susan Hanson (Minneapolis: University of Minnesota Press, 1993), 384. Emphasis added. For a counterargument positioning "neutrality" as a strategic political response to decolonization in postwar France, see Daniel Just, *Literature, Ethics, and Decolonization in Postwar France: The Politics of Disengagement* (New York: Cambridge University Press, 2015).

82. Blanchot, *The Infinite Conversation*, 384. While Blanchot does not discuss focalization per se, his parallel theory of narrative voice adopts "*il*," which is often translated as "he," also indicative of a neuter or neutral "it."

83. In other words, Genette would like us to believe that the narrating instance is ontologically prior to focalization. But the genius of his system, if pushed to its logical conclusion, actually means quite the opposite.

84. Many critics have argued the same of narrative space in the case of cinema. See, for example, Stephen Heath's seminal essay, "Narrative Space," in *Questions of Cinema* (Bloomington: University of Indiana Press, 1981), 19–75.

85. Alan Williams, "Is Sound Recording Like a Language?" *Yale French Studies* 60 (1980): 61.

86. While the phrase "horn's mouth" appears commonly in the US nascent trade press in the cylinder era of the 1890s and 1900s, "horned mouth" is a phrase I draw from Charles Grivel, "The Phonograph's Horned Mouth," in *Wireless Imagination: Sound, Radio, and the Avant-Garde*, ed. Douglas Kahn and Gregory Whitehead (Cambridge, MA: MIT Press, 1992), 31–62. Grivel invites two senses, both a vaginal opening (hearing) and a phallic penetration (inscribing) that, in playback, violates the speaker's sense of interiority. Recording for Grivel is feminizing in its event. Throughout the book, I use his phrase so as to keep these senses in play. Thanks to Kyle Barnett for helpful discussion.

87. "The phonograph does not hear as do ears that have been trained immediately to filter voices, words, and sounds out of noise; it registers acoustic events as such,"

Friedrich A. Kittler writes in *Gramophone, Film, Typewriter*, trans. Geoffrey Winthrop-Young and Michael Wutz (Stanford, CA: Stanford University Press, 1999), 23. Thank you to Clara Latham for bringing this quotation to my attention.

88. One of few reflections on sound in relation to focalization is Melba Cuddy-Keane, "Modernist Soundscapes and the Intelligent Ear: An Approach to Narrative through Auditory Perception," in *A Companion to Narrative Theory*, ed. James Phelan and Peter J. Rabinowitz (New York: John Wiley & Sons, 2007), 382–98. Cuddy-Keane proposes to replace the term focalization with "diffusion" and "auscultation." I am addressing the dimension of focalization that most determines colonial sound: selection.

89. Sanjay Krishnan, "Seeing the Animal: Colonial Space and Movement in Joseph Conrad's *Lord Jim*," *Novel* 37, no. 3 (November 1, 2004): 336. These sounds have little to do with the central action: Marlow notes them nonetheless, making them to some extent "deselected," that is, focalized in order to be marginalized. For further discussion of deselection in relation to race and narrative, see my "Elliptical Sound."

90. Also see my "Elliptical Sound," where I describe "deselection" in relation to Ernest Hemingway's representation of black timbre and sound.

91. Kittler, *Gramophone, Film, Typewriter*, 23.

92. See, for example, Kittler's discussion of Jimi Hendrix (*Gramophone, Film, Typewriter*, 111). Kittler also links the hallucinatory sound of bells in Pink Floyd to an 1898 recording that promised to give listeners the authentic sound of "Negro plantation" life. For a related critique of Kittler, see Benjamin Steege, "Between Race and Culture: Hearing Japanese Music in Berlin," *History of Humanities* 2 (2017): 361–74.

93. The term "soundscape" originated in R. Murray Schafer's 1977 *Tuning of the World*, republished as *The Soundscape: Our Sonic Environment and the Tuning of the World* (Rochester, VT: Destiny, 1994). The book perpetuates imperial conceptions of space derived from ethnology and field recording while also valuing "natural sound" over "noise." The shout of a subaltern woman is not part of the vivifying reality that Schafer invests in the soundscape nor can it be analyzed by means of what Stephen Feld, a seminal ethnomusicologist, names "acoustemology," a concept he summarizes in "Acoustemology," in *Key Words in Sound*, ed. David Novak and Matt Sakakeeny (Durham, NC: Duke University Press, 2015), 12–21. It is a method of listening to place that binds acoustics to anthropology and epistemology. As a concept, soundscape cannot accommodate the sounds of colonial ruination, sounds that, if attended to, attack the liberated subject position of the auditor whose audition is itself a form of aggressive capture. For an incisive critique of Schafer, see Marie Thompson, *Beyond Unwanted Sound: Noise, Affect, and Aesthetic Moralism* (New York: Blooms-bury, 2017).

94. Kittler, *Discourse Networks*, 27.

95. Kittler, *Discourse Networks*, 26.

96. Kittler, *Discourse Networks*, 26.

97. Christopher L. Miller, *Blank Darkness: Africanist Discourse in French* (Chicago: University of Chicago Press, 1985), 6.

98. See Ann Laura Stoler, ed., *Imperial Debris: On Ruins and Ruination* (Durham, NC: Duke University Press, 2013), 1–38.

99. Stoler, ed., *Imperial Debris*, 3.

100. Ann Laura Stoler, *Along the Archival Grain: Epistemic Anxieties and Colonial Common Sense* (Princeton, NJ: Princeton University Press, 2010), 2.

101. Barthes locates two modes of *tacere*, the silence of the discreet man and that of the skeptic who has a moral obligation to withhold or refrain from a position. The ecological claim to a right to silence or to be rid of noise, Barthes argues, fails to address the true pollutant, which is speech. Roland Barthes, *The Neutral: Lecture Course at the College de France (1977–1978)*, trans. Rosalind Krauss and Denis Hollier (New York: Columbia University Press, 2005), 21–26.

102. See Nancy Rose Hunt, "An Acoustic Register, Tenacious Images, and Congolese Scenes of Rape and Repetition," *Cultural Anthropology* 23, no. 2 (2008): 245. For Hunt, this sound is "constitutive of reproductive ruination" during the rubber regime, many women across multiple generations left unable to bear children after being raped (245). I return to such sounds in Chapter 3.

103. Saidiya V. Hartman, "Venus in Two Acts," *Small Axe* 12, no. 2 (2008): 1.

104. Douglas Kammen, "Conrad and Coal," *Los Angeles Review of Books*, December 11, 2019, https://lareviewofbooks.org/article/conrad-and-coal/. Kammen argues that Conrad replaces coal with Almayer's pursuit of a gold deposit in order to heighten a poetic dichotomy with the forest. For an example, see *AF*, 4.

105. Hartman, "Venus in Two Acts," 1, 2–3.

106. Hunt, "An Acoustic Register," 229.

107. David E. Wellbery, foreword to Kittler, *Discourse Networks*, xii.

108. Ian Watt, *Conrad and the Nineteenth Century* (Berkeley: University of California Press, 1979), 270–86. Watt concentrates on the visual dimension of Conrad's decoding, but its contours are also acoustical. In *Lord Jim*, Jim believes he hears a slur being addressed to him (we later learn it's meant for a dog). When Jim's ship meets with disaster, Conrad presents the event elliptically as a vibration, "less than a sound." For a discussion of this vibration, see my "'A Sinister Resonance': Vibration, Sound, and the Birth of Conrad's Marlow," *Qui Parle* 21 no. 2 (2013): 69–100.

109. See GoGwilt, *The Passage of Literature*, 162. Elaborating Spivak's theory of the subaltern, GoGwilt also invokes terminology from the work of Laurie Sears and Judith Butler.

110. GoGwilt, *The Passage of Literature*, 153–76.

111. GoGwilt, *The Passage of Literature*, 161.

112. GoGwilt, *The Passage of Literature*, 163.

113. What I've called the "unsaid" in this novel is not the same as what is diffi-

cult to say, as a language of the closet. Harpham (*One of Us*, 121–22) argues that Lingard's transaction with Almayer is homosexual and that his desire for Almayer is only neutralized by a transaction with a woman. Harpham doesn't address the fact that "Mrs. Almayer" is kept, essentially, as a concubine and slave by Lingard before she is exchanged to become Almayer's wife (presumably acting as Lingard's surrogate).

114. The spatiotemporal displacement of the *nyai* figure—a displacement that is, for GoGwilt, coproductive of English and Indonesian modernisms—bears crucially on William Faulkner's presentations of interracial desire. The black woman, as the object of white desire and violence in Faulkner, is routed through his reception of the *nyai* figure in Conrad, though he would not have had such a name for her. In other words, Faulkner contacts the subaltern uncanny of Conrad's novel. Faulkner names a character in *As I Lay Dying* "Jewel," the name of the *nyai* in *Lord Jim*. Faulkner's Jewel is the product of Addie's affair with Whitfield. Peter Lancelot Mallios, *Our Conrad: Constituting American Modernity* (Stanford, CA: Stanford University Press, 2010), persuasively argues that Addie's internal monologue, which reports the affair, is shot through with her unstated desire for blackness. But is not such a desire also routed through the Pacific? Indeed, as Almayer watches "drifting logs," they rush from the river into the sea "through the impenetrable gloom" (*AF*, 11) a phrase that Conrad later echoes and reanimates in relation to the Congo in *Heart of Darkness*. The Pacific, an Archipelagic America, haunts the Faulknerian sense of place, which will become more apparent when, later in this present chapter, I discuss his *Sanctuary*.

115. In this vein Robyn R. Warhol, "Narrating the Unnarratable: Gender and Metonymy in the Victorian Novel," *Style* 28, no. 1 (1994): 74–94, theorizes a feminine counterpart to Gerald Prince's notion of the "unnarrateable," or what can't be told because it is tedious, taboo, or exceeds language. For Prince, the latter can be marked by phrases like "I cannot put into words the emotion," a reticence that Warhol argues to be gendered in Victorian fiction (79).

116. "Dutch colonial archival documents serve less as stories for a colonial history than as active, generative substances with histories as documents with itineraries of their own." Stoler, *Archival Grain*, 1.

117. See Carson, "The Gender of Sound."

118. Cited in David Novak and Matt Sakakeeny, eds., *Keywords in Sound* (Durham, NC: Duke University Press, 2015), 1. "Sound is vibration that is perceived and becomes known through its materiality" (1). This definition functions via a similar tautology.

119. See Jacques Rancière, *The Politics of Aesthetics: The Distribution of the Sensible*, trans. Gabriel Rockhill (New York: Continuum, 2004). In a Platonic vein, he writes of "the system of *a priori* forms determining what presents itself to sense experience. It [aesthetics] is a delimitation of spaces and times, of the visible and the invisible, of speech and noise, that simultaneously determines the place and the stakes of politics as a form of experience" (13). My claim, of course, is not on behalf of the a

priori but rather a colonial history that determines the distribution of the sensible as a colonial distribution or sensorium.

120. In among the first sustained reflections on sound in Conrad, the composer and writer David Toop, *Sinister Resonance: The Mediumship of the Listener* (New York: Continuum, 2010), 200, describes "the base condition of a hypothetical space in which sound and light are absent." Toop draws attention to the impossibility of absolute silence or stillness in Conrad's sensory spaces, noting *The Secret Sharer* (1910) and "the auditory tension of the story, in which all sound is treated as an unnatural, if inevitable rupture of stillness (the cup before it breaks), questions the notion of silence as a possible absolute" (199–200).

121. Aaron Fogel, "The Mood of Overhearing in Conrad's Fiction," *Conradiana* 15, no. 2 (1984): 134.

122. The sound of the voice, for Cavarero in *For More Than One Voice*, is tantamount to a proper name. In Chapter 2, we will find Conrad to be both longing for and highly suspicious of vocal ontology.

123. Dain is not a proper name, Peter Lancelot Mallios describes in an annotation, but rather "a title of distinction among the Bugis, a Malay tribe." See Joseph Conrad, *Almayer's Folly: A Story of an Eastern River* (New York: Modern Library, 2002), 167n3.

124. "The Malay term 'Tuan' (in both *Lord Jim* and *Almayer's Folly*) encodes an effaced reference to the term 'nyai'. . . . Since the term 'nyai' is a transcription and translation from the Javanese into Malay, the volatile racial and sexual problems of entitlement it encodes in the corresponding term 'tuan' emerge from a crossing over between at least three different scriptings of Malay: *Kawi* (Old Javanese), *Jawi* (Arabic) and *Rumi* (Roman)." Christopher GoGwilt, "Conrad and Romanised Print Form: From Tuan Almayer to 'Prince Roman,'" in *Conrad and Language*, ed. Katherine Isobel Baxter and Robert Hampson (Edinburgh: Edinburgh University Press, 2016), 130n12. GoGwilt describes how "Tuan" enters the *OED* by way of Conrad, but only to be (mis)translated as "lord," i.e., a word of colonial subservience.

125. What Chatman calls "degrees of audibility" is a metaphor for a narrator's shifting "presence" to or implication in the action (*Story and Discourse*, 196). Such audibility may be "covert," i.e., "we hear a voice speaking of events, characters, and setting, but its owner remains hidden in the discursive [*sic*] shadows" (197). In a different vein, Pooja Rangan, *Immediations: The Humanitarian Impulse in Documentary* (Durham, NC: Duke University Press, 2017), explores the audibility of subaltern subjects to humanitarian documentary film practice, that is, its fantasmatic effort to "give a voice" to the "voiceless."

126. See Gayatri Chakravorty Spivak, "Can the Subaltern Speak?" in *Colonial Discourse and Postcolonial Theory: A Reader*, ed. Patrick Williams and Laura Chrisman (New York: Columbia University Press, 1994), 66–111.

127. Spivak, "Can the Subaltern Speak?" 82–83.

128. Gayatri Chakravorty Spivak elaborates this claim in a different essay, "Echo," *New Literary History* 24, no. 1 (1993): 17–43, which I take up in Chapter 2.

129. Gemma Corradi Fiumara, *The Otherside of Language: A Philosophy of Listening* (New York: Routledge, 1990), 2.

130. Cavarero, *For More Than One Voice*, 33–41, describes how Aristotle splits the notion of *logos* from its dependency on sound, originally defined in the *Poetics* as both *phone* (sound) and *semantike* (words).

131. Levin writes in related ways of "occluded representation" in Conrad and brings his general aesthetic principle to bear upon what she calls a "nontractable nonbeing" (*Tracing the Aesthetic Principle*, 8, 3). In my estimation, such occlusion is fundamentally traumatic.

132. Thank you to Christopher GoGwilt, who suggested this point to me in correspondence. This section gained enormously from his insights.

133. Conrad doesn't explicitly engage British colonialism until "Karain: A Memory." The British are only marginally present in *Almayer's Folly* through disnarration.

134. Gerald Prince, "The Disnarrated," *Style* 22, no. 1 (1988): 3.

135. I also invoke Genette's vastly consequential typology of novelistic duration in its suppressed choreographic potential. The "rhythms" of narrative can suddenly become "discontinuous," Genette writes, "syncopated, built of enormous scenes separated by immense gaps," departing from the norms of isochronism (*Narrative Discourse*, 93).

136. See Harilaos Stecopoulos, "South to the World: William Faulkner and the American Century," in *William Faulkner in Context*, ed. John Matthews (New York: Cambridge University Press, 2015), 147–55. In this stunning essay, Stecopoulos notes how "the theme of US global power often only emerges as peculiar marginalia in Faulkner's stories and novels" that "accrue" significance through recurrence; they are decentered from the narrative proper (150) but also its space. References to the American archipelago are scattered about the novel not only as metonyms but as elliptical moments of dialogue, as when it is revealed that Goodwin killed a man in the Pacific over a "nigger woman." Such moments require a mode of double listening. Faulkner had read Conrad in ways attuned to the problem of US colonial expansion.

137. North, *The Dialect of Modernism*, 57–58, describes how the language spoken on the *Vidar*, "on the decks of which Conrad learned virtually everything factual that went into his early Malay novels," must have been what the Dutch called "gibberish Malaya" maritime pidgin. This section gained greatly from Paul Nadal's insights.

138. GoGwilt ("Conrad and Romanised Print Form," 128) draws this phrase, which indexes the novel's otherwise occluded linguistic struggle, from the anonymous narrator's observation of the decaying sign "Lingard and Co."

139. The facts of decolonization include scripts as they pass into each other in "the space of print" (GoGwilt, *Passage of Literature*, 23). GoGwilt recalls, for example, how Benedict Anderson historicizes print capitalism's arrival in the East Indies after

the mid-century, such that "the language [a lingua franca Malay] moved out into the marketplace and media." Anderson, qtd. in GoGwilt, "Conrad and Romanised Print Form," 120. By 1928, GoGwilt continues, "A central part of this story is the way Romanised print Malay displaced the form of Arabic script traditionally used to write Malay since at least the sixteenth century. These different forms of writing Malay— *Jawi* and *Rumi*, Arabic and Roman—coexisted throughout the nineteenth century (their relative linguistic prestige carrying a different weight in British-controlled Malaysia and the Dutch-controlled East Indies)" (121).

140. I say "occlusion" not only because most readers of the novel will have little ready access to the contested history of Malay script. This history has been occluded, quite literally, from the *OED*. In its most current digital version, GoGwilt describes, the *OED* no longer includes the Arabic script for another key Malay word in Conrad's lexicon, one that stands in important relation to the *nyai*: "Tuan." When dialoging with an earlier published version of this present chapter (see Julie Beth Napolin, "'A Sinister Resonance': Joseph Conrad's Malay Ear and Auditory Cultural Studies," *Sounding Out! The Sound Studies Blog*, 9 July 2015, http://web.archive.org/web/2019 1219153239/https://soundstudiesblog.com/?s=Conrad%27s+malay+ear), GoGwilt notes that the opening shout of *Almayer's Folly* has yet to be decoded in relation to the "form of revolutionary Malay that will forge the language of anti-colonial Indonesian nationalism" (GoGwilt, "Conrad and Romanised Print Form," 129). Here I am arguing that, in its acoustics, the shout does not offer itself to be "decoded" per se. These thoughts and the chapter in general represent a formative and ongoing dialogue with GoGwilt.

141. Trinh, *Woman, Native, Other*, 53.

142. See Walter Benjamin's comments at the end of *The Origin of German Tragic Drama*, trans. John Osborne (New York: Verso, 2009), where he argues against this notion, retrieving the page in its thingliness.

143. Stephen Best and Sharon Marcus, "Surface Reading: An Introduction," *Representations* 108, no. 1 (2009): 1–21, note that the sounds of words are part of a text's "surface." But such a "surface" is immediately fractured when we no longer presume a text's monolingualism.

144. GoGwilt, "Conrad and Romanised Print Form," 128.

145. Clifford influentially introduces the notion of "salvage" ethnography in relation to its rhetoric of a disappearing object. "The other is lost . . . but saved in text." James Clifford, "On Ethnographic Allegory," in *Writing Culture: The Poetics and Politics of Ethnography*, ed. James Clifford and George E. Marcus (Berkeley: University of California Press, 1986), 112. Also see Christopher GoGwilt, *The Invention of the West: Joseph Conrad and the Double-Mapping of Europe and Empire* (Stanford, CA: Stanford University Press, 1995), which examines Conrad's logic of salvage ethnography in relation to the development of British anthropology. "Conrad adjusted the 'Malay' subject of his early work to participate in this problem of representation, omitting the

array of ethnographic detail one finds in [Sir Hugh] Clifford's text, to create a carefully misrepresented Malay fiction" (72).

146. See Edwin C. Hill Jr., *Black Soundscapes White Stages: The Meaning of Francophone Sound in the Black Atlantic* (Baltimore, MD: Johns Hopkins Press, 2013), 3. He who listens with imperial ears is an auditory analogue to "the white male subject of European landscape discourse—he whose imperial eyes passively look out and possess." Mary Louise Pratt, *Imperial Eyes: Travel Writing and Transculturation* (New York: Routledge, 1992), 9; qtd. in Hill, *Black Soundscapes*, 3). In Chapter 3, I discuss at length how listening, like the gaze, is split by pleasure and death but also by Du Boisian recognition.

147. The "murmur" annotates Du Chaillu's sense of untranslatable tongues but also what GoGwilt (*The Passage of Literature*, 232) argues to be the "philological presumption" of the human sciences from which Conrad breaks: "that language is the 'human expression' of a people" or that language and landscape are anthropologically tied. In *Heart of Darkness*, Conrad writes of the murmur as escaping the moment of its inscription: "The rapids were near, and an uninterrupted, uniform, headlong, rushing noise filled the mournful stillness of the grove, where not a breath stirred, not a leaf moved, with a mysterious sound—as though the tearing pace of the launched earth had suddenly become audible" (*HD*, 66). These and other sounds make Conrad's novel, for Homi K. Bhabha, *The Location of Culture* (New York: Routledge, 2004), 123–38, a prime example of the fantasy of colonial nonsense; I hear them differently.

148. Du Chaillu, qtd. in Pratt, *Imperial Eyes*, 209. It is important to note that I cite Pratt at cross-purposes with her own interpretation of Conrad as a "hyphenated white man" making an "imperialist internal critique" (213). I'm arguing that if we recuperate Conrad's sound effects, we recuperate a different anti-imperial inflection.

149. Among the most sensitive and psychoanalytic engagements with this dimension of the novel is Christopher Lane, "Almayer's Defeat: The Trauma of Colonialism in Conrad's Early Work," *Novel: A Forum on Fiction* 32, no. 3 (1999): 401–28.

150. See Sterne, *Audible Past*.

151. Summarizing the tradition of novel theory that rests upon the ontological referent of the voice (including Chatman and Roy Pascal), Hale writes, "When a character speaks, the narrator only seems silent; if one listens closely, one can hear his 'voice' as an intonation within another voice" (Hale, *Social Formalism*, 96). Hale summarizes Dorrit Cohn's reliance upon metaphors of the voice: "Fiction . . . has progressed from 'vocal to hushed authorial voices, from dissonant to consonant relations.'" (97). My claim is that these theorists never engage resonance as the relationship between text and sound, reading consciousness and listening consciousness, as if the "voice" of narrative can be bracketed from the inner "voice" of reading, which can in turn be bracketed from factual resonances. Also see Rey Chow, "Listening after 'Acousmaticity': Notes on a Transdisciplinary Problematic," in *Sound Objects*, ed. James A. Steintrager and Rey Chow (Chapel Hill, NC: Duke University Press, 2019), 114–29. While this

essay was published after I completed this manuscript, it is essential to consider. In ways that unfold from Chow's long critical trajectory—from her interrogation of the desire for native speech in *Writing Diaspora* (1993) to her critique of monolingualism in *Not Like a Native Speaker* (2014)—Chow persuasively revisits Husserl's investment in a pure inner voice to underscore how the method of phenomenological reduction, or "bracketing," coincides historically with widespread anxiety about the voice's reproducibility. The phenomenological effort is a *nativist* one, Chow argues, or an attempt to "salvage a virginal voice" untainted by the outside ("Listening after 'Acousmaticity,'" 114). In a final section of this tour-de-force essay, one with far-reaching and transdisciplinary consequences, Chow briefly pinpoints free indirect discourse as a technique of vocal estrangement in relation to Bakhtin's theory of double voicing (a theory I turn to in later chapters). She asks, and I hope that *The Fact of Resonance* may be read as one sustained response, "to what extent could such literary scholarship be shared—or, perhaps, adapted—for comparative study of the voice in the realm of sound theory? To what extent might literary studies be regarded, if somewhat belatedly, as partaking of the transdisciplinary discourse about acousmaticity?" (123).

152. I draw this phrase from Chow's sense that, given political-economic relations and the deployment of *desire* in the realm of knowledge, the languages of the Third World "are more likely [than Western languages] to submit to forcible transformation in the translation" (*Primitive Passions*, 178).

153. Pratt, *Imperial Eyes*, 222.

154. "'Romanticism,' we realize again and again in Conrad," Fogel writes, "is the literary expression of imperialism" ("The Mood of Overhearing," 134). Robert Hampson, *Cross-Cultural Encounters in Joseph Conrad's Malay Fiction: Writing Malaysia* (London: Palgrave, 2000), 1, shows how there was already a place for Borneo within the "popular imagination" of Conrad's readership, Conrad's Malay trilogy drawing upon existing myths of imperial heroes. For Frederic Jameson, *The Political Unconscious: Narrative as a Socially Symbolic Act* (Ithaca, NY: Cornell University Press, 1981), 206–80, the first part of *Lord Jim* is a feat of postmodern écriture, and the second part, which takes place in the fictional Malay island of Patusan, falls back on comfortable tropes of romance. Jameson does not consider the anticolonial valences of Patusan, chiefly communicated through the figure of the *nyai*.

155. I take up Du Bois in the Intersonority. For a foundational discussion of the relationship between double consciousness and double voicing see Hale, *Social Formalism*, 197–220.

156. See Jacques Derrida, *Monolingualism of the Other; or, The Prosthesis of Origin*, trans. Patrick Mensah (Stanford, CA: Stanford University Press, 1998).

157. Silverman, *The Acoustic Mirror*, 72; Rosolato, qtd. in Silverman, *The Acoustic Mirror*, 72.

158. Gustave Flaubert, *The Letters of Gustave Flaubert: 1830–1857*, ed. and trans. Francis Steegmuller (Cambridge, MA: Harvard University Press, 1980), 154.

159. Flaubert, *Letters*, 154.

160. Gustave Flaubert, "On Realism," in *Documents of Modern Literary Realism*, ed. George J. Becker (Princeton, NJ: Princeton University Press, 1963), 94.

161. Fredric Jameson, "Criticism in History," in *Weapons of Criticism: Marxism in America and the Literary Tradition*, ed. Norman Rudich (Palo Alto, CA: Stanford University Press, 1976), 35.

162. Jameson elides the acoustical techniques of the novel, as when "Across the silence that filled the village, a harrowing cry travelled through the air [*Au milieu de silence qui emplissait le village, un cri déchirant traversa l'air*]," a sound of amputation that Flaubert presents as surrounding but not penetrating a self-absorbed Emma. Gustave Flaubert, *Madame Bovary*, trans. Geoffrey Wall (New York: Penguin, 2003), 171. Thank you to Nathan Brown for suggesting this passage. This and other sounds drift into Conrad. Flaubert begins the book with Charles Bovary's stutter in another exquisitely sonic scene that Conrad seems to rewrite whenever he introduces a character whose speech fails to be understood.

163. For a discussion of the overdetermination of the letter "K" in Conrad, including self-accusation, see Chris GoGwilt, "Conrad's Accusative Case: Romanization, Changing Loyalties, and Switching Scripts," *Conradiana* 46, nos. 1–2 (2014): 53–62.

164. The Basmala is a daily prayer recited before many chapters of the Qu'ran. GoGwilt notes the eventual erasure of Arabic script from the *OED* entry on *bi-smi llāhi*, which appears in Conrad's text in English translation (see GoGwilt, "Conrad and Romanised Print Form"). Abdulla would have uttered to himself in Arabic. Conrad's ending is a double occlusion of Arabic script and of Romanized, transliterated *sound*. In that occlusion, there is a black Atlantic sound, for the movement of the sun in the novel, tracing a course from East to West, resonates Arab Africa. The opening of Mrs. Almayer's shout calls across that distance.

165. For Lacan, language means separation; we have the word because we don't have the thing. Here, however, the cut is memorably allegorized by the textual beginnings of *Lord Jim* in the torn-out endpapers of an 1819 family volume of Polish poetry copied out in Conrad's maternal grandmother's hand. It's not known when Conrad wrote these pages, but Eloise K. Hay, "*Lord Jim*: From Sketch to Novel," *Comparative Literature* 12, no. 4 (1960): 298, has suggested as early as the summer of 1896. Hay imagines that the leather notebook was among his keepsakes carried in a trunk to the Congo, along with the half-finished manuscript of *Almayer's Folly*.

166. Ford Madox Ford, *Joseph Conrad: A Personal Remembrance*, https://gutenberg.ca/ebooks/fordfm-josephconrad/fordfm-josephconrad-00-h-dir/fordfm-josephconrad-00-h.html.

167. James Clifford, *The Predicament of Culture* (Cambridge, MA: Harvard University Press, 1988), 96.

168. Edward W. Said, *Orientalism* (New York: Vintage, 1979), 6.

169. Jameson, "Criticism in History," 35.

170. Chow, *Primitive Passions*, 184.

171. Chow, *Primitive Passions*, 184.

172. Chow, *Primitive Passions*, 185.

173. Bhabha has connected Conrad's political discourse to English liberal values. But equally central to the foundation of liberal discourse is this question of consent.

174. Seyla Benhabib, *The Reluctant Modernism of Hannah Arendt*, rev. ed. (New York: Rowman and Littlefield, 2003), 79. Writing of Arendt's *The Origins of Totalitarianism*, Benhabib suggests a contradictory principle at the heart of the establishment of the modern nation-state, which must dominate and expand while requiring the "consent of the governed" (79).

175. GoGwilt, *The Invention of the West*, 81. Also see Lane, "Almayer's Defeat." Tracing the interracial unconscious of Conrad's narrative, Lane diagnoses "a type of passion that pushes for intimacy—often destroying it—[and] severs connection entirely" (416). Such passion, I've argued, is operative at the symbolic, linguistic, and acoustical registers of reading.

176. In the case history of Dora, who famously terminates her treatment, Freud recalls Dora's cough and introduces the possibility of its origin in the "uncanny sounds" that "reach" the ears of children. Sigmund Freud, *Dora: An Analysis of a Case of Hysteria*, ed. Philip Rieff (New York: Simon & Schuster, 1997), 71. Flagging his material as incomplete, Freud conjectures that the labored breathing of her father was heard by Dora emanating from her parent's bedroom, transferred to and reembodied by Dora. Freud provides, in other words, a sonic etiology of her hysteric dyspnea. "In this small recollection there must be the trace of an allusion."

177. "Classical rhetoric mentions anacoluthon especially with regard to the structure of periodical sentences. . . . It designates any grammatical or syntactical discontinuity in which a construction interrupts another before it is completed." De Man, *Allegories of Reading*, 289.

178. de Man, *Allegories of Reading*, 288.

179. Hunt, "An Acoustic Register," 243.

180. Hunt, "An Acoustic Register," 243, underscores reappropriation.

181. According to North, *The Dialect of Modernism*, 50, "the international maritime pidgin that had been current in the East Indies since the time of the Portuguese" contributed the word "nigger" to English. I return to the circulation of this slur in Chapter 2.

182. Jean-Luc Nancy, *Listening*, trans. Charlotte Mandell (New York: Fordham University Press, 2007), 13.

183. For example, Siem Reap was controlled by the Thai Kingdom of Siam in the eighteenth century before being returned to Cambodia in 1907. The term Siamese is both "nationally and racially marked," GoGwilt notes, and Taminah's name is already "Javanese-sounding" (*The Passage of Literature*, 170). The name is a sonic trace of geopolitics, which heightens the uncanny effect of Akerman's use of lip sync.

184. Khmer is part of the family of languages shared by the Malay Peninsula— Akerman recodes the novel's own meditation on script. Perhaps Akerman wishes to suggest a vague Pacific "setting." Artistic intentions aside, the vertiginous effect is clear: Akerman incites sensorial issues of legibility, exoticism, and identification. The issue of legibility will become important in the Intersonority, when I describe the optics of musical notation for those who can't read music.

185. David Toop, *Ocean of Sound: Aether Talk, Ambient Sound, and Imaginary Worlds* (London: Serpent's Tail, 1995), xii. Toop describes how Debussy's father had wanted him to be a sailor. In a reverse corollary of Conrad, Debussy instead found in music a "dedication to a life in the imagination" (16).

186. Jacques Attali, *Noise: The Political Economy of Music*, trans. Brian Massumi (Minneapolis: University of Minnesota Press, 1984), 3.

187. Paul de Man, "Dialogue and Dialogism," *Poetics Today* 4 (1983): 103.

188. See Paul de Man, "Autobiography as De-Facement," in *The Rhetoric of Romanticism* (New York: Columbia University Press, 1984), 67–82. Readers of the novel will recall that, to facilitate Nina and Dain's escape, Mrs. Almayer scratches out the face of another man's corpse, placing Dain's ring on his finger; it allows for the ruse that Dain is dead. See Michael Fried, "Almayer's Face: On 'Impressionism' in Conrad, Crane, and Norris," *Critical Inquiry* 17, no. 1 (1990): 193–236. My view is that, in escape, Nina chooses preoedipal identification with the Malay mother rather than castrated identification with the white father, an escape whose meaning would not have been lost on Akerman.

189. For a discussion of the recurrent place of maternal reconstitution in Akerman's films, avowed by Akerman herself, see Alisa Lebow, "Identity Slips: The Autobiographical Register in the Work of Chantal Akerman," *Film Quarterly* 70, no. 1 (Fall 2016): 54–60.

190. Dominic Pettman, "Pavlov's Podcast: The Acousmatic Voice in the Age of Mp3s," *Differences* 22, nos. 2–3 (December 1, 2011): 141.

191. See Cavarero, *For More Than One Voice*, 171.

192. For a discussion of "original mimesis," see Philippe Lacoue-Labarthe, *Typography: Mimesis, Philosophy, Politics*, trans. Christopher Fynsk (Cambridge, MA: Harvard University Press, 1989). Also see Nidesh Lawtoo, *Conrad's Shadow: Catastrophe, Mimesis, Theory* (East Lansing: Michigan State University Press, 2016); and *The Phantom of the Ego: Modernism and the Mimetic Unconscious* (East Lansing: Michigan State University Press, 2013), who places mimesis at the center of Conrad's project.

193. See Silverman, *Acoustic Mirror*, 42–71, for her analysis of lip sync and the postdubbing of female voices in *Singin' in the Rain* and other films.

194. Trinh T. Minh-ha, *When the Moon Waxes Red: Representation, Gender, and Cultural Politics* (New York: Routledge, 1991), 67.

195. Similarly, in the "Club Silencio" sequence of *Mulholland Drive*, David Lynch

capitalizes on the capacity for such revelation in concealment or audibility in silencing.

2. THE ECHO OF THE OBJECT

1. Sigmund Freud, *Beyond the Pleasure Principle*, trans. James Strachey (New York: Norton, 1989), 12.

2. Freud, *Beyond the Pleasure Principle*, 13–14.

3. Freud, *Beyond the Pleasure Principle*, 15.

4. Freud, *Beyond the Pleasure Principle*, 14. While this specific text is not part of his study, Daniel Heller-Roazen provides in *Echolalias: On the Forgetting of Language* (New York: Zone, 2005) a remarkable analysis of the appearance and disappearance of speech and linguistic community, including in Freud's essays on aphasia.

5. Homi K. Bhabha, *The Location of Culture* (New York: Routledge, 2004), 177.

6. In Lacan's estimation in *The Four Fundamental Concepts of Psychoanalysis: The Seminar of Jacques Lacan, Book XI*, ed. Jacques-Alain Miller, trans. Alan Sheridan (New York: Norton, 1998), 62, mastery of the mother's comings and goings is "of secondary importance" to *fort-da*. Instead, the scene is paradigmatic of how the *object a* is separated (or "cut") from the maternal body. The oscillating space between the two phonemes allows the child to represent himself as an object who is separated from the other. Echo would seem to be there in the background of this analysis. The neglect of Echo and, with her, of history and politics is the crux of Spivak's critique of Freud and Lacan's citation under erasure of Ovid's myth across various texts, for example, in Jacques Lacan, *Anxiety: The Seminar of Jacques Lacan, Book X*, ed. Jacques-Alain Miller (Malden, MA: Polity, 2016), 183. "Freud leaves Ovid alone. . . . In one Freudian articulation at least, primary narcissism is an 'absolute self-suffienc[cy] from which we step, toward noticing a changeful world outside and the beginnings of finding objects, by being born [*mit dem Geborenwerden*].' Here the mother is nothing but, in Luce Irigaray's word, an 'envelope.' By contrast, in Ovid Liriope's womb has a history. It comes to envelop Narcissus by a primary rape by Cephisus, demidivine violence as sexual violence that does not offend the political economy of the gods. The entire pretext of Tiresias and Echo as major players is crosshatched by a story of punishment and reward. When Freud and Lacan use the narrative as psychoethical instantiations they ignore this framing." Gayatri Chakravorty Spivak, "Echo," *New Literary History* 24, no. 1 (1993): 22. Ovid's Narcissus emerges, Spivak continues, "from a scene of responsibility and punishment," which is omitted from the "modern Narcissus" for whom primary narcissism is jubilant and auto-erotic (22). In Chapter 1, we found that Conrad includes in the opening shout of *Almayer's Folly* a trace of rape, a mere echo within Almayer, who focalizes the shout. Conrad understood the myth well, and just like Ovid indicates the nymph's rape in two lines, Conrad renders it in just a few words. Conrad reorganizes the subjective coordinates of this myth *and* its violent frame when the slave girl, Taminah, rustles in the bushes, Mrs. Almayer calling out, "Who's there?"

7. René Descartes, *Discourse on Method and Mediations on First Philosophy*, ed. David Weissman (New Haven, CT: Yale University Press, 1996), 64.

8. In conversation with Jean-Luc Nancy, Jacques Derrida recalls Descartes's "insistence on pronunciation, on the ineluctable pronouncement of 'Ego sum, ego existo'—and on time, on this 'each time' of the proffered utterance [*profération*]. . . . Words seem to be carried [*portée*] by the mouth beyond their mere discursive reach [*portée*]." Jacques Derrida, *On Touching—Jean-Luc Nancy*, trans. Christine Irizarry (Stanford, CA: Stanford University Press, 2005), 33. Derrida's elliptical comments appear to be based on the importance of the proposition (and its Latin term, *pronuntiatum*) in Descartes's second meditation. In a feminist vein, Frances Dyson, "The Genealogy of Radio Voice," in *Radio Rethink: Art, Sound, and Transmission*, ed. Daina Augaitis and Dan Lander (Banff: Walter Phillips Gallery, 1994), describes how Descartes seeks silence away from worldly "flux" and corporeality, or what Veit Erlmann, *Reason and Resonance: A History of Modern Aurality* (New York: Zone, 2010), calls a "soundproof space" free of noise and breath, which "entangle" the philosopher's ego "in a web of uncanny affinities" (32).

9. Adriana Cavarero, *For More Than One Voice: Toward a Philosophy of Vocal Expression*, trans. Paul A. Kottman (Stanford, CA: Stanford University Press, 2005), 171.

10. Cavarero, *For More Than One Voice*, 171.

11. Cavarero, *For More Than One Voice*, 171.

12. Cavarero, *For More Than One Voice*, 168.

13. Cavarero chooses the biblical story of the voice of Jacob as the philosophical ground of her book. Attempting to steal the blessing from his brother, Esau, Jacob applies fake fur to his arms to fool the blind Isaac that he is Esau. Hearing Jacob speak, Isaac replies, "The voice is the voice of Jacob." It is a perfect relation, circular and genitive. In Cavarero's view, the story teaches that "Artifice cannot capture the voice." Cavarero, *For More Than One Voice*, 24. In the Overture, I described double listening in W. E. B. Du Bois as an alternative ground for a theory of listening, one that I shall return to in the Intersonority.

14. Jacques Derrida, *Writing and Difference*, trans. Alan Bass (Chicago: University of Chicago Press, 1978), 217, suggests that the fundamental characteristic of the scene of writing is "*spacing*" as "linear consecution" on the page but also a temporal break with the site of inscription. "Arche-writing" is the name Derrida gives to the intrusion of difference into self-presence, such that any spoken event is always already "writing."

15. Rey Chow, *Not Like a Native Speaker: On Languaging as a Postcolonial Experience* (New York: Columbia University Press, 2014), eloquently describes a series of postcolonial experiences with accent and intonation, taking up therein what she calls "the open and unhealed wounds of language" (11). Such wounds, she continues, speak to the "ongoing unevenness among languages and cultures."

16. See "echolocation, n.," *OED Online*.

17. Eve Kosofsky Sedgwick, "Paranoid Reading and Reparative Reading, or, You're

So Paranoid, You Probably Think This Essay Is About You," in *Touching Feeling: Affect, Pedagogy, Performativity* (Durham, NC: Duke University Press, 2003), 149.

18. Sigmund Freud, *Civilization and its Discontents*, trans. James Strachey (New York: Norton, 1989), 13. When the breast is unavailable, the infant screams. "There is for the first time set over against the ego an 'object,' in the form of something which exists 'outside' and which is only forced to appear by a special action" (14).

19. But colonialism itself is also unthinkable. See David Eng, in "Colonial Object Relations," *Social Text* 34, no. 1 (2016): 1–19. The *fort-da* scene, Eng notes, already "presents us with a more general problem of *difference* in objects," or "the urgent question of why some objects are thrown away *and* retrieved while others or not" (4).

20. We forget that anti-Semitism was already on the rise in fin-de-siècle Vienna and that Freud had been denied a professorship for being Jewish, two contexts that spurred his imaginative flight into *The Interpretation of Dreams*. See Charles E. Schorske, *Fin-De-Siècle Vienna: Politics and Culture* (New York: Vintage, 1980).

21. In relation to Fanon's title, Fred Moten writes of his own mistranslation ("The Case of Blackness," *Criticism* 50, no. 2 [2008]: 177–218) as a form of what he has elsewhere called "analytic precision" (see his "Blackness and Nothingness (Mysticism in the Flesh)," *South Atlantic Quarterly* 112, no. 4 [October 2013]: 738).

22. In Chapter 1, we found these communicational theories of narrative to suppress acoustics.

23. Also see Nico Israel, *Outlandish: Writing Between Exile and Diaspora* (Stanford, CA: Stanford University Press, 2000), for an account of Conrad's exile.

24. A major background to my account is Philippe Lacoue-Labarthe, "The Echo of the Subject," in *Typography: Mimesis, Philosophy, Politics*, trans. Christopher Fynsk (Cambridge, MA: Harvard University Press, 1989), 139–207. While I address his essay at greater length in Chapter 3, I do not take it up here for the simple fact that he brackets politics. Some readers might also hear resonances with Fred Moten's concept of "the resistance of the object." I return to this concept in Chapter 3. The "object" in Moten's case is the commodity, while in this present chapter we are taking up the ego—though in the coda we will find them to be inextricable.

25. Gayatri Chakravarty Spivak, *The Critique of Postcolonial Reason: Toward a History of the Vanishing Present* (Cambridge, MA: Harvard University Press, 1999), 126.

26. Spivak, *The Postcolonial Critique of Reason*, 127.

27. Anne Anlin Cheng, *The Melancholy of Race: Psychoanalysis, Assimilation, and Hidden Grief* (New York: Oxford University Press, 2001), 11.

28. Cheng, *The Melancholy of Race*, 13.

29. Sigmund Freud, "Mourning and Melancholia," in *The Standard Edition of the Complete Psychological Works of Sigmund Freud*, ed. James Strachey (London: Hogarth, 1971), 14:257.

30. Freud, "Mourning and Melancholia," 14:256. Qtd. in Kaja Silverman, *The*

Acoustic Mirror: The Female Voice in Psychoanalysis and Cinema (Bloomington: Indiana University Press, 1988), 158.

31. See Michael North, *The Dialect of Modernism: Race, Language, and Twentieth-Century Literature* (New York: Oxford University Press, 1998), 57–58.

32. Ovid *Metamorphoses* 3.337.

33. See Joan W. Scott, "Fantasy Echo: History and the Construction of Identity," *Critical Inquiry* 27, no. 2 (2001): 284–304. Scott found the title of her essay through an English-speaking student who misheard Scott's rendering of the phrase *fin-de-siècle* in her German accent. Reading and puzzling over the appearance of "fantasy echo" in the student's paper (on the topic of European history), Scott realized it was a provocative phrase, worthy of theorization in relation to identity, solidarity, and the category of "women."

34. Qtd. in Scott, "Fantasy Echo," 288.

35. Rose, qtd. in Scott, "Fantasy Echo," 289.

36. I borrow this phrase from Kathleen McClusky's rare and technical account of the linguistic structure of sound in Virginia Woolf, another modernist whose sentences work through phonemes and sonic repetition. McClusky writes, "Since the reading of novels is primarily a visual experience having a silent 'auditory' dimension rather than an oral one, I have indicated in places the participation of visual echoes in the patterns (for example in 'a large grimy dog' where the soft g participates visually in the pattern although its sound is different). Thus the term phoneme includes grapheme as well." Kathleen McClusky, *Reverberations: Sound and Structure in the Novels of Virginia Woolf* (Ann Arbor: UMI Research Press, 1986), 129n7.

37. Michael H. Levenson, *A Genealogy of Modernism: A Study of English Literary Doctrine, 1908–1922* (New York: Cambridge University Press, 1986), 1–9, focuses on the narrator's shift in pronoun and titles his discussion "The Modernist Narrator on a Victorian Sailing Ship."

38. Cavarero, *For More Than One Voice*, 168–69, discusses *logos* stripped of the semantic in the process of repetition until it becomes purely vocalic.

39. Again, this silence is pivotal for Spivak, who, in "Echo," works to recover a different reality for the female subject, who, according to Freud and Lacan, tends toward narcissism.

40. In *Beyond the Pleasure Principle*, Freud's topographical model of the ego is largely supplanted by the economic theory of the drives. Freud had figured the censor in *Interpretation of Dreams* (1900) as an activity or power (*Macht*), but in "On Narcissism" (1914) he begins to think of it as speaking in a "voice" (*Stimme*). It is only later in *The Ego and the Id* that this censoring entity will be apportioned its own place and normalizing function in the structure of the psyche, the so-called superego. In that work, Freud continues to figure the censor in vocalic terms, the superego regulating psychic life through commanding voices that also narrate, as if in a voiceover, one's

actions and thoughts. The mother's voice is the first object a newborn recognizes, and "vocal and aural abilities precede visual aptitude." Aimée Boutin, *Maternal Echoes: The Poetry of Marceline Desbordes-Valmore and Alphonse de Lamartine* (Newark: University of Delaware Press, 2001), 17. Boutin notes how the primordial place of the mother's voice, suggestive of a maternal identification that predates both the Lacanian mirror stage and the place of the mother's face (in its "mirror-role") is discussed at length by the French psychoanalysts Didier Anzieu and Guy Rosolato.

41. Spivak, "Echo," 32.

42. I am not alone in this. When browsing a used book auction, I found that the previous owner of one set of the complete works had placed a large "X" over the slur on the book's spine.

43. Freud writes that the dream "has above all to evade the censorship, and with that end in view, the dream-work makes use of *displacement of psychical intensities* to the point of a transvaluation of all psychical values." But there are, he continues, "*considerations of representability.*" The dream must draw from acoustical and visual traces; however, "little attention is paid to the logical relations between the thoughts; those relations are ultimately given a disguised representation in certain *formal* characteristics of dreams." Sigmund Freud, *The Interpretation of Dreams*, trans. James Strachey (New York: Avon, 1998), 506. In this same way, I am suggesting that Wait is "there" even when he is absent; that is, he is present in the formal consideration of narrative voice in Conrad, or what through Conrad becomes the participant-observer of American modernism.

44. See Christina Sharpe, *In the Wake: On Blackness and Being* (Durham, NC: Duke University Press, 2016). Wake work is the specific yet pervasive work of mourning opened up by the Middle Passage, which I explore in more detail in Chapter 3. For Sharpe, wake work opens up the possibility of black ontology as such.

45. English borrows from "*monēre*" to derive "monitor," not simply a signal or indicator but, by the 1930s, a loudspeaker system used to broadcast a performance or output the signal to an engineer or performer who is listening for and adjusting disturbances. But the word never loses its now archaic sense of ecclesiastical authority, where to listen in is also to watch and surveil, such that one can also watch on a monitor; to monitor is to control (visually and acoustically) from afar. Importantly, "monument" is also derived from *monēre*; it is, then, both prescriptive and postscriptive in its meanings.

46. See David Copenhafer, "Overhearing (in) *Touch of Evil* and *The Conversation*: From 'Real Time' Surveillance to Its Recording," *Sound Studies* 4, no. 1 (2018): 2–18.

47. Those who work in sound design know that Hitchcock might have used a piece of recorded sound that was neither rain nor a running faucet. It is not important which is the "real" source, notwithstanding the fact that it would undecidable anyway, since the investigator is already hearing one through the memory of the other.

48. Thank you to Copenhafer for this expression.

49. Walter Benjamin, *Illuminations*, ed. Hannah Arendt, trans. Harry Zohn (New York: Schocken, 1968), 94.

50. For North, such moments are "vocal blackface" that reflect not simply modernism's primitivism but the problem of standardizing English (*The Dialect of Modernism*, 6).

51. Gérard Genette, *Narrative Discourse: An Essay in Method*, trans. J. E. Lewin (Ithaca, NY: Cornell University Press, 1972), 211.

52. Mikhail Bakhtin, "Discourse in the Novel," in *Literary Theory: An Anthology*, ed. Julie Rivkin and Michael Ryan (Malden, MA: Blackwell, 2004), 677.

53. Lacan adds to this structure the category of the ideal ego, or *Ideal-Ich*, which he associates with the imaginary rather than the symbolic. It first strikes the subject during the mirror stage, which presents the beholder a *Gestalt*, or seemingly whole image, with which the infant identifies.

54. Sigmund Freud, "On Narcissism: An Introduction," in *The Standard Edition of the Complete Psychological Works of Sigmund Freud*, ed. James Strachey (London: Hogarth, 1957), 14:90.

55. Albert J. Guerard, "The Nigger of the 'Narcissus'," *Kenyon Review* 19, no. 2 (1957): 215.

56. Guerard, "The Nigger of the 'Narcissus'," 215. "What this something is—more specific than a 'blackness'—is likely to vary with each new reader," Guerard continues. In this brilliant essay, Guerard notes that Vernon Young detected in "Wait" a play on the word ("Wait, *weight*, burden"), such that "symbolic potentialities exist from the start" (215). Guerard goes on to insist, however, upon Wait's "concrete reality" as black man, just as Moby Dick is a "real whale" (216). But blackness in Conrad opens up something like the substitutability of the symbol in general; as concretion, it has everything to do with the relay between the particular and the universal (since Guerard's moment of writing, Rogin has also argued for the racialized concretion of the "whiteness" of the whale).

57. See Ivan Krielkamp, "A Voice without a Body: The Phonographic Logic of 'Heart of Darkness,'" *Victorian Studies* 40, no. 2 (1997): 211–44; Vincent Pecora, "*Heart of Darkness* and the Phenomenology of Voice," *ELH* 52, no. 4 (1985): 993–1015; and Bette Lynn London, *The Appropriated Voice: Narrative Authority in Conrad, Forster, and Woolf* (Ann Arbor: University of Michigan Press, 1990).

58. Eric Lott, "Love and Theft: The Racial Unconscious of Blackface Minstrelsy," *Representations* 39 (Summer 1992): 33.

59. We learn from Freud that the object is recalcitrant because of the failed work of mourning. In "Mourning and Melancholia," Freud differentiates between two forms of grief that he thought to be corollaries. Freud famously observes, "In mourning it is the world which has become poor and empty; in melancholia it is the ego itself" (246). As a condition, melancholia (*Melancholie*) is characterized by the metaphoric recurrence of symptoms, among them a loss of all interest in the world and a "profoundly painful

dejection." As an affect, mourning (*Traurigkeit*) is responsive to and expressive of an event of loss, and it begins in the admission that there has been the loss of an object, one that is nameable and knowable. Recognizing that one has lost someone or "some abstraction," such as nation or an ideal, we expect grief and, with it, its cries to pass with time. Mourning accepts a reality principle that the love object is gone, freeing the libido to become reattached to new objects. Cheng shows that Freud was never able to think through what happens to the object once it is thoroughly debased. We can say, in turn, that displacement of loss haunts Freud as the one who would give us the theoretical tools to articulate it; displacement infects the theory of displacement, loss the theory of loss.

60. Freud, "Mourning and Melancholia," 247.

61. Freud writes of "the laments which always sound the same and are wearisome in their monotony" ("Mourning and Melancholia," 256). We forget that Freud was writing in the age of Edison, and he regarded himself as having "the gift of a phonographic memory," particularly in the recall of case histories. See Sigmund Freud, *New Introductory Lectures on Psycho-Analysis*, trans. James Strachey (New York: Norton, 1990), 5.

62. Freud, "Mourning and Melancholia," 249, 256.

63. Freud, "Mourning and Melancholia," 257. The German translation is as provided by Judith Butler, *The Psychic Life of Power: Theories in Subjection* (Palo Alto, CA: Stanford University Press, 1997), 175.

64. Butler, *The Psychic Life of Power*, 176.

65. Most notably by Judith Butler in *Excitable Speech: A Politics of the Performative* (New York: Routledge, 2013), where she argues that injurious speech can also be subversively seized.

66. Cheng, *The Melancholy of Race*, 200n22. Ranjana Khanna describes a similar structure in *Dark Continents: Psychoanalysis and Colonialism* (Durham, NC: Duke University Press, 2003), writing of "colonial melancholia."

67. Cheng, *The Melancholy of Race*, 11.

68. Frantz Fanon, *Black Skin, White Masks*, trans. Charles Lam Markmann (London: Pluto Press, 1986), 20.

69. Fanon, *Black Skin, White Masks*, 21.

70. Roland Barthes, *Responsibility of Forms: Critical Essays on Music, Art, and Representation*, trans. Richard Howard (Berkeley: University of California Press, 1997), 271.

71. Kristeva, qtd. in Barthes, *Responsibility of Forms*, 270.

72. Barthes, *Responsibility of Forms*, 271.

73. Barthes, *Responsibility of Forms*, 273, 270.

74. Fanon, *Black Skin, White Masks*, 21. This kind of criticism was also launched against James Baldwin. In a famous televised debate, William F. Buckley Jr. accused Baldwin of having stolen his intonation (from white men like Buckley).

75. Fanon, *Black Skin, White Masks*, 111–12. What is translated by Markmann as "Sho' good eatin'" is in the original French "Y a bon banania": The translation anglicizes the phrase into a minstrel phrase, since the minstrel voice, appetitive and in dialect, is one that would be readily available in the American and British readerly acoustical imaginary. But there are other differences, as well. Edwin C. Hill Jr., in *Black Soundscapes White Stages: The Meaning of Francophone Sound in the Black Atlantic* (Baltimore, MD: Johns Hopkins Press, 2013), provides part of the text in French: "Je promenai sur moi un regard objectif, découvris ma noirceur, mes caractères ethniques,—et me défoncèrent le tympan l'anthropophagie, l'arriération mentale, le fétichisme, les tares raciales, les négriers, et surtout, et surtout: 'Y a bon banania.'" Hill writes: "'*Tympan*' here means eardrum, not 'tom-tom' (the punctuation also suggests '*tympan*' is not part of the list of agents, but part of the body as a direct object of violence). The '*tympan*' constitutes an intimate barrier between self and other, not one that naturally remains open. '*Défoncer*,' denotes not just a beating but a puncturing or penetration of this membrane or inner skin" (25–26). In his translation of Fanon's book, Richard Philcox translates *défoncer* as "deafened." There is a violent opening and splitting apart.

What Hill does not say is that Markmann's translation racializes the sound that breaks Fanon open. He is, in Markmann's understanding, being battered down by an echo that includes a racialized music. Some sound, heard in advance as stereotype, echoes back to Fanon before he might even talk to this boy (who doesn't address him). Overhearing the slur breaks in upon the eardrum to reproduce consciousness as racial consciousness. *Tam-tam* (tom-tom) is, in fact, among the most unifying yet multivalent figures of Fanon's text. Across his translation of Fanon, Philcox translates *tam-tam* simply as "drum," dampening its resonances with hybridized traditional music, for example in Fanon's phrase, "*Eia! le tam-tam baragounie le message cosmique.*" See *Peau noire, masques blancs* (Paris: Éditions du Seuil, 1952), 100. As will I turn to in Chapter 3, Conrad, to some extent, contributes to that echo in writing of drumming in *Heart of Darkness*, what becomes a universalized, racialized sound, one that Ralph Ellison also references—via Conrad—in the epilogue to *Invisible Man*.

76. Also see Pierre Macherey, "Figures of Interpellation in Althusser and Fanon," *Radical Philosophy*, May/June 2012, https://www.radicalphilosophy.com/article/figures-of-interpellation-in-althusser-and-fanon. According to Macherey, Althusser never references Fanon, who published his book two decades before Althusser's 1970 "Ideology and Ideological State Apparatuses." But the two were contemporaries, and Althusser, born in Algeria, likely read Fanon. What becomes possible to trace, in other words, is the acoustical displacement of Fanon by Althusser. This displacement allows Althusser to posit a universalizing scene of subjectivation that echoes into his inheritors such that it becomes possible to think of a "body" of a subject without skin. Understood in this way, *The Psychic Life of Power* is a companion to a book like Saidiya Hartman's *Scenes of Subjection*.

77. Butler, *The Psychic Life of Power*, 112.

78. Hill, *Black Soundscapes White Stages*, 25.

79. Fanon, *Black Skin, White Masks*, 111.

80. See Frantz Fanon, "This Is the Voice of Algeria," in *A Dying Colonialism*, trans. Haakon Chevalier (New York: Grove, 1965), 69–98. Also see Ian Baucom, "Frantz Fanon's Radio: Solidarity, Diaspora, and the Tactics of Listening," *Contemporary Literature* 42, no. 1 (2001): 15–49.

81. It is in relation to interpellation that Butler recalls the middle voice, as between the passive and active states. See *The Psychic Life of Power*, 108.

82. Fanon, *Black Skin, White Masks*, 109.

83. Isaac Julien's film *Frantz Fanon: Black Skin White Mask* memorably begins with Fanon (played by Colin Salmon) pressing his ear against a radio, listening to Creole broadcasts as a child. According to Baucom, "Frantz Fanon's Radio," 15, it "rehearses Fanon's biography in miniature" while it also "allegorizes one of his most important writing strategies"—to present "a compilation of those voices to which he has inclined his ear and a record of his responses."

84. Alice Cherki, *Frantz Fanon: A Portrait*, trans. Nadia Benabid (Ithaca, NY: Cornell University Press, 2006), 27.

85. Cheng, *The Melancholy of Race*, 162.

86. See Jean Laplanche, *Essays on Otherness*, ed. John Fletcher (New York: Routledge, 1999), 194, who writes, for example, that the paradigm of revelation means that "God is a god who speaks and compels the hearer to listen" in the call, "Hear, O Israel!" But this call is also enigmatic and "compels one to translate."

87. Fanon, *Black Skin, White Masks*, 217. Emphasis mine.

88. Fanon, *Black Skin, White Masks*, 120 (in French, 97).

89. Fanon, *Black Skin, White Masks*, 109.

90. Fanon, *Black Skin, White Masks*, 140 (in French, 113). Such waiting includes watching. Fanon here describes the moment before a crushing cinematic stereotype will appear for audiences who both expect and demand it.

91. The quotations include Langston Hughes (translated into French), "The Negro Speaks of Rivers," a poem that Peter Lancelot Mallios, *Our Conrad: Constituting American Modernity* (Stanford, CA: Stanford University Press, 2010) has convincingly routed through Conrad. It is unclear to me if Fanon read *Le Nègre du Narcisse*, Robert d'Humières's now standard 1913 translation of Conrad's novel (André Gide, who ushered Conrad into French letters, also translated the book in 1909). But Conrad was enormously popular in 1950s France. D'Humières's translation describes Wait as coming from "Antilles" yet retains Wait's name in English: "Wait! cria une voix pleine e retentissante. . . . Qu'est-ce que c'est? Qui a dit Wait" Quel . . ." (Joseph Conrad, *Le Nègre du Narcisse*, trans. Robert d'Humières [Paris: Gallimard, 1913], 14). In the section where Fanon writes, "I wait for me," he references the English title of

the American writer Chester Himes's novel *If He Hollers Let Him Go*, about a black shipyard worker.

92. Butler, *The Psychic Life of Power*, 111.

93. Butler, *The Psychic Life of Power*, 108.

94. The spatial acoustic produces the political possibility of pretending not to hear someone who injures you. "The nigger seemed not to hear," says the narrator of the slur, which is not addressed directly to James Wait. Conrad's narrator is the one who hears it; he reports the men's murmur but does not himself join in, triangulating the scene. On the heels of this scene, Wait asks another mate if the ship's cook is also a "colored man," disappointed to learn he is not. This passing moment of dialogue overheard by the narrator indicates his attunement to Wait's solitude and the foreclosed possibility of racial community. Wait will only ever be heard aboard ship by white ears. But Wait's ability to dissimulate throughout the novel is acute. Conrad, in other words, is keenly aware of the black mate's strategies of racialized survival. Along these same lines, "'I heard nothing strange,'" Langston Hughes says in the "Haunted Ship" section of *The Big Sea: An Autobiography* (New York: Hill and Wang, 1993), 96. In *Our Conrad*, this brief section proves to be of major importance to Mallios's discussion of Conrad and African American literature. While working in the New York port, tending to "dead ships," the white men dare Hughes to sleep on the ship that creaks at night; that same winter the poet wrote "The Weary Blues." They expect Hughes to be terrified, like the black men represented in films. Needless to say, he gets through the night by pretending not to hear the ghostly sounds. While staying on the ship, he read Conrad's *Heart of Darkness*.

95. Mieke Bal, *Narratology: Introduction to the Theory of Narrative*, 3rd ed. (Toronto: University of Toronto Press, 2009), 30.

96. North, *The Dialect of Modernism*, 40.

97. Qtd. in Michael Greaney, *Conrad, Language, and Narrative* (Cambridge: Cambridge University Press, 2005), xi.

98. These defacements are memorably theorized by Michael Fried in "Almayer's Face: On 'Impressionism' in Conrad, Crane, and Norris," *Critical Inquiry* 17, no. 1 (1990): 193–236, which I discuss at length in Chapter 3.

99. Laurence Davies, "Afterword," in *Conrad and Language*, ed. Katherine Isobel Baxter and Robert Hampson (Edinburgh: Edinburgh University Press, 2016), 205.

100. Qtd. in North, *The Dialect of Modernism*, 40.

101. See Christopher GoGwilt, *The Passage of Literature: Genealogies of Modernism in Conrad, Rhys, and Pramoedya* (New York: Oxford University Press, 2011), 13. GoGwilt calls this moment the "authorial primal scene" not simply for Conrad but of a creolized conception of modernism.

102. Davies, "Afterword," 205.

103. It is unclear to me whether such an egoic scenario is, in the end, essentially

white. Such a question would require a more extensive analysis of the echoes in Fanon. In reciting the textual voices of the colonial past, Fanon attempts to "liquidate" them (*Black Skin, White Masks*, 122). But citing them involves preserving them. Frank B. Wilderson III, "The Narcissistic Slave," in *Cinema and the Structure of US Antagonisms* (Durham, NC: Duke University Press, 2010), 55–91, argues that Fanon—a reader of Lacan—shows us that Lacanian "full speech" is a white project, one that "crowd[s] out the White subject's realization . . . of violence" (84). "Black narcissism" is a fallacy because the Lacanian analysand is not aiming to free himself from the emptiness of social stereotype but from projection by the self onto others (85).

104. For a discussion of Conrad's influence on Fitzgerald and his generation, see Mallios, *Our Conrad*, 221–64. According to Mallios, Fitzgerald described reading *The Nigger of the "Narcissus"* and sitting down immediately to begin *Gatsby*.

105. In the Reprise, I return to this reflexive phrase, "to shape itself," which recurs across Conrad's early corpus in multiply conjugated ways. The French and Polish languages here left their trace in Conrad's English, but this trace—resonance—is one through which Marlow is born.

106. This fact of resonance is borne out by Conrad's compositional history. It is widely thought that his first piece of fictional writing was the unpublished story "The Black Mate." It begins with an incredible irony and ambiguity, when the narrator says, "Here comes the black mate." It takes several paragraphs to learn that he is named thus for the darkness of his hair, Conrad capitalizing on the missing image of reading.

107. Benjamin, *Illuminations*, 85. For the proper quotation, see Freud, *Beyond the Pleasure Principle*, 28. Though it is rarely recognized as such, the often-quoted misquotation means that Benjamin was either citing from memory or from the old notes described by Sigrid Wiegel, *Body- and Image-Space: Re-reading Walter Benjamin*, trans. Georgina Paul with Rachel McNicholl and Jeremey Gaines (New York: Routledge, 1996), 107. According to Wiegel, Freud writes *an Stelle*, or "instead of," while Benjamin writes *an der Stelle*, or "in the place of." Thanks to Nell Wasserstrom for bringing this issue to my attention.

108. Joseph Conrad, *Notes on Life and Letters: The Collected Works*, vol. 3 (Garden City, NY: Doubleday, Page, 1926), 12–14. Emphasis added.

109. Ian Watt, *Conrad in the Nineteenth Century* (Berkeley: University of California Press, 1979), 90.

110. Jacques Derrida, *Dissemination*, trans. Barbara Johnson (Chicago: University of Chicago Press, 1981), 109.

111. Conrad labored over the completion of *The Rescue*, taking up and leaving the demanding project numerous times. *Heart of Darkness* and *Lord Jim* were but two reprieves from its composition. While he was able to compose *Heart of Darkness* rather quickly, *Lord Jim* proved to be a painful interruption within the interruption.

112. Joseph Conrad and David Storrar Meldrum, *Letters to William Blackwood and David S. Meldrum* (Durham, NC: Duke University Press, 1958), 27.

113. Edward Said, *The World, the Text, and the Critic* (Cambridge, MA: Harvard University Press, 1983), 90.

114. Said, *The World, the Text, and the Critic*, 90.

115. When Said revised and republished "Conrad: The Presentation of Narrative" for *The World, the Text, and the Critic*, he omitted the epigraph altogether.

116. Roland Barthes, *Image, Music, Text*, trans. Stephen Heath (New York: Hill and Wang, 1977), 142. It is a bit odd to translate the phrase "le noir-et-blanc" as "negative," though it is true that the contrast bears within itself a dialectical (negating) relation. Barthes's original sense might have been the blank (white) page, which then bears black ink. But given that black-and-white is stated as if in union, it is difficult not to hear a prelude to Barthes's future thinking on photography. In relation to postwar France and decolonization, it is also hard not to hear an occluded racial other. This play is of course testimony to his central thesis. For a compelling discussion of how loss of identity in Barthes may in fact represent a calculated response to colonial Algeria and a refusal of domination, see Daniel Just, *Literature, Ethics, and Decolonization in Postwar France: The Politics of Disengagement* (New York: Cambridge University Press, 2015), 24–44. I return to these issues in Chapter 3.

117. Kaja Silverman, *The Threshold of the Visible World* (New York: Routledge, 1996), 73.

118. Silverman, *The Threshold of the Visible World*, 73. Ideality is the recognition, Silverman describes, accorded to the master by the slave. But that dynamic is itself suggestive because it places Conrad—not Wait—in the position of slave.

119. The source of the title in Shakespeare's *Macbeth* is more quickly recognized but also more easily accredited. This issue of source is at the heart of the novel's displaced confrontation with slavery and the problem of the exchange value of human life. The echo of a dying James Wait into Faulkner (via Shakespeare and blackface) has also caught the rigorous attention of John T. Matthews, "Dialect and Modernism," in *The Sound and the Fury: An Authoritative Text, Backgrounds and Contexts, Criticism*, ed. Michael Gorra (New York: Norton, 2014), 487.

120. In Lacoue-Labarthe's phrase, an echo is "catacoustic" (from Greek *kata*, or through, down, or against). For Christina Sharpe in *In the Wake*, the Middle Passage is *the* catastrophe on which modernity turns: In Faulkner, what Sharpe calls, after Maurice Blanchot, "writing the disaster" demands a shattered chronology (as does colonialism in Conrad).

121. William Faulkner, *Collected Stories* (New York: Vintage International, 1990), 862.

122. I draw these details from Mallios, *Our Conrad*.

123. I adapt this phrase from the work of Mallios, who rereads twentieth-century American literature through the often ignored yet constituting force of Conrad, Mallios taking up what he calls the "metaliterary." Faulkner's *As I Lay Dying* becomes the primary example of "a critical anatomy of the invisibility of race within white Southern

residual hegemonic formations" (*Our Conrad*, 361), which I return to in Chapter 3. For further discussion of the weight of Conrad and race in Faulkner's ouevre, see my "The Acoustics of Narrative Involvement: Modernism, Subjectivity, Voice," PhD diss., UC Berkeley, 2010, https://escholarship.org/uc/item/1ws2f1tr, 107–80. The relationship between the two writers has long been understudied, with a few major exceptions: Albert J. Guerard, *Conrad the Novelist* (Cambridge, MA: Harvard University Press, 1958); and Stephen M. Ross, "Conrad's Influence on Faulkner's *Absalom, Absalom!*," *Studies in American Fiction* 2, no. 2 (1974): 199–209. On the heels of Mallios's study, there has been a burst of scholarship. See, for example, Maurice Ebileeni, *Conrad, Faulkner, and the Problem of Nonsense* (New York: Bloomsbury Academic, 2015), who discusses Benjy's cry in terms of Conrad and Lacan. The cry is not "nonsense," in my view, but the melancholic sound of the withdrawal and preservation of a racial love object.

124. The cry between Benjy and Bon echoes still further if we consider the sound of Nancy, the African American caregiver in Faulkner's "That Evening Sun" (1931), one of the Compson stories. She issues a recurring cry. Benjy does not appear in this story, Nancy to some extent occupying his place (or Benjy her place—it is not known what year Faulkner began this short story). I discuss this resonance at greater length in "The Expropriated Voice," in *Faulkner and Slavery*, ed. Jay Watson and James G. Thomas Jr. (Oxford: University of Mississippi Press, forthcoming).

125. Sigmund Freud, *The Psychopathology of Everyday Life*, trans. Alan Tyson (New York: Norton, 1990), 14.

126. Such an effect is related to what Garrett Stewart, *Reading Voices: Literature and the Phonotext* (Berkeley: University of California Press, 1990), 7, calls "sound defects," where a word during silent reading can become substitutable, "yielding at its boundary."

127. Freud used the German word *Überdeterminiertheit* in his discussions of overdetermination, but his sound map invites the relation to *Stimme*.

128. Freud, *The Psychopathology of Everyday Life*, 15.

129. In Faulkner, intimacy is often maintained by the women who substitute for the mother. Dilsey, like Nancy, is an African American caregiver of the Compson children, and Caddy, Benjy's sister, also "hears" Benjy. But their hearing is not symmetrical. Dilsey, residing in a former slave cabin, labors in the Compson household, and her care involves an asymmetrical relationship of exchange. After Caddy leaves, Dilsey is the only one there to comfort Benjy at the novel's end, to hear and recognize his cry. The disavowed black maternal contains in Faulkner's imaginary such that it gives shape to the possibility of novelistic form. For a discussion of disavowal of the black maternal love object, see Judith Sensibar, *Faulkner and Love: The Women Who Shaped His Art, a Biography* (New Haven, CT: Yale University Press, 2010), 19–128.

130. In describing this scene in his seminal *Doubling and Incest/Repetition and Revenge: A Speculative Reading of Faulkner*, expanded ed. (Baltimore, MD:

Johns Hopkins University Press, 1996), John Irwin says that the shadow has "Negro resonances in his mind" (37). This extremely thoughtful account of psychodynamics doesn't question the ease with which darkness ("the dark self, the ego shadowed by the unconscious") slides into blackness in Faulkner. Irwin turns quickly away from the issue of race to return to the problem of incest. But the overarching problem of incest in the novel is in fact grounded in miscegenation (the two words sharing an etymological root). For an influential and structuralist discussion of the relationship between incest and miscegenation in American literary and legal discourse, see Werner Sollers, "Incest and Miscegenation," in *Neither Black nor White yet Both: Thematic Explorations of Interracial Literature* (New York: Oxford University Press, 1997), 285–335. Sollers begins this chapter with a quotation from Faulkner: "—So it's the miscegenation, not the incest, which you can't bear" (285). The two words continually chime in Faulkner.

131. In his essay on Fanon, "The Case of Blackness," Moten argues that a persistent sense of "black pathology" constitutes "the background against which all representations of blacks, blackness, or (the color) black take place." This background includes "the regulatory metaphysics that undergirds interlocking notions of sound and color in aesthetic theory" (177).

132. Alexander G. Weheliye, *Phonographies: Grooves in Sonic Afro-Modernity* (Durham, NC: Duke University Press, 2005), 101, similarly describes how, without the graphic or visual accompaniment of the human body, the circulation of recorded music often "sought to yoke" sound and visual source together by other means. A parallel yet inverted act is to *displace* the black body as visual source. See, for example Mark Goble, *Beautiful Circuits: Modernism and the Mediated Life* (New York: Columbia University Press, 2010), 179, who describes how the image of the phonograph metonymized otherwise absent bodies of black musicians in the white popular musical imaginary at the turn of the last century.

133. Conrad, in this way, is more foundational to Faulkner's techniques of consciousness than James Joyce.

134. G. Jean-Aubrey, *Joseph Conrad: Life and Letters*, 2 vols. (Garden City, NY: Doubleday, Page, and Co., 1927), 77; qtd. in Watt, *Conrad in the Nineteenth Century*, 90.

135. Watt, *Conrad in the Nineteenth Century*, 90.

136. Jean-Aubrey, *Joseph Conrad*, 77; qtd. in Watt, *Conrad*, 90.

137. William Faulkner, *Essays, Speeches, and Public Letters* (New York: Random House, 2011), 263. My emphases. This 1934 essay was first published in January 1973 by Joseph Blotner in the *Yale University Library Gazette*, as "William Faulkner's Essay on the Composition of *Sartoris*."

138. The word "sorrow" bears crucially on Conrad's lexicon in *The Nigger of the "Narcissus"* but also on Du Bois's thinking of song, which I shall discuss in the Intersonority. In the final chapter of *The Sound and the Fury*, when Dilsey takes Benjy to

a black church with her, she is said to "moan" with him: Benjy's sound becomes what it hasn't been anywhere else in the novel. It becomes audible as black music, a sound in the spiritual tradition. It redefines the previous instances of the cry, such that one wonders if Benjy hadn't been singing at times, imitating Dilsey's musication. It circles back to the beginning of the narrative and redefines its modes of perception.

139. Toni Morrison, "Unspeakable Things Unspoken: The Afro-American Presence in American Literature," Tanner Humanities Center, University of Utah, https://tanner lectures.utah.edu/_documents/a-to-z/m/morrison90.pdf, 136.

140. Faulkner, qtd. in *Faulkner and the Literature of the Black Americas*, ed. Jay Watson and James G. Thomas Jr. (Jackson: University Press of Mississippi, 2016), xi.

141. Faulkner, qtd. in *Faulkner and the Literature of the Black Americas*, xi.

142. F. Scott Fitzgerald, *The Great Gatsby* (New York: Scribner, 2003), 138. For a related discussion of Fitzgerald and Faulkner in relation to American race relations, see Walter Benn Michaels, *Our America: Nativism, Modernism, and Pluralism* (Durham, NC: Duke University Press, 1995), 1–15. Also see Mallios, *Our Conrad*, 221–64.

143. Jim's final, parting utterance to Marlow in *Lord Jim* is somewhere between a stutter and an interrupted fragment; it populates Marlow's discourse about Jim, the phrase "I said nothing" recurring.

INTERSONORITY: UNCLAIMED VOICES CIRCUM-1900, OR SOUND AND SOURCELESSNESS IN *THE SOULS OF BLACK FOLK*

1. Frantz Fanon, *Black Skin, White Masks*, trans. Charles Lam Markmann (London: Pluto Press, 1986), 128. Such a relation, Fanon says, is opposed to that of the white man, who "wants the world" (128).

2. I draw this rhetorical concept from Judith Butler, "Introduction," *Soul and Form*, trans. Anna Bostock (New York: Columbia University Press, 2010), 11. In this way, Du Bois resonates with Georg Lukács's concern for the loss of communicability, except that, for Du Bois, communicability for African Americans had not yet been won, the loss being a priori: the Middle Passage. What Lukács will later call "transcendental homelessness" can be recast by Du Bois and Conrad as forms of narrative where homelessness owes itself to real experiences of migration.

3. Stéphane Mosès, "Émile Benveniste and the Linguistics of Dialogue," *Revue de Métaphysique et de Morale* 32 (2001): 509–25, https://www.cairn-int.info/focus-E _RMM_014_0509-emile-benveniste-and-the-linguistics-of.htm.

4. Julia Kristeva, "The Speaking Subject," in *On Signs*, ed. Marshall Blonsky (Baltimore, MD: Johns Hopkins University Press, 1985), 212.

5. Catherine Malabou, *The Heidegger Change: On the Fantastic in Philosophy*, trans. Peter Skafish (Albany: SUNY Press, 2011), 31. Change "always means at once *change of route* and *change of form*" (*The Heidegger Change*, 19). Again, readers of the early work of Lukács will recognize Du Bois as his near contemporary. According

to Butler, "Introduction," 4, forms "are reinvented for the purposes of conveying a very specific condition, at once existential and historical."

6. See Philippe Lejeune, *On Autobiography*, trans. Katherine Leary (Minneapolis: University of Minnesota Press, 1988), 3–30. In Chapter 3, I return to the concept of the autobiographical pact.

7. Theories of enunciation are, Kristeva writes, "incapable of taking into account, first, sense as practice; not a phenomenon but a process of which presupposes a permanent dialectic (position and destruction) of the identity (which is as much the identity of the speaking subject as the identity of the signification produced for communication)." Kristeva, "The Speaking Subject," 212.

8. Adell, qtd. in Hortense J. Spillers, "'Born Again': Faulkner and the Second Birth," in *Fifty Years after Faulkner*, ed. Jay Watson and Ann J. Abadie (Jackson: University Press of Mississippi, 2016), 63. Adell here draws from Joel Williamson. Spillers also remarks upon the notes Du Bois made during the last William James lecture he audited. Double consciousness thus "sustains a preeminent transatlantic exchange" during important times of Du Bois's own biography (65). There is a sizeable body of scholarship on Hegel and Du Bois, the most concentrated study being Odesa M. Weatherford-Jacobs's unpublished dissertation, which provides a history of Du Bois's "journey toward the phenomena of Hegel" through James as well as a detailed account of Hegel's philosophical system as reflected in Du Bois. The topic remains understudied in relation to listening. Discussing the impact of Hegel's thought on Du Bois during his time as a student at Humboldt, Gilroy argues for the centrality of slave experience and song in transatlantic culture and modernity. Paul Gilroy, *The Black Atlantic: Modernity and Double Consciousness* (Cambridge, MA: Harvard University Press, 1993), 111–45. For a more recent discussion of Du Bois and music vis-à-vis Hegel, see Eli Zaretsky, *Political Freud: A History* (New York: Columbia University Press, 2015), 38–79.

9. As a hybrid genre work, the book pluralistically addresses the senses, Mary Zamberlin suggests, after the manner of Du Bois's teacher at Harvard, William James, who encouraged his students to listen to lectures in the way that one "receives a song." Du Bois's techniques involve a "micro-politics of sound," one whose many registers cannot be easily interpreted or exhausted. Mary Zamberlin, "Disseminating the Eaches: The Micro-Politics of Sound in *The Souls of Black Folk*," in *Rhizosphere: Gilles Deleuze and the "Minor" American Writing of William James, W. E. B. Du Bois, Gertrude Stein, Jean Toomer, and William Faulkner* (New York: Routledge, 2006), 81, 85.

10. Spillers, "'Born Again': Faulkner and the Second Birth," 63.

11. Spillers, "'Born Again': Faulkner and the Second Birth," 63. Du Bois brings his "immense learning to bear upon the critical conditions that African Americans are called upon to confront" amid the failure of Reconstruction, Spillers writes, including "the irrevocable advance of white backlash, disenfranchisement, and the vicious outbreak of domestic terrorism" (63).

12. Martine Syms, "Black Vernacular: Reading New Media," http://martinesyms.com/black-vernacular-reading-new-media/.

13. See Dorothy J. Hale, *Social Formalism: The Novel in Theory from Henry James to the Present* (Stanford, CA: Stanford University Press, 1998), 197–220.

14. Also see Cheryl A. Wall, "Resounding Souls: Du Bois and the African American Literary Tradition," *Public Culture* 17, no. 2 (May 2005). Wall argues for the paramount importance of return in Du Bois, a re-sounding of the literary and musical past.

15. Fanon, *Black Skin, White Masks*, 109.

16. Peter Coviello, "Intimacy and Affliction: Du Bois, Race, and Psychoanalysis," *Modern Language Quarterly* 60, no. 1 (2003): 4. Coviello attends to the work of Spillers as a sensitive critic of this dimension of Du Bois's thought, including "Mama's Baby, Papa's Maybe," an essay I discuss in Chapter 3. Also see Zaretsky, *Political Freud*, 41, who argues that Du Bois, like Freud, "placed memory at the center of all human strivings toward freedom."

17. Fanon, *Black Skin, White Masks*, 217.

18. Fanon, *Black Skin, White Masks*, 217.

19. The colonial master demands "not recognition but work" such that "every ontology is made unattainable in a colonized and civilized society" (Fanon, *Black Skin, White Masks*, 220n8, 109).

20. Fanon, *Black Skin, White Masks*, 217.

21. In his translation of Fanon, Richard Philcox suggests that *ferme* be translated as "shut off."

22. Kara Keeling, *The Witch's Flight: The Cinematic, the Black Femme, and the Image of Common Sense* (Durham, NC: Duke University Press, 2007), 10.

23. Fanon, *Black Skin, White Masks*, 217, quotes Hegel as writing, "what is to happen can only be brought about by means of both"; *they recognize themselves as mutually recognizing each other.*"

24. Kevin Quashie, *The Sovereignty of Quiet: Beyond Resistance in Black Culture* (New Brunswick, NJ: Rutgers University Press, 2012), 12.

25. Quashie, *The Sovereignty of Quiet*, 13.

26. Quashie, *The Sovereignty of Quiet*, 14.

27. Fanon, *Black Skin, White Masks*, 112.

28. Herbert Marcuse, *Reason and Revolution* (New York: Beacon, 1960), 123.

29. Spillers, "'Born Again': Faulkner and the Second Birth," 64.

30. In *Absalom, Absalom!*, Faulkner writes a scene of Thomas Sutpen as a boy splitting into two voices after he is turned away by a slave from delivering a message from his father to the planter. The resonances between Faulkner, Du Bois, and Hegel were not lost on Spillers, who brings these figures together into stunning relation account in "'Born Again': Faulkner and the Second Birth." Also see my "The Acoustics of Narrative Involvement: Modernism, Subjectivity, Voice," PhD diss., UC Berkeley,

2010, https://escholarship.org/uc/item/1ws2f1tr, where I also read the splitting of Sutpen in relation to Du Bois, but specifically along the axis of failed listening.

31. See Peter Szendy, *All Ears: The Aesthetics of Espionage* (New York: Fordham University Press, 2016). Szendy concentrates his comments on the drive in relation to surveillance. In this present chapter, we find in Du Bois an alternative primal scene, one that relates to double consciousness and the Middle Passage. I return to this split in listening and the Freudian primal scene in Chapter 3.

32. Ross Posnock, *Color and Culture: Black Writers and the Making of the Modern Intellectual* (Cambridge, MA: Harvard University Press, 2000), 91.

33. See Eric J. Sundquist, *To Wake the Nations: Race in the Making of American Literature* (Cambridge, MA: Belknap, 1998), a seminal account of Du Bois and sorrow song that draws upon the work of the anthropologist Franz Boas and his theory, captured by the phrase "alternating sounds," that one hears through categories in ways that prevent communication across cultures. Though Du Bois was trained as a sociologist, the alternating-sounds theory is at cross-purposes with the universalist premise that grounds Du Bois's account of listening, particularly as presented in the primal scene of double consciousness. The girl cannot "hear" Du Bois not because of categorical cultural difference but because of an as yet unfilled or false universality that continually tilts Du Bois's text toward the future. This tense is easily effaced by the text's more overt preservationist and ethnographic impulse. The silence of the musical epigraphs that begin each of Du Bois's chapters are caught up in that double movement.

34. Fanon, *Black Skin, White Masks*, 218.

35. The most extensive account of Schaeffer's thought and largely untranslated treatise can be found in Brian Kane, *Sound Unseen: Acousmatic Sound in Theory and Practice* (New York: Oxford University Press, 2014). I return to his work in Chapter 3. For further discussion of the sound object in relation to critical theory, see Rey Chow and James A. Steintrager, "In Pursuit of the Object of Sound: An Introduction," *differences* 22, nos. 2/3 (2011): 1–9.

36. Henry David Thoreau, *Walden and Civil Disobedience* (New York: Penguin, 1986), 168. Thank you to David Copenhafer for suggesting this passage to me. Two mediating intellectual conjunctions that link Du Bois and Thoreau are Ralph Waldo Emerson and William James. William sent his novelist brother, Henry, a copy of Du Bois's book. A trace of Du Bois can perhaps be apprehended in Henry James's 1908 preface to the New York edition of *The Portrait of a Lady* (a novel that underwent extensive revision after its initial publication), when James names Isabel Archer not a protagonist but a "center of consciousness," a consciousness that proves to be agonized in the novel.

37. Thoreau, *Walden and Civil Disobedience*, 169.

38. Thoreau, *Walden and Civil Disobedience*, 168.

39. It is a "transperception." See Douglas Kahn, *Earth Sound Earth Signal: Energies and Earth Magnitude in the Arts* (Berkeley: University of California Press, 2013), 162.

40. Barbara Johnson, "Animation, Abortion, Apostrophe," *Diacritics* 16, no. 1 (1986): 31.

41. Though Symons was born in Wales, he was of Cornish descent and largely educated in Europe. Symons's poem nonetheless resonates with the expropriation of Welsh as a native language under the British Empire, but also the very fact of diaspora, which underscores Jahan Ramazani's conviction in *A Transnational Poetics* (Chicago: University of Chicago Press, 2009) that poetic forms are in themselves transnational, voicing the grief of dispersal.

42. Wall, "Resounding Souls," 219.

43. See my "On Banishing Socrates' Wife: The Interiority of the Ear in *Phaedo*," in *Poiesis*, ed. Nathan Brown and Petar Milat (Zagreb: Multimedijalni Institute, 2017), 156–75. There I describe Socrates's argument that a lyre's music is produced not by wood, vibration, and touch but by the theory of harmony that ontologically precedes it. In this section of the *Phaedo*, Socrates contests his Pythagorean interlocutor on the way to a larger demonstration of the immortality of the soul. Wood, vibration, and touch—these are mortal and temporal things.

44. For an extensive reading of the genitive case of sound ("the sound of"), see Naomi Waltham-Smith, *The Sound of Life* (New York: Fordham University Press, forthcoming). I return to these issues in Chapter 3.

45. Christian Metz, "Aural Objects," trans. Georgia Gurrieri, *Yale French Studies* 60 (1980): 27–28. This essay represents among the first critical adaptations of the theory of the sound object for film studies, but its implications for literature have yet to be explored.

46. The first publication of the songs as arranged for and performed by the Jubilee Singers was in 1873. According to Sara Marcus, *Political Disappointment: A Partial History* (Cambridge, MA: Harvard University Press, forthcoming), in Du Bois's moment, these songs had already "made numerous appearances in writing," particularly in white edited collections, such as *Slave Songs of the United States* (1867) and *Hampton and Its Students* (1874), from which Du Bois drew this and several others of his musical epigraphs. A common presumption of many anthologies, Marcus notes, was of "the songs' immunity to notation." Thank you to Marcus for sharing parts of her unpublished manuscript with me.

47. Jacques Lacan, *The Four Fundamental Concepts of Psychoanalysis: The Seminar of Jacques Lacan, Book XI*, ed. Jacques-Alain Miller, trans. Alan Sheridan (New York: Norton, 1998), 81.

48. Lisa Gitelman, *Scripts, Grooves, and Writing Machines: Representing Technology in the Edison Era* (Stanford, CA: Stanford University Press, 2000), shows how the first copyright case—one that would help cement the laws that now determine

ephemeral sound as property—involved "coon songs" and the industry's "hungry mimesis" (124). Stephen Michael Best, *The Fugitive's Properties: Law and the Poetics of Possession* (Chicago: University of Chicago Press, 2004), takes up this same case, but in order to unfold the problem of the slave (as possession) at the heart of the philosophical project of liberalism. Also see David Suisman, *Selling Sounds: The Commercial Revolution in American Music* (Cambridge, MA: Harvard University Press, 2010).

49. Sundquist, *To Wake the Nations*, 482. Also see Daphne A. Brooks, *Bodies in Dissent: Spectacular Performances of Race and Freedom, 1850–1910* (Durham, NC: Duke University Press, 2006), 281–342. Brooks argues that readings of the Jubilee's songs tend to focus on white enjoyment rather than on the experience of black performers. For Jennifer Lynn Stoever, *The Sonic Color Line: Race and the Cultural Politics of Listening* (New York: New York University Press, 2016), 26, it is crucial that Du Bois seizes representational control of the memory of slavery when the white imaginary increasingly focuses on the "authentic" and suffering. For further discussion of Du Bois and Douglass in relation to vernacular culture in musical romanticism, see Ronald Radano, "Denoting Difference: The Writing of the Slave Spirituals," *Critical Inquiry* 22, no. 3 (1996): 506–44.

50. Sundquist, *To Wake the Nations*, 476. Du Bois relied for his transcriptions upon the anthologies of white figures such as William E. Barton (1899) and Thomas Wentworth Higginson (1867). Sundquist argues that Du Bois discredits through literary style the simpleminded notion that it was white anthologists who had taught African Americans to take pride in spirituals. Although he studied and copied the bars of melody from existing anthologies, to my eyes he also altered them, transposing "You May Bury Me in the East" into another key.

51. Sundquist, *To Wake the Nations*, 476.

52. Kane, *Sound Unseen*, 105. According to Kane, Wagner designed elaborate mechanisms for concealing the orchestra at Bayreuth. Du Bois first heard Wagner performed in the United States, and then in 1936, the year that Jesse Owens won the gold medal at the Olympics in Germany, Du Bois took a much-longed-for pilgrimage to Bayreuth. This experience must have been intensely ambivalent, particularly with the intensification of Wagner's racism in his daughter, who was at that point directing Bayreuth. See Alex Ross, *The Rest Is Noise: Listening to the Twentieth Century* (New York: Farrar, Straus and Giroux, 2007).

53. It is has not escaped critics that John is, to some extent, a stand-in for Du Bois, John becoming estranged from his peers through education. But Du Bois chose the genre of fiction for this particular installment. The final moment of sound heightens the fictional element, one made uncannier by the fact that the wedding march appears rather late in the opera but John is ushered out quite early—he never would have heard this part of the opera.

54. Du Bois's editors note the difference in translation (154n2).

55. Posnock, *Color and Culture*, 89.

56. Du Bois, qtd. in Peter Lancelot Mallios, *Our Conrad: Constituting American Modernity* (Stanford, CA: Stanford University Press, 2010), 203. Noting the quotation, one that Du Bois both cites and reverses in value, Mallios asks "what construction of *Conrad*" underlies the allusion, describing also the heightened polyvocality of Du Bois's essay, which makes its significance unclear (203).

57. For a discussion of Harris, see Sharon Sliwinski, *Human Rights on Camera* (Chicago: University of Chicago Press, 2011). Du Bois was also writing in the era that lynching rose along with the kinds of communications technology that announced it. Lynching photographs were frequently disseminated as postcards (violent images were outlawed only in 1908 by the United States Postal Service).

58. When in 1926 Du Bois reviewed Carl Van Vechten's "Nigger Heaven," he calls it a "blow to the face." "'Nigger' is an English word of wide use and definite connotation. As employed by Conrad, Sheldon, Allen, and even Firbank it was justifiable. But the phrase, 'Nigger Heaven,' as applied to Harlem is a misnomer." Du Bois, qtd. in Mallios, *Our Conrad*, 200.

59. For a provocative discussion of the drum in relation to the "skin ego," or the skin as a "relational frontier," see John Mowitt, *Percussion: Drumming, Beating, Striking* (Durham, NC: Duke University Press, 2002), 18–19.

60. Spillers notes that Du Bois revised the title from "Strivings of the Negro People," published in 1897 in *Atlantic Monthly* (the same year as *The Nigger of the "Narcissus,"* making the texts companion pieces in an acoustic mirror). In the revised title, the emphasis is now on the first-person-plural possessive, but just who the "we" is that it refers to is uncertain or, rather, universalized. This gesture of universalization is underscored by Du Bois's addition of "spiritual," multiple in its registers.

61. For a sense of the role of musical literacy in the nineteenth century, see Thomas Christensen, "Four-Hand Piano Transcription and Geographies of Nineteenth-Century Musical Reception," *Journal of the American Musicological Society* 52, no. 2 (Summer 1999): 259. "Before the advent of the phonograph and radio—and more specifically, the long-playing record—piano transcription was the primary means by which a literate musical public could come to know this music" (259). "It made acoustically accessible a repertory to which most musicians had only occasional access in live performance" (259).

62. See Marcus, *Political Disappointment*, for a historical discussion of the shifting and complex attitudes among African Americans that the old songs ought not to be sung, not only because of their beginnings in slavery but because white audiences seemed to gain so much enjoyment from them. The Jubilee Singers added sorrow songs to their original repertoire of European songs in order to help pay the bills. For Marcus, Du Bois's book marks a pivotal moment of aspirational return to sorrow songs.

63. See Roland Barthes's essay of this title in *The Responsibility of Forms: Critical*

Essays on Music, Art, and Representation, trans. Richard Howard (Berkeley: University of California Press, 1997).

64. "A musical score has no immediate acoustical content, only the immediate visual content of lines and dots and the immediate tactile content of the smooth, thin pages, but it does directly specify a sequence of actions that, if followed, produces actually audible content." Elaine Scarry, *Dreaming by the Book* (New York: FSG, 1999), 6.

65. In *Being and Time*, Dasein is "entangled," or "initially and for the most part *alongside* the 'world' [*das Dasein ist zunächst und zumeist* bei *der besorgten 'Welt'*]." Martin Heidegger, *Being and Time*, trans. Joan Stambaugh (Albany: State University of New York Press, 1996), 164; in German, 175; italics in original. Here I modify Stambaugh's translation of *bei* from "together with" to "alongside" the world, a commonplace in textual commentaries of Heidegger.

66. Sundquist, *To Wake the Nations*, 470.

67. See Angela Davis, *Blues Legacies and Black Feminism: Gertrude "Ma" Rainey, Bessie Smith, and Billie Holiday* (New York: Vintage, 1999), 5.

68. Frederick Douglass, *The Narrative of the Life of Frederick Douglass, an American Slave, Written by Himself*, 21st ed. (Chapel Hill: University of North Carolina Press, 1999), https://docsouth.unc.edu/neh/douglass/douglass.html.

69. See Davis, *Blues Legacies and Black Feminism*, 4–5.

70. Sundquist, *To Wake the Nations*, 470.

71. Sundquist, *To Wake the Nations*, 476.

72. The sublating transformativity of this structure of feeling thus includes, Marcus suggests in *Political Disappointment*, vast "disappointment," a feeling Du Bois names in the book's opening essay. Disappointment, for Marcus, is a politically productive moment, one in which a future praxis has not yet been disclosed. Essential to its disclosure is returning to the songs of older political movements, an argument Marcus begins to lay out in "Untimely Feedback," *Artforum*, December 7, 2016, https://www.artforum.com/slant/mourning-after-sara-marcus-on-the-us-presidential-election-65119. In this same vein, Jonathan Flatley, *Affective Mapping: Melancholia and the Politics of Modernism* (Cambridge, MA: Harvard University Press, 2009), describes an "affective mapping" in Du Bois through which songs disclose the historicity of feelings. Du Bois hears in songs the fact of his being bound to other people who feel and have felt like he does before (146). Songs' political potential is "nascent and unrealized" (106).

73. Also see Stoever, *The Sonic Color Line*. In her discussion of the Jubilee Singers, Stoever places special emphasis upon vibration in the physical act of collective singing, a vibration that cannot be transcribed or contained by white structures.

74. Marcus, "Untimely Feedback." Also see Naomi Waltham-Smith, who argues in *Music and Belonging between Revolution and Restoration* (New York: Oxford University Press, 2017) that musical and political revolution are tied up with restoration and return.

75. I am aware of the racializing dangers of this distinction. My intention is not to attribute to Du Bois a kind of romanticized "life" missing from Conrad. We are considering instead the different yet twinned afterlives of a printed book. *The Souls of Black Folk* is not without its echoes and "sinister" resonances, chief among them the cry, an issue I take up in Chapter 3.

76. In relation to "the ephemeral (music, sound) and the material (inscription)" and, with it, the "materiality of the ephemeral," Weheliye anachronistically likens Du Bois to a turntablist, cutting and mixing songs in ways that recall the dialectical methods of Walter Benjamin, for whom quotations were at the center of the practice of writing. Alexander Weheliye, *Phonographies: Grooves in Sonic Afro-Modernity* (Durham, NC: Duke University Press, 2005), 101.

77. Here, Du Bois also includes the musical notation, which I have omitted.

78. Walter Benjamin, *Illuminations*, ed. Hannah Arendt, trans. Harry Zohn (New York: Schocken, 1968), 46.

79. See Kodwo Eshun, *More Brilliant Than the Sun: Adventures in Sonic Fiction* (London: Quartet, 1998).

80. See Frances Dyson, "The Genealogy of Radio Voice," in *Radio Rethink: Art, Sound, and Transmission*, ed. Daina Augaitis and Dan Lander (Banff: Walter Phillips Gallery, 1994), 172. This tradition, Dyson describes, "splits" the voice between the metaphysical and the physical, or the voice of the mind and the voice of the body.

81. This phrase comes from Shane Butler's remarkable translation of Aristotle in *The Ancient Phonograph* (Cambridge, MA: MIT Press, 2015), 41. Butler calls attention to Aristotle's use of the figure of the waxed tablet, "antiquity's paradigmatic writing material," the soul (*psukhe*) being "imagined as impressionable material."

82. Gilroy, *The Black Atlantic*, 112–13.

83. In this vein, Weheliye calls the book an "extended echo chamber in which traces of the spirituals reverberate with and against each other." Qtd. in Jennifer Lynn Stoever, "Fine-Tuning the Sonic Color-Line: Radio and the Acousmatic Du Bois," *Modernist Cultures* 10, no. 1 (2015): 101.

84. G. W. F. Hegel, *Aesthetics*, trans. T. M. Knox (Oxford: Clarendon, 1975), 2: 890.

85. Du Bois posits the black artisan who, split by double aims and strivings, "could not articulate the message of another people" (*SBF*, 12). The history of this split is laid out in a series of concepts that Du Bois names (after Macbeth) a "shape." First, in bondage, freedom was the "shout," "the message in his own plaintive cadences": "'Shout, O children!'" (12). Decades pass after Emancipation, and yet "In vain do we cry," which finally ossifies with time into an "old cry" with no new word to replace it (13). The protagonist demands the ballot and then books; finally, and in ways that bring us to the present, he devotes time to social analysis, but before prejudice he "stands . . . well-nigh speechless" (15). "Whispering and portents" set upon him, that he must always be a servant, which "the Nation echoed" in a kind of political resolu-

tion of turmoil in resignation until "the sound of conflict" again rends his soul. It is the moment that culminates the chapter in its textual impetus, the end circling back to motivate the beginning: "that men may listen" (16). The essay is a shape of sounds.

86. For a discussion of the figure of the cry as textually unifying, see Zamberlin, "Disseminating the Eaches," 85.

87. Benjamin, *Illuminations*, 98.

88. For a discussion of Alexander von Humboldt's ethnographic work in relation to indigenous sound, see Ana María Ochoa Gautier, *Aurality: Listening and Knowledge in Nineteenth-Century Colombia* (Durham, NC: Duke University Press, 2014).

89. Alexander Rehding, "The Quest for the Origins of Music in Germany circa 1900," *Journal of the American Musicological Society* 53, no. 2 (July, 2000): 346. This moment in Germany has been described in wonderful detail by Rehding. The first full professorial chairs in musicology (*Musikwissenschaft*) were established in this moment in Vienna (in 1879 and 1898) and Strasbourg (in 1897) (363).

90. The most extensive discussion of Freud's interest in archeology can be found in Richard H. Armstrong, *A Compulsion for Antiquity: Freud and the Ancient World* (Ithaca, NY: Cornell University Press, 2005). For an illuminating reading of Conrad in relation to Freud's archeological theory of the psyche, see Vassiliki Kolocotroni, "1899, Vienna, and the Congo: The Art of Darkness," in *The Edinburgh Companion to Twentieth-Century Literatures in English* (Edinburgh: Edinburgh University Press, 2006), 11–22.

91. For a pathbreaking discussion of the concept of the circum-Atlantic in relation to performance, see Joseph R. Roach, *Cities of the Dead: Circum-Atlantic Performance* (New York: Columbia University Press, 1996).

92. Africa becomes in his thinking a *kulturvolk*. But through black listening consciousness, Du Bois discards the false binary between *natur* and *kultur* in *volk*. For a discussion of these categories in relation to Alexander von Humboldt's travel diaries, see Ana María Ochoa Gautier, *Aurality: Listening and Knowledge in Nineteenth-Century Colombia* (Durham, NC: Duke University Press, 2014).

93. See Philippe Lacoue-Labarthe, *Typography: Mimesis, Philosophy, Politics*, trans. Christopher Fynsk (Cambridge, MA: Harvard University Press, 1989), 191. Though I return to these texts in Chapter 3, here I exclude further discussion of Lacoue-Labarthe's remarkable recuperation of Theodor Reik's largely forgotten work *The Haunting Melody* for the reason that he stops short of geopolitics, which is so pronounced in Du Bois's conception of song (but also in Conrad's and Fanon's conceptions of echo). We forget that Reik wrote this text in English in America as a Jewish émigré from war; to be haunted by melody was to be haunted by a Vienna that could not be retrieved.

94. Indeed, when Adriana Cavarero wrote *For More Than One Voice: Toward a Philosophy of Vocal Expression*, trans. Paul A. Kottman (Stanford, CA: Stanford University Press, 2005), her study of sonorousness, it was arguably as a companion to *Relating*

Narratives: Storytelling and Selfhood, trans. Paul A. Kottman (Stanford, CA: Stanford University Press, 2000). This early text gives us the remarkable concept of the "necessary other."

95. Édouard Glissant, *Poetics of Relation*, trans. Betsy Wing (Ann Arbor: University of Michigan Press, 1997), 15.

96. Saidiya Hartman, "Venus in Two Acts," *Small Axe* 12, no. 2 (2008): 2–3.

97. Jacques Lacan, *Écrits: The First Complete Edition in English*, trans. Bruce Fink (New York: Norton, 2006), 394. Thank you to Amanda Holmes for recommending and discussing this passage with me.

98. Rizvana Bradley, "Vestiges of Motherhood: The Maternal Function in Recent Black Cinema," *Film Quarterly* 71, no. 2 (2017): 46–52. For Bradley, the black maternal—a missing body lost to representation in the afterlives of slavery—sustains itself in black aesthetic form in the manner of an unthought: vertiginous gaps, sinkholes of memory, and cuts between sound and image.

99. Saidiya Hartman, *Lose Your Mother: A Journey along the Atlantic Slave Route* (New York: Farrar, Straus, and Giroux, 2007), 39.

100. It is in relation to the phonemes "Do ba-na co-ba" that we can "see" on the page an anachronic future as what Brent Hayes Edwards, *Epistrophies: Jazz and the Literary Imagination* (Cambridge, MA: Harvard University Press, 2017), 37, calls "a story about the inception of what we call 'jazz singing.'" Edwards is interested in scat as a "falling" of words into phonemes.

101. See Aaron Carter-Ényì, "'Music More Ancient Than the Words': W. E. B. Du Bois's Theories on Africana Aurality," *Sounding Out!: The Sound Studies Blog*, August 27, 2019, https://soundstudiesblog.com/2018/08/27/music-more-ancient-than -words-w-e-b-du-boiss-theories-on-africana-aurality/.

102. Benjamin, *Illuminations*, 90.

103. Benjamin, *Illuminations*, 90.

104. Mladen Dolar, *A Voice and Nothing More* (Cambridge, MA: MIT Press, 2006), argues of the primal scene, "The time between hearing and understanding is precisely the time of construction of fantasies, desires, symptoms, all the basic structures which underlie and organize the vast ramifications of human enjoyment" (137). I return to this concept at length in Chapter 3.

105. Roland Barthes, *Image, Music, Text*, trans. Stephen Heath (New York: Hill and Wang, 1977), 188, 182.

106. See Alexander G. Weheliye, *Habeas Viscus: Racializing Assemblages, Biopolitics, and Black Feminist Theories of the Human* (Durham, NC: Duke University Press, 2014), 33–45.

107. Hortense J. Spillers, "Mama's Baby, Papa's Maybe: An American Grammar Book," *Diacritics* 17, no. 2 (Summer 1987): 67.

108. In the Overture, I referenced Julia Kristeva's theory of the *chora*, which is also central to Barthes's theorization of the "grain of the voice," particularly in relation to

what he calls "geno-song," or the part of a song that is not in service of the "message." See Barthes, *Image, Music, Text*, 182.

109. Fred Moten, "The Case of Blackness," *Criticism* 50, no. 2 (2008): 182.

110. Seyla Benhabib, *The Reluctant Modernism of Hannah Arendt*, rev. ed. (New York: Rowman and Littlefield, 2003), 107.

111. Wall uses the term "hieroglyphs" in a pejorative sense in relation to Du Bois's inclusion of melodies—but they are *notes*. It is worth recalling the contrasting role played by the figure "hieroglyph" in Adorno's essay "The Form of the Phonograph Record," which discloses for Adorno a messianic "true language," a first and last sound. Theodor W. Adorno, *Essays on Music*, ed. Richard Leppert, trans. Susan H. Gillespie (Berkeley: University of California Press, 2002), 277–82.

3. SINISTER RESONANCE

1. Ingrid Burrington, Twitter post, October 9, 2018, 9:31AM. https://twitter.com/life winning/status/1049653649562132482

2. For a description of the six-step supply chain of conflict minerals, see John Prendergast and Shasha Lezhnev, "From Mine to Mobile Phone: The Conflict Mineral Supply Chain," *The Enough Project*, December 10, 2019, https://enoughproject.org /files/minetomobile.pdf.

3. "Niobe, n.," *OED Online*.

4. In the *Cratylus*, Plato conjectures that language begins in onomatopoeia, or the mimetic resonance between things and their names. Thinking of Tantalus, among many of Plato's speculative etymologies, he conjectures an inheritance from *talas*, or wretched.

5. Qtd. in Christopher L. GoGwilt, *The Passage of Literature: Genealogies of Modernism in Conrad, Rhys, and Pramoedya* (New York: Oxford University Press, 2011), 218. This sense was already deemed "rare" by the late nineteenth century, which, according to GoGwilt, saw the splitting of this ideal "master science" into the separate disciplines of linguistics and literature before the sense was once again revived.

6. There are numerous postcolonial adaptations of *Heart of Darkness*, including V. S. Naipaul's *A Bend in the River* and Tayeb Salih's *Season of Migration to the North*. In "The Blank Spaces in Conrad's *Heart of Darkness*" (a keynote address for "Conradian Crosscurrents: Creativity and Critique," delivered in 2017 at Fordham University), Margaret Cezair-Thompson described how she is developing a novel told from the perspective of Kurtz's unnamed "Intended."

7. Conrad, qtd. in Chinua Achebe, "An Image of Africa: Racism in Conrad's *Heart of Darkness*," in *Heart of Darkness: A Norton Critical Edition*, 4th ed., ed. Paul B. Armstrong, 336–48 (New York: Norton, 2005), 344.

8. Here I gesture to Fred Moten, *In the Break: The Aesthetics of the Black Radical Tradition* (Minneapolis: University of Minnesota Press, 2003), 173, when he writes,

"The repression of the knowledge of the hole in the signifier is shadowed by another, not so easily sensed repression of the knowledge of the whole in the signifier. This is a repression of amplification, of sound and, most especially, of *abounding*, in the sense that Derrida employs, where the whole expands beyond itself in the manner of an ensemble that pushes conventional ontological formulation over the edge."

9. Christopher L. Miller, *Blank Darkness: Africanist Discourse in French* (Chicago: University of Chicago Press, 1985), 6.

10. Miller, *Blank Darkness*, 10.

11. Achebe notes that, when the ill-informed describe indigenous speech, they often call it "dialect," never language ("An Image of Africa," 349).

12. Ngugi wa Thiong'o recalls how Conrad indignantly recited his literary agent's painful remarks in a letter addressed to him: "You told me that 'I did not speak English' to you." Reflecting on Conrad, who had come to English as an outsider and, contemporary globalization, Ngugi writes that *Heart of Darkness* "still has strong resonance today." See Ngugi wa Thiong'o, "The Contradictions of Joseph Conrad," *New York Times*, November 21, 2017, https://www.nytimes.com/2017/11/21/books/review/dawn-watch-joseph-conrad-biography-maya-jasanoff.html.

13. Also see Debra Romanick Baldwin, "Marlow, Socrates, and an Ancient Quarrel in *Chance*," in *Centennial Essays on Joseph Conrad's* Chance, ed. Allan H. Simmons and Susan Jones (Boston: Brill, 2015), 53–65. Baldwin shows the profound impact of Platonic dialogues on Conrad during his classical education, noting his references to Socrates in *Chance* and the role of the Platonic aporia across his narratives. Conrad's classical orientation grounds my claim that he immanently critiques the dialogue as *the* central medium of the rational tradition.

14. Plato, *Phaedo*, trans. Eva Brann, Peter Kalkavage, and Eric Salem (Newburyport, MA: Focus, 1998), 59e8–60a6.

15. Hélène Cixous, "Castration or Decapitation," trans. Annette Kuhn, *Signs* 7, no. 1 (1981): 49, writes, "they do utter a little, but they don't speak. Always keep in mind the distinction between speaking and talking. It is said, in philosophical texts, that women's weapon is the word, because they talk, talk endlessly, chatter, overflow with sound, mouth-sound: but they don't actually *speak*, they have nothing to say. They always inhabit the place of silence, or at most make it echo with their singing. And neither is to their benefit, for they remain outside knowledge."

16. See Sarah Ahmed, "Feminist Complaint," *Feminist Killjoys*, April 29, 2014, https://feministkilljoys.com/2014/12/05/complaint/.

17. https://www.etymonline.com/word/complain. Originally cited by Ahmed, "Feminist Complaint."

18. Plato, *Phaedo*, 103c2–3.

19. See John Llewelyn, *Margins of Religion: Between Kierkegaard and Derrida* (Bloomington: Indiana University Press, 2008), 278. In Chapter 1, I referenced in relation to what I am calling "modernist doxa," how Cassin notes that *doxa* is from

dokeó, "to appear," and is in the same family as *dechomai*. Barbara Cassin et al., eds., *Dictionary of Untranslateables: A Philosophical Lexicon* (Princeton, NJ: Princeton University Press, 2014), 228.

20. Llewelyn, *Margins of Religion*, 278. The Greek underpinnings of making room are sonic. *Chōreō* recalls the importance of movement and dance in Nietzsche's theory of the somatic dimension of hearing. See P. Christopher Smith, *The Hermeneutics of Original Argument: Demonstration, Dialectic, Rhetoric* (Chicago: Northwestern University Press, 1998), 354n1. "Making room" is a preoccupation in Heidegger's *Being and Time*, in his writings on Parmenides, and throughout his late work. In his (1969) *Art and Space*, trans. Charles Siebert (The Hague: Nijhoff, 1973), 6, he writes, "How does clearing-away [*Räumen*] happen? Is it not making-room [*Einräumen*], and this again in a twofold manner as granting and arranging [*des Zulassens und des Einrichtens*]? First, making-room admits something [*Einmal gibt das Einräumen etwas zu*]." For Heidegger there is no issue of exclusion, except in sculpture, which is first constituted by making a border in space.

21. It is true that, in *The Birth of Tragedy*, Nietzsche's responds to *Phaedo* and wrests from Plato and Aristotle a suppressed ritualistic dimension of listening by an audience (or *akouontes*, from *akou*, to hear). But to the extent that the Nietzschean *chorus* is gendered masculine, despite being a site of phenomena's "birth" (*Geburt*), we are thrown back into a listening without the feminine principle of support. *Chora* is a principle that appears only to disappear.

22. Hortense J. Spillers, "Mama's Baby, Papa's Maybe: An American Grammar Book," *Diacritics* 17, no. 2 (Summer 1987): 73.

23. Saidiya V. Hartman, *Lose Your Mother: A Journey along the Atlantic Slave Route* (New York: Farrar, Straus, and Giroux, 2007), 39.

24. Hartman, *Lose Your Mother*, 81.

25. "resonance, n.," *OED Online*.

26. Sigmund Freud, *Dora: An Analysis of a Case of Hysteria*, ed. Philip Rieff (New York: Simon & Schuster, 1997), 71.

27. When the boy is confronted with the first vision of female genitalia, he imagines there to be a missing penis, one he fantasizes to have been cut off by an enraged father. The work of the fetish, constitutive of heterosexual male desire for Freud, is to fill that lack with a substitute object that, making woman whole again, also remakes her in his image (male heterosexual desire moving through homosexual coordinates as part of its operation).

28. Spillers, "Mama's Baby, Papa's Maybe," 65.

29. Spillers, "Mama's Baby, Papa's Maybe," 67.

30. Sigmund Freud, *The Question of Lay Analysis*, trans. James Strachey (New York: Norton, 1990), 38.

31. Barbara Johnson, *The Feminist Difference: Literature, Psychoanalysis, Race, and Gender* (Cambridge, MA: Harvard University Press, 2000), 19.

32. Mary Ann Doane, *Femme Fatales: Feminism, Film Theory, Psychoanalysis* (New York: Routledge, 1991).

33. The title is, to some extent, attributable to the voice of the novel's unnamed narrator. When Marlow's recitation ends, the narrator looks into the distance to see the offing—the part of the sea that can be seen from land and where a ship first becomes visible as approaching. As a figure, the "offing" moves from nautical language to mean an immanent event. In the offing, the unnamed narrator sees "the heart of an immense darkness," the moment from which, presumably, the title of the novel first makes itself known to him as its imputed scribe. But it is Marlow who first suggests the phrase when he describes his journey along another river, the Congo, saying, "'We penetrated deeper and deeper into the heart of darkness.'" The title, in other words, can't be said to originate, repeated in its first instance. For a time, Conrad considered including the definite article in the title, but omitted it.

34. When I first quoted this sentence in the Coda to Chapter 2, I noted his silence on colonial Algeria. These meanings all seem to come together in his reading of the young black boy saluting the "tri-colour" in *Mythologies*. See Moten's critique of Barthes's reference to the photograph of Emmett Till's mutilated face (*In the Break*, 192–211). For Moten, Barthes cannot fathom the black maternal or the irreducible sound of that photograph, one to which a "black mo'nin" inheres.

35. See Tonya Blowers, "The Textual Contract: Distinguishing Autobiography from the Novel," in *Representing Lives*, ed. Allison Donnell and Pauline Polkey (London: Palgrave Macmillan), 105.

36. Emphasis added. The 1917 "Author's Note" was included in the Doubleday edition of *Youth and Two Other Stories*. Much of what follows in the Reprise to this book concerns the reverberation of this note in the work of Faulkner, who owned this edition. Also see my "Music's Unseen Body: Conrad, Cowell, Du Bois, and the Beginnings of American Experimental Music," *Conradiana* 48, nos. 2–3 (2016): 143–62. There I discuss how, through this note, *Heart of Darkness* can be located in the theory and practice of American experimental music via Henry Cowell's seminal work for piano "Sinister Resonance" (1930).

37. Katherine Bergeron, *Decadent Enchantments: The Revival of Gregorian Chant at Solesmes* (Berkeley: University of California Press, 1998), 19.

38. Consider, for example, the piano. Composition must, to some extent, continually undo its most resonant qualities, dampening the note through the pedal (later, the composer Morton Feldman described a form of composition for piano that lets notes live and die of their own accord, striving for a long duration between them, the pianist not striking a new note until the previous one has become almost inaudible). The sinister resonance is after the note, its vibratory and still-sounding residue.

39. Michael Gallope, *Deep Refrains: Music, Philosophy, and the Ineffable* (Chicago: University of Chicago Press, 2017), 71.

40. Gallope, *Deep Refrains*, 71.

41. See Benjamin Steege, *Helmholtz and the Modern Listener* (New York: Cambridge University Press, 2012). Helmholtz's experiments with resonance are also central to Veit Erlmann, *Reason and Resonance: A History of Modern Aurality* (New York: Zone, 2010).

42. Gallope, *Deep Refrains*, 71.

43. GoGwilt, *The Passage of Literature*, 231. It's on this basis that GoGwilt asks his reader to rethink Conrad's "refusal to accord a language to the people depicted" in *Heart of Darkness* not as "an anthropology of racism" (which it is for Achebe) but rather as "a psychological insight" (which it is for Naipaul).

44. A major commentator on this aspect of Conrad's work is J. Hillis Miller. See, for example, his "Should We Read *Heart of Darkness?*" in *Heart of Darkness*, 4th Norton Critical ed., ed. Paul B. Armstrong, 463–73 (New York: Norton, 2006). I will discuss Miller later in the chapter.

45. For a lengthier discussion of the beginnings of Marlow in such vibration, see my "'A Sinister Resonance': Vibration, Sound, and the Birth of Conrad's Marlow," *Qui Parle* 21, no. 2 (2013): 69–100.

46. See Cathy Caruth, *Unclaimed Experience: Trauma, Narrative, and History* (Baltimore, MD: Johns Hopkins University Press, 1996), 1–9.

47. "There is a striking contrast in the words which in most Indo-European languages designate the two sides. While there is a single term for 'right' which extends over a very wide area and shows great stability, the idea of 'left' is expressed by a number of distinct terms, which are less widely spread and seem destined to disappear constantly in the face of new words." Robert Hertz, "The Pre-Eminence of the Right Hand: A Study in Religious Polarity," *HAU: Journal of Ethnographic Theory* 3, no. 2 (2013): 342. With thanks to James Clifford, who suggested the essay to me.

48. Hertz, "The Pre-Eminence of the Right Hand," 343.

49. Hertz, "The Pre-Eminence of the Right Hand," 343.

50. Hertz, "The Pre-Eminence of the Right Hand," 343, 345.

51. Hertz, "The Pre-Eminence of the Right Hand," 347–48.

52. Rizvana Bradley, "Living in the Absence of a Body: The (Sus)Stain of Black Female (W)holeness," *Rhizomes* 29 (2016), http://www.rhizomes.net/issue29/pdf/bradley.pdf, 9, 5. According to Bradley, central to the racing of sexual difference is also what Spillers calls the "ungendering" of black women, also described at length by Angela Davis in her account of slave households.

53. See Geoffrey H. Hartman, "I. A. Richards and the Dream of Communication," in *The Fate of Reading and Other Essays*, 20–40 (Chicago: Chicago University Press, 1975). This concept will be familiar to readers of Lacan's *Seminar II*, in which, when coming upon the question of a universal structure of language, he pauses to consider the telephone: "The Bell Telephone Company needed to economise, that is to say, to pass the greatest number of communications down one single wire," Lacan writes. "But one communicates, one recognises the modulation of a human voice, and as a

result one has the experience of understanding which comes from the fact that one recognises words one already knows." All messages pass indiscriminately through the circuit, which underscores what "one always forgets, namely that language, this language which is the instrument of speech, is something material." In this forgetting, some fundamental experience of speech finds its orientation in fantasy: "The things of the heart, the conviction passed on from one individual to another, comes over in its entirety." The sense of mediation disappears. Jacques Lacan, *The Ego in Freud's Theory and in the Technique of Psychoanalysis, 1954–1955: The Seminar of Jacques Lacan, Book II*, ed. Jacques-Alain Miller, trans. Sylvana Tomaselli (New York: Norton, 1991), 82, 83. Avital Ronell explores this section of Lacan at length in *The Telephone Book: Technology, Schizophrenia, Electric Speech* (Lincoln: University of Nebraska Press, 1989).

54. It also requires context "seizable by the addressee, and either verbal or capable of being verbalized" and contact or "a physical channel and psychological connection between the addresser and the addressee" that allows entrance into and continuation of communication. Roman Jakobson, "Linguistics and Poetics," in *Style in Language*, ed. Thomas A. Sebeok (New York: John Wiley and Sons, 1960), 353.

55. Ferdinand de Saussure, *Course in General Linguistics*, trans. Roy Harris (New York: Bloomsbury, 2013), 139; in French, 164.

56. Moten begins *In the Break* with the scream of Frederick Douglass's Aunt Hester, which orients his pathbreaking critique of Saussure's reliance on a theory of value. In the autobiography that recalls this sound—a writing that is, for Moten, not simply graphic in its violence but phonographic, a graphic sound—Douglass recalls the defining New World injury of being without a mother.

57. Saussure, *Course in General Linguistics*, 14.

58. Saussure, *Course in General Linguistics*, 14.

59. Saussure, *Course in General Linguistics*, 168.

60. Gayatri Chakravorty Spivak, "Echo," *New Literary History* 24, no. 1 (1993): 22.

61. We think of the Lacanian scopic drive as the desire to take in, but really what the scopic seeks is mastery, not consumption (the visual object, Hegel describes, *persists* in its "peaceful" and separate existence).

62. Joseph Conrad, *Mirror of the Sea* (Marlboro, VT: Marlboro, 1988), 136.

63. Gérard Genette, *Narrative Discourse: An Essay in Method*, trans. J. E. Lewin (Ithaca, NY: Cornell University Press, 1972), 236. Dorothy J. Hale, *Social Formalism: The Novel in Theory from Henry James to the Present* (Stanford, CA: Stanford University Press, 1998), argues that Genette overrelies on an idea of linguistic materiality, which allows levels to stay in place despite the way that they might register one another; they retain their ontological autonomy. In email correspondence with me, Hale stated it thus: "The narrating instance interrupts narrative; narrative enacts its closeness or distance from story—levels make themselves visible by their material qualities or effects."

64. Thomas A. Edison, "The Phonograph and Its Future," *North American Review* 126, no. 262 (1878): 527.

65. I am thinking here of the existential implications of boredom in Heidegger but also of the negative aesthetic to be found in the modernist "anti-operas" of this moment, particularly Debussy's *Pelléas* (1902), a work that thinks through Wagner's *Tristan*. See Lydia Goehr, "Radical Modernism and the Failure of Style: Philosophical Reflections on Maeterlinck-Debussy's *Pelléas et Mélisande*," *Representations* 74, no. 1 (2001): 58.

66. G. W. F. Hegel, *Aesthetics*, trans. T. M. Knox (Oxford: Clarendon, 1975), 2:890. For the German, I am relying upon Gallope, *Deep Refrains*, 79–81.

67. T. M. Knox translates Hegel's use of *Ton* "variously as sound, note, and tone, depending on the context," writes Gallope (*Deep Refrains*, 273n19). But Gallope describes how, across Hegel's writings, these three terms work in tandem. The first, *Schall* (sound), is a "primitive" substratum, which Gallope links to a broader evolutionary thinking in German Romanticism. But where others were content to posit this "primitive substratum," it was for Hegel by no means the most archaic. Hegel was exactingly dialectical in his thinking of tone (*Ton*), positing in his *Naturphilosophie* (1830) a "heavy matter" of *Klang* ("natural sound") that, despite being inhuman, Gallope writes, "a product of the 'determinations of materiality,'" is nonetheless "dialectical in that it undergoes a process of becoming independent, ideal, and relatively free from materiality as an 'inner vibration of the body within itself'" (77). Gallope directs us, for example, to Wilhelm Heinrich Wackenroder's 1798 essay on musical aesthetics as an important antecedent of Hegel. Drumming was for Wackenroder a primordial *Schall* that, in Gallope's phrase, "developed historically into a music," an evolutionary teleology (73).

68. "It [*Klang*] is something like a *Schall* without human hands, one that takes shape as an elastic vibration between bodies—an ideal but ephemeral form of cohesion." Gallope, *Deep Refrains*, 77. In Hegel's phrase, *Klang* is "The ideality posited in elasticity," or a "double negation" of "two mutually sublating determinations," whereby ideality's negated materiality is itself negated. Hegel, qtd. in Gallope, *Deep Refrains*, 78. In *Lectures on Aesthetics*, Hegel maintains this logic of double negation, but now, Gallope writes, "what is negated is no longer just the divided externality of indifferent matter, but the spatiality" of painting (79).

69. Gallope, *Deep Refrains*, 73.

70. Hegel, qtd. in Gallope, *Deep Refrains*, 78.

71. Walter Benjamin, *Illuminations*, ed. Hannah Arendt, trans. Harry Zohn (New York: Schocken, 1968), 90–91. For an important discussion of Conrad's oral communities in relation to Benjamin, see Michael Greaney, *Conrad, Language, and Narrative* (Cambridge: Cambridge University Press, 2005).

72. Benjamin, *Illuminations*, 91.

73. Benjamin, *Illuminations*, 86.

74. Benjamin does not mention Freud in his essay, but he is clearly invoking *Beyond the Pleasure Principle*. Freud begins his famous book with the problem of shell-shock, perhaps because total war points to some limit in the talking cure as a form of counsel. Freud posits in this text the repetition compulsion whereby one repeats what one cannot remember; through Benjamin, we can add that one only remembers where one tells the story, or converts raw experience into narrative, remembering and converting into narrative being coextensive.

75. Catherine Malabou explained this point in her seminar, "Heidegger and Foucault," April 2, 2007, at the University of California, Berkeley.

76. Michel Foucault, *The Hermeneutics of the Subject: Lectures at the Collège de France 1981–1982*, ed. Frédéric Gros, trans. Graham Burchell (New York: Picador, 2005), 334. Foucault's book doesn't replicate a phonocentric event, however. He shows notetaking to have been a central component of listening for the Greeks.

77. For a discussion of Plutarch, see Foucault, *The Hermeneutics of the Subject*. Though he does not discuss Plutarch, an extensive study of the tension between reason and resonance in the rational tradition after Descartes can be found in Erlmann, *Reason and Resonance*.

78. Benjamin, *Illuminations*, 107.

79. Of course, that is Genette's communicational premise with which Ann Banfield and others take issue. For Banfield, there is no prior oral event to which the writing refers; there are simply written sentences that are, in their grammatical character, "unspeakable." But even if we are to shed this conceptual dependence on the oral, I'm suggesting, there is the fact of the past tense and its unfolding effects.

80. Martin Heidegger, *Being and Time*, trans. Joan Stambaugh (Albany: State University of New York Press, 1996), 153 (*SUZ 164*). Thank you to Naomi Waltham-Smith for recommending this quotation to me, which she theorizes at length in relation to Derrida in *The Sound of Life* (New York: Fordham University Press, forthcoming). As a preface to this remark, Heidegger writes that "acoustic perception [*akustische Vernehmen*] is based on hearing [*Hören*]," an issue that Waltham-Smith deftly takes up in relation to Derrida's "Heidegger's Ear."

81. Kaja Silverman, *The Threshold of the Visible World* (New York: Routledge, 1996), 93. In this section of Silverman's text, she draws from Benjamin's concept of the aura of the traditional work of art, which she suggests is a kind of "irradiation" from afar, or an idealization through which a thing drops its "fourth wall." Benjamin's conception of the story is essentially auratic. In fact, he preferred *aural* as the adjectival form in German, which underscores its acoustical properties in his thinking. *Heart of Darkness* radiates, too, but as an experience of dependence upon a repudiated other afar.

82. Qtd. in Mark L. McPherran, "Introducing a New God: Socrates and His *Daimonion*," in *Socrates' Divine Sign: Religion, Practice, and Value in Socratic Phi-*

NOTES TO PAGES 170–172

losophy, ed. Pierre Desirée and Nicolas D. Smith (Kelowna, BC: Academic Printing and Publishing, 2005), 114.

83. As Achebe suspects . . .

84. Giorgio Agamben, "History," in *Potentialities: Collected Essays in Philosophy*, ed. and trans. Daniel Heller-Roazen (Palo Alto, CA: Stanford University Press, 1999), 118.

85. Robert Laynton, *Behind the Masks of God*, rev. and exp. 2nd ed. (Straffordshire, UK: Stoke-on-Trent, 2016), 48. Mladen Dolar turns to the daimon as one Western origin of the acousmatic in *A Voice and Nothing More* (Cambridge, MA: MIT Press, 2006), but in his concern for the Lacanian object voice he does not comment on this modal dimension, the way the daimon cuts what is and what could be. That is why the daimon is not seen by oneself, a fact Conrad marks in *Lord Jim* when Jim experiences being watched by Marlow: "This fellow—ran the thought—looks at me as though he could see somebody or something behind my back" (*LJ*, 33). The peculiar nature of the daimon is to be behind one's back, visible only to others. Hannah Arendt, *The Human Condition*, 2nd ed. (Chicago: University of Chicago Press, 1998), 192. The famous command of the daimon in *Phaedo* is "to make music," which has bearing on the aural form of Marlow's narratives. For further discussion of the daimon, see my "On Banishing Socrates' Wife: The Interiority of the Ear in *Phaedo*," in *Poiesis*, ed. Nathan Brown and Petar Milat (Zagreb: Multimedijalni Institute, 2017), 156–75. There I describe how Plato suppresses these more ritualistic dimensions of the daimon in favor of a different etymology. For example, Laynton argues against Plato's etymology in the *Cratylus* and postulates the daimon as being closer to *daiō* ("to divide, to distribute destinies, to allot") (48).

86. A sinister resonance directs us to the ways that spoken word (*parole*)—one with the political weight of what Philippe Lacoue-Labarthe, "The Horror of the West," in *Conrad's "Heart of Darkness" and Contemporary Thought: Revisiting the Horror with Philippe Lacoue-Labarthe*, ed. Nidesh Lawtoo (London: Bloomsbury, 2012), 113, calls "testimony"—first depends on an abstract conveyance, or a physical channel that might host its event of irradiation: For there to be testimony, there must first be an opening, an audibility and communicability.

87. Frantz Fanon, *Black Skin, White Masks*, trans. Charles Lam Markmann (London: Pluto Press, 1986), 217.

88. "resonator, n." *OED Online*. For a nuanced account of the resonator and its impact on modern understandings of the physics and psychology of listening, see Steege, *Helmholtz and the Modern Listener*, 43–79. In Helmholtz's early experiments with tone generation and resonance, for example, in striking a tuning fork against the string of a monochord, he found that only those tones "common to both" will swell loudly.

89. Laynton, *Behind the Masks of Gods*, 48–49.

90. Ngugi wa Thiong'o, "The Contradictions of Joseph Conrad," *New York Times*, November 21, 2017, https://www.nytimes.com/2017/11/21/books/review/dawn-watch -joseph-conrad-biography-maya-jasanoff.html. This relation between Ngugi and Conrad interests GoGwilt in *The Passage of Literature*. Also see Michaela Bronstein in *Out of Context: The Uses of Modernist Fiction* (New York: Oxford University Press, 2018), which chimes with my account, in "The Acoustic of Narrative Involvement," of the anachronic relation between Conrad and Faulkner, described in Chapter 2 and the Reprise to this book.

91. Stefan Helmreich, "Transduction," in *Keywords in Sound*, ed. David Novak and Matt Sakakeeny (Durham, NC: Duke University Press, 2015), 222.

92. Helmreich, "Transduction," 222.

93. Garrett Stewart, *Reading Voices: Literature and the Phonotext* (Berkeley: University of California Press, 1990), 222, might call this "two phonemic messages in one scriptive form."

94. I draw this phrase from Jennifer Janechek, "The Horror of the Primal Sound: Proto-telephony and Imperialism in 'Heart of Darkness,'" *The Conradian* 41, no. 2 (2016): 8–27.

95. See Jacques Lacan, *The Four Fundamental Concepts of Psychoanalysis: The Seminar of Jacques Lacan, Book XI*, ed. Jacques-Alain Miller, trans. Alan Sheridan (New York: Norton, 1998), 79–90.

96. It has gone largely unnoticed that when Sartre theorizes the gaze in *Being and Nothingness*, or the feeling that "someone is looking at me," a crucial prelude to the experience is the rustle in the branches. He hears a sound, which signals he is seen (a dynamic that places the scene well within the range of the Ovidian myth, Echo also making a noise that catches Narcissus's attention). This moment in Sartre is key for Fanon, adapted to his discussion of the boy who points at him such that being is no longer for itself but for the other. Fanon is the echo of that sound.

97. Jacques Derrida, *Of Grammatology*, corrected ed., trans. Gayatri Chakravorty Spivak (Baltimore, MD: Johns Hopkins University Press, 1997), 166.

98. Freud concluded that the dream was grounded in the young boy's traumatic experience of overhearing his parents having sex. Calling it the "primal scene," Freud conjectured that there must have been sounds the young boy could not understand. In the letters he exchanged with Fliess, Freud had begun to attend to the strange things heard in childhood as the basis for fantasy life and, with it, sexuality. See Sigmund Freud, "From the History of an Infantile Neurosis," in *The Standard Edition of the Complete Psychological Works of Sigmund Freud*, ed. James Strachey (London: Hogarth, 1955), 17:1–124.

99. Freud, "From the History of an Infantile Neurosis," 17:38.

100. Following Lacan, Mladen Dolar but also Michel Chion and Slavoj Žižek return to the domain of infantile listening—the auditory acts that occur before a person has

fully entered into speech and language—to explain the most psychologically troubling effects of the acousmatic, of hearing without seeing.

101. See Dolar, *A Voice and Nothing More.*

102. Vincent Cornu, qtd. in Nikolai Duffy, introduction to *Gap Gardening: Selected Poems*, by Rosmarie Waldrop (New York: New Directions, 2016), 2. Duffy likens its experience to the "vision without visual consciousness" that perceives a blank spot on the page. Thank you to my student Paige Smucker for introducing me to this text.

103. In "The Horror of the West," Lacoue-Labarthe writes beautifully and in passing of a "minimal diegesis" that holds the "we" of Conrad's narrative address together, stating that Plato's categories are "the only ones we have" (113). The most sustained discussions of mimesis in Conrad are to be found in Nidesh Lawtoo, *Conrad's Shadow: Catastrophe, Mimesis, Theory* (East Lansing: Michigan State University Press, 2016).

104. Pierre Schaeffer, "Acousmatics," in *Audio Culture: Readings in Modern Music*, ed. Christoph Cox and Daniel Warner (New York: Continuum, 2004), 77, writes that the acousmatic situation "gives back to the ear alone the entire responsibility of a perception that ordinarily rests on other senses." In this situation and its "concealment of causes . . . it is the listening itself that becomes the origin of the phenomenon" (77).

105. Schaeffer, "Acousmatics," 78.

106. The most extensive historical account of and critical intervention in the implications of Schaeffer's largely untranslated treatise can be found in Brian Kane, *Sound Unseen: Acousmatic Sound in Theory and Practice* (New York: Oxford University Press, 2014).

107. Adriana Cavarero, *For More Than One Voice: Toward a Philosophy of Vocal Expression*, trans. Paul A. Kottman (Stanford, CA: Stanford University Press, 2005), 171.

108. Welles's sound design is, however, much more substantial, and it surrounds the dialogue with ethnographic recordings of singing in ways that were radical for this moment in radio history, song being at nearly the same volume as speech.

109. Benjamin, *Illuminations*, 255.

110. See Susan Buck-Morss, *The Dialectics of Seeing: Walter Benjamin and the Arcades Project* (Cambridge, MA: MIT Press, 1989), 210: "The truth which the dialectical image illuminates is historically fleeting." Conrad makes an appearance in Benjamin's *Arcades Project*, where he discusses Conrad's *The Shadow-Line*. This literary "passage" forms the basis of GoGwilt's account of Benjamin's aesthetic of *mise-en-abyme* in Conrad's engagement with opera. GoGwilt, *The Passage of Literature*, 43–47.

111. Qtd. in Goehr, "Radical Modernism and the Failure of Style," 57.

112. See Moten, *In the Break*, 13. He writes, "Marx's counterfactual ('If the commodity could speak it would say . . .') is broken by the trace of a subjectivity born in objection that he neither realizes nor anticipates." The commodity that speaks, that

is, the slave, contradicts "the thesis on value—that it is not intrinsic—that Marx assigns it."

113. James Hutchinson Stirling, *The Secret of Hegel: Being the Hegelian System in Origin, Principle, Form, and Matter* (London: Longman, Roberts, and Green, 1865), 2:2–3. In among the earliest English-language interpretations of Hegel, Stirling wrote in 1865 that *"Stimme* means *voice,* and the action of *Bestimmen* is to supply voice to what previously had none." *Bestimmung* is "a sort of naming of Adam" (2:2).

114. Ivan Krielkamp, "A Voice without a Body: The Phonographic Logic of 'Heart of Darkness,'" *Victorian Studies* 40, no. 2 (1997): 229.

115. See Adrian Daub, *Four-Handed Monsters: Four-Handed Piano Playing and Nineteenth-Century Culture* (New York: Oxford University Press, 2014), 24–55.

116. Jonathan Sterne, *Audible Past: Cultural Origins of Sound Reproduction* (Chapel Hill, NC: Duke University Press, 2003), 290, 292.

117. Sterne, *Audible Past,* 290.

118. Theodor W. Adorno, *Essays on Music,* ed. Richard Leppert, trans. Susan H. Gillespie (Berkeley: University of California Press, 2002), 278–79.

119. Freud's move is to split the drive between pleasure and death, and Peter Szendy suggests the same of listening in *All Ears: The Aesthetics of Espionage* (New York: Fordham University Press, 2016).

120. It is the same space with which Henry James begins "The Turn of the Screw," where Douglas reads aloud from a diary. But James abruptly ends the story without returning back to that space, showing having killed the space of telling, so to speak.

121. For example, see Ashon Crawley, *Blackpentecostal Breath: The Aesthetics of Possibility* (New York: Fordham University, 2017), 139–96, who articulates "what the black object hears around itself" (144). Crawley insists that groans be heard and understood as "joyful noise" sounding out against objectification and toward other aesthetic possibilities.

122. Edward W. Said, *Culture and Imperialism* (New York: Vintage, 1994), 51.

123. Said, *Culture and Imperialism,* 51. Emphasis mine. Also see Edward W. Said, "Conrad and Nietzsche," in *Reflections on Exile and Other Essays* (Cambridge, MA: Harvard University Press, 2000), 70–82, which focuses on the shared place of *melos* in their writings. The Greeks, we have seen with Plato, were continually thinking about musical forms that might contain and exclude the most troubling forces of sound (but also racial others: the origin of "barbarian," meaning "not Greek" and "uncivilized," is simply babble or the incomprehensible speech of the foreigner).

124. Michael Rogin, *Blackface, White Noise: Jewish Immigrants in the Hollywood Melting Pot* (Berkeley: University of California Press, 1998), 20–22. Rogin concentrates his reading on an advertisement for blackface in the United States: "The 'cry was that we have no NATIVE MUSIC,' proclaimed the preface to an antebellum book of 'plantation songsters,' 'until our countrymen found a triumphant and vindicating

APOLLO in the genius of E. P. Christy, who . . . was the first to catch our *native airs* as they floated wildly, or hummed in the balmy breezes of the sunny south'" (22).

125. One important exception to the dearth of scholarship on Reik is, of course, "The Echo of the Subject," Philippe Lacoue-Labarthe's major essay in *Typography: Mimesis, Philosophy, Politics*, trans. Christopher Fynsk (Cambridge, MA: Harvard University Press, 1989). More recently, John Mowitt redresses this gap in *Sounds: The Ambient Humanities* (Berkeley: University of California Press, 2015), 40–57.

126. Joseph Conrad, *Collected Letters*, vol. 9: *Uncollected Letters and Indexes*, ed. Laurence Davies, Owen Knowles, Gene M. Moore, and J. H. Stape (New York: Cambridge University Press, 2008), 208. Thank you to Laurence Davies for recommending this letter to me.

127. In 1894 Conrad wrote to Marguerite Poradowska that his novel-in-progress, *Almayer's Folly*, begins with a *trio* of three characters and ends with a long *solo* in the manner of Wagner's *Tristan*. Laurence Davies suggests that Poradowska must have been in Brussels with him, Conrad speaking of a recent shared experience. See Conrad, *Collected Letters*, vol. 9, 208n5. This reference carries the sense that the solo could also be conjured in her memory, if not in precise melodic content, then in its sonority, a penumbra of duration and feeling. Conrad never went to Bayreuth, and La Monnaie De Munt, the federal opera house where Conrad attended *Tristan and Isolde*, was not retrofitted in the Wagnerian style. But his memory and knowledge of opera would have been nurtured by long discussions with his writing partner and close friend Ford Madox Ford, the son of Francis Heuffer, a devoted Wagnerian who, as a German expatriate, made his pilgrimage return to the Bayreuth festival each year, as did many of Conrad's contemporaries. For a discussion of that relationship and Wagner's influence, see John Lewis DiGaetani, *Richard Wagner and the Modern British Novel* (Rutherford, NJ: Fairleigh Dickinson University Press, 1978), 23–57. According to Vincent Pecora, "*Heart of Darkness* and the Phenomenology of Voice," *ELH* 52, no. 4 (1985): 993–1015, Conrad had studied Schopenhauer's theory of music, a major touchstone for Nietzsche, in *The World as Will and Idea*. George Butte, "What Silencus Knew: Conrad's Uneasy Debt to Nietzsche," *Comparative Literature* 41, no. 2 (Spring 1989): 113–208, argues that Conrad's writings betray an intimate knowledge of nihilism in Nietzsche's *Birth of Tragedy*. Butte seems to assume that Conrad had read Nietzsche's text before 1900. According to a very helpful summary in Mary Anne Frese Witt, "D'Annunzio's Dionysian Women: The Rebirth of Tragedy in Italy," in *Nietzsche and the Rebirth of the Tragic*, ed. Mary Anne Frese Witt (Rutherford, NJ: Fairleigh Dickinson University Press, 2007), 101n15, the earliest complete French translation (Conrad could not read German) was Jean Marnold and Jacques Morland, trans., *L'origine de la tragédie* (Paris: Mercure de France, 1901). It's possible that Conrad encountered anthologized fragments of Nietzsche's book in Henri Lichtenberger's *Friedrich Nietzsche: Aphorismes et fragments choisis* (Paris: Felix Alcan, 1899), a

translation also cited in Frese Witt, 101n15. It's perhaps more likely that Conrad
gained familiarity with Nietzschean themes through their shared reading of Calderon's
La vida es sueña, a major source for the German Romantics.

128. Kane, *Sound Unseen*, 105.

129. Christopher Bollas, *The Evocative Object World* (New York: Routledge,
2008), 51.

130. Moten, *In the Break*, 16.

131. The first audio recording of *Tristan und Isolde* was 1924, the year of Conrad's
death. Of course, if we follow the implications of what I am calling retroaudition, then
one could read the text through the sonic present of that recording's widespread
availability.

132. Adorno, *Essays on Music*, 285.

133. Anne Cheng, *Second Skin: Josephine Baker and the Modernist Surface* (New
York: Oxford University Press, 2013), 67.

134. Lawtoo, *Conrad's Shadow*, 143. It is Chinua Achebe who relates the otherwise unnamed people in Conrad's text to the Fang, "living just north of Conrad's River
Congo" ("An Image of Africa," 347). On this basis, Lawtoo brilliantly traces Conrad's
observations of music and movement to Fang ritual and the preeminent place of
trance, drawing out the implications for contemporary politics. While Lawtoo similarly
regards Conrad's observations of sound as among the first ethnographies of music in
the Congo, I take Conrad's techniques to be inseparable from both the racial unconscious and Conrad's critique of colonial knowledge production.

135. See Yolanda Covington-Ward, *Gesture and Power: Religion, Nationalism,
and Everyday Performance in Congo* (Durham, NC: Duke University Press,
2016). Here, I am taking up an anachronic dimension of resonance to consider what
will happen to the sound space of the Belgian Congo in Conrad's lifetime. Covington-
Ward traces the history of spirit-induced trembling (*zakama*) by female prophets in
the Lower Congo in the colonial period (c. 1921) through the decades leading up to
independence (Conrad traveled several hundred miles from what is now Kinshasa in
the DRC to Kisangani). The *kingunza* (prophetic) movement—"singing, drumming,
and more important, trembling"—was a war fought "with music, prayer, and bodies" (Covington-Ward, 72), not unlike the Civil Rights movement in the New World,
where old spirituals—freedom songs—were retrieved and recast. Lawtoo notes the
central role of the female prophet in Achebe's *Things Fall Apart* (*Conrad's Shadow*,
181–84). The black woman in *Heart of Darkness* has been called variously "mistress"
and "concubine" by critics, but never a prophet, and yet Marlow recalls her profound
gestural authority.

136. Benjamin, *Illuminations*, 98.

137. For a psychoanalytically inflected discussion of this moment in recording history, see Roshanak Kheshti, *Modernity's Ear: Listening to Race and Gender in World
Music* (New York: NYU Press, 2015).

138. For a discussion of the role of blackface minstrelsy in Victorian culture, see Michael Pickering, "The Blackface Clown," in *Black Victorians/Black Victoriana*, ed. Gretchen Holbrook (New Brunswick, NJ: Rutgers University Press, 2003), 159–74.

139. See Pecora, *"Heart of Darkness* and the Phenomenology of Voice," who makes it clear that the voice of Kurtz speaks in *Heart of Darkness* on the other side of some epistemic break (as theorized by both Schopenhauer and Nietzsche) such that the voice Marlow seeks is no longer available. I am interested in what it means to (re)route that episteme, which ostensibly begins with Plato and Homer, through the Middle Passage, colonialism, and exile.

140. Qtd. in Ian Watt, "Conrad's Preface to *The Nigger of the 'Narcissus,'"* *NOVEL: A Forum on Fiction* 7, no. 2 (1974): 101.

141. Michael North, *The Dialect of Modernism: Race, Language, and Twentieth-Century Literature* (New York: Oxford University Press, 1998), 39, 57.

142. Lowell, qtd. in GoGwilt, *The Passage of Literature*, 11.

143. GoGwilt, *The Passage of Literature*, 10.

144. According to Watt, Conrad uses the term "temperament" in its English sense to mean "elements in the total personality which control its response to sensory, emotional, intellectual and aesthetic experience," though it may have originated in Conrad's readings of Guy de Maupassant, who used the term to mean "sensibility" and "soul." Watt, "Conrad's Preface," 108. The term "solidarity" entered English by way of French in 1848 (making it, to some extent, a revolutionary term). Like Conrad's (mis)use of "temperament," it would have struck Conrad's English readers as strange if not foreign. These words' "ring" for contemporary English readers would counteract the very sentiment they were to express. Furthermore, the notion of solidarity or "kinship" nowhere appears in novel theory as it was developing in England at the time. The fact that Conrad wished to be included in that popular debate is evident in the title he chose for the American publication of the preface, "The Art of Fiction," that is, the same title of Henry James's essay that, by all accounts, galvanized novel theory in England, James also being Conrad's voice ideal. Because editors had not included Conrad's preface in the novel's original publication, he paid for it at his own expense. The Doubleday edition of Conrad's novel—the first edition to include the preface *as* a preface—introduces it through another note, "To My Readers in America," which ends with the remarkable phrase, "And here is the Suppressed Preface." Conrad begins the preface with the notion that art "appeals" to the senses, which can be routed via the French *appeler*, to call or to plea. Conrad privileges hearing as the condition of the novel becoming a means of solidarity but registers a doubt about its being received, which for Conrad means *to be heard*.

145. For Rousseau, figurative language retains traces of a *sensual* truth that contradicts fact.

146. In this last phrase, Conrad appears to cite (as if from memory) a quotation from Anatole France's "Aristos and Polyphilos on the Language of Metaphysics." France

writes, "What is this if not a collection of little symbols, much worn and defaced, I admit, symbols which have lost their original brilliance, and picturesqueness, but which still, by the nature of things, remain symbols?" Derrida uses this same quotation from France to help ground his theory of "white mythology," neatly summarized by Joseph Adamson, "White Mythology," in *Encyclopedia of Contemporary Literary Theory: Approaches, Scholars, Terms*, ed. Irene Rima Makaryk (Toronto: University of Toronto Press, 1993), 652, as the "philosophical dream of a language cleansed of all figurative stain and made absolutely approximate to its signified."

147. Cheng, *Second Skin*, 68.

148. Goehr, "Radical Modernism and the Failure of Style," 63.

149. Conrad, *Collected Letters*, vol. 3, 94–5.

150. See Krielkamp, "A Voice without a Body."

151. Thank you to Steege for pointing out this relationship to me. While critical commentary on Symbolist vibration is not extensive, a helpful discussion of sound and rhythm that situates *vers libre* in the intellectual history of scientific aesthetics may be found in Robert Michael Brain, *The Pulse of Modernism: Physiological Aesthetics in Fin-de-Siècle Europe* (Seattle: University of Washington Press, 2015), 150–73. Brain also describes the importance of "the multitonal tone of Wagner" and the theories of Charles Henry, a mathematician and aestheticist writing in the orbit of experimental phonetics, physiology, and linguistics.

152. Brain, *The Pulse of Modernism*, 151.

153. The phonograph is scriptural, the writing of waves. Peter Szendy, *Listen: A History of Our Ears* (New York: Fordham University Press, 2008), shows that among the earliest fears of composers regarding mechanical reproduction, as "machine-language" and reading, was that it might replace notation and compositional authority over sound. Yet, in conceiving of the phonograph's script as a bearer of the spiritual *lingua franca* of vibration, Conrad is perhaps closer to Walter Benjamin's thinking regarding the inscription of sound as theorized by the physicist Johann Wilhelm Ritter (here I quote directly from Benjamin's citation of Ritter, including the ellipses), as "a light pattern, fire-writing . . . Every sound would then have its own letter directly to hand . . . That inward connection of word and script—so powerful that we write when we speak . . . has long interested me. Tell me: how do we transform the thought, the idea, into the word; and do we ever have a thought or an idea without its hieroglyph, its letter, its script? Truly it is so." Ritter, qtd. in Walter Benjamin, *The Origin of German Tragic Drama*, trans. John Osborne (New York: Verso, 2009), 213. For Conrad, the idea vibrates in the reader, who, before she can see it, must first hear and feel it, written language being a fire-writing in the other. When Conrad seeks the novel's communicability, what he seeks is its vibration. For further discussion of Benjamin and Ritter, see Erlmann, *Reason and Resonance*.

154. Also, see Jonathan Sterne and Tara Rodgers, "The Poetics of Signal Processing," *Differences* 22, nos. 2–3 (January 1, 2011): 31–53. They describe how the

poetics of signal processing draws from the lexicon of the nineteenth-century sea voyage. We speak of sound "waves" and "channels," its electric "current" and "flow." But Conrad helps us understand the entanglement of colonialism, trade, and empire within the linguistic and sonic; these were not voyages toward but for.

155. In the conclusion of *Matter and Memory*, trans. N. M. Paul and W. S. Palmer (Brooklyn: Zone, 1988), Henri Bergson writes, "matter thus resolves itself into numberless vibrations, all linked together in uninterrupted continuity, all bound up with each other, and traveling in every direction like shivers through an immense body" (208). Thank you to Alexis Nalley, who referenced this quotation in her 2010 senior thesis on Faulkner and Bergson at the University of California, Berkeley.

156. Marx and Engels, qtd. in Alan Williams, "Is Sound Recording Like a Language?" *Yale French Studies* 60 (1980): 52.

157. The notion of the "innumerable" betrays readings of Schopenhauer translated into English and, with it, a reception of his thinking of music not as a copy or representation of phenomenon but the will itself. "All the innumerable conceivable phenomena and conditions of things, might be coexistent in boundless space, without limiting each other, or might be successive in endless time without interfering with each other." See Arthur Schopenhauer, *The World as Will and Idea*, vol. 1, trans. R. B. Haldane and J. Kemp, http://www.gutenberg.org/files/38427/38427-h/38427-h .html. Conrad writes in the preface to *The Nigger of the "Narcissus"* of "the latent feeling of fellowship with all creation—and to the subtle but invincible conviction of solidarity that knits together the loneliness of innumerable hearts" as stimulated by the work of art. What is remarkable about the echo of Schopenhauer, however, is that the notion and its phrasing live quite a different life in Nietzsche than they do in Conrad, two writers who have been connected through a shared thinking of music and suffering by Said, Lawtoo, and Henry Stanten. My point is that Conrad—in his contact with the colonies—hears a different tenor in Schopenhauer's representation of suffering and the will: He hears the world-constituting displacement of the Middle Passage.

158. Édouard Glissant, *Poetics of Relation*, trans. Betsy Wing (Ann Arbor: University of Michigan Press, 1997), 5.

159. Glissant, *Poetics of Relation*, 5.

160. Across his early work, Conrad rewrites for empire a sound and listening consciousness inscribed by Gustave Flaubert, *Madame Bovary*, trans. Geoffrey Wall (New York: Penguin, 2003), 172: "the last cries from the amputation which issued in a slow heavy wail, broken by jagged screeching, like the far-off bellow of some creature being slaughtered." Flaubert's characters hear the cry but will not listen to it. Faulkner receives this sound (through Conrad) for Benjy.

161. Eli Friedlander, "On the Musical Gathering of Echoes of the Voice: Walter Benjamin on Opera and the *Trauerspiel*," *Opera Quarterly* 21, no. 4 (2005): 631.

162. For example, Aaron Fogel, *The Coercion to Speech: Conrad's Poetics of*

Dialogue (Cambridge, MA: Harvard University Press, 1985), notes that Wait's typhoid cough continually chimes with the strange, punctuating noise made by chief mate Baker, "Ough. Ough."

163. Comparative literature represents a turn away from the texual fragment—the basis of philology as a "science of language"—toward the "deposit of multiple, overlapping, and contested literary systems of culture" (GoGwilt, *The Passage of Literature*, 218). GoGwilt also notes here the connection, according to Hugh Kenner, between the growth of the *OED* and "the collaborative process of the English modernists, Joyce, Pound, and Eliot."

164. Gaston Bachelard, *The Poetics of Space*, trans. Maria Jolas (Boston: Beacon, 1994), 176.

165. William Faulkner, *As I Lay Dying*, corrected text ed. (New York: Vintage, 1990), 171–72. In *Our Conrad: Constituting American Modernity* (Stanford, CA: Stanford University Press, 2010), Peter Lancelot Mallios convincingly argues this novel to have a displaced relationship to blackness, chiefly through its appositional relationship to Conrad. "Carcassonne" ends with "an immensity of silence and darkness." William Faulkner, *Collected Stories* (New York: Vintage, 1990), 900. For John T. Matthews, "Recalling the West Indies: From Yoknapatawpha to Haiti and Back," *American Literary History* 16, no. 2 (April 13, 2004): 238–62, "Carcassonne" is one of many stories where Faulkner works out an early preoccupation with US expansion in the West Indies as being descended from the Southern plantation design.

166. The "abyss" is a central figure in Glissant, *Poetics of Relation*.

167. Cavarero, *For More Than One Voice*, 169.

168. In this way, Conrad's thinking is quite close to that of Rousseau in "The Essay on the Origin of Languages," where he argues that before there was literal language, there was the figure, and before there was the figure, there was the cry, a passionate communication.

169. Joseph Conrad, *The Mirror of the Sea* (Marlboro, VT: Marlboro, 1988), 69, 70, passim.

170. Conrad, *The Mirror of the Sea*, 137.

171. Paul de Man, *The Rhetoric of Romanticism* (New York: Columbia University Press, 1984), 76.

172. See Lacoue-Labarthe, *Typography*, 139–207.

173. Conrad, qtd. in Said, *The World, the Text, and the Critic*, 93. "Solitude overpowers me; it absorbs me. I see nothing, I read nothing. It is like a kind of tomb, at the same time a hell, where one has to write, write, write" (Conrad, *The Collected Letters of Joseph Conrad*, vol. 3: *1903–1907*, ed. Frederick R. Karl and Laurence Davies [New York: Cambridge University Press, 1988], 53).

174. Flaubert, "On Realism," 93. Flaubert, *Correspondance* (Paris: L. Conard, 1910), 394.

175. This term is a technical one from linguistics. See Kathleen McClusky, *Rever-*

berations: Sound and Structure in the Novels of Virginia Woolf (Ann Arbor, MI: UMI Research Press, 1986).

176. Several critics have made this same observation of Lacan's title *Écrits*. See Alice Lagaay, "Between Sound and Silence: Voice in the History of Psychoanalysis," *Episteme* 1, no. 1 (2008): 58n3.

177. John Hollander, *Vision and Resonance: Two Senses of Poetic Form*, 2nd ed. (New Haven, CT: Yale University Press, 1985), 121, argues that words can sound like nature only because they sound like each other.

178. Michael Fried, "Almayer's Face: On 'Impressionism' in Conrad, Crane, and Norris," *Critical Inquiry* 17, no. 1 (1990): 199.

179. In *What Was Literary Impressionism?* (Cambridge, MA: Harvard University Press, 2018), Michael Fried again underscores the visual dimension of Conrad's composition. The return occurs earlier, however, most notably in Bill Brown's critique of Fried on the question of race, "Writing, Race, and Erasure: Michael Fried and the Scene of Reading," *Critical Inquiry* 18, no. 2 (1992): 387–402; but also Fried's sharp rebuttal, "Response to Bill Brown," *Critical Inquiry* 18, no. 2 (1992): 403–10.

180. "What wonder then that during the long blank hours the doubt creeps into the mind and I ask myself whether I am fitted for that work. The worst is that while I am thus powerless to produce my imagination is extremely active: whole paragraphs, whole pages, whole chapters pass through my mind. Everything is there: descriptions, dialogue, reflexion—everything—everything but the belief, the conviction, the only thing needed to make me put pen to paper." Joseph Conrad and David Storrar Meldrum, *Letters to William Blackwood and David S. Meldrum* (Durham, NC: Duke University Press, 1958), 27.

181. Conrad and Meldrum, *Letters*, 26–27.

182. For Freud, the twists and turns of the child's fantasy first involve that of watching another child being beaten, then that of watching oneself being beaten.

183. Conrad, qtd. in Fried, "Almayer's Face," 214.

184. Conrad, qtd. in Fried, "Almayer's Face," 214.

185. Fried emphasizes the defacement at the center of *Almayer's Folly*. Mrs. Almayer scratches off the face of a drowned man washed ashore, placing Dain's bracelet on his wrist so that, in finding the corpse, Almayer might think Dain is dead. Nina can then run away with Dain unimpeded. Fried does not explore the Oedipal anguish driving this scene, Mrs. Almayer intervening in Kaspar's desire to retain Nina as his own in an effort to preserve her whiteness in preventing her attachment to Dain as a substitute that mars her racial identity.

186. An English translation of the letter as it was finally sent exists in the *Collected Letters*, but, lamenting that the editors did not plan to include either the original Polish or its draft (a rarity), Jean Szczypien transcribed and published the draft, framed by an eloquent contextualization of the familial and fraternal ties associated with it. See

Jean M. Szczypien, "A Draft of a Polish Conrad Letter in the Manuscript of 'Almayer's Folly,'" *Polish Review* 43, no. 3 (1998): 355–59.

187. Wendy Xu made this point in her lecture at the New School, "Writing Home: Diasporic Language and the Poetics of Immigrant Memory," on April 4, 2019.

188. Conrad, qtd. in Szczypien, "A Draft of a Polish Conrad Letter," 358.

189. Thank you to Mateusz Halawa for his help with Conrad's Polish.

190. J. Hillis Miller calls it a catachrestic prosopopoeia ("Should We Read 'Heart of Darkness'?," 467).

191. Jean-Jacques Rousseau, *"The Discourses" and Other Early Political Writings*, ed. Victor Gourevitch (Cambridge: Cambridge University Press, 1997), 268.

192. Rousseau, *"The Discourses" and Other Early Political Writings*, 268. "En nous transportant hors de nous-mêmes; en nous identifiant avec l'être souffrant. Nous ne souffrons qu'autant que nous jugeons qu'il souffre; ce n'est pas dans nous, c'est dans lui que nous souffrons."

193. Derrida, *Of Grammatology*, 166, argues that the signifier seems not to fall into the world. "It is in the context of this possibility that one must pose the problem of the cry," he writes.

194. Glissant, *Poetics of Relation*, 15.

195. The dancer Owkui Okpokwisili made this provocative comment during her public talk, "The Unruly Body," on April 27, 2018, at the Graduate Institute for Design, Ethnography, and Social Thought.

196. Rogin, *Blackface, White Noise*, 20. Here, Rogin writes of a character in an Alphra Behn play but the figure is applicable to Conrad.

197. See Susan McClary, *Feminine Endings: Music, Gender, and Sexuality* (Minneapolis: University of Minnesota Press, 2002), 10–11.

198. Casement, qtd. in Nancy Rose Hunt, "An Acoustic Register, Tenacious Images, and Congolese Scenes of Rape and Repetition," *Cultural Anthropology* 23, no. 2 (2008): 239. Conrad and Casement encountered each other in the Congo; they were there at the same time.

REPRISE: REVERBERATION, CIRCUMAMBIENCE, AND FORM-SEEKING SOUND (*ABSALOM, ABSALOM!*)

1. Theodor W. Adorno, *Essays on Music*, ed. Richard Leppert, trans. Susan H. Gillespie (Berkeley: University of California Press, 2002), 141.

2. William Faulkner, *Light in August*, corrected text ed. (New York: Vintage, 1993), 119.

3. Here I gesture to John T. Matthews, "Recalling the West Indies: From Yoknapatawpha to Haiti and Back," *American Literary History* 16, no. 2 (April 13, 2004): 238–62. Matthews shares my sense that Faulkner writes through a kind of penumbra, references to the West Indies scattered on the surface of the text. Many of Matthews's elected examples trade in auditory figures, though his argument is visualistic.

4. Walter Benjamin, *Illuminations*, ed. Hannah Arendt, trans. Harry Zohn (New York: Schocken, 1968), 83.

5. Ian Baucom, *Specters of the Atlantic: Finance Capital, Slavery, and the Philosophy of History* (Durham, NC: Duke University Press, 2005), 311. Here, Baucom writes in a Benjaminian vein.

6. The year 1833, when Sutpen arrives in town, is the past of the narrative, when most of events discussed take place; it is the year of the Slavery Abolition Act. The year 1909 is the narrating present, when the narrators speak of the past, and it places the novel's timeline just before that of *The Sound and the Fury*. The year 1936 is Faulkner's moment of writing, two years after the United States ends its ongoing occupation of Haiti.

7. See Benjamin, "Theses on the Philosophy of History," *Illuminations*, 253–64. I draw this particular interpretation of the text from Max Haiven, *Revenge Capitalism: The Ghosts of Empire, the Demons of Capital, and the Settling of Unpayable Debts* (London: Pluto, 2020).

8. Édouard Glissant, *Faulkner, Mississippi* (New York: Farrar, Straus and Giroux, 1999), 98.

9. William Faulkner, *Faulkner in the University*, ed. Frederick Landis Gwynn and Joseph Leo Blotner (Charlottesville: University of Virginia Press, 1959), 20. For further discussion of this moment in Faulkner's seminar, see my "The Acoustics of Narrative Involvement: Modernism, Subjectivity, Voice," PhD diss., UC Berkeley, 2010, https://escholarship.org/uc/item/1ws2f1tr, 107–80.

10. Faulkner, *Faulkner in the University*, 20.

11. Faulkner, *Faulkner in the University*, 142.

12. Thanks to Benjamin Steege, with whom discussions of Heidegger were invaluable to the development of this section.

13. Martin Heidegger, *Being and Time*, trans. Joan Stambaugh (Albany: State University of New York Press, 1996), 128.

14. Heidegger, *Being and Time*, 127.

15. Michael Milgate, *Faulkner's Place* (Athens: University of Georgia Press, 1997), provided an important intervention in Faulkner studies by suggesting that Faulkner was of "two voices," as *Absalom* itself is split between Quentin, a Southerner, and Shreve, his principal interlocutor, an outsider. Faulkner's art is structured by a "regionalist's need to map his region" and to create a world legible to those "to whom the region will specifically, and almost by definition, be unfamiliar" (77).

16. Faulkner, qtd. in Milgate, *Faulkner's Place*, 30.

17. Quentin Anderson, qtd. in Carolyn Porter, *Seeing and Being: The Plight of the Participant-Observer in Emerson, James, Adams, and Faulkner* (Middletown, CT: Wesleyan University Press, 1981), 6. Anderson speaks specifically of the nineteenth-century European thinkers Hegel, Nietzsche, Marx, and Freud. See especially chapter 1 of Porter's influential text, "American Ahistoricism" (3–22), in which she argues

against the notion of what C. Van Woodward first called the "irony of southern history" (3). As Toynbee writes, "history is something that happens to other people" (qtd. in Porter, *Seeing and Being*, 4).

18. William Faulkner and Jean Stein, "William Faulkner: The Art of Fiction No. 12," *Paris Review* 12 (Spring 1956), https://www.theparisreview.org/interviews/4954 /william-faulkner-the-art-of-fiction-no-12-william-faulkner.

19. Arendt was a reader of Faulkner. She mentions him twice in her corpus, first in *The Human Condition*, 2nd ed. (Chicago: University of Chicago Press, 1998), 181n5, in a reference to the "unknown solider" as a memorial to a war that disclosed no one, no "who." She elaborates in this work the politics of the "space of appearance," an issue I took up in Chapter 1. The second reference appears in Hannah Arendt, *On Revolution* (New York: Penguin, 2006). Americans are plagued by "ignorance, oblivion, and a failure to remember," she writes. Arguing for the politics of speech as a politics of "future reference," Arendt contends in a brief footnote that the work of Faulkner represents the shape that an American memory might take: "How such guideposts for future reference and remembrance arise out of this incessant talk, not, to be sure, in the form of concepts but as single brief sentences and condensed aphorisms, may best be seen in the novels of William Faulkner. Faulkner's literary procedure, rather than the content of his work, is highly 'political,' and, in spite of many limitations, he has remained, as far as I can see, the only author to use it" (*On Revolution*, 307n4). She doesn't elaborate, but the essential premise is a Faulknerian one: Words, once spoken aloud, linger in thought and space and are unpredictable in their memory and political impact. Faulkner, however, makes the same case for written words; whenever they take up a delayed memory, they take on what I've called an acousticality, one whose political dimension is the delayed repercussion.

20. Jean-Luc Nancy, *Listening*, trans. Charlotte Mandell (New York: Fordham University Press, 2007), 17, writes, "If temporality is the dimension of the subject (ever since St. Augustine, Kant, Husserl, and Heidegger), this is because it defines the subject as what separates *itself* and retains *itself*, not only from the other or from the pure 'there,' but also from self: insofar is it waits for *itself* and retains *itself*, insofar as it desires (itself) and forgets (itself), insofar as it retains, but repeating it, its own empty unity and its projected . . . or ejected unicity." Ellipsis in original.

21. The multiplicities of meanings of the French *sonner*, including to summon, is there in Conrad as well, but not in a "play," as Nancy's translator notes (*Listening*, 75n43), but rather in a being caught between languages, a *broken* resonance. Quentin receives a note from Rosa, "a summons, out of another world almost" (*AA*, 5).

22. Joseph Conrad, *An Outcast of the Islands* (Garden City, NY: Doubleday, Page, 1925), 17.

23. For a discussion of overtonal montage in Faulkner and Eisenstein, see my "The Fact of Resonance: An Acoustics of Determination in Faulkner and Benjamin," *Symploke* 24, nos. 1–2 (2016): 171–86.

24. See Judith Butler, *The Psychic Life of Power: Theories in Subjection* (Palo Alto, CA: Stanford University Press, 1997). Butler describes the turning back that characterizes the Nietzschean will but also the literary trope.

25. Denise Riley, *The Words of Selves: Identification, Solidarity, Irony* (Stanford, CA: Stanford University Press, 2000), 12.

26. Emily Ann Thompson, *Soundscape of Modernity: Architectural Acoustics and the Culture of Listening in America, 1900–1933* (Cambridge, MA: MIT Press, 2004), 3. In the historical period covered by Thompson (1900–1933), reverberation became all important in architectural considerations, a "new, nonreverberant criterion" taking hold, as technologies and strategies reduced reverberation, such that "the many different places that made up the modern soundscape began to sound alike" (3).

27. William Faulkner's *Sanctuary*, corrected text ed. (New York: Vintage, 1993), begins with a shattered image in water, "broken and myriad," and a hidden yet nearby sound of a bird, "meaningless and profound out of suspirant and peaceful following silence which seemed to isolate the spot" (4, 8).

28. See Sami Khatib, "The Messianic without Messianism: Walter Benjamin's Materialist Theology," *Anthropology & Materialism* 1 (2013), http://journals.openedition .org/ am/159.

29. Several other scholars also have noted that Faulkner separates sound and image in ways related to cinema. See Sarah Gleeson-White, "Auditory Exposures: Faulkner, Eisenstein, and Film Sound," *PMLA* 128, no. 1 (January 2013): 87–100; and Jay Watson, "The Unsynchable William Faulkner," in *William Faulkner in the Media Ecology*, ed. Julian Murphet and Stephan Solomon (Baton Rouge: Louisiana State University Press, 2015).

30. Mladen Dolar, *A Voice and Nothing More* (Cambridge, MA: MIT Press, 2006), 138, writes of the primal scene, "There is a temporal vector between the voice (the incomprehensible, the traumatic) and the signifier (the articulation, the rationalization)," fantasy arising as the "junction" between the two. Faulkner's art, however, lies in the historical determination of such scenes and of the gap between hearing and understanding.

31. In Russell West's incredibly beautiful and underappreciated *Conrad and Gide: Translation, Transference, and Intertextuality* (Atlanta, GA: Rodopi, 1996), 42, he comments on Marlow's appearance in *Lord Jim* (which strikes us as already repeated), "Marlow is obliged to tell Jim's story again and again, trying to close the gap between *what was* and *what might have been*. I don't mean to suggest that Rosa's experience, as a white woman, is at all analogous to Fanon's, but they do share an inquiry into the social fact of listening and the desire to convert necessity. That sharing is itself cause for considering the slackening of boundaries in sound.

32. Also see Hortense J. Spillers, "'Born Again': Faulkner and the Second Birth," in *Fifty Years after Faulkner*, ed. Jay Watson and Ann J. Abadie (Jackson: University Press of Mississippi, 2016).

33. Jean-François Lyotard, *The Postmodern Condition*, trans. Geoff Bennington and Brian Massumi (Minneapolis: University of Minnesota Press, 1984), 22.

34. Heidegger, *Being and Time*, 42, asserts that in ancient ontology, it is in the world that beings are encountered and accessed. In the world, being becomes "comprehensible" as what is always and already in each being. To recognize this categorical determination is also to say it to a being, "so to speak, right in the face."

35. Frantz Fanon, *Black Skin, White Masks*, trans. Charles Lam Markmann (London: Pluto Press, 1986), 109, 112.

36. Fanon, *Black Skin, White Masks*, 113.

37. Faulkner developed Yoknapatawpha in the same period that Zora Neale Hurston conceived of eye-dialect in writing black Floridian vernacular, Hurston also documenting voices and tall tales on the verge of disappearance and in ways honed by her experience as an ethnographer. This was the same period that John and Alan Lomax took their equipment to the Delta to record the blues for the Library of Congress, the rise of mass distributed recordings also bringing black music into expanded sites of contact.

38. Jonathan Sterne, *Audible Past: Cultural Origins of Sound Reproduction* (Chapel Hill, NC: Duke University Press, 2003), 4.

BIBLIOGRAPHY

Achebe, Chinua. "An Image of Africa: Racism in Conrad's *Heart of Darkness*." In *Heart of Darkness: A Norton Critical Edition*, 4th ed., ed. Paul B. Armstrong, 336–49. New York: Norton, 2006.

Adamson, Joseph. "White Mythology." In *Encyclopedia of Contemporary Literary Theory: Approaches, Scholars, Terms*, ed. Irene Rima Makaryk, 652. Toronto: University of Toronto Press, 1993.

Adorno, Theodor W. *Essays on Music*. Ed. Richard Leppert. Trans. Susan H. Gillespie. Berkeley: University of California Press, 2002.

Agamben, Giorgio. "History." In *Potentialities: Collected Essays in Philosophy*, ed. and trans. Daniel Heller-Roazen. Palo Alto, CA: Stanford University Press, 1999.

Ahmed, Sarah. "Feminist Complaint." *Feminist Killjoys blog*. April 29, 2014. https://feministkilljoys.com/2014/12/05/complaint/.

Anderson, Benedict. *Imagined Communities: Reflections on the Origin and Spread of Nationalism*. Rev. ed. New York: Verso, 2016.

Arendt, Hannah. *The Human Condition*. 2nd ed. Chicago: University of Chicago Press, 1998.

———. Introduction to *Illuminations*, by Walter Benjamin, ed. Hannah Arendt, trans. Harry Zohn, 1–55. New York: Schocken, 1968.

———. *On Revolution*. New York: Penguin, 2006.

Armstrong, Richard H. *A Compulsion for Antiquity: Freud and the Ancient World*. Ithaca, NY: Cornell University Press, 2005.

Attali, Jacques. *Noise: The Political Economy of Music*. Trans. Brian Massumi. Minneapolis: University of Minnesota Press, 1984 [1977].

Bachelard, Gaston. *The Poetics of Space*. Trans. Maria Jolas. Boston: Beacon, 1994.

Bakhtin, Mikhail. "Discourse in the Novel." In *Literary Theory: An Anthology*, ed. Julie Rivkin and Michael Ryan, 674–85. Malden, MA: Blackwell, 2004.

Bal, Mieke. *Narratology: Introduction to the Theory of Narrative*. 3rd ed. Toronto: University of Toronto Press, 2009.

Banfield, Ann. *Unspeakable Sentences: Narration and Representation in the Language of Fiction*. Boston: Routledge & Kegan Paul, 1992.

Barthes, Roland. *Camera Lucida: Reflections on Photography*. Trans. Richard Howard. New York: Macmillan, 1981.

——. *Image, Music, Text*. Trans. Stephen Heath. New York: Hill and Wang, 1977.

——. *The Neutral: Lecture Course at the College de France (1977–1978)*. Trans. Rosalind Krauss and Denis Hollier. New York: Columbia University Press, 2005.

——. *Responsibility of Forms: Critical Essays on Music, Art, and Representation*. Trans. Richard Howard. Berkeley: University of California Press, 1997.

——. *The Rustle of Language*. Trans. Richard Howard. Berkeley: University of California Press, 1989.

Baucom, Ian. "Frantz Fanon's Radio: Solidarity, Diaspora, and the Tactics of Listening." *Contemporary Literature* 42, no. 1 (2001): 15–49.

——. *Specters of the Atlantic: Finance Capital, Slavery, and the Philosophy of History*. Durham, NC: Duke University Press, 2005.

Bauman, H-Dirksen. "Listening to Phonocentrism with Deaf Eyes: Derrida's Mute Philosophy of (Sign) Language." *Essays in Philosophy* 9, no. 1 (2008).

Baxter, Katherine Isobel, and Robert Hampson, eds. *Conrad and Language*. Edinburgh: Edinburgh University Press, 2016.

Beckett, Samuel. *Nohow On: Company, Ill Seen Ill Said, Worstward Ho: Three Novels*. New York: Grove, 1996.

Benjamin, Walter. *Illuminations*. Ed. Hannah Arendt. Trans. Harry Zohn. New York: Schocken, 1968.

——. *The Origin of German Tragic Drama*. Trans. John Osborne. New York: Verso, 2009.

Benhabib, Seyla. *The Reluctant Modernism of Hannah Arendt*. Rev. ed. New York: Rowman and Littlefield, 2003.

Bennett, Jane. *Vibrant Matter: A Political Ecology of Things*. Durham, NC: Duke University Press, 2010.

Benn Michaels, Walter. *Our America: Nativism, Modernism, and Pluralism*. Durham, NC: Duke University Press, 1995.

Benveniste, Émile. *Problems in General Linguistics*. University of Miami Press, 1971.

Bergeron, Katherine. *Decadent Enchantments: The Revival of Gregorian Chant at Solesmes*. Berkeley: University of California Press, 1998.

Bergson, Henri. *Matter and Memory*. Trans. N. M. Paul and W. S. Palmer. Brooklyn: Zone, 1988.

Best, Stephen Michael. *The Fugitive's Properties: Law and the Poetics of Possession*. Chicago: University of Chicago Press, 2004.

Best, Stephen, and Sharon Marcus. "Surface Reading: An Introduction." *Representations* 108, no. 1 (2009): 1–21.

Bhabha, Homi K. *The Location of Culture*. New York: Routledge, 2004.

Blanchard, Marc E. "The Sound of Songs: The Voice in the Text." In *Hermeneutics and Deconstruction*, ed. Hugh J. Silverman and Don Ihde, 122–35. Albany: State University of New York Press, 1985.

Blanchot, Maurice. *The Infinite Conversation*. Trans. Susan Hanson. Minneapolis: University of Minnesota Press, 1993.

Blowers, Tonya. "The Textual Contract: Distinguishing Autobiography from the Novel." In *Representing Lives*, ed. Allison Donnell and Pauline Polkey, 105–16. London: Palgrave Macmillan.

Bollas, Christopher. *The Evocative Object World*. New York: Routledge, 2008.

Boutin, Aimée. *Maternal Echoes: The Poetry of Marceline Desbordes-Valmore and Alphonse de Lamartine*. Newark: University of Delaware Press, 2001.

Bradley, Rizvana. "Living in the Absence of a Body: The (Sus)Stain of Black Female (W)holeness." *Rhizomes* 29 (2016). http://www.rhizomes.net/issue29/pdf/bradley .pdf.

———. "Vestiges of Motherhood: The Maternal Function in Recent Black Cinema." *Film Quarterly* 71, no. 2 (2017): 46–52.

Brady, Erika. *A Spiral Way: How the Phonograph Changed Ethnography*. Jackson: University Press of Mississippi, 1999.

Brain, Robert Michael. *The Pulse of Modernism: Physiological Aesthetics in Fin-de-Siècle Europe*. Seattle: University of Washington Press, 2015.

Bronstein, Michaela. *Out of Context: The Uses of Modernist Fiction*. New York: Oxford University Press, 2018.

Brooks, Daphne A. *Bodies in Dissent: Spectacular Performances of Race and Freedom, 1850–1910*. Durham, NC: Duke University Press, 2006.

Brooks, Peter. *Reading for the Plot: Design and Intention in Narrative*. Cambridge, MA: Harvard University Press, 1992.

Brown, Bill. "Writing, Race, and Erasure: Michael Fried and the Scene of Reading." *Critical Inquiry* 18, no. 2 (1992): 387–402.

Buck-Morss, Susan. *The Dialectics of Seeing: Walter Benjamin and the Arcades Project*. Cambridge, MA: MIT Press, 1989.

Burkert, Walter. *Greek Religion*. Cambridge, MA: Harvard University Press, 1985.

Butler, Judith. *Excitable Speech: A Politics of the Performative*. New York: Routledge, 2013 [1997].

———. Introduction to *Soul and Form*, by Georg Lukács, trans. Anna Bostock, ed. John T. Sanders and Katie Terezakis. New York: Columbia University Press, 2010.

———. *The Psychic Life of Power: Theories in Subjection*. Palo Alto, CA: Stanford University Press, 1997.

Butler, Shane. *The Ancient Phonograph*. Cambridge, MA: MIT Press, 2015.

Butte, George. "What Silencus Knew: Conrad's Uneasy Debt to Nietzsche." *Comparative Literature* 41, no. 2 (Spring, 1989): 113–208.

Carson, Anne. "The Gender of Sound." In *Audio Culture: Readings in Modern Music*, rev. ed., ed. Christoph Cox and Daniel Warner, 43–60. New York: Bloomsbury, 2017.

Carter-Ényì, Aaron. "'Music More Ancient Than the Words': W. E. B. Du Bois's Theories on Africana Aurality." *Sounding Out!: The Sound Studies Blog*. August 27, 2019. https://soundstudiesblog.com/2018/08/27/music-more-ancient-than-words-w-e-b-du -boiss-theories-on-africana-aurality/.

Caruth, Cathy. *Unclaimed Experience: Trauma, Narrative, and History*. Baltimore, MD: Johns Hopkins University Press, 1996.

Cassin, Barbara, Emily Apter, Jacques Lezra, and Michael Wood, eds. *Dictionary of Untranslateables: A Philosophical Lexicon*. Princeton, NJ: Princeton University Press, 2014.

Cavarero, Adriana. *For More Than One Voice: Toward a Philosophy of Vocal Expression*. Trans. Paul A. Kottman. Stanford, CA: Stanford University Press, 2005.

———. *Relating Narratives: Storytelling and Selfhood*. Trans. Paul A. Kottman. Stanford, CA: Stanford University Press, 2000.

Christensen, Thomas. "Four-Hand Piano Transcription and Geographies of Nineteenth-Century Musical Reception." *Journal of the American Musicological Society* 52, no. 2 (Summer 1999): 255–98.

Cheng, Anne Anlin. *The Melancholy of Race: Psychoanalysis, Assimilation, and Hidden Grief*. New York: Oxford University Press, 2001.

———. *Second Skin: Josephine Baker and the Modernist Surface*. New York: Oxford University Press, 2013.

Cherki, Alice. *Frantz Fanon: A Portrait*. Ithaca: Cornell University Press, 2006.

Chion, Michel. *The Voice in Cinema*. Trans. Claudia Gorbman. New York: Columbia University Press, 1999.

Chow, Rey. *Not Like a Native Speaker: On Languaging as a Postcolonial Experience*. New York: Columbia University Press, 2014.

———. *Primitive Passions: Visuality, Sexuality, Ethnography, and Contemporary Chinese Cinema*. New York: Columbia University Press, 1995.

Chow, Rey, and James A. Steintrager. "In Pursuit of the Object of Sound: An Introduction." *differences* 22, nos. 2/3 (2011): 1–9.

Cixous, Hélène. "Castration or Decapitation." Trans. Annette Kuhn. *Signs* 7, no. 1 (1981): 41–55.

Clifford, James. "On Ethnographic Allegory." In *Writing Culture: The Poetics and Politics of Ethnography*, ed. James Clifford and George E. Marcus, 98–121. Berkeley: University of California Press, 1986.

———. *The Predicament of Culture*. Cambridge, MA: Harvard University Press, 1988.

Conrad, Joseph. *Almayer's Folly: A Story of An Eastern River* (New York: Modern Library, 2002).

———. *The Collected Letters of Joseph Conrad*, vol. 3: *1903–1907*. Ed. Frederick R. Karl and Laurence Davies. New York: Cambridge University Press, 1988.

———. *The Collected Letters of Joseph Conrad*, vol. 9: *Uncollected Letters and Indexes*. Ed. Laurence Davies, Owen Knowles, Gene M. Moore, and J. H. Stape. New York: Cambridge University Press, 2008.

———. *An Outcast of the Islands*. Garden City, NY: Doubleday, Page, and Co., 1936.

———. *Le Nègre du Narcisse*. Trans. Robert d'Humières. Paris: Gallimard, 1913.

———. *The Mirror of the Sea*. Marlboro, VT: Marlboro Press, 1988.

———. *Notes on Life and Letters: The Collected Works*, vol. 3. Garden City, NY: Doubleday, Page and Co., 1926.

Conrad, Joseph, and David Storrar Meldrum. *Letters to William Blackwood and David S. Meldrum*. Durham, NC: Duke University Press, 1958.

Copenhafer, David. "Overhearing (in) *Touch of Evil* and *The Conversation*: From 'Real Time' Surveillance to Its Recording." *Sound Studies* 4, no. 1 (2018): 2–18.

Copjec, Joan. *Read My Desire: Lacan against the Historicists*. Brooklyn: Verso, 2015.

Coviello, Peter. "Intimacy and Affliction: Du Bois, Race, and Psychoanalysis." *Modern Language Quarterly* 60, no. 1 (2003): 1–32.

Covington-Ward, Yolanda. *Gesture and Power: Religion, Nationalism, and Everyday Performance in Congo*. Durham, NC: Duke University Press, 2015.

Crawley, Ashon. *Blackpentecostal Breath: The Aesthetics of Possibility*. New York: Fordham University, 2017.

Cuddy-Keana, Melba. "Modernist Soundscapes and the Intelligent Ear: An Approach to Narrative through Auditory Perception." In *A Companion to Narrative Theory*, ed. James Phelan and Peter J. Rabinowitz, 382–98. New York: John Wiley & Sons, 2007.

Dames, Nicholas. *The Physiology of the Novel: Reading, Neuroscience, and the Form of Victorian Fiction*. New York: Oxford University Press, 2007.

Daston, Lorraine, and Peter Galison. *Objectivity*. New York: Zone, 2010.

Davies, Laurence. "Afterword." In *Conrad and Language*, ed. Katherine Isobel Baxter and Robert Hampson, 204–12. Edinburgh: Edinburgh University Press, 2016.

———. "Clenched Fists and Open Hands: Conrad's Unruliness." *The Conradian* 32, no. 2 (2007): 23–35.

Davis, Angela. *Blues Legacies and Black Feminism: Gertrude "Ma" Rainey, Bessie Smith, and Billie Holiday*. New York: Vintage, 1999.

Daub, Adrian. *Four-Handed Monsters: Four-Handed Piano Playing and Nineteenth-Century Culture*. New York: Oxford University Press, 2014.

de Man, Paul. *Allegories of Reading: Figural Language in Rousseau, Nietzsche, Rilke, and Proust*. New Haven, CT: Yale University Press, 1979.

———. "Autobiography as De-Facement." In *The Rhetoric of Romanticism*, 67–82. New York: Columbia University Press, 1984.

———. "Dialogue and Dialogism." *Poetics Today* 4 (1983): 99–107.

de Saussure, Ferdinand. *Course in General Linguistics*. Trans. Roy Harris. New York: Bloomsbury Academic, 2013.

Derrida, Jacques. *Archive Fever: A Freudian Impression*. Trans. Eric Prenowitz. Chicago: University of Chicago Press, 1998.

——. *Dissemination*. Trans. Barbara Johnson. Chicago: University of Chicago Press, 1981.

——. "*Khōra*." In *On The Name*, ed. Thomas Dutoit, trans. David Wood, John P. Leavey Jr., and Ian McLeod, 89–130. Palo Alto, CA: Stanford University Press, 1995.

——. *Margins of Philosophy*. Trans. Alan Bass. Chicago: University of Chicago Press, 1982 [1972].

——. *Monolingualism of the Other; or, The Prosthesis of Origin*. Trans. Patrick Mensah. Stanford, CA: Stanford University Press, 1998.

——. *Of Grammatology*. Corrected ed. Trans. Gayatri Chakravorty Spivak. Baltimore, MD: Johns Hopkins University Press, 1997.

——. *On Touching—Jean-Luc Nancy*. Trans. Christine Irizarry. Stanford, CA: Stanford University Press, 2005.

——. *Speech and Phenomena, and Other Essays on Husserl's Theory of Signs*. Trans. David Allison. Chicago: Northwestern University Press, 1973.

——. *Writing and Difference*. Trans. Alan Bass. Chicago: University of Chicago Press, 1978.

Descartes, René. *Discourse on Method and Meditations on First Philosophy*. Ed. David Weissman. New Haven, CT: Yale University Press, 1996.

DiGaetani, John Louis. *Richard Wagner and the Modern British Novel*. Rutherford, NJ: Fairleigh Dickinson University Press, 1978.

Dimock, Wai Chee. "A Theory of Resonance," *PMLA* 112, no. 5 (1997): 1060–71.

Doane, Mary Ann. *Femmes Fatales: Feminism, Film Theory, Psychoanalysis*. New York: Routledge, 1991.

Dolan, Emily. *The Orchestral Revolution: Haydn and Technologies of Timbre*. New York: Cambridge University Press, 2013.

Dolar, Mladen. *A Voice and Nothing More*. Cambridge, MA: MIT Press, 2006.

Douglass, Frederick. *The Narrative of the Life of Frederick Douglass, an American Slave, Written by Himself*. 21st ed. Chapel Hill: University of North Carolina Press, 1999. https://docsouth.unc.edu/neh/douglass/douglass.html.

Du Bois, W. E. B. *The Souls of Black Folk*. Ed. Henry Louis Gates Jr. and Terri Hume Oliver. New York: Norton, 1999.

Duffy, Nikolai. Introduction to *Gap Gardening: Selected Poems*, by Rosmarie Waldrop. New York: New Directions Books, 2016.

Dyson, Frances. "The Genealogy of Radio Voice." In *Radio Rethink: Art, Sound, and Transmission*, ed. Daina Augaitis and Dan Lander. Banff: Walter Phillips Gallery, 1994.

Ebileeni, Maurice. *Conrad, Faulkner, and the Problem of NonSense*. New York: Bloomsbury Academic, 2015.

Edison, Thomas A. "The Phonograph and Its Future." *North American Review* 126, no. 262 (1878): 527–36.

Edwards, Brent Hayes. *Epistrophies: Jazz and the Literary Imagination*. Cambridge, MA: Harvard University Press, 2017.

Eidsheim, Nina Sun. *The Race of Sound: Listening, Timbre, and Vocality in African American Music*. Durham, NC: Duke University Press, 2019.

Ellis, Nadia. *Territories of the Soul: Queered Belonging in the Black Diaspora*. Durham, NC: Duke University Press, 2015.

Eng, David. "Colonial Object Relations." *Social Text* vol. 34, no. 1 (2016): 1–19.

Erlmann, Veit. *Reason and Resonance: A History of Modern Aurality*. New York: Zone, 2010.

Eshun, Kodwo. *More Brilliant Than the Sun: Adventures in Sonic Fiction*. London: Quartet, 1998.

Fanon, Frantz. *Black Skin, White Masks*. Trans. Charles Lam Markmann. London: Pluto Press, 1986.

——. *Peau noire, masques blancs*. Paris: Éditions du Seuil, 1952.

——. "This Is the Voice of Algeria." In *A Dying Colonialism*, trans. Haakon Chevalier, 69–98. New York: Grove, 1965.

Faulkner, William. *Absalom, Absalom!*. Corrected text ed. New York: Vintage, 1990.

——. *As I Lay Dying*. Corrected text ed. New York: Vintage, 1990.

——. *Essays, Speeches, and Public Letters*. New York: Random House, 2011.

——. *Faulkner in the University*. Ed. Frederick Landis Gwynn and Joseph Leo Blotner. Charlottesville: University of Virginia Press, 1959.

——. *Sanctuary*. Corrected text ed. New York: Vintage, 1993.

——. *The Sound and the Fury*. Corrected text ed. New York: Vintage, 1984.

Faulkner, William, and Jean Stein. "William Faulkner: The Art of Fiction No. 12." *Paris Review* 12 (Spring 1956). https://www.theparisreview.org/interviews/4954/william-faulkner-the-art-of-fiction-no-12-william-faulkner.

Feld, Stephen. "Acoustemology." In *Key Words in Sound*, ed. David Novak and Matt Sakakeeny, 12–21. Durham, NC: Duke University Press, 2015.

Fiumara, Gemma Corradi. *The Otherside of Language: A Philosophy of Listening*. New York: Routledge, 1990.

Fitzgerald, F. Scott. *The Great Gatsby*. New York: Scribner, 2003.

Flatley, Jonathan. *Affective Mapping: Melancholia and the Politics of Modernism*. Cambridge, MA: Harvard University Press, 2009.

Flaubert, Gustave. *Correspondance*. Paris: L. Conard, 1910.

——. *The Letters of Gustave Flaubert: 1830–1857*. Ed. and trans. Francis Steegmuller. Cambridge, MA: Harvard University Press, 1980.

——. *Madame Bovary*. Trans. Geoffrey Wall. New York: Penguin, 2003.

——. "On Realism." In *Documents of Modernist Literary Realism*, ed. George J. Becker, 89–96. Princeton, NJ: Princeton University Press, 1963.

Fogel, Aaron. *The Coercion to Speech: Conrad's Poetics of Dialogue*. Cambridge, MA: Harvard University Press, 1985.

——. "The Mood of Overhearing in Conrad's Fiction." *Conradiana* 15, no. 2 (1984): 127–41.

Ford, Ford Madox. *Joseph Conrad: A Personal Remembrance*. https://gutenberg.ca /ebooks/fordfm-josephconrad/fordfm-josephconrad-00-h-dir/fordfm-josephconrad -00-h.html.

Foucault, Michel. *The Hermeneutics of the Subject: Lectures at the Collège de France 1981–1982*. Ed. Frédéric Gros. Trans. Graham Burchell. New York: Picador, 2005.

Frese Witt, Mary Anne. "D'Annunzio's Dionysian Women: The Rebirth of Tragey in Italy." In *Nietzsche and the Rebirth of the Tragic*, ed. Mary Anne Frese Witt, 72–103. Rutherford, NJ: Fairleigh Dickinson University Press, 2007.

Freud, Sigmund. *Beyond the Pleasure Principle*. Trans. James Strachey. New York: Norton, 1989.

——. *Civilization and its Discontents*. Trans. James Strachey. New York: Norton, 1989.

——. "'A Child Is Being Beaten': A Contribution to the Study of the Origin of Sexual Perversions." In *The Standard Edition of the Complete Psychological Works of Sigmund Freud*, ed. James Strachey, 17:175–204. London: Hogarth, 1955.

——. *Dora: An Analysis of a Case of Hysteria*. Ed. Philip Rieff. New York: Simon & Schuster, 1997.

——. "From the History of an Infantile Neurosis." In *The Standard Edition of the Complete Psychological Works of Sigmund Freud*, ed. James Strachey, 17:1–124. London: Hogarth, 1955.

——. *The Interpretation of Dreams*. Trans. James Strachey. New York: Avon, 1998.

——. "Mourning and Melancholia." In *The Standard Edition of the Complete Psychological Works of Sigmund Freud*, ed. James Strachey, 14:237–58. London: Hogarth, 1971.

——. *New Introductory Lectures on Psycho-Analysis*. Trans. James Strachey. New York: Norton, 1990.

——. "On Narcissism: An Introduction." In *The Standard Edition of the Complete Psychological Works of Sigmund Freud*, ed. James Strachey, 14:67–102. London: Hogarth, 1957.

——. "Two Encyclopedia Articles." In *The Standard Edition of the Complete Psychological Works of Sigmund Freud*, ed. James Strachey, 18:235–59. London: Hogarth, 1975.

——. "'Psychoanalyse' und 'Libidotheorie.'" In *Gesammelte Werke*, 13:211–33. London, 1940.

——. *The Psychopathology of Everyday Life*. Trans. Alan Tyson. New York: Norton, 1990.

——. *The Question of Lay Analysis*. Trans. James Strachey. New York: Norton, 1990.

——. "Trauer und Melancholie." In *Gesammelte Werke*, 10:428–46. London: Imago, 1991.

Fried, Michael. "Almayer's Face: On 'Impressionism' in Conrad, Crane, and Norris." *Critical Inquiry* 17, no. 1 (1990): 193–236.

——. "Response to Bill Brown," *Critical Inquiry* 18, no. 2 (1992): 403–10.

——. *What Was Literary Impressionism?* Cambridge, MA: Harvard University Press, 2018.

Friedlander, Eli. "On the Musical Gathering of Echoes of the Voice: Walter Benjamin on Opera and the *Trauerspiel*." *Opera Quarterly* 21, no. 4 (2005): 631–46.

Gasché, Rodolphe. *Of Minimal Things: Studies on the Notion of Relation*. Stanford, CA: Stanford University Press, 1999.

Gallope, Michael. *Deep Refrains: Music, Philosophy, and the Ineffable*. Chicago: University of Chicago Press, 2017.

Genette, Gérard. *Narrative Discourse: An Essay in Method*. Trans. J. E. Lewin. Ithaca, NY: Cornell University Press, 1972.

Gilroy, Paul. *The Black Atlantic: Modernity and Double Consciousness*. Cambridge, MA: Harvard University Press, 1993.

Gitelman, Lisa. *Scripts, Grooves, and Writing Machines: Representing Technology in the Edison Era*. Stanford, CA: Stanford University Press, 2000.

Gleeson-White, Sarah. "Auditory Exposures: Faulkner, Eisenstein, and Film Sound." *PMLA* 128, no. 1 (January 2013): 87–100.

Glissant, Édouard. *Caribbean Discourse: Selected Essays*. Trans. J. Michael Dash. Charlottesville: University Press of Virginia, 1989.

——. *Faulkner, Mississippi*. New York: Farrar, Straus and Giroux, 1999.

——. *Poetics of Relation*. Trans. Betsy Wing. Ann Arbor: University of Michigan Press, 1997.

Goble, Mark. *Beautiful Circuits: Modernism and the Mediated Life*. New York: Columbia University Press, 2010.

Goehr, Lydia. "Radical Modernism and the Failure of Style: Philosophical Reflections on Maeterlinck-Debussy's *Pelléas et Mélisande*." *Representations* 74, no. 1 (2001): 55–82.

GoGwilt, Christopher L. "Conrad and Romanised Print Form: From Tuan Almayer to 'Prince Roman.'" In *Conrad and Language*, ed. Katherine Isobel Baxter and Robert Hampson, 117–31. Edinburgh: Edinburgh University Press, 2016.

——. "Conrad's Accusative Case: Romanization, Changing Loyalties, and Switching Scripts." *Conradiana* 46, nos. 1–2 (2014): 53–62.

——. *The Invention of the West: Joseph Conrad and the Double-Mapping of Europe and Empire*. Stanford, CA: Stanford University Press, 1995.

——. *The Passage of Literature: Genealogies of Modernism in Conrad, Rhys, and Pramoedya*. New York: Oxford University Press, 2011.

Greaney, Michael. *Conrad, Language, and Narrative*. Cambridge: Cambridge University Press, 2005.

Greenblatt, Stephen. "Resonance and Wonder." *Bulletin of the American Academy of Arts and Sciences* 43, no. 4 (1990): 11–34.

Grivel, Charles. "The Phonograph's Horned Mouth." In *Wireless Imagination: Sound, Radio, and the Avant-Garde*, ed. Douglas Kahn and Gregory Whitehead, 31–62. Cambridge, MA: MIT Press, 1992.

Guerard, Albert J. *Conrad the Novelist*. Cambridge, MA: Harvard University Press, 1958.

——. "The Nigger of the Narcissus." *Kenyon Review* 19, no. 2 (1957): 205–32.

Haiven, Max. *Revenge Capitalism: The Ghosts of Empire, the Demons of Capital, and the Settling of Unpayable Debts*. London: Pluto, 2020.

Hale, Dorothy J. *Social Formalism: The Novel in Theory from Henry James to the Present*. Stanford, CA: Stanford University Press, 1998.

——. "Structuralism, Narratology, Deconstruction." In *The Novel: An Anthology of Criticism and Theory, 1900–2000*, ed. Dorothy J. Hale, 186–204. Malden, MA: Blackwell, 2006.

Hampson, Robert. *Cross-Cultural Encounters in Joseph Conrad's Malay Fiction: Writing Malaysia*. London: Palgrave, 2000.

Harpham, Geoffrey Galt. *One of Us: The Mastery of Joseph Conrad*. Chicago: University of Chicago Press, 1996.

Hartman, Geoffrey. "I. A. Richards and the Dream of Communication." In *The Fate of Reading and Other Essays*, 20–40. Chicago: University of Chicago Press, 1975.

Hartman, Saidiya. *Lose Your Mother: A Journey along the Atlantic Slave Route*. New York: Farrar, Straus, and Giroux, 2007.

——. "Venus in Two Acts." *Small Axe* 12, no. 2 (2008): 1–14.

Hay, Eloise K. "Lord Jim: From Sketch to Novel." *Comparative Literature* 12, no. 4 (1960): 289–309.

Heath, Stephen. "Narrative Space." In *Questions of Cinema*, 19–75. Bloomington: University of Indiana Press, 1981.

Hegel, G. W. F. *Aesthetics*. Vol. 2. Trans. T. M. Knox. Oxford: Clarendon, 1975.

——. *Phenomenology of Spirit*. Trans. Arnold V. Miller. Oxford: Clarendon, 1977.

Heidegger, Martin. *Art and Space*. Trans. Charles Siebert. The Hague: Nijhoff, 1973.

——. *Being and Time*. Trans. Joan Stambaugh. Albany: State University of New York Press, 1996.

——. *On the Way to Language*. Trans. Peter D. Hertz. New York: Harper & Row, 1971.

——. *Sein und Zeit*. Tubingen: Max Niemerer Verlag, 1993.

Heller-Roazen, Daniel. *Echolalias: On the Forgetting of Language*. New York: Zone, 2005.

Helmreich, Stefan. "Transduction." In *Keywords in Sound*, ed. David Novak and Matt Sakakeeny, 222–31. Durham, NC: Duke University Press, 2015.

Hertz, Robert. "The Pre-Eminence of the Right Hand: A Study in Religious Polarity." *HAU: Journal of Ethnographic Theory* 3, no. 2 (2013): 335–57.

Hill, Edwin C., Jr. *Black Soundscapes White Stages: The Meaning of Francophone Sound in the Black Atlantic*. Baltimore, MD: Johns Hopkins Press, 2013.

Hochman, Brian. *Savage Preservation: The Ethnographic Origins of Modern Media Technology*. Minneapolis: University of Minnesota Press, 2014.

Hollander, John. *The Figure of Echo: A Mode of Allusion in Milton and After*. Berkeley: University of California Press, 1984.

———. *Vision and Resonance: Two Senses of Poetic Form*. 2nd ed. New Haven, CT: Yale University Press, 1985.

Hughes, Langston. *The Big Sea: An Autobiography*. New York: Hill and Wang, 1993.

Hunt, Nancy Rose. "An Acoustic Register, Tenacious Images, and Congolese Scenes of Rape and Repetition." *Cultural Anthropology* 23, no. 2 (2008): 220–53.

Ingarden, Roman. *The Literary Work of Art: An Investigation on the Borderlines of Ontology, Logic, and the Theory of Literature*. Trans. George G. Grabowicz. Evanston, IL: Northwestern University Press, 1973.

Irwin, John T. *Doubling and Incest/Repetition and Revenge: A Speculative Reading of Faulkner*. Expanded ed. Baltimore, MD: Johns Hopkins University Press, 1996.

Iser, Wolfgang. *The Act of Reading: A Theory of Aesthetic Response*. Baltimore, MD: Johns Hopkins University Press, 1980.

Israel, Nico. *Outlandish: Writing between Exile and Diaspora*. Stanford, CA: Stanford University Press, 2000.

Jakobson, Roman. "Linguistics and Poetics." In *Style in Language*, ed. Thomas A. Sebeok, 350–77. New York: John Wiley and Sons, 1960.

James, Henry. *The Art of Fiction and Other Essays*. Oxford: Oxford University Press, 1948.

———. *The Portrait of a Lady*. 2nd Norton Critical ed. New York: Norton, 1995.

Jameson, Fredric. "Criticism in History." In *Weapons of Criticism: Marxism in America and the Literary Tradition*, ed. Norman Rudich, 31–50. Palo Alto, CA: Stanford University Press, 1976.

———. *The Political Unconscious: Narrative as a Socially Symbolic Act*. Ithaca, NY: Cornell University Press, 1981.

Janechek, Jennifer. "The Horror of the Primal Sound: Proto-telephony and Imperialism in 'Heart of Darkness.'" *The Conradian* 41, no. 2 (2016): 8–27.

Jean-Aubrey, G. *Joseph Conrad: Life and Letters*. 2 vols. Garden City, NY: Doubleday, Page, and Co., 1927.

Johnson, Barbara. "Animation, Abortion, Apostrophe." *Diacritics* 16, no. 1 (1986): 28–47.

———. *The Feminist Difference: Literature, Psychoanalysis, Race, and Gender*. Cambridge, MA: Harvard University Press, 2000.

Just, Daniel. *Literature, Ethics, and Decolonization in Postwar France: The Politics of Disengagement*. New York: Cambridge University Press, 2015.

Kahn, Douglas. *Earth Sound Earth Signal: Energies and Earth Magnitude in the Arts*. Berkeley: University of California Press, 2013.

Kammen, Douglas. "Conrad and Coal." *Los Angeles Review of Books*, December 11, 2019. https://lareviewofbooks.org/article/conrad-and-coal/.

Kane, Brian. "Jean-Luc Nancy and the Listening Subject." *Contemporary Music Review* 31, nos. 5–6 (2012): 439–47.

———. *Sound Unseen: Acousmatic Sound in Theory and Practice*. New York: Oxford University Press, 2014.

Keeling, Kara. *The Witch's Flight: The Cinematic, the Black Femme, and the Image of Common Sense*. Durham, NC: Duke University Press, 2007.

Khanna, Ranjana. *Dark Continents: Psychoanalysis and Colonialism*. Durham, NC: Duke University Press, 2003.

Khatib, Sami. "The Messianic without Messianism: Walter Benjamin's Materialist Theology." *Anthropology & Materialism* 1 (2013). http://journals.openedition.org /am/159.

Kheshti, Roshanak. *Modernity's Ear: Listening to Race and Gender in World Music*. New York: NYU Press, 2015.

Kincaid, Jamaica. "Flowers of Evil." *New Yorker*, October 5, 1992, 154–59.

Kittler, Friedrich A. *Discourse Networks, 1800/1900*. Trans. Michael Metteer and Chris Cullens. Stanford, CA: Stanford University Press, 1992.

———. *Gramophone, Film, Typewriter*. Trans. Geoffrey Winthrop-Young and Michael Wutz. Stanford, CA: Stanford University Press, 1999.

Kolocotroni, Vassiliki. "1899, Vienna, and the Congo: The Art of Darkness." In *The Edinburgh Companion to Twentieth-Century Literatures in English*, 11–22. Edinburgh: Edinburgh University Press, 2006.

Kreilkamp, Ivan. "A Voice without a Body: The Phonographic Logic of 'Heart of Darkness.'" *Victorian Studies* 40, no. 2 (1997): 211–44.

Krishnan, Sanjay. "Seeing the Animal: Colonial Space and Movement in Joseph Conrad's *Lord Jim*." *Novel* 37, no. 3 (November 1, 2004): 326–35.

Kristeva, Julia. *Revolution in Poetic Language*. Trans. Margaret Waller. New York: Columbia University Press, 1984.

———. "The Speaking Subject." In *On Signs*, ed. Marshall Blonsky, 210–20. Baltimore, MD: Johns Hopkins University Press, 1985.

Lacan, Jacques. *Écrits: The First Complete Edition in English*. Trans. Bruce Fink. New York: Norton, 2006.

———. *The Ego in Freud's Theory and in the Technique of Psychoanalysis, 1954–1955:*

The Seminar of Jacques Lacan, Book II. Ed. Jacques-Alain Miller. Trans. Sylvana Tomaselli. New York: Norton, 1991.

——. *The Four Fundamental Concepts of Psychoanalysis: The Seminar of Jacques Lacan, Book XI*. Ed. Jacques-Alain Miller. Trans. Alan Sheridan. New York: Norton, 1998.

Lacoue-Labarthe, Philippe. "The Horror of the West." In *Conrad's "Heart of Darkness" and Contemporary Thought: Revisiting the Horror with Phillipe Lacoue-Labarthe*, ed. Nidesh Lawtoo. London: Bloomsbury, 2012.

——. *Typography: Mimesis, Philosophy, Politics*. Trans. Christopher Fynsk. Cambridge, MA: Harvard University Press, 1989.

Lagaay, Alice. "Between Sound and Silence: Voice in the History of Psychoanalysis." *Episteme* 1, no. 1 (2008): 53–62.

Lane, Christopher. "Almayer's Defeat: The Trauma of Colonialism in Conrad's Early Work." *Novel* 32, no. 3 (Summer 1999): 401–28.

Laplanche, Jean. *Essays on Otherness*. Ed. John Fletcher. New York: Routledge, 1999.

Lawtoo, Nidesh. *Conrad's Shadow: Catastrophe, Mimesis, Theory*. East Lansing: Michigan State University Press, 2016.

——. *The Phantom of the Ego: Modernism and the Mimetic Unconscious*. East Lansing: Michigan State University Press, 2013.

Laynton, Robert. *Behind the Masks of God*. Rev. and exp. 2nd ed. Straffordshire, UK: Stoke-on-Trent, 2016.

Lebow, Alisa. "Identity Slips: The Autobiographical Register in the Work of Chantal Akerman." *Film Quarterly* 70, no. 1 (Fall 2016): 54–60.

Lejeune, Philippe. *On Autobiography*. Trans. Katherine Leary. Minneapolis: University of Minnesota Press, 1988.

Levenson, Michael H. *A Genealogy of Modernism: A Study of English Literary Doctrine, 1908–1922*. New York: Cambridge University Press, 1986.

Levin, Yael. *Tracing the Aesthetic Principle in Conrad's Novels*. New York: Palgrave Macmillan, 2002.

Llewelyn, John. *Margins of Religion: Between Kierkegaard and Derrida*. Bloomington: Indiana University Press, 2008.

London, Bette Lynn. *The Appropriated Voice: Narrative Authority in Conrad, Forster, and Woolf*. Ann Arbor: University of Michigan Press, 1990.

Lordi, Emily J. *Black Resonance: Iconic Women Singers and African American Literature*. New Brunswick, NJ: Rutgers University Press, 2013.

Lott, Eric. "Love and Theft: The Racial Unconscious of Blackface Minstrelsy." *Representations* 39 (Summer 1992): 23–50.

Lowe, Lisa. *The Intimacies of Four Continents*. Durham, NC: Duke University Press, 2015.

Lubbock, Percy. *The Craft of Fiction*. Project Gutenberg. https://www.gutenberg.org
/files/18961/18961-h/18961-h.htm.

Lukács, Georg. *The Theory of the Novel: A Historico-Philosophical Essay on the Forms
of Great Epic Literature*. Trans. Anna Bostock. Cambridge, MA: MIT Press, 1971.

Lyotard, Jean-François. *The Postmodern Condition*. Trans. Geoff Bennington and
Brian Massumi. Minneapolis: University of Minnesota Press, 1984.

Macherey, Pierre. "Figures of Interpellation in Althusser and Fanon." *Radical Philosophy*, May/June 2012, https://www.radicalphilosophy.com/article/figures-of
-interpellation-in-althusser-and-fanon.

Mallios, Peter Lancelot. *Our Conrad: Constituting American Modernity*. Stanford, CA:
Stanford University Press, 2010.

Marcus, Sara. *Political Disappointment: A Partial History*. Cambridge, MA: Harvard
University Press, forthcoming.

———. "Untimely Feedback." *Artforum*, December 7, 2016. https://www.artforum.com
/slant/mourning-after-sara-marcus-on-the-us-presidential-election-65119.

Marcuse, Herbert. *Reason and Revolution*. New York: Beacon, 1960.

Matthews, John T. "Dialect and Modernism." In *The Sound and the Fury: An Authoritative Text, Backgrounds and Contexts, Criticism*, ed. Michael Gorra, 484–93.
New York: Norton, 2014.

———. "Recalling the West Indies: From Yoknapatawpha to Haiti and Back." *American
Literary History* 16, no. 2 (April 13, 2004): 238–62.

McClary, Susan. *Feminine Endings: Music, Gender, and Sexuality*. Minneapolis: University of Minnesota Press, 2002.

McCluskey, Kathleen. *Reverberations: Sound and Structure in the Novels of Virginia
Woolf*. Ann Arbor: UMI Research Press, 1986.

McEnaney, Tom. *Acoustic Properties: Radio, Narrative, and the New Neighborhood of
the Americas*. Evanston, IL: Northwestern University Press, 2017.

McGurl, Mark. *The Program Era: Postwar Fiction and the Rise of Creative Writing*.
Cambridge, MA: Harvard University Press, 2009.

McPherran, Mark L. "Introducing a New God: Socrates and His *Daimonion*." In
Socrates' Divine Sign: Religion, Practice, and Value in Socratic Philosophy, ed.
Pierre Desirée and Nicolas D. Smith, 13–30. Kelowna, BC: Academic Printing and
Publishing, 2005.

Metz, Christian. "Aural Objects." Trans. Georgia Gurrieri. *Yale French Studies* 60
(1980): 24–32.

———. *The Imaginary Signifier: Psychoanalysis and the Cinema*. Trans. Celia Britton,
Annwyl Williams, Ben Brewster, and Alfred Guzzetti. Bloomington: Indiana University Press, 1982.

Miller, Christopher L. *Blank Darkness: Africanist Discourse in French*. Chicago: University of Chicago Press, 1985.

Miller, J. Hillis. "Should We Read 'Heart of Darkness'?" In *Heart of Darkness*, 4th Norton Critical ed., ed. Paul B. Armstrong, 463–73. New York: Norton, 2006.

Millgate, Michael. *Faulkner's Place*. Athens: University of Georgia Press, 1997.

Morrison, Toni. *Tar Baby*. 1st Vintage International ed. New York, Vintage, 2004.

———. "Unspeakable Things Unspoken: The Afro-American Presence in American Literature." Tanner Humanities Center, University of Utah. https://tannerlectures.utah.edu/_documents/a-to-z/m/morrison90.pdf.

Mosès, Stéphane. "Émile Benveniste and the Linguistics of Dialogue." *Revue de Métaphysique et de Morale* 32 (2001): 509–25. https://www.cairn-int.info/focus-E_RMM_014_0509-emile-benveniste-and-the-linguistics-of.htm.

Moten, Fred. "Blackness and Nothingness (Mysticism in the Flesh)." *South Atlantic Quarterly* 112, no. 4 (October 2013): 737–80.

———. "The Case of Blackness." *Criticism* 50, no. 2 (2008): 177–218.

———. *In the Break: The Aesthetics of the Black Radical Tradition*. Minneapolis: University of Minnesota Press, 2003.

Mowitt, John. *Percussion: Drumming, Beating, Striking*. Durham, NC: Duke University Press, 2002.

———. *Sounds: The Ambient Humanities*. Berkeley: University of California Press, 2015.

Naddaff, Ramona. *Exiling the Poets: The Production of Censorship in Plato's Republic*. Chicago: University of Chicago Press, 2002.

Nadelhaft, Ruth. *Joseph Conrad: A Feminist Reading*. Atlantic Highlands, NJ: Humanities Press International, 1991.

Nancy, Jean-Luc. *Listening*. Trans. Charlotte Mandell. New York: Fordham University Press, 2017.

———. "Récit Recitation Recitative." In *Speaking of Music: Addressing the Sonorous*, ed. Keith Chapin and Andrew H. Clark, trans. Charlotte Mandell, 243–55. New York: Fordham University Press, 2013.

Napolin, Julie Beth. "The Acoustics of Narrative Involvement: Modernism, Subjectivity, Voice." PhD diss., UC Berkeley, 2010. https://escholarship.org/uc/item/1ws2f1tr.

———. "Elliptical Sound: Audibility and the Space of Reading." In *Sounding Modernism: Rhythm and Sonic Mediation in Modern Literature and Film*, ed. Helen Groth Murphet and Penelope Hone. Edinburgh: Edinburgh University Press, 2017.

———. "The Expropriated Voice." In *Faulkner and Slavery*, ed. Jay Watson and James G. Thomas Jr. Oxford: University of Mississippi Press, forthcoming.

———. "The Fact of Resonance: An Acoustics of Determination in Faulkner and Benjamin." *Symploke* 24, nos. 1–2 (2016): 171–86.

———. "Music's Unseen Body: Conrad, Cowell, Du Bois and the Beginnings of Experimental Music." *Conradiana* 48, nos. 2–3 (2016): 143–62.

———. "On Banishing Socrates' Wife: The Interiority of the Ear in *Phaedo*." In *Poiesis*, ed. Nathan Brown and Petar Milat, 156–75. Zagreb: Multimedijalni Institute, 2017.

———. "'A Sinister Resonance': Joseph Conrad's Malay Ear and Auditory Cultural Studies." In *Sounding Out! The Sound Studies Blog*, July 9, 2015. http://web.archive.org/web/20191219153239/https://soundstudiesblog.com/?s=Conrad%27s+malay+ear.

———. "'A Sinister Resonance': Vibration, Sound, and the Birth of Conrad's Marlow." *Qui Parle* 21 no. 2 (2013): 69–100.

Napolin, Julie Beth, and Mariana Rosenfeld. "The Politics of the Musical Situation." *Continent* 5, no. 3 (2016) http://continentcontinent.cc/index.php/continent/article/view/266.

Ngugi wa Thiong'o. "The Contradictions of Joseph Conrad." *New York Times*, November 21, 2017. https://www.nytimes.com/2017/11/21/books/review/dawn-watch-joseph-conrad-biography-maya-jasanoff.html.

North, Michael. *The Dialect of Modernism: Race, Language, and Twentieth-Century Literature*. New York: Oxford University Press, 1998.

Novak, David, and Matt Sakakeeny. Introduction to *Keywords in Sound*, ed. David Novak and Matt Sakakeeny, 1–11. Durham, NC: Duke University Press, 2015.

Ochoa Gautier, Ana María. *Aurality: Listening and Knowledge in Nineteenth-Century Colombia*. Durham, NC: Duke University Press, 2014.

Ovid, *Metamorphoses*. http://perseus.uchicago.edu/perseus-cgi/citequery3.pl?dbname=LatinAugust2012&query=Ov.%20Met.&getid=1.

Patron, Sylvie. "Homonymy, Polysemy, and Synonymy: Reflections on the Notion of Voice." In *Strange Voices in Narrative Fiction*, ed. Krogh Hansen, Stefan Iversen, Henrik Skov Nielsen, and Rolf Reitan, 13–36. Berlin: Walter de Gruyter, 2011.

Pecora, Vincent. "*Heart of Darkness* and the Phenomenology of Voice." *ELH* 52, no. 4 (1985): 993–1015.

Penman, Ian. *On the Mic: How Amplification Changed the Voice for Good*. New York: Continuum, 2002.

Pettman, Dominic. "Pavlov's Podcast: The Acousmatic Voice in the Age of Mp3s." *Differences* 22, nos. 2–3 (December 1, 2011): 140–67.

Pickering, Michael. "The Blackface Clown." In *Black Victorians/Black Victoriana*, ed. Gretchen Holbrook, 159–74. New Brunswick, NJ: Rutgers University Press, 2013.

Plato. *Phaedo*. Trans. Eva Brann et al. Newburyport, MA: Focus, 1998.

Porter, Carolyn. *Seeing and Being: The Plight of the Participant-Observer in Emerson, James, Adams, and Faulkner*. Middletown, CT: Wesleyan University Press, 1981.

Poulet, Georges. "The Phenomenology of Reading." *New Literary History* 1, no. 1 (1969): 53–68.

Pratt, Mary Louise. *Imperial Eyes: Travel Writing and Transculturation*. New York: Routledge, 1992.

Prendergast, John, and Shasha Lezhnev. "From Mine to Mobile Phone: The Conflict

Mineral Supply Chain." *The Enough Project*. December 10, 2019. https://enough
project.org/files/minetomobile.pdf.

Prince, Gerald. *A Dictionary of Narratology*. Rev. ed. Lincoln: University of Nebraska
Press, 2003.

———. "The Disnarrated." *Style* 22, no. 1 (1988): 1–8.

———. "On a Postcolonial Narratology." In *A Companion to Narrative Theory*, ed.
James Phelan and Peter J. Rabinowitz, 372–81. Malden, MA: Blackwell, 2005.

Quashie, Kevin. *The Sovereignty of Quiet: Beyond Resistance in Black Culture*. New
Brunswick, NJ: Rutgers University Press, 2012.

Radano, Ronald. "Denoting Difference: The Writing of the Slave Spirituals." *Critical
Inquiry* 22, no. 3 (1996): 506–44.

Ramazani, Jahan. *A Transnational Poetics*. Chicago: University of Chicago Press, 2009.

Rancière, Jacques. *The Politics of Aesthetics: The Distribution of the Sensible*. Trans.
Gabriel Rockhill. New York: Continuum, 2004.

Rangan, Pooja. *Immediations: The Humanitarian Impulse in Documentary*. Durham,
NC: Duke University Press, 2017.

Rehding, Alexander. "The Quest for the Origins of Music in Germany circa 1900."
Journal of the American Musicological Society 53, no. 2 (July, 2000): 345–85.

Richardson, Brian. "Silence, Progression, and Narrative Collapse in Conrad."
Conradiana 46 no. 1 (2015): 109–21.

Riley, Denise. "'A Voice without a Mouth': Inner Speech." *Qui Parle* 14, no. 2 (2004):
57–104.

———. *The Words of Selves: Identification, Solidarity, Irony*. Stanford, CA: Stanford
University Press, 2000.

Roach, Joseph R. *Cities of the Dead: Circum-Atlantic Performance*. New York: Columbia University Press, 1996.

Rogin, Michael. *Blackface, White Noise: Jewish Immigrants in the Hollywood Melting
Pot*. Berkeley: University of California Press, 1998.

Romanick Baldwin, Debra. "Marlow, Socrates, and an Ancient Quarrel in *Chance*." In
Centennial Essays on Joseph Conrad's Chance, ed. Allan H. Simmons and Susan
Jones, 53–65. Boston: Brill Rodopi, 2016.

Ronell, Avital. *The Telephone Book: Technology, Schizophrenia, Electric Speech*. Lincoln: The University of Nebraska Press, 1989.

Rose, Jacqueline. *States of Fantasy: The Clarendon Lecture in English Literature,
1994*. New York: Oxford University Press, 1996.

Ross, Alex. *The Rest Is Noise: Listening to the Twentieth Century*. New York: Farrar,
Straus and Giroux, 2007.

Ross, Stephen M. "Conrad's Influence on Faulkner's *Absalom, Absalom!*" *Studies in
American Fiction* 2, no. 2 (1974): 199–209.

———. *Fiction's Inexhaustible Voice: Speech and Writing in Faulkner*. Athens: University of Georgia Press, 1989.

Rousseau, Jean-Jacques. *Rousseau: "The Discourses" and Other Early Political Writings*. Ed. Victor Gourevitch. Cambridge: Cambridge University Press, 1997.

Said, Edward W. *Beginnings: Intention and Method*. New York: Columbia University Press, 1985 [1975].

———. "Conrad and Nietzsche." In *Reflections on Exile and Other Essays*, 70–82. Cambridge, MA: Harvard University Press, 2000.

———. "Conrad: The Presentation of Narrative." *Novel: A Forum on Fiction* 7, no. 2 (Winter 1974): 116–32.

———. *Culture and Imperialism*. New York: Vintage, 1994.

———. *Joseph Conrad and the Fiction of Autobiography*. New York: Columbia University Press, 2008.

———. *Orientalism*. New York: Vintage, 1979 [1978].

———. *The World, the Text, and the Critic*. Cambridge, MA: Harvard University Press, 1983.

Saint-Amour, Paul K. "*Ulysses* Pianola." *PMLA* 130 (2015): 15–36.

Scarry, Elaine. *Dreaming by the Book*. New York: FSG, 1999.

Schaeffer, Pierre. "Acousmatics." In *Audio Culture: Readings in Modern Music*, ed. Christoph Cox and Daniel Warner, 76–81. New York: Continuum, 2004.

Schafer, R. Murray. "The Music of the Environment." In *Audio Culture: Readings in Modern Music*, ed. Christoph Cox and Daniel Warner, 29–39. New York: Continuum, 2004.

———. *The Soundscape: Our Sonic Environment and the Tuning of the World*. Rochester, VT: Destiny, 1994.

Schmid, Wolf. "Narratee." In *The Living Handbook of Narratology*. http://www.lhn.uni -hamburg.de/article/narratee.

Schopenhauer, Arthur. *The World as Will and Idea*. Vol. 1. Trans. R. B. Haldane and J. Kemp. Project Gutenberg. http://www.gutenberg.org/files/38427/38427-h/38427 -h.html.

Schor, Naomi. *Reading in Detail: Aesthetics and the Feminine*. New York: Routledge, 2007.

Schorske, Charles E. *Fin-De-Siècle Vienna: Politics and Culture*. New York: Vintage, 1980.

Scott, Joan W. "Fantasy Echo: History and the Construction of Identity." *Critical Inquiry* 27, no. 2 (2001): 284–304.

Sedgwick, Eve Kosofsky. "Paranoid Reading and Reparative Reading, or, You're So Paranoid, You Probably Think This Essay Is About You." In *Touching Feeling: Affect, Pedagogy, Performativity*, 123–51. Durham, NC: Duke University Press, 2003.

Serpell, C. Namwali. *Seven Modes of Uncertainty*. Cambridge, MA: Harvard University Press, 2014.

Sewlall, Harry. "Writing from the Periphery: The Case of Ngugi and Conrad." *English in Africa* 30, no. 1 (2003): 55–69.

Sharpe, Christina. *In the Wake: On Blackness and Being*. Durham, NC: Duke University Press, 2016.

Silverman, Kaja. *The Acoustic Mirror: The Female Voice in Psychoanalysis and Cinema*. Bloomington: Indiana University Press, 1988.

———. *The Threshold of the Visible World*. New York: Routledge, 1996.

Sliwinski, Sharon. *Human Rights on Camera*. Chicago: University of Chicago Press, 2011.

Smith, P. Christopher. *The Hermeneutics of Original Argument: Demonstration, Dialectic, Rhetoric*. Chicago: Northwestern University Press, 1998.

Sollors, Werner. "Incest and Miscegenation." In *Neither Black nor White yet Both: Thematic Explorations of Interracial Literature*, 285–335. New York: Oxford University Press, 1997.

Spillers, Hortense J. "'Born Again': Faulkner and the Second Birth." In *Fifty Years after Faulkner*, ed. Jay Watson and Ann J. Abadie, 57–79. Jackson: University Press of Mississippi, 2016.

———. "Mama's Baby, Papa's Maybe: An American Grammar Book." *Diacritics* 17, no. 2 (Summer 1987): 64–81.

Spivak, Gayatri Chakravorty. "Can the Subaltern Speak?" In *Colonial Discourse and Postcolonial Theory: A Reader*, ed. Patrick Williams and Laura Chrisman, 66–111. New York: Columbia University Press, 1994.

———. *The Critique of Postcolonial Reason: Toward a History of the Vanishing Present*. Cambridge, MA: Harvard University Press, 1999.

———. "Echo." *New Literary History* 24, no. 1 (1993): 17–43.

Stecopoulos, Harilaos. "South to the World: William Faulkner and the American Century." In *William Faulkner in Context*, ed. John Matthews, 147–55. New York: Cambridge University Press, 2015.

Steege, Benjamin. "Between Race and Culture: Hearing Japanese Music in Berlin." *History of Humanities* 2 (2017): 361–74.

———. *Helmholtz and the Modern Listener*. New York: Cambridge University Press, 2012.

Sterne, Jonathan. *Audible Past: Cultural Origins of Sound Reproduction*. Chapel Hill, NC: Duke University Press, 2003.

Sterne, Jonathan, and Tara Rodgers. "The Poetics of Signal Processing." *Differences* 22, nos. 2–3 (January 1, 2011): 31–53.

Stewart, Garrett. *Reading Voices: Literature and the Phonotext*. Berkeley: University of California Press, 1990.

Stirling, James Hutchinson. *The Secret of Hegel: Being the Hegelian System in Origin, Principle, Form, and Matter*. Vol. 2. London: Longman, Roberts, and Green, 1865.

Stoever, Jennifer Lynn. "Fine-Tuning the Sonic Color-Line: Radio and the Acousmatic Du Bois." *Modernist Cultures* 10, no. 1 (2015): 99–118.

——. *The Sonic Color Line: Race and the Cultural Politics of Listening*. New York: New York University Press, 2016.

Stoler, Ann Laura. *Along the Archival Grain: Epistemic Anxieties and Colonial Common Sense*. Princeton, NJ: Princeton University Press, 2010.

——. *Carnal Knowledge and Imperial Power: Race and the Intimate in Colonial Rule*. Berkeley, CA: University of California Press, 2002.

——, ed. *Imperial Debris: On Ruins and Ruination*. Durham, NC: Duke University Press, 2013.

——. *Race and the Education of Desire: Foucault's History of Sexuality and the Colonial Order of Things*. Durham, NC: Duke University Press, 1995.

Suisman, David. *Selling Sounds: The Commercial Revolution in American Music*. Cambridge, MA: Harvard University Press, 2010.

Sundquist, Eric J. *To Wake the Nations: Race in the Making of American Literature*. Cambridge, MA: Belknap, 1998.

Syms, Martine. "Black Vernacular: Reading New Media." http://martinesyms.com/black-vernacular-reading-new-media/.

"Syncopation." *Grove Music Online*. https://doi.org/10.1093/gmo/9781561592630.article.27263.

Szczypien, Jean M. "A Draft of a Polish Conrad Letter in the Manuscript of 'Almayer's Folly.'" *Polish Review* 43, no. 3 (1998): 355–59.

Szendy, Peter. *All Ears: The Aesthetics of Espionage*. New York: Fordham University Press, 2016.

——. *Listen: A History of Our Ears*. New York: Fordham University Press, 2008.

Taussig, Michael. *Mimesis and Alterity: A Particular History of the Senses*. New York: Routledge, 1993.

Thompson, Emily Ann. *The Soundscape of Modernity: Architectural Acoustics and the Culture of Listening in America, 1900–1933*. Cambridge, MA: MIT Press, 2004.

Thompson, Marie. *Beyond Unwanted Sound: Noise, Affect, and Aesthetic Moralism*. New York: Bloomsbury, 2017.

Thoreau, Henry David. *Walden and Civil Disobedience*. New York: Penguin, 1986.

Toop, David. *Ocean of Sound: Aether Talk, Ambient Sound, and Imaginary Worlds*. London: Serpent's Tail, 1995.

——. *Sinister Resonance: The Mediumship of the Listener*. New York: Continuum, 2010.

Trinh, Minh-ha T. *Cinema Interval*. New York: Routledge, 1999.

——. *Reassemblage*. New York: Women Make Movies, 1983. DVD.

——. *When the Moon Waxes Red: Representation, Gender, and Cultural Politics*. New York: Routledge, 1991.

——. *Woman, Native, Other: Writing Postcoloniality and Feminism*. Bloomington: Indiana University Press, 1989.

Wall, Cheryl A. "Resounding Souls: Du Bois and the African American Literary Tradition." *Public Culture* 17, no. 2 (May 2005): 217–34.

Waltham-Smith, Naomi. *Music and Belonging between Revolution and Restoration.* New York: Oxford University Press, 2017.

———. *The Sound of Life.* New York: Fordham University Press, forthcoming.

Warhol, Robyn R. "Narrating the Unnarratable: Gender and Metonymy in the Victorian Novel." *Style* 28, no. 1 (1994): 74–94.

Watson, James Gray. *William Faulkner, Letters and Fictions.* Austin: University of Texas Press, 1987.

Watson, Jay. Introduction to *Faulkner and the Literature of the Black Americas,* ed. Jay Watson and James G. Thomas Jr., vii–xxiv. Jackson: University Press of Mississippi, 2016.

———. "The Unsyncable William Faulkner." In *William Faulkner in the Media Ecology,* ed. Julian Murphet and Stephan Solomon. Baton Rouge: Louisiana State University Press, 2015.

Watt, Ian. *Conrad in the Nineteenth Century.* Berkeley: University of California Press, 1979.

———. "Conrad's Preface to *The Nigger of the 'Narcissus.'*" *NOVEL: A Forum on Fiction* 7, no. 2 (1974): 101–15.

Weatherford-Jacobs, Odesa M. "Hegel and Du Bois: A Study of the Influence of G. W. F. Hegel on the Early Writings of W. E. B. Du Bois (1896–1903)." PhD diss., St. Louis University, 2002.

Wiegel, Sigrid. *Body- and Image-Space: Re-reading Walter Benjamin,* trans. Georgina Paul with Rachel McNicholl and Jeremey Gaines. New York: Routledge, 1996.

Weheliye, Alexander G. *Habeas Viscus: Racializing Assemblages, Biopolitics, and Black Feminist Theories of the Human.* Durham, NC: Duke University Press, 2014.

———. *Phonographies: Grooves in Sonic Afro-Modernity.* Durham, NC: Duke University Press, 2005.

Wellbery, David E. Foreword to *Discourse Networks, 1800/1900,* trans. Michael Metteer and Chris Cullens, vii–xxxiii. Stanford, CA: Stanford University Press, 1992.

Welty, Eudora. *One Writer's Beginnings.* Boston: Faber and Faber, 1983.

West, Russell. *Conrad and Gide: Translation, Transference, and Intertextuality.* Atlanta, GA: Rodopi, 1996.

Wilderson, Frank B. III. "The Narcissistic Slave." In *Cinema and the Structure of US Antagonisms,* 55–91. Durham, NC: Duke University Press, 2010.

Williams, Alan. "Is Sound Recording Like a Language?" *Yale French Studies* 60 (1980): 51–66.

Witt, Mary Anne Frese, ed. *Nietzsche and the Rebirth of the Tragic.* Rutherford, NJ: Fairleigh Dickinson University Press, 2007.

Zamberlin, Mary. "Disseminating the Eaches: The Micro-Politics of Sound in *The Souls of Black Folk*." In *Rhizosphere: Gilles Deleuze and the "Minor" American Writing of William James, W. E. B. Du Bois, Gertrude Stein, Jean Toomer, and William Faulkner*, 69–106. New York: Routledge, 2006.

Zaretsky, Eli. *Political Freud: A History*. New York: Columbia University Press, 2015.

INDEX

JULIE BETH NAPOLIN is Assistant Professor of Digital Humanities in the Literature Program at The New School. She has published on sound, media, and literature in *qui parle*, *Symploke*, *Sounding Out!*, and *Social Text* and in such volumes as *Vibratory Modernism*, *Sounding Modernism*, and *Fifty Years after Faulkner*. In 2012 she was awarded a Bruce Harkness Young Scholar Award by the Joseph Conrad Society of America.

Printed and bound by CPI Group (UK) Ltd, Croydon, CR0 4YY

09/06/2025

14685656-0005